CRIME AND SOCIAL CONTROL IN ASIA AND THE PACIFIC

A Cross-Border Study

Victor N. Shaw

University Press of America,® Inc.
Lanham · Boulder · New York · Toronto · Plymouth, UK

Copyright © 2007 by
University Press of America,® Inc.
4501 Forbes Boulevard
Suite 200
Lanham, Maryland 20706
UPA Acquisitions Department (301) 459-3366

Estover Road
Plymouth PL6 7PY
United Kingdom

Library of Congress Control Number: 2006938182
ISBN-13: 978-0-7618-3679-7 (clothbound : alk. paper)
ISBN-10: 0-7618-3679-9 (clothbound : alk. paper)
ISBN-13: 978-0-7618-3680-3 (paperback : alk. paper)
ISBN-10: 0-7618-3680-2 (paperback : alk. paper)

Contents

Part IV Crime and Social Control: Larger Institutions, Processes, and
         Contexts

Introduction

The region of Asia and the Pacific constitutes the major part of the world. Asia is the largest continent, accounting for nearly one third of the landmass on earth. The Pacific Ocean holds the largest body of water, making up almost half of the earth's ocean surface. The Pacific alone, representing more than one third of the earth's total surface area, is often considered as the principal physical feature of the planet (Jacobs, LeVasseur, Kinsella, and Feldman 2004).

The majority of the human population lives across Asia and the Pacific (Newbold 2006; World Almanac 2006). Asia hosts six of the ten most populous countries in the world: China, India, Indonesia, Pakistan, Bangladesh, and Japan. The United States, the third of the ten most populated countries, sits on the Eastern coast of the Pacific. Russia, another member of the top ten, stretches eastward through Northern Asia into the Northwestern Pacific. Immediately following the top ten, there are other populous countries in the region, such as Mexico, the Philippines, Iran, and Thailand, in Asia, on the Pacific Rim, or across the Pacific Ocean.

In terms of economic development, the region of Asia and the Pacific embraces an entire spectrum of varying productive forces (World Bank 2006). There are economic superpowers, newly industrializing hopefuls, as well as underdeveloped societies in the region. Canada, Japan, Russia, and the United States are members of the dominant Group-8 of Great Industrial Countries in the global economy. South Korea, Taiwan, Hong Kong, and Singapore have gained reputations for their miraculous economic growth as the "four little dragons" in Asia (Xu 1996; Biggart and Mauro 1999). China has in recent years achieved one of the highest GNP increases in the world. On the other hand, North Korea is close to an economic collapse. Aboriginal societies in isolated Asian hinterlands and Pacific islands lag far behind in economic and social development. So do war-afflicted countries, such as Afghanistan, Cambodia, and Sri Lanka.

On the geopolitical map of the United States, Asia and the Pacific has been overshadowed by Europe, the Middle East, and other regions over the twentieth century. From the battlefields of World War II in Europe emerged the North Atlantic Treaty Organization (NATO). The ensuing Cold War and continuing turmoil in the Middle East added to the strategic significance of Europe in the global policies of the United States. As a result, most American foreign contacts have been made across the Atlantic Ocean. Evidence of this directional contact can be seen conspicuously in the system schedules of the major American air carriers.

The twenty-first century will be quite different. It will be the century of Asia and the Pacific. All possible expected changes in the world will be on display in this region (Andersson and Gunnarsson 2003; Rigg 2003; Sievers 2003). Politically, there will be transitions from socialism to capitalism, from ideological fanaticism to social pluralism, from totalitarian dictatorship to coalitional alliance, and from authoritarianism to a democratic form of government (Shaw 1996; Ware and Kisriev 2001). Economically, there will be transformations of state planning, corporate monopoly, and public intervention into market rationality, open competition, and individual entrepreneurship (Xu 1996; Kohli, Moon, and Sorensen 2003). Socially, there will be a rise of the middle-class, a valuing of public opinion, and an expansion of civil society, as well as a switch of social solidarity from the mechanical to the organic (Durkheim 1964; Morley 1993). Social networking and everyday life for people in Asia and the Pacific will be shaped increasingly and saliently by the division of labor, bureaucratic arrangement, and professional associations rather than by family mandates, group affinities, and community togetherness (Durkheim 1964; Weber 1968; Beeson 2002).

These changes are becoming evident in both large societies and small communities across Asia and the Pacific. The major remaining socialist countries on the planet—China, North Korea, and Vietnam—all located in this region, are either voluntarily undertaking reform or being pressured to change their economic and political systems (Goodman 1988; Shaw 1996; Zhou 2000; Lawrance 2003; McCargo 2004). Even traditional societies, such as Asian mountainous tribes and Pacific island communities, are beginning to look to the West or their more advanced neighbors for models of modernization and development. With these forces converging for social change, Asia and the Pacific will definitely be the most dynamic region in the world in the new century.

The United States sits geographically on the East Coast of the Pacific. With its global military and economic strengths as well as its leadership role in science and technology, the United States will continue to be a major stakeholder in the era of Asia and the Pacific. Unlike its role in the Cold War of the twentieth century, the new role of the United States will be more that of an active participant in terms of economic, political, and diplomatic input. There may be occasional or regional arms competitions and military confrontations. But hostility is not expected to be a dominant feature of this era. Similar to its experience with Europe in the past decades, the United States will see a massive expansion of contacts across the Pacific Ocean in the twenty-first century. It will also seek to formalize and solidify its power and influence in the region through international or NATO-like multinational organizations, such as the newly formed Asia-Pacific Economic Cooperation (APEC).

This study focuses on crime and social control amid many other aspects in the Asia and Pacific era dynamics (Shaw 2003). Crime and social control are obviously shaped by larger social forces within an historical era. In time of war, crime is likely to involve treason, espionage, genocide, hostage taking, or weaponry dealing. Social control often looms in the form of fear, terror, threat, victory, or defeat. In time of peace, on the other hand, crime is likely to center on economic interests or activities: politicians corrupt, businessmen cheat, and civilians steal. Social control often comes in the form of fines, property confiscation, loss of benefits, and imprisonment. Throughout the Asia and Pacific era, crime and social control will to a large degree be determined by geopolitical alignments, economic dealings, cultural exchanges, diplomatic maneuverings, and civilian contacts among nations and societies in the region. An overwhelming emphasis on economic competition and development will mean that national, territorial, group, and individual interests will be at center stage as both cause and consequence, both means and ends for crime and social control across Asia and the Pacific in the new century.

This study seeks to examine crime and social control in the context of country-to-country, system-to-system, ideology-to-ideology, and civilization-to-civilization interactions in Asia and the Pacific. Structurally, it divides into four major parts. Part I lays the groundwork. It develops a theoretical framework appropriate for the study of crime and social control inside and outside national borders, provides information about the fieldwork and data collection done by the author in Asia and around the Pacific Rim, and states the major goals and specific objectives for the study. Part II focuses on crime. It identifies and explores both existent and emergent crimes that have significant impacts upon national, regional, and international dynamics in Asia and the Pacific. Specifically, the study describes and analyzes crime resulting from social disorganization, crimes of opportunity, corporate and entrepreneurial crime, governmental and bureaucratic crime, smuggling and the drug trade, human trafficking and illegal immigration, organized crime, and crimes of terror. Part III concentrates upon social control. It examines and analyzes change of control ideologies, transfer of control technologies, professionalization of control forces, modernization of control systems, cross-border collaboration and cooperation, international organization and coordination, as well as civil penetration and global synchronization for crime control across Asia and the Pacific. To help the reader gain a systematic understanding, Part IV explores changing dynamics between major contrasting social forces, including capitalism and socialism, Eastern civilizations and Western development, democratic forms of government and patriarchal leadership, citizen initiative and state authority, formalism and informalism, procedural fairness and control effectiveness. It attempts to assess and clarify possible impacts of larger social processes on crime and social control in Asia and the Pacific. The study concludes with both a review of its contributions and limitations and suggestions for future research and policy initiatives concerning cross-border crime and social control across Asia and the Pacific as well as around the world.

Part I

GROUNDWORK:
THEORIES, METHODS, AND OBJECTIVES

It is natural to expect that a wide range of social forces will make their debut and then their full-scale multifaceted display in an era of transformational change. It is sensible to anticipate that crime and social control will emerge as a challenging social problem amid rapid fundamental change in a dynamic region. To understand fully the changing social dynamics in the Asia and Pacific era, however, it is necessary to lay a firm foundation in both theoretical and methodological dimensions.

1

Concepts, Themes, and Theories

In examining cross-border crime and social control in Asia and the Pacific, this study first calls for clarification, identification, and application of a number of concepts and theories.

CONCEPTS

While Asia and the Pacific Ocean are each well defined in geographical terms, Asia and the Pacific as a geopolitical region is in need of a formal definition. Physically, the region of Asia and the Pacific encompasses the Continent of Asia, Oceania, and the Pacific Ocean. However, the Pacific Ocean brings ambiguity as well as challenge to the definition of the whole geopolitical region or entity. Although numerous Pacific islands are indisputably Pacific, countries sitting along the Eastern shoreline of the Pacific Ocean through North, Central, and South Americas can be arguably Pacific or non-Pacific, wholly Pacific or partially Pacific. For example, Chile, Panama, and Peru, each of which has its East farthest point to the Pacific Ocean measured in only a few hundred of miles or less, can qualify as fully Pacific in a purely geographical sense. On the other hand, Canada, Mexico, and the United States, all of which have massive land areas expanding thousands of miles from the Pacific shorelines to their Eastern borders, may see

Pacific characteristics and influences only in their Western coastal provinces, states, or territories. Using the nation-state and its political or administrative entity as the unit of analysis, however, Asia and the Pacific refers to a geopolitical region that includes all the countries or territories around the Pacific Rim, across the Pacific Ocean, and throughout the expansive hinterland of Asia.

As countries vary immensely from developing to developed economies, democratic to non-democratic polities, and traditional to modern societies, crime understandably takes on different meanings across Asia and the Pacific. Crime, in its most original and general sense, refers to individual or group behaviors that a society considers serious enough to threaten its existence. Environmental, economic, and social conditions of specific societies are obviously determining factors in their respective definitions of crime. In ancient Peru, destruction of a bridge was considered a horrendous crime because the bridge was an indispensable means of connection in a land crisscrossed by ravines and canyons. Among North American Plains Indians, theft of a horse or a blanket was deemed one of the most serious wrongs because a person deprived of his horse or blanket could face immediate danger of death. Generally, people in simple, primitive, and homogeneous societies relate to each other directly. They usually have little property to be concerned about. Crime against the person may be limited to visibly severe injuries to the human body or a total loss of life. Abuse, internal sufferings, quarrels, fights, and minor to moderate injuries may all be brushed aside as part of growing-up or a customary way of life. On the other hand, people in complex, advanced, and heterogeneous societies tend to maintain some distance from one another. They often have a wide range of individual interests to acquire, defend, and protect. Crime against the person may include any threat, stress, or discomfort inflicted upon one citizen by another. Libel, harassment, stalking, and discrimination become criminal acts when citizens claim the protection of private space and interpersonal distance.

This study takes into account individual countries and their respective definitions of crime in describing and explaining crime, its causes and consequences, within national boundaries. The study goes beyond territorial jurisdictions and their corresponding legal interpretations while examining criminal acts of international scope and significance, such as human trafficking, drug smuggling, organized crime, abuse of human rights, genocide, terrorism, and misdeeds by multinational corporations. The international community, symbolized by the United Nations and similar worldwide organizations, is primarily dominated by Western powers composed of developed capitalist countries. Thus, crime and its international definitions to a large degree reflect the values, standards, and expectations in Western society.

Reaction to crime goes hand in hand with the definition of crime. Therefore social control differs tremendously, from jurisdiction to jurisdiction, from territory to territory, and from nation to nation, throughout Asia and the Pacific. There are traditional, closely knit, undeveloped, and geographically isolated rural settlements where economic interdependence, mutual surveillance, customary prohibitions, and communal ways of life serve well to keep deviance, crime, and other problematic behavior in check. There are modern, loosely clustered, developed, and spatially open urban sprawls where rampant crime and staggering social problems, such as vagrancy, prostitution, and homelessness, constantly call for social intervention, stretching an often inadequately equipped and organized social control system to its limit.

This study examines social control in both prevention and intervention dimensions. Social control therefore refers not only to formal control apparatuses or mechanisms, such as law enforcement agencies, courts, and correctional facilities, but also to informal networks or activities, including kinship, neighborhood watch, and workplace surveillance (Shaw 1996). In discussing each type of social control, this study evaluates its roots, evolutional change, effectiveness and efficiency, and challenges in the context of larger social structure and process. For example, reaction to theft can be informal or private in societies that have not developed the concept of property or in places where a few items of property in existence can be easily replaced or exchanged. However, in capitalist economies where capital, profit, and ownership take center stage, social regulation of contract, taxation, labor compensation, inheritance, and other interest-related matters calls into operation a formal governmental bureaucracy. Social control of theft, fraud, price fixing or gouging, tax evasion, and other economic violations constitute the principal activities of a large-scale civil and criminal justice system. In general, as society changes from the simple to the complex, the undeveloped to the developed, the homogeneous to the heterogeneous, the communal to the organizational, or the mechanical to the organic, social control becomes more formal than informal, more public than private, more reactive than preventive, more legal than commonsensical, and more in accordance with the correctness of bureaucratic procedure than with the fullness of human interest.

Finally, the concept of cross-border sits at the center of this study. The idea of border assumes a national, territorial, or jurisdictional boundary within which crime is defined under a specific rationale and social control is mounted in a particular manner. Cross-border considerations involve contrasts, conflicts, or confrontations between or among jurisdictions, territories, or countries in the definition of criminal behavior as well as in the social reaction to crime. For example, citizens of one country may enter another country without permission to escape from political oppression, religious persecution, economic hardship, cultural intolerance, childbearing restrictions, or criminal punishment. Are all such entries crimes? How should one kind of entry be designated as criminal and another as permissible and legal? Business entities often relocate to other countries. Multinational corporations generally make their decisions on business registration, branch location, material supply, equipment purchase, product distribution, shipment, and other production matters in response to policies and regulations by individual nations in which they operate. Their goal is usually to avoid environmental protection laws, bypass labor regulations, and minimize tax contributions they would be subject to in their home country. At the system level, one country may invade another, committing crimes of war, genocide, or terror against humanity. One country may impose economic sanctions against another, driving millions of ordinary people into hardship, hunger, and misery. One country may harbor prominent political dissidents, powerful business tycoons, and influential intellectual figures from another, creating a state of uncertainty, instability, and even chaos in the latter. The concept of cross-border obviously calls for an international definition of crime on the basis of humanity and universal justice and, correspondingly, an international forum of social control premised on mutual respect for sovereignty, peace, and co-existence.

   In general, Asia and the Pacific constitutes a significant part of the world, illustrating the extent of diversity as well as the intensity of dynamism in economic development, political practice, social organization, culture, and ways of life. Crime and its definition vary from time to time. Reaction to crime and overall social control differ from place to place. The idea of cross-border not only highlights differences but can also create clashes among jurisdictions, territories, or countries in crime and social control. There is a clear need for international or multinational efforts in defining, fighting, and treating deviance, crime, and other problematic behavior amid constant exchanges of people, information, and material across jurisdictional, territorial, or national borders.

THEMES AND THEORIES

Deviance, crime, and social control are part of everyday human living in all societies. Specific explanations for deviations from social norms abound, varying from time to time and from place to place. In the West, explanations for crime are multiple and overlapping, ranging from anomie, career, conflict, functionalist, rational choice, social control, social disorganization, social learning, and societal reaction theories to subculture perspectives (Shaw 2002). Each theory or perspective emerges from a particular social or historical context and may find some application in Asia and the Pacific. The anomie perspective builds upon Emile Durkheim's conception of anomie as moral confusion and Robert Merton's conception of anomie as social strain. According to Durkheim (1952), when individuals are caught in a normative vacuum between the remote state and unscrupulous individualism, they are likely to exhibit anomic deviancy or fall victim to anomic suicide. Merton (1957), on the other hand, posited that people turn to nonconformity, including innovation, ritualism, retreatism, and rebellion, when they become mired in the structured disparity between promises of achievable prosperity and lack of real-life opportunities to realize those promises.

In the new Asia and Pacific era, moral confusion can go hand in hand with social strain as cause for deviance and crime when more and more individuals grow up with a Western-style education. While these individuals may be inspired with ideas of individualism, material affluence, personal freedom, and self-actualization, they may still have to subject themselves to family mandates, group pressures, governmental controls, and various other reality restraints. For example, an official returning to a developing country after a period of diplomatic assignment in a developed capitalist country knows how creative, careful, and persistent he or she has to be in stealing just enough money from various sources under his or her control in order to build and maintain a lifestyle comparable to what common citizens of an affluent society enjoy.

The career perspective examines how criminal identity evolves over an individual lifespan. Criminal identity involves identification with criminal values, acquisition of criminal skills, and attainment of criminal status. Some individuals take crime as a business undertaking or a way of life while others view it as a mistake or a misfortune in their overall conventional life. Some are disciplined professionals while others are unpolished amateurs. Some are seasoned members of established criminal groups while others act out of random human impulsivity.

Across Asia and the Pacific, there is obviously the widest possible range of individual offenders and organized criminal groups in terms of sophistication, maturity, and career pathway. However, what is important is to follow individual career or non-career offenders in their changing social environment to understand how individual variations derive from differential influences from tradition, differential exposures to the outside world, and differential levels of economic development among societies or nation states in the region.

The conflict perspective includes a variety of theoretical arguments surrounding various interests possessed and pursued by individuals and groups in their social survival. Some of those arguments are radical in suggestion of reformative actions whereas others are just critical in analysis of realistic issues. Beginning with Karl Marx and Friedrich Engels (1979), the private ownership of means of production is first blamed for the rampant spread of crime and social ills over the era of economic surplus, wealth accumulation, and class division. In capitalist society, the worst crime or evil of all is not street violence but the exploitation of workers by the bourgeoisie, the ruling class of capitalism. There is then conflict between and among groups, subcultures, traditions, communities, or societies. As one group becomes dominant, it is likely to impose its version of reality upon others, making the latter and much of their behavior deviant, illegal, and subject to punishment (Wirth 1931; Sellin 1938; Gold 1958; Dahrendorf 1959). Further, there are differences between men and women and among people within the same social class or the same interest group. While both men and women are abused by the capitalist system, crime against and by women is caused by male aggression, as well as by men's attempt to control and subordinate women (Daly and Chesney-Lind 1988). While the poor, the uneducated, and the powerless are exploited generally by the rich, the educated, and the powerful, they are often persistently victimized by street criminals from their own social class (Lea and Young 1984; Schwartz and DeKeseredy 1993).

Throughout Asia and the Pacific, culture conflict used to figure saliently in the process of colonization in which Western imperialists imposed their "civilized" outlook upon indigenous cultures, subjecting the latter to harsh, punitive control measures. Now in the era of open competition for economic development and social advancement, the old problems of culture conflict, discrimination, and unfair treatment will not soon abate when migrants attempt to adapt to alien cultures, developing societies struggle to compete with developed economies by way of cheap labor or raw materials, and small, backward, or resource-lacking countries manage to play by the rules of nations set by a few large military and economic powers in the world.

The functionalist perspective explores how deviance and crime are necessitated by a social system and what they offer to the functional operation, maintenance, and progression of the social system. Durkheim (1964) considered crime as an inevitable, normal, and integral part of all healthy societies. Among its various contributions to social order, crime helps set moral boundaries, strengthen in-group solidarity, allow for adaptive innovation, and reduce internal societal tensions. Parsons (1951) viewed deviance or crime as both generating its own control and renewing a system's equilibrium. Merton (1957) noted that not all functions of deviance or crime are recognized, intended, or negative. It is important to examine various unrecognized, unintended, or positive functions by deviance or crime as well. A recent comprehensive effort is seen in Shaw's exposition of substance use and abuse. Shaw (2002) explores six critical dimensions for understanding various possible functions substance serves for users, substance users serve for specific groups, and substance use serves for society. The dimensions are these: function versus dysfunction, manifest versus latent functions, material versus moral functions, short-term versus long-term functions, peripheral versus core functions, and alternative functions. For example, in the eyes of some nationalist radicals, substances, such as heroin and cocaine, symbolize their nation's power to counteract the omnipresent dominance of Western capitalist countries in the world.

With regard to the geodynamics of Asia and the Pacific, cross-border crime certainly reflects the gap, the imbalance, and the clash among nations or territories in economic development, social modernization, and bilateral exchange. It may solidify unilateral positions and trigger international cooperation in social control. It may even serve as a safety valve, reducing or mitigating tensions from trade, territorial disputes, or diplomatic frictions. From a theoretical point of view, rampant crime and its various symptomatic manifestations within and outside national borders often represent clear and loud warnings about deeper and broader social problems facing the whole region.

The rational choice perspective begins with classical criminology, and more generally, utilitarianism. Cesare Beccaria (1963) viewed humans as rational hedonists who explore and assess available alternatives to maximize pleasure and minimize pain. Jeremy Bentham (1967) expounded the calculative nature of human actions, showing how every human act is calculated in accordance with its likelihood to produce advantage, pleasure, and happiness or to avoid mischief, pain, and unhappiness. Assuming that pleasure is gained from crime, both Beccaria and Bentham argued that punishment ought to be meted out rationally and proportionately to inflict pain in amounts greater than the pleasure achieved from the criminal act. The contemporary rational choice perspective, while sharing the general spirit of classical theory, is specific, concrete, and practical in its theoretical analysis. It follows routine activities by ordinary human actors. It examines personal factors, such as needs for material gains, thrills, or revenge, criminal skills, and individual access to legitimate avenues for success. It also investigates situational factors, ranging from the vulnerability of the target, the location of the operation, the reward of the criminal undertaking, and the risk of apprehension, to the severity of punishment. By combining or contrasting personal with situational factors, the perspective pinpoints how people choose to commit or forgo crime in every possible rational manner.

The era of Asia and the Pacific will surely provide testimony to one of the central propositions in the rational choice theory. That is, crime is a product of criminal opportunity. What criminal opportunities are being created by a sweeping economic development across the region? Not only are there market lures, widening varieties of goods, and increasing flows of people, but also legal loopholes, lags in regulation, and corrupt social control agents. What kinds of people are being thrown into the evolving scene of criminal opportunities? There are throngs of people, such as propertyless, homeless, or penniless migrants or vagrants, who are driven by their economic loss, job failure, social dislocation, cultural disorientation, or survival desperation. There is no lack of people, such as instant celebrities and upstart millionaires, who are motivated by material gain, business success, advantageous social positioning, self-perceived smartness or supremacy, misguided ambition, or winner's pride. For example, a few upstarts in a growing economy may rationalize their offensive behavior above and beyond the law when they attempt to dominate the market, interfere in the politics, threaten the mass media, or manipulate the populace within their national or territorial boundary.

The social control perspective attempts to identify all possible social entities or forces that keep people in line. An obvious observation is that most people do not commit crime. The reason can be simple: Most people have internalized mainstream social norms. Walter Reckless (1961), in his containment theory, assumes that for every individual there exist a containing external structure and a protective internal structure, both of which provide defense, protection, and insulation against deviant behavior. Travis Hirschi (1969) presents a social bonds theory in which he explores how social bonds, such as attachment, commitment, involvement, and belief, engage youth in conventional lines of activity. Gresham Sykes and David Matza (1957) even posit that deviant or criminal actors may have already known the wrongfulness of their wayward or lawbreaking acts. Because they know the difference between right and wrong, they develop techniques of neutralization, including denial of responsibility, denial of injury, denial of the victim, condemnation of the condemner, and appeal to higher loyalties, to rationalize their deviant behavior, to defuse their inner sense of guilt, and to ward off possible social attacks. Victor Shaw (1996) provides a comprehensive analysis of social control in formal versus informal, primary versus secondary, internal versus external, social versus organizational, regulative versus suggestive, and Western versus non-Western dimensions. According to Shaw, social control refers to "any mechanism or practice for securing individual compliance, maintaining collective order and normative consistency, or dealing with problematic or deviant situations" (1996: 26).

Throughout Asia and the Pacific, tradition, social custom, religion, family, kinship, mediation, and communal interrelatedness continue to serve as sources of social control while legal codes, justice systems, and state bureaucracies are poised to take dominance. There is miscommunication, conflict, or even chaos when the two types of social forces come into contact with each other. There is cooperation, complementarity, or interdependence when one source lends aid or support to the other. For instance, the state-run justice system may rely upon various familial, kinship, tribal, or community-based conflict management forums to discipline wayward individuals, resolve civil disputes, keep local order, and sustain long-term stability in remote areas. On the other hand, many age-old forces or practices may pose serious challenges to the state and its criminal or civil justice system in applying the law equally and equitably to every citizen in every jurisdiction across the country.

The social disorganization perspective relates people to their living era and environment. It studies why and how deviance, crime, and other social problems tend to increase in a time and a place where change occurs abruptly. Beginning at the University of Chicago in the early twentieth century, a wide variety of empirical studies were conducted to explore the meaning of life as experienced by people in the time or in an environment of social disorganization. W. I. Thomas and Florian Znaniecki (1920) followed Polish peasants from Europe to America and found that many of these immigrants were caught in the lack of normative guidance between their old and new worlds. With an "anything goes, nothing works" attitude that so typically developed among them, some easily drifted into deviance, mental disorder, crime, and other forms of unruly behavior. Robert Park (1936), in cooperation with Ernest Burgess, developed an ecological model to capture the interrelationships of people and their environment in the time of social disorganization. For the city of Chicago, they identified five concentric zones, each of which has its own unique structure, organizations, inhabitants, and cultural features. Applying the model, Clifford Shaw and Henry McKay (1969) found that delinquency, along with other community problems, such as infant mortality, truancy, mental disorder, deviance, and crime, occurred mostly in the areas nearest the central business zone. Recently, Victor Shaw (2002) examines the cause, manifestation, and outcome of social disorganization in his systematic application of the social disorganization perspective to the phenomenon of substance use and abuse. As he points out, change as the primary cause for social disorganization may take place at both individual and social levels, and in the form of migration, immigration, and environmental change. When it occurs, social disorganization may manifest itself in not only material but also spiritual dimensions. As a result of social disorganization, a society or system may collapse, fall into disequilibrium, or reorganize for a new state of affairs.

The Asia and Pacific era seems to provide a prime testing ground for the social disorganization perspective. Migrants flock from hinterlands to coastlines, from countryside to metropolis, or from the backwater of economy to the frontline of development. Immigrants cross national borders from repressive regimes to democratic forms of government, from developing or undeveloped economies to developed affluent consumer markets, or from traditional, primitive, or unicultural territories to modern, advanced, and multicultural societies. In their new environments, they are likely to gather at crossroads, transportation hubs, urban ghettos, or ethnic enclaves with mobile population segments in unstable and unpleasant neighborhoods. They not only miss their loved ones and old ways of life at home, but also face immediate challenges of survival, finding a job, making a living, staying away from danger, and adapting to the new environment. As modernization continues in varying phases by varying speeds, migration across territorial or national borders will remain strong and constant for a long time in Asia and the Pacific. Social disorganization and its resultant social problems, such as crime, delinquency, substance abuse, and divorce, will inevitably exist as one of the most salient social issues for all concerned scholars and policymakers in the region.

The social learning perspective focuses on the acquisition of criminal motives and skills as a human learning experience. Like any other human behavior, crime is learned. An offender is not born capable of committing a crime. In order to successfully carry out criminal offenses, the offender must internalize some basic values favorable to crime and master some critical skills essential to certain criminal undertakings. With regard to the mode of learning, the differential association argument emphasizes face-to-face contact between novice or amateur and experienced or professional criminals under one roof, in the same group, or in the same community (Sutherland 1947). The differential association argument, on the other hand, attests to the effect of the mass media in spreading deviant or criminal messages, images, models, and identities across the population. People learn by identification. In other words, one does not have to physically associate with one's favorite role models or reference groups to become identified with them in criminal offending or other behavior (Glaser 1956). With relevance to both arguments, differential reinforcement figures in the process of learning. Deviance or crime is likely to be repeated if it leads to positive, pleasurable, or desirable outcomes, such as the presence of rewards and the removal of punishment. It is likely to be discontinued if it results in negative, painful, or undesirable consequences, such as the presence of punishment and the removal of rewards (Burgess and Akers 1966). More generally, nature versus nurture, interest versus experience, subculture versus social climate are also issues of critical importance in understanding the foundation, the stage, and the context of learning about criminal and other human behaviors (Shaw 2002).

The social learning perspective finds its obvious application in the Asia and Pacific era as industrialization, urbanization, and continuing development increase the flow of people, information, and consumer goods across national or territorial borders in the region. Migrants learn from migrants by association because they come from comparable backgrounds and gather in similar places. Immigrants learn from immigrants by identification because they share similar dreams and face common problems or challenges. Hollywood entertainment feeds curious audiences in developing countries, providing them with vivid portrayals of Western-style sex, violence, and extravagance. In a smaller scope yet in a similar manner, movies from undeveloped or developing societies find audiences in the developed world, offering them glimpses of non-Western practices or lifestyles, such as martial arts and totem worship. People emulate their favorite stars in sports and entertainments. They look for inspiration in battlefield confrontations, feudal feuds, or urban warfare featured in entertainment products. Physically, people travel from culture to culture, from territory to territory, and from country to country. They mingle with local people, learning how to drink, how to smoke, how to use drugs, or how to enjoy services by prostitutes. As for social control, legal loopholes, lack of coordination in border areas, inadequate training for justice officials, outdated technology, budget shortfalls, and equipment backwardness may allow a considerable number of offenders to escape arrest and prosecution for their various lawbreaking behaviors. The situation can be especially salient in developing countries where absence of punishment or lack of deterrence often serves to encourage people who are thinking about engaging in deviant or criminal activities.

The societal reaction perspective eyes social reaction to crime and explores its possible effect on an individual's further slide into criminality. The central argument of the perspective is that crime is socially defined, criminal identity is assigned and acquired through a social process, and individuals may be inadvertently pushed into a deviant way of life or a criminal career by social treatment. Frank Tannenbaum (1938) first discovered a gradual shift, or a process of tagging, "from the definition of the specific acts as evil to a definition of the individual as evil" in his study of social treatment of offenders (17). Edwin Lemert (1951) then made an explicit distinction between primary and secondary deviations. While primary deviations occur when individuals are still in the role of conformists, secondary deviations take place only when individuals assume deviant roles imputed to them through social reaction and behave in accordance with their so-altered self-concepts. Howard Becker (1963) further introduced the notion of a developmental process that moves from attainment of a deviant identity to devoted participation in a deviant career as he followed marijuana users in their use progression through three related stages. As pointed out unequivocally by David Ward and Charles Tittle (1993), "sanctioning and labeling of norm violators significantly affect the likelihood that an offender will develop a deviant identity and that such identities significantly affect the likelihood of recidivism" (60).

What can be learned from the societal reaction perspective? Should there be lesser social reaction because social reaction is oftentimes an inevitable factor in an offender's further slide into criminality? The answer is not standard or uniform for different societies in Asia and the Pacific. There should be lesser social reaction because there are traditional, customary, or community-based forms of social control that target mind, spirit, or self-image through collective surveillance, public shaming, or self-blaming. While these measures work effectively as general deterrence on the side of prevention, they can be quite counterproductive and sometimes even destructive on the matter of treatment. For instance, when an individual is forced to leave his or her community due to negative labeling, he or she is likely to encounter much more grave circumstances in a new environment outside: homelessness, vagrancy, dependency, a criminal career, or suicide. There should be no lesser social reaction because social control is simply inadequate in many developing countries across Asia and the Pacific. It is rarely excessive control that pushes people into deviance or criminality. It is often lack of control that spawns deviant acting and criminal offending. A general reaction to the warning raised by the societal reaction theory is, therefore, to strengthen, specify, and sharpen social control, making it equitable in terms of law, objective with regard to evidence, standard across the population, specific to the act, and essentially neutral to the actor.

Finally, the subculture perspective turns to culture, specifically subcultures as the social milieu for developing and sustaining deviant and criminal ideas, values, norms, skills, and behaviors. Work by Frederick Thrasher on gangs (1927) and William Whyte (1943) on immigrant slums represents some of the earliest writings on subcultures. The subculture explanation develops into a full-fledged theoretical paradigm through a series of landmark studies on various groups or subcultures, including Albert Cohen's (1955) study of delinquent boys, Richard Cloward and Lloyd Ohlin's (1960) identification of criminal, conflict, and retreatist gangs or subcultures among youth, Marvin Wolfgang and Franco Ferracuti's (1967) examination of a subculture of violence prevailing in some lower-class urban communities, and Walter Miller's (1958) inquiry into the lower-class culture or subculture as a whole in American society. Hans Sebald (1968) offers a comprehensive inventory of what elements there are in a subculture and what functions a subculture may serve for its participants in his study of adolescent subculture. According to him, youth subculture provides young people with common values and norms, unique lingo and argot, common styles and fads, distinctive forms of mass media, distinctive criteria for status, a sense of belonging, gratification of specific needs, protection from adult control, and general social support.

Approaching Asia and the Pacific as an entire region that to some degree shares a common cultural orientation, the subculture perspective can first look into different nation-based or territory-based cultural systems to see how each of them breeds and sustains a unique political economy, a distinctive social practice, and an exclusive pattern of deviant or criminal behavior. For instance, while family-centered entrepreneurship flourishes in some of the Eastern cultures, individualism is often to blame for various egoistic crimes and deviances committed in Western cultural contexts. Within a national culture, there are obviously various subcultures, such as rural versus urban, upper-class versus lower-class, rebelling versus conforming, and migrant versus settler groups or subcultures, that may be linked to specific attitudes, customs, or practices. For example, upper- and middle-class residents may develop a negative attitude toward lower-class migrants, blaming the latter for all the social ills they see in their everyday experiences. Most important, the subculture perspective points to the possibility that deviant or criminal subcultures form or dissolve above and beyond national cultures across Asia and the Pacific. An immediate observation is this: international prostitutes working in Hong Kong, Los Angeles, or Tokyo are subject to the subculture of sex, sex trade, and sex industry no matter in what country these individuals originate, what language they speak, or what national culture they carry.

While each of these theories can find meaningful applications in Asia and the Pacific, it is critically important to go beyond specific explanations in order to examine how broader and larger social forces impact and are impacted by crime and social control throughout a dynamic region in a time of rapid change.

This study examines crime and social control in the context of sweeping social dynamics, such as economic development, political democratization, social liberalization, and cultural diversification, across Asia and the Pacific. Following these major social dynamics automatically affords a complete view of the clash and fusion between tradition and modernity, poverty and prosperity, scarcity and affluence, socialism and capitalism, communality and constitutionality, collectivism and individualism, conservatism and liberalism, as well as Eastern civilization and Western development. Theoretically, modernization, dependency, world system, and other macro schools of thought shed critical light on large social structures and processes. But empirical observation, everyday life narrative, commonsensical reasoning, and vulgar analysis of conventional wisdom are always necessary to perceive, sensitize, and understand individual experiences with deviance, crime, social problems, and social control in a changing environment (So 1990; So and Chiu 1995; Findlay 1999).

Focusing on economic development, for instance, allows the researcher to differentiate a region into developed and undeveloped territories; a country into industrialized or urbanized and unindustrialized or un-urbanized areas; a city into upper-class neighborhoods and lower-class slums; and a population into haves and have-nots. Exploitation, manipulation, discrimination, and mistreatment occur when people from undeveloped regions seek employment and take low-paying jobs in private households and labor-intensive sectors in developed societies. Concentration of wealth in the hands of the haves and their conspicuous consumption provide immediate targets for crime whereas unemployment, poverty, and loss of hope on the part of the have-nots can supply instant motivation for offending. Clashes between traditional and modern, rural and urban, communal and organizational forces figure in the puzzling question whether it is the rich, the educated, and the powerful who exploit and abuse the poor, the uneducated, and the powerless, or it is the latter who steal from, rebel against, or otherwise victimize the former. As for culture, civilization, and social system, conflict between Eastern and Western cultures or civilizations may be a factor to consider when a Chinese immigrant entrepreneur in Canada disciplines his or her employees to a degree that he or she violates their civil liberties. Confrontation between socialism and capitalism may be a line of reason to explore when a Cuban business owner who openly claims loyalty to Fidel Castro finds his or her business in the United States boycotted and even vandalized by American customers and Cuban immigrant clients.

2

Interviews, Fieldwork, and Data Collection

This study began in 1996. In the past ten years, the author collected data on various aspects of crime, deviance, and social control through his extensive personal and professional network in Asia and the Pacific.

First, the author sought assistance from officials and scholars in Asia and the Pacific in obtaining statistics, documents, reports, and case stories. Second, the author traveled extensively across Asia and the Pacific to collect firsthand information. In his numerous fieldwork trips, he visited a representative range of countries or territories, including Hong Kong, Indonesia, Israel, Japan, Mainland China, Malaysia, the Philippines, Singapore, South Korea, Taiwan, and Thailand in Asia, Australia and New Zealand in Oceania, Canada, Mexico, and the United States in North America, Colombia, Ecuador, and Peru in South America, and Guam and Hawaii in the Pacific. For instance, the author observed border-crossings in Hong Kong, explored drug trafficking routes near the Golden Triangle, visited villages in hinterland China, sat in criminology classes in various Asian and Pacific universities, conducted formal group meetings with officials and scholars in different Asian and Pacific countries, talked to pimps and prostitutes in Australia, Malaysia, the Philippines, Thailand, and the United States, and interviewed a sample of former drug addicts from Southeast Asia who now live in the San Joaquin Valley, California. Third, the author reads Chinese newspapers, watches Chinese television news, and listens to Chinese radio operated by

Chinese Americans in the United States on a daily basis. He continuously gathers news items on crime, deviance, and social control from these and various other related sources. Most important, he tries to remain on top of major developments in societies across Asia and the Pacific.

INTERVIEWS

The author conducted both casual talks and formal interviews with officials, scholars, and research subjects regarding crime, deviance, and social control in Asia and the Pacific. He examined pictures and documents at the time of conversation with officials, service professionals, and crime victims. He sometimes received papers and electronic messages from scholars and experts following facto-face consultations.

First, the author interviewed organized crime leaders, prostitution ring organizers, sex establishment owners, drug dealers, and cross-border offenders in his various fieldwork trips to Asia and the Pacific. Contact with established groups and their leaders was usually arranged with an insider's formal introduction. Interviews lasted as briefly as less than an hour in a hotel lobby or as long as half a day at the leader's private ranch. Questions were always open, free from inquisitorial pressure or moral connotation, and posed in a way not only appropriate to the situation but also with an attempt to understand. For instance, taking the role of the interviewee, the author often asks a leader or owner such questions as "What does it take to survive and succeed in the business?" and "What thoughts and feelings do you typically have following a long day of hard work?" Talk with sex-related establishment owners, for a few times, took place as simple tourist encounters. The author walked through a well-known red light district in the city. When approached by an English-speaking business solicitor, the author stopped, chatting with him about the district, the business, his job, and his employer. In Bangkok, Tokyo, and other major Asian cities, the author saw Nigerians, Senegalese, South Africans, Canadians, Americans, and Europeans working as solicitors, handlers, or security guards for strippers' clubs, massage parlors, and other sex-centered businesses. In Tokyo, for example, the author through a Senegalese street solicitor had the opportunity to talk to an alleged owner of two sex-related establishments. To the author's surprise, the self-claimed owner is an American who went to Japan initially as an English teacher.

The most dramatic contact was with a prostitution ring organizer in Malaysia in 2003. It came totally by accident. The author saw a middle-aged man pleading with the hotel clerk for a couple of rooms while checking in at an airport hotel. The man, who spoke Chinese, said he had stayed there a few times without reservation in the past and asked why suddenly there was no room this time. The author stepped in to offer help, as the hotel clerk kept saying he did not understand Chinese. Acting as a Chinese-English translator between the man and the hotel clerk, the author managed a smooth communication that led to the finding of two rooms for the man. The man was obviously thankful to the author. He took the author to his companions who were waiting in a corner in the hotel lobby. With shock and disbelief, the author saw eleven young good-looking girls as his companions who would stay with him in two small hotel rooms; the author had previously stayed at this hotel on two separate nights on his multinational fieldwork trips! The man, noticing the author's surprise, explained that he was a tourist guide leading the group of girls in a trip to Malaysia. Later in the night, the author secured a chance to talk to the man. From the conversation, the author learned that the man owned a dance hall or nightclub in Northeastern China, that he recruited young women from his city and took them regularly on short trips to Malaysia, Indonesia, Singapore, Hong Kong, and other Asian destinations, that girls included in each trip are scheduled to perform in nightclubs under arrangement by local Chinese in the host society, and that he aspired to cover Australia and other Western markets where there is a growing Chinese immigrant population. At the end of the conversation, the man left the author with his cellular number, requesting the author to help him expand his business to Canada and the United States.

Second, the author interviewed drug users, prostitutes, illegal immigrants, and other cross-border violators or victims in various settings across Asia and the Pacific. While jails, reformatories, and temporary detention facilities are known places to reach officially caught or identified offenders or victims, the actual bases where people make deals or create problems, often without the attention of the law, are likely to be border crossings, transportation hubs, and city streets. For example, the author learns about an important cross-border transaction, marriage dealing, through purely civil contact. At the author's home party, one of his friends brought her newly met workmate who came to the United States through a kind of marriage scam. The author later interviewed the woman on her whole experience, and through her reached her former "husband" as well as a few more women who went through similar marriage experiences. From those interviews, the author was able to develop a general assessment of marriage dealing by individuals within the Unites States and individuals within other less developed countries. In a typical story about marriage dealing, an American man, through his family connection, goes to a foreign country to look for young women to marry; he sponsors his newly wed wife to immigrate to the United States immediately upon marriage; he helps his wife apply for permanent residency in the Unites States; he divorces his wife about two years after when she can legally stay in the United States; he then enters into another round of search for another young woman to marry. The deal is this: The man collects fees once or at different milestones—upon marriage, upon arrival in the United States, upon filing of application for an immigrant visa, or upon approval of permanent residency. The woman is usually coerced to work to support the man and his family while being sponsored for her green card application.

Third, the author conversed with officials, lawyers, court clerks, helping professionals, and service workers on various occasions on trips throughout Asia and the Pacific. Contact with these sources benefited tremendously from the author's extensive professional network forged, maintained, and expanded through study and work. For example, with assistance from various alumni associations at the East-West Center in Hawaii, where he studied from 1989 to 1993, the author secured a series of interviews with important officials in Southeast Asia. In Indonesia, the author held a long conversational interview with an official whose national commission on violence against women is poised to assist female migrant workers in their miseries, not only at home but also overseas. She showed me dozens of photos she had gathered of migrant workers and informed me about their living conditions, work routines, and gathering places, as well as the injuries they suffer from labor, abuse, or punishment. In the Philippines, the author met with a university professor who directs a government-designated or authorized program to screen and train migrant workers for work overseas. Using standardized psychological tests, the program seems to attempt to identify and prepare only those who are physically strong as well as mentally sound, mainly in terms of intelligence, for working in a foreign, potentially hostile environment.

The author even benefited directly from his classmates, students, and friends who work in law, law enforcement, and government in countries in Asia and the Pacific. For example, the author was able to travel in an official vehicle bearing the police seal across a border region and engage in in-depth dialogues with county police chiefs and other important law enforcement officials through a classmate who now works in a police college administered by a provincial bureau of public security in China. The author has a few classmates who practice immigrant law in the United States. One of them specializes in refugee and political asylum. While they feed the author with interesting cases from time to time, the most helpful source seems to be a non-lawyer friend who works as a Chinese-English translator in a federal court. Some stories the author has heard from her served as a real eye-opener to the growing variety of cross-border violations or problems between the United States and a fast-developing China.

Fourth, the author discussed crime, deviance, and social control in Asia and the Pacific with concerned scholars and experts in major international conferences in Australia, Brazil, Canada, Finland, France, Germany, Iceland, Israel, Japan, Mexico, Poland, Puerto Rico, Taiwan, and the United States. Using the conference program as a search tool, the author first identified sessions pertaining to Asia and the Pacific, especially crime and social control in the region. He then attended the sessions where related papers were presented. Following the presentation, the author talked to the speaker, and when appropriate, asked for a special meeting in which he could clarify or verify with the speaker specific details regarding particular cross-border transactions. For example, the author held a dinner meeting with a Russian scholar in Poland to talk about domestic problems as well as international crimes following the collapse of the Soviet Union. Sometimes, opportunities arose by accident during the social hours sponsored by the conference organizer. In Canada, the author came upon a sociologist from Singapore at the conference welcome party. The author obtained from him critical insights into a wide range of social issues in Southeast Asia. In Taiwan, the author happened to sit, in a conference tour bus, next to a scholar who specializes in international migration across the Pacific Rim. The author engaged in a highly fruitful conversation with him concerning migration, crime, economic development, and political liberalization. In addition to spontaneous exchanges at conference venues, the author often followed up scholarly contacts with emails, postcards, or formal letters of appreciation. Papers, abstracts, or statistical tables were often received following face-to-face meetings at the conference.

Finally, the author telephoned friends and colleagues in Asia and the Pacific, verifying stories or incidents reported over various channels of the mass media. The author navigated websites, read newspapers and magazines, listened to radio, and watched television programs in both English and Chinese. When he came across a case or story in the media that did not sound immediately credible, the author called his friends or relatives for verification or second opinion. Regarding specific incidents, the author asked directly if it indeed occurred or happened as it was portrayed in the media. Answers were usually clear and straightforward: "It did happen," "It did not happen at all", or "It happened but not as dramatized in the media." As far as some stories were concerned, the author could only seek for a kind of opinion. Responses varied obviously from person to person. For instance, when the author asks if it is possible, if it is true, that there is an instance in which a Mainland China company opens a nominal business in Hong Kong in order to convert and transfer funds from Chinese *Yuan* to American dollars, he can only expects such variable answers as "I think so," "I do not know anything about it," or "I know people who do just that."

OBSERVATIONAL VISITS

It is the author's belief that an author must have some live visual impressions about a city, a country, or a region when he or she starts to write anything about it. To fill and enrich his background experience with Asia and the Pacific, the author has made numerous visits to the region. During each of his visits, the author made serious efforts to mingle with the crowd of ordinary people, to follow the routine of their daily lives, and to feel the pulse of their common concerns and sentiments.

There are obviously layers of observation for a researcher beginning as a simple tourist in a foreign country. In the first layer is the cleanliness, orderliness, or general sanitary conditions of city streets, public places, and ports of transportation. In the second layer is the concentration or distribution of commercial establishments, multinational corporations, and high-rise buildings. The third layer is the city transportation system. Is there orderly coverage by bus, subway, ferry, or light rail? Does each line of transportation run on schedule or erratically? The fourth layer is the cost of living, and in close relationship, the quality of life. How much do ordinary people spend on food, clothes, transportation, and other daily articles? How much do they earn as factory workers, hotel staff, sales clerks, corporate managers, police officers, or schoolteachers? Further or deeper in the observation is the spirit of people through the mannerisms they exhibit and the fashions they wear. Answers are sometimes explicit in what is seen, such as prices listed on merchandises displayed in marketplaces. They are sometimes implicit in what people do or how things are taken care of. Questioning may be necessary, in addition to simple observations, to obtain a satisfactory answer or develop a general picture.

In the author's experience, he is able to develop an immediate impression of the level of economic and social development of a region from a short visit, much like that of a tourist. The author obtains a bird's-eye view of a major city and its surrounding area from an aircraft just before it lands. On a sunny day, the author can get a clear picture of the city, its streets, residential houses, office buildings, production facilities, and general layout. At the airport, the author takes notice of the scale, complexity, and level of commercial service. On the way to the city center, the author usually rides on bus, rail, and other public transportation that most local travelers take into the city. Whenever possible, the author chats with local people sitting next to him, asking questions about nearby streets or establishments glimpsed as he travels. Upon arrival in the city, the author first finds a highest point, the top of a high-rise building for example, where he can have a panoramic view of the city. He then walks around in major districts, oftentimes bumping into people in the downtown business area or a suburban shopping mall. To approximate experience in the perspective of local residents, the author uses public transportation from one point of interest to another throughout the city. For example, the author has walked hours through main thoroughfares, waterfronts, beachfronts, or otherwise well-known streets in Bangkok, Manila, and Jakarta. He saw passengers clinging to running buses, motor-driven vehicles spewing choking smokes all over the city, pedestrians running through the busy traffic, teenagers swimming in filthy water, children begging for money, streets littered with trash, blocks lined with dilapidated houses, rivers clogged with industrial waste, and parks dotted by piles of burning garbage. The author also took long walks through the centers or waterfronts of Singapore, Taipei, Tokyo, Osaka, Nagoya, and Yokohama. Besides lines of commercial establishments and mountains of skyscrapers, he was able to enjoy various spots of well-manicured gardens, plazas, and parks in the middle of the city. The difference in development among countries can be immediately and clearly seen in traveling through capitals, major ports, and large metropolises.

The author often develops during an observational visit an impression of the acceptance of governmental controls even in such easily noticeable areas as traffic regulation or trash disposal. The impression is not based simply upon the presence of police officers, security guards, military personnel, royal images, or government signs at ports of transportation, public offices, commercial establishments, or city streets. The author also looks into areas where such control is less apparent. For instance, the author wonders whether there is a rational system of traffic rules or an effective enforcement of such rules on vehicles and pedestrians when he sees taxi drivers, including the one he hires, weave through lines of automobiles or throngs of people in city streets without much regard for traffic signs or signals. The author wonders about the level of involvement and of effectiveness of municipal authority when he walks by streets strewn with trash, through tourist attractions or public plazas filled with graffiti, or along rivers or lakes contaminated by industrial or human waste. The author questions the rule of law or the role of government when he is approached for money or an unusual trade in public places or when he is sent to visit some commercial establishments or left nowhere in the city by operators of some unique form of city transportation, one after another. Ironically, the author seems to have seen more officers or guards in uniform in countries where he has every reason to believe that the government is inherently weak or just does not do an effective job in serving the interest of the general public. In contrast, the author remembers seeing fewer police officers in city streets and public places where he can sense clearly a strong role played by the government in regulating public behavior and keeping social order.

The author also attempts to form an impression about the prevalence and severity of social problems in a region during his tour of the region. On the surface, the author pays attention to whatever he can see as an ordinary tourist: polluted rivers, contaminated beaches, exposed mountains, eroded lands, dilapidated houses, shanty towns, overcrowded streets, unattended parks, homeless people sleeping in public places, children or handicapped individuals begging for help on the sidewalk, and trash piled up at street corners. Beyond these immediate observations, the author takes every opportunity to reach out to people from different walks of life, asking them specific questions about crime, deviance, and victimization. In the Philippines, the author talked to a security guard on a wide range of issues when he had difficulty falling asleep in the middle of the night at the Manila Hotel. In Indonesia, the author was able to hire an English-speaking taxi driver for a whole day. The driver took the author to many different places in Jakarta, offering much information about the city and its various physical and social aspects. The author sometimes visits high-profile places, such as red-light districts, slums, transit stations, and downtown help centers, in a city. Whenever possible, the author mingles with people in the setting, chatting with them either as a participant or a visitor. For example, the author stayed overnight at some railway stations in Asia. Besides obtaining clues about social problems among migrants, the author gained critical insights about people in transit or crowds in public places from those real life experiences. A common observation at the train station is that passengers naturally or automatically make efforts to balance the instincts to guard themselves and their belongings from strangers with the need to know others and their surroundings in an unfamiliar place. Among a crowd of people sitting or sleeping on the floor at the station, there are always transactions over space, information, entertainments, tickets, travel-related needs, daily articles, and miscellaneous matters. While the majority of passengers focus on dealing with a common concern or problem they share, such as a train delay or a need to save money on lodging, a few attempt to take advantage of the situation for profit or other gains by offering an exchange of tickets or sharing some valuable amenities. Most noticeably, local merchants and cheap lodging operators walk around to lure customers with allegedly huge discounts or specials.

An important impression the author believes he can reasonably derive from observational visits is about the pace and scale of social change in a society. The most obvious way to achieve the goal is to make multiple visits to the same society over a period of time. Comparisons between earlier and later trips may point to the pace of change, which is often witnessed in the physical layout of a city, the system of transportation across the city, the neatness of city streets, parks, and plazas, the clustering of residential compounds, and the distribution of commercial establishments. With no reference to official statistics, physical changes sometimes are so evident in a society that the author, like any similarly-minded tourist observers, may be seized with a sudden impulse to utter his surprise: "What a society! Becoming more prosperous every day!" Change, its scope, speed, and nature, may also be detected in spontaneous observations. For example, seeing construction take place from community to community, seeing truck or shiploads of raw materials or products move on land or through waterways, and seeing buses or trainloads of people travel between cities and rural areas, the author can obtain a vivid picture of economic development that is underway in a society. Hearing people talk about changing jobs, pursuing education in foreign countries, expanding business on domestic markets or overseas, keeping maids in their private household, hiring an interior design team for their home project, entertaining mistresses, or feeding bodyguards can give the author insight into the change of culture, customs, institutions, and the general social mosaic. It is also through all these manifestations that the author observes individuals and learns about their attitudes toward education, work and career, marriage and family, consumption and leisure, personal safety, wealth, power, and morality.

Lastly, a common yet revealing impression the author always has following an observational visit to a society is about its people and their spirit. Are people in that society optimistic or pessimistic? Are they forward looking or backward looking? Are they open-minded? Are they friendly, unfriendly, or even hostile among themselves or toward outsiders? Do they work hard or do they take a generally easy approach to life? Are they motivated or do they seem not to care much about where they are in the world of nations? Do they enjoy life or are they seemingly stressed with every aspect of life? While he senses a great deal of commonality in the way people think and act across Asia and the Pacific, the authors also sees country or territory-specific attitudes and behaviors among people who adhere to different cultural traditions, operate under different social systems, and strive for prosperity in different levels of economic development throughout the region.

For instance, there seem to be three different types of people with reference to economic development, national character, or a combination of both. People of the first type tend to pack and confine themselves in a box. They yield to each other automatically, to some degree neurotically, as if concession or self-containment is built into their mindset. From public greetings or the physically omnipresent gesture of courtesy among this type of people, it is difficult to detect or even speculate what they feel: pain or happiness, modesty or pride, and stress or comfort. Observations made by the author in public places across a few major Asian and Pacific financial centers are illustrative: even the unprivileged who are either homeless or cannot afford to pay for lodging on their trip to the city seemed to have made a conscientious effort to keep themselves and their belongings clean, neat, and confined within the boundary of the mat on which they sleep. People of the second type appear to always have the world in their everyday perspective. They naturally ask questions about their country's place in the world as the basic reference to position themselves in relation to outsiders or foreigners. The stranger in the public arena may find these people shockingly rude, mean-spirited, or perhaps cold and unfriendly. Only when one is viewed or treated as a friend in their home or workplace, can one see these people as actually warm, open, and kind, or cheerfully accommodating, supporting, and caring. People of the third type still swing back and forth between extreme states of mind: pessimism versus optimism, sadness versus happiness, or being worrisome versus being carefree. On the one hand, these people often lament the meager income they earn, the polluted and congested city in which they live, the rampant social problems they face, or, generally, the level of economic development their country has attained. On the other hand, they look genuinely content when they take low-status domestic jobs around the world; they appear transcendentally worry-free when they produce full houses of children one family after another; they remain amply joyful when they jump into contaminated water for a bath; and they seem brazenly careless when they ravage a public plaza with trash, graffiti, and human waste in a celebrative event.

3

Issues, Objectives, and Implications

Given the nature, scope, and complexity of the issue to be explored, it is necessary to clarify what objectives this study is intended to achieve. As far as research methodology is concerned, it is important to point out what limitations this study has.

First, this study attempts to serve as an alarm that certain crimes have moved beyond national borders, becoming a regional problem across Asia and the Pacific. For this purpose, the study is obliged to identify and explain major types of cross-border crimes and their general characteristics. Specifically, what are cross-border crimes? Are they conventional crimes, such as murder, robbery, forcible rape, burglary, and larceny, that just move beyond national or territorial borders? Are they categorically different crimes that germinate only in borderlands and cross-border transactions? Are cross-border crimes prevalent or serious enough for formal definitions or reactions from countries that share borders or from the international community as a whole? Cross-border violations are currently defined and handled by individual countries or territories. While there are so-called international surveys or statistics on criminal offenses, findings or results are always compiled or presented by individual countries or territories as they are collected and stored. While this study uses live cases it finds available in the public domain, it must leave to future scholarly inquiries to delve, with the appropriate tools, into the specific nature, incidence, pattern, and trend of those crimes within nations and those that could be classified as cross-border crimes.

Second, this study aims to offer a warning that social control must be not only a national responsibility, but also an international effort. With this goal, the study tries to pinpoint what one country may learn from another in fighting crime and securing a safe environment for its citizens. Specifically, what is cross-border social control? What crime, problem, or issue falls under cross-border control? What does cross-border control entail? Does it necessarily require one country to yield to another in sovereignty, defense, or national pride? Does it occur only when there is a common threat and a shared interest in facing the common threat between or among countries? Is it unavoidably difficult for one country to hand over its citizen for prosecution by another country where that citizen is charged with a serious crime? Is it against self-interest for one country to prevent its citizens from leaving home to seek economic fortunes in other more developed countries? Although it sounds plausible that cross-border crimes call for cross-border control, it remains true that differences or gaps in social control lie behind most violations or offenses that occur between or among countries. The truth points to an urgent need for mutual understanding, respect, and support among different social control systems throughout the international community. This study focuses on common social control protocols across national borders in Asia and the Pacific. It is for other empirical investigations to examine control cooperation between or among countries and to explore different control measures taken in response to various international crimes in the region and around the world.

Third, this study aspires to show that crime and social control mesh inexorably with larger social forces in a somewhat unbreakable cause-effect chain of interaction. In this abstract yet important mission of enlightenment, the study connects crime and social control to basic social structures and fundamental social processes in Asia and the Pacific. On the level of human evolution, there is a contrast between Western and Eastern civilizations. Whereas Western civilizations attempt a technological understanding and control of nature, Eastern civilizations orient people to peace and harmony among themselves as well as with their natural environment. On the level of social system, there is a confrontation between capitalism and socialism. Whereas capitalism upholds private ownership and individual prosperity, socialism advocates collective control of means of production by the state on behalf of all people for the sake of the common welfare. On the level of active social forces, people always exhibit ambivalence in their attitudes toward tradition versus modernity. While tradition may invoke pride, sufficiency, and comfort, modernity brings about challenge, prosperity, and excitement. There is also a struggle between the state and the civil society. While the state tends to garner power in its hand, civil society constantly strives for difference, diversity, and individuality. A selective interest in or a differential emphasis on means over ends, or vice versa, is always at issue. For example, people not only think about their strategies or tactics when they hunt down and capture a target enemy, but also reflect upon their legal, ethical, or professional conduct even when they have their target enemy in custody. This study is the first adventure through wild and rough terrains of humanity, civilization, ideology, political economy, law, power, conflict, domination, and social order for intellectual insights and enlightenments. It hopes to motivate many more daring, stimulating, and thought-provoking research endeavors to fully appreciate and understand both general dynamics and specific mechanisms of cross-border crime and social control throughout Asia and the Pacific and around the world.

Fourth, this study does not claim to be representative. Most academic inquires find their legitimacy by being representative. A research project becomes legitimate or significant if it presents findings or results applicable to all units of analysis in the universe of its subjects. Scientifically, representation is ensured by random selection of units of analysis in a study. With respect to this research, what is the unit of analysis? Is it an individual country or an individual institution or an individual person within each selected country? Obviously, such an issue was not even raised when the author embarked on the study. The author just wanted to know what was going on when he made observational visits to major spots and talked to people from different walks of life in each country or in each territory across Asia and the Pacific. From a research point of view, however, what he sees, whom he sees, what he asks about, and to whom he asks questions are essentially accidental in the large context of a country or territory. Information gathered from accidental visits and conversations is technically valid and true only at the time when and in the place where the author made his observations and conducted his interviews. Analysis derived from such an effort may therefore be insightful only for understanding similar events or similar groups of people. While it sounds critically modest or discouraging, that is all the utility this exploration study may possibly offer. On the issue of legitimacy, this study can seek its justification only by way of uniqueness. The core of an argument for uniqueness is that something is noticeable because it is different from anything else. More generally, something is worthy of academic attention simply because it exists, even at an isolated place for a limited time.

Another disclaimer about this study is that it does not purport to be a source of information for statistical summation or any other practical purpose. If one is interested in knowing about crime and crime rates in a particular country or comparing social control and social control measures among jurisdictions in a region, one probably should begin with official crime or criminal justice statistics collected and compiled by a governmental authority. If one is interested in following a particular cross-border crime to see how frequently it takes place or how seriously it causes injury or inflicts damage to the people, properties, or jurisdictions involved, one probably ought to design or conduct a study of the crime at a specific location within a specific time frame. If one wants to portray cross-border crime and social control with live images, accurate numbers, or reliable statistics, one may have to wait until some ad hoc international entity is formed and commissioned to collect such information for a duration of time. As to this study, one can see it only as a source of inspiration to explore crime, deviance, and other social problems in the larger social dynamics of a region, to examine law, control, and social order amid the greater social forces of an era, and to reflect upon crime and social control along the recurrent themes of the general human evolution.

Furthermore, this study does not claim to be a reference for whatever one wants to know about crime and social control in Asia and the Pacific. Crime is a complex social issue. It is defined differently across jurisdictions. There are conventional crimes, such as homicide, robbery, and theft, and unconventional crimes, such as terrorism, political persecution, and witch hunts. A type of crime may increase, decline, or remain steady over time. If one wants to follow common crimes in Asia and the Pacific, one can delve into crime statistics for individual countries or territories to see how some crimes become commonplace under specific circumstances or within a set time frame. Social control lies in the hand of an authority in a particular country or territory. There is informal control in the form of persuasion, guidance, and exemplary influence, and formal control in the form of restitution, retribution, and reformation. Social control may be permissive here, restrictive there, or become neutral or ineffective in some places for some time. If one hopes to study effective social control measures or models, one can best satisfy one's desires by entering individual jurisdictions to find out how some control measures or models are effectively developed and fine-tuned. Crime intertwines with social control. Crime, with its changing prevalence, seriousness, and consequence, calls variably for social control. Social control, by its varying certainty, severity, and celerity, feeds differentially back on crime. If one wishes to investigate the interactive relationship between crime and social control, one can best serve one's interest by choosing a particular crime or a particular form of social control to see how one results in or from the other within an identifiable jurisdiction. One can take this study only as a point of departure or as a source of motivation for detailed, in-depth research into crime, deviance, social control, and their interactions in a particular country or territory or over a peculiar region composed of a limited number of interrelated nations or jurisdictional entities.

Despite the shortcomings it has in research and research methodology, this study attempts to be general and systematic in theory. In categorizing various types of cross-border crime and social control, it strives to be complete. In explaining each type of crime and social control across national borders, it aims to be critical, and hopefully, insightful. In analyzing large social forces, it attempts to be historical and holistic. Ideal types are described and explained often beyond the limitation of empirical observations and experiences. Causes and effects are explored and pinpointed to the extent that is possible in an observational study. Structures and processes are delineated and specified always in the spirit of scientific logic and sociological imagination. While it does not provide definite information about any particular type of crime and social control within and outside particular countries or territories, this study hopes to serve as a beginning, a reference, or a motivator for any country-specific study of crime and social control in Asia and the Pacific and for inquiries into cross-border crime, control, and social dynamics around the world.

Part II

CRIME AND DEVIANCE:
TYPES, PATTERNS, AND CHARACTERISTICS

Industrialization, urbanization, and economic development can improve material conditions and the quality of life. But they also increase opportunities for deviance and criminal behavior. As conventional crimes climb, unconventional social deviance and new crime make their debut as well. In rapidly developing countries across Asia and the Pacific, it is no surprise to see growth in both the volume of conventional crimes and the type of new criminal activities (Xu 1995; Zvekic 1995; Findlay 1999; Newman 1999; Goddard 2001; Schiray 2001; Oldenburg 2002).

4

Crime Resulting from Social Disorganization

Social disorganization is a social condition that appeared during the early stage of Western industrialization and urbanization (Durkheim 1952; Park, Burgess, and McKenzie 1967). In the new era of development and modernization across Asia and the Pacific, migrants not only move from rural villages to urban areas, but also cross national borders from the Philippines to Saudi Arabia, from Thailand to Japan, from Central Asia to Northwestern China, or from China to Australia, Canada, and the United States (Jayasuriya and Sang 1991; Shaw 2003). Social disorganization therefore takes both domestic and international forms.

BCKGROUND

The idea of social disorganization was conceived at the University of Chicago in the 1920s. Following rapid industrialization and extensive urbanization at the turn of the century, Chicago sociologists were poised to survey and understand omnipresent manifestations of unprecedented changes in the vast landscape of the United States.

W. I. Thomas and Florian Znaniecki (1920) studied Polish immigrants in America and their relatives in Poland. They found that immigrants have difficulty assimilating the norms and values of their new social environments, while seeing that what used to work for them in their rural communities of a different cultural tradition no longer served their new needs of living in the midst of industrializing cities. Caught in the lack of normative guidance between their old and new worlds, immigrants develop an "anything goes, nothing works" attitude. With that attitude, they could easily drift into divorce, deviance, mental disorder, and other forms of socially undesirable behavior.

Thomas and Znaniecki's study provides a classical statement of the social disorganization perspective. Using similar methods, such as observations, interviews, and personal documents, Chicago scholars ventured into various dynamics of social disorganization to illustrate "the process by which the authority and influence of an earlier culture and system of social control are undermined and eventually destroyed" (Park, Burgess, and McKenzie 1967: 107). Thomas (1923) himself examined the life of a prostitute in *The Unadjusted Girl*. Nels Anderson (1923) studied homelessness in *The Hobo: The Sociology of the Homeless Man*. Ernest Mowrer (1927) analyzed disorganized families in *Family Disorganization*. Louis Wirth (1928) and Harvey Zorbaugh (1929) focused on slums in their respective works: *The Ghetto* and *The Gold Coast and the Slum*. Frederick Thrasher (1927) researched gangs and gang activities in *The Gang*. Clifford Shaw (1930) followed the story of a delinquent boy in *The Jack Roller*. He later cooperated with Maurice Moore (1931) in *The Natural History of a Delinquent Career* and James McDonald (1938) in *Brothers in Crime*. Other scholars who concentrated on the "seamy side" of city life in the perspective of social disorganization included Paul Cressey (1932), *The Taxi-Dance Hall*; Norman Hayner (1936), *Hotel Life*; and Edwin Sutherland (1937), *The Professional Thief*.

While being persistent in their internal-subjective approaches, Chicago scholars also emphasized efforts to measure objectively external factors that affect both the process and consequence of social disorganization. Robert Park (1936), in cooperation with Ernest Burgess, studied the physical layout of Chicago and developed an ecological model of five concentric zones to capture the interrelationships of people and their environment in the city. At the center is the downtown business district occupied by commercial establishments, law and governmental offices, and business headquarters. In the outer reaches of the city is the commuter zone of satellite towns lived in by people with bountiful social and economic resources. In between are the transition zone, the zone of workingmen's homes, and the residential zone. The zone of workingmen's homes provides blue-collar workers with easy access to jobs and city transportation networks. The residential zone features single-family homes owned by small entrepreneurs, professionals, and managerial personnel. The zone in transition, however, gathers poor and unskilled beggars, bums, vagabonds, and other rootless people in dilapidated tenements next to old factories, warehouses, and red-light businesses. Being pushed by the growing business district, it bears and exemplifies most of the bruises and wounds of urban social change: truancy, delinquency, prostitution, gambling, substance abuse, homelessness, mental illness, suicide, and criminal activities.

The ecological model soon became the hallmark of the social disorganization perspective. Applying the model, Clifford Shaw and Henry McKay (1969) explored the ecological distribution of delinquency. A systematic examination of juvenile court records revealed these findings: (a) delinquency, along with infant mortality, truancy, mental disorder, and other community problems, takes place differentially throughout the city, with the highest rates of occurrence in the areas nearest the central business zone; (b) areas of high delinquency are characterized by a high percentage of immigrants, nonwhites, or families on relief, and a low percentage of home ownership; and (c) some areas consistently suffer from high delinquency, regardless of the ethnic composition of residents. In a similar spirit, Robert Faris and Warren Dunham (1939) mapped the ecological distribution of public hospitalization for serious mental disorders. According to them, "the highest rates for schizophrenia are in hobohemia, the rooming-house, and foreign-born communities close to the center of the city ... as these communities represent areas of some disorganization due to their close proximity to the steel factories"(Faris and Dunham 1939: 95).

Social disorganization theorizing continued after the Chicago School era. Within the United States, Bernard Lander (1954) conducted representative research in Baltimore, Maryland, David Bordua (1959) in Detroit, Michigan, and Roland Chilton (1964) in Indianapolis, Indiana. All these area studies show that ecological conditions, such as substandard housing, low income, and unrelated people living together, predict high incidence of delinquency. Concerning immigration, Richard Sollenberger (1968) invoked social disorganization imagery to explain why children in Chinatown, the tightly knit, family-oriented Chinese-American enclave, do not become delinquents. Outside the United States, especially in developing societies, Kirson Weinberg (1976) examined juvenile delinquency in Accra, Ghana. He found that delinquent youths are concentrated in areas characterized by physical deterioration, disintegration of traditional family structures, poor education, unskilled labor, poverty, alcoholism, and high rates of adult crime. Marshall Clinard and Daniel Abbott (1976) studied property crime in Kampala, Uganda. Comparing radically different rates of property offenses in two physically similar slums, they discovered that the low-crime slum has greater homogeneity in population, more family stability, a larger degree of sharing in tribal customs, more intimate interactions among residents, and a higher level of participation in community organizations.

Toward the 1980s and 1990s, interest began to shift away from traditional emphasis on conflict in values. The new generation of social ecologists focuses more on the relationship of community deterioration and economic decline to criminality (Byrne and Sampson 1985). Among various physical, economic, and social conditions examined are abandoned buildings, deserted houses, apartments in poor repair, trash and litter, graffiti, boarded-up storefronts, noise, congestion, lack of employment, limited job opportunities, population turnover, poverty concentration, and life cycles in community change. For instance, Ralph Taylor and Jeanette Covington (1988) followed the life cycle in urban areas, from the increase in population density to changes in racial or ethnic make-up, to population thinning, and from housing construction to residential decline or decay, to housing replacement and upgrade or neighborhood gentrification. They pointed out that community fear and crime rates increase when urban areas undergo such cyclical change (1993). To a lesser degree though, social ecologists also look into the nonmaterial dimension of disorganized neighborhoods. Community fear, siege mentality, the effect of poverty concentration, and social altruism are conceptualized to explain why crime and social problems spread, persist, or decrease in response to prevalent sentiments shared by residents in the community (Wilson 1987; Anderson 1990; Chamlin and Cochran 1997; Holloway 1998).

CAUSE

Social disorganization relates inherently to change and its nature, scale, pace, duration, and impact. As rapid change occurs in a short period of time and rural people flock to urban centers to seek economic fortunes, a large portion of the population become spiritually disoriented. Although they see that the old values, lifestyles, and community relations they bring with them no longer serve their needs for belonging and togetherness, they also find that it is difficult to acquire new rules, norms, and ways of living in the current environment. They feel that anything goes but nothing works. This attitude facilitates a drift to deviance and crimes.

Underlying the general portrayal of social disorganization and its connection to individual deviations, there is a need to identify and analyze fundamental causes for social disorganization at both societal and individual levels. For society as a whole, war, revolution, modernization, natural disaster, an epidemic, a change of system, a change in government, a change of culture, and a change of lifestyle are usually events that can cause the state of social disorganization. War erupts in a country when it is invaded by another country or countries or when it is divided by two or more domestic forces fighting for dominance in its territory. In the midst or aftermath of a war, private properties are destroyed, people are forced to flee from place to place, cities lie in ruins, and the entire country falls into a political vacuum. There is moral ambiguity or confusion: Justice or injustice seems to be determined by the results of warfare. There is material decay or loss when one side attacks the other by bombs, fires, and other destructive forces. There is social chaos or anarchy as people run away, speculate on goods, services, or securities, or steal foods and other daily articles out of their instincts for survival. Across Asia and the Pacific, war seemed never to cease to make its impact in the twentieth century and now into the twenty-first century. At the multilateral level, World War II, the Korean War, and the Vietnam War involved multiple countries, including major powers such as China and the United States, in the region. Bilaterally, China fought along its border areas with India, the former Soviet Union, and Vietnam. Cambodia was taken over by Vietnam. Iraq battled Iran, invaded Kuwait, and is now occupied by an American-led foreign force. Within individual countries, ethnic conflict, religious confrontation, and regional strife often flare up to full-scale warfare. In Sri Lanka, the Tamil Tigers have been fighting for decades for control over the Northern and Eastern parts of the island country. In Indonesia, the newly formed province of North Maluku is still recovering from a period of communal violence that began as an ethnic conflict in the late 1999s and raged on as a religious war through the early 2000s. Afghanistan has yet to consolidate itself as a united country after its lengthy sufferings of a bitter civil war among tribes since the Soviet withdrawal in the late 1980s.

Revolution takes place around ideas that have their origin in ideology, religion, government, economy, and culture. Transforming a society or country on a grand scale, revolution often invokes heated ideological debates, confrontational social movements, and even bloody wars in the battlefield. Social values, norms, and beliefs change in form, style, and substance as one side rises to dominance and the other becomes muted. Population groups switch or rotate by political power, economic interest, or social leverage when some take control and others become disfranchised. Physical infrastructure, production facilities, city properties, and material life may fall into total destruction amid revolutionary conflicts or begin to take shape following a revolution-inspired reconstruction. As for cross-border movement, political dissidents are sent to exile in foreign countries when a revolutionary regime pursues radical policies or becomes simply repressive. Civilian refugees are pushed into border regions or international destinations as domestic turmoil continues unabatedly. Throughout Asia and the Pacific, the most sweeping revolution is undoubtedly the communist revolution that divides China across the Taiwan Strait, militarizes the Koreas on the Korean Peninsula, unifies Vietnam between the South and the North, and pits Cuba against its giant neighbor, the United States. The communist revolution also fuels, penetrates, or intertwines with other revolutions. The Great Cultural Revolution that sent hundreds of thousands of urban youths to the countryside for reeducation through labor is part of the larger communist revolution in China. The Iranian Revolution that revived Islamic Fundamentalism in the Middle East began as a workers' revolution against an autocratic monarchy supported by capitalist and landlord classes. Even the Asian Industrial Revolution, a different kind of revolution that took Japan to the apex of the second largest economy in the world and turned South Korea, Hong Kong, Taiwan, and Singapore into four little dragons in Asia, came about through defensive strategies devised by Western powers against possible communist expansion.

Modernization has been a thematic force of human evolution in the past three hundred years since the Industrial Revolution first began in England. Modernization features industrialization, urbanization, bureaucratization, specialization, and social differentiation. In the process of modernization, older generations cling to traditional values, family-based farming or craftsmanship, communal interconnectedness, age-old social groupings, and customary ways of life while younger generations are educated with scientific beliefs, knowledge, and skills for work on specialized jobs on mass production lines or in bureaucratized environments throughout cities. Moral confusion is tremendous in the beginning and remains salient even when a society settles well into later phases of modernization. Physical disorder is massive at the initial stage and may exist as a chronic condition as the society struggles to catch up with its more advanced neighbors. Social dislocation becomes constant as economic sectors expand and contract, interest groups rise and fall, and social fashions or lifestyles gain currency and lose favor. With an enormous gap in modernization among countries or territories, the region of Asia and the Pacific exhibits all the manifestations of social disorganization, not only over the historical flow of time but also in spatial existence. While a significant number of people in Hong Kong, Japan, Singapore, and the United States face the challenge of discovery and innovation in technology, organizational management, and job skills in a largely modernized physical environment, a considerable proportion of the population in Afghanistan, Bangladesh, Cambodia, and the Philippines still have to deal with the immediate urgency of finding and securing water, foods, and shelters for survival in urban ghettos, deserted villages, or dust-shrouded crossroads. In between, people in China, Chile, India, and Indonesia are spread throughout the whole spectrum from one extreme to the other. There are highly bureaucratized organizations in advanced areas where research, marketing, and management personnel engage in tense competition with their counterparts in high-tech and other fast-changing arenas around the world. There are also utterly disorganized communities in backward hinterlands where residents will pawn some of their children for money or pieces of property on which they can live and maintain life for their extended family.

Natural disasters occur by the force of nature. In forms from epidemic, typhoon, hurricane, earthquake, flood, drought, fire, famine, and heat wave to snowstorm, they result most commonly in massive property damage or human loss. A specific natural disaster may fall upon a particular area, country, or continent. It may involve a whole region or half of the world. Natural disasters change people's immediate living environment. They challenge humans' desired version of the world or preferred way of life. For a short period of time and in the shock of a mighty natural force, people are not only prompted to think abstractly about the nature of environment, the essence of social order, and the meaning of life, but also forced to plan practically for their own survival, adjustment, and adaptation. Social disorganization therefore manifests itself in both physical devastations and emotional, spiritual, or intellectual shakeups, following a major natural disaster. Asia and the Pacific, due to its sheer size and unique geographic characteristics, seem to bear most of the bruises and wounds of natural disasters in the world. Of the most explosive and deadly natural disasters that ever strike human societies, an overwhelming majority takes place in Asia or around the Pacific Rim. Depending upon where it hits and how severe and widespread it is, a natural disaster may cause massive dislocation within a country or involve a number of countries in a border region to deal with a large flow of refugees. When it combines with war, revolution, and other human atrocity, a natural disaster may even send masses of people in one country into another country for indefinite resettlement. For example, Northeast China has become a gathering ground for hundreds of thousands of Korean refugees who fled from years of drought, famine, and dictatorship in North Korea. Hong Kong, Singapore, and even Taiwan are often sought-after destinations by Afghanis, Bangladeshis, Indians, Pakistanis, Sri Lankans, and Chinese who are displaced by natural disasters or other turmoil in their respective homelands.

Following war, revolution, modernization, and natural disasters, there are often changes as drastic and disruptive as a change of social system or a change of government, or as gradual and fundamental as a change of culture or a change of lifestyle. A change of social system may feature a transformation from kingdom, monarchy, or chiefdom to representative, elective, or democratic polities, from household, communal, or controlled productions to open, free, or market economies, or from feudalism or colonialism to capitalism or socialism. A change of government accompanies a change of social system but may occur routinely under the same system, from conservative to liberal, from one party to another, and from the old guard to elements of an emergent force. A change of culture results from a change of social system or a change of government when old beliefs, values, norms, and practices are discouraged or prohibited in favor of a new ideology, a new code of morality, a new social order, and a new way of life. A change of lifestyle is reflected essentially in the evolving standard of living, level of material affluence, availability of scientific knowledge, and even degree of social tolerance. Only in an open, free, and affluent society, can lifestyle become an individual choice on the basis of science rather than social dictation from tradition or custom.

No matter whether it is drastic or gradual, a change of social system, government, culture, or lifestyle creates a situation where choices and adjustments have to be made between contrasting or opposing forces. Social disorganization occurs. So do social disorganization-derived deviance, crime, and social problems. Across Asia and the Pacific, the Chinese Communist Revolution sent widespread shockwaves when communists came into power, turning Mainland China from a partly feudal and partly colonial society into a fully socialist country. Filipinos received close attention when they staged a people's revolution to bring down the Marcos regime for a more meaningful form of democratic government. Cambodians fled in thousands and died in millions when a culture of genocide took dominance under the radically ideologized Khmer Rouge. As modernization continues, people in Asia and the Pacific become more and more aware of both the benefits and the dangers associated with economic development, material affluence, and individualistic lifestyle. Change is in the making when people take a more and more balanced approach toward nature, society, and their own way of life.

At the individual level, people make choices in work and life. They move from place to place, not only due to dramatic events that happen in the immediate environment, but also in response to opportunities that exist in remote locations. There are migrants who leave rural areas to work in urban centers, who deal goods along transportation lines, who follow production seasons from one job to another, and who launch business adventures in hinterlands. When they cross national borders to settle in foreign lands for opportunities in work, business, or family life, migrants become immigrants to their adopted nations or emigrants from their countries of origin. By specific category, migrants first include students who come from the countryside or Third World countries to acquire knowledge and skills in cities or advanced capitalist nations. As they are socialized into and prepared for working and living in organizational environments with scientific knowledge, contemporary values, and technical skills, students are likely to stay in cities or advanced societies where they study. In China, for example, millions of high school graduates leave home in various parts of the country each year for colleges and universities in cities. Thousands of Chinese college graduates seek study opportunities in developed Western countries, such as Australia, Britain, Canada, France, Germany, Japan, and the United States. Although it is not widely recognized and properly understood by migration studies, migration by way of study and training is the most original, fundamental, and important form of population change and shift within and outside national borders.

There are also job seekers, takers, or performers who move from one place to another in response to employment opportunities or due to job assignment. Missionaries travel to remote areas or aboriginal societies to spread the word of God. Soldiers fight a guerrilla war in the mountains or serve as mercenary troops on faraway battlefields. Diplomats live in a foreign country to represent and promote the interests of their homeland. Anthropologists, archeologists, geographers, and other scientific explorers spend years in the wild or away from home to study subjects of interest to them. While all these older types of migrant workers continue their stints, they are far outnumbered by the large army of people on job assignment from multinational corporations and state-owned and operated military forces, diplomatic corps, business conglomerates, and organizational bureaucracies. For example, multinational corporations in Australia, Canada, Japan, and the Unites States send hundreds of technical, marketing, and management personnel from their home countries to the factories, stores, or service stations they operate in Bangladesh, China, Indonesia, or Thailand. Thousands of American service men and women work on military bases in Japan, South Korea, and Turkey, and now in posts in Afghanistan and Iraq as well, or on aircraft carriers or submarines across the Pacific Ocean. While China has teams of engineers, mechanics, medical professionals, and laborers on various contract projects in the Middle East, Indonesia and the Philippines both supply a large number of domestic workers to the same region. Migration by way of work, organizationally sponsored or individually initiated, is undoubtedly the most common yet significant movement of people on both domestic and international fronts.

With wealth accumulated over lifetime or concentrated in a family fortune, there appears a growing leisure class of people who are free from labor and able to live within any country throughout the international community. In the past, only kings, queens, emperors, warlords, or business tycoons could send their children, spouses, mistresses, relatives, confidants, or maids to exclusive resorts or exotic lands for seasonal resettlement, recreational getaway, or longtime vacation. In contemporary society where the overall level of material affluence is high, communication is advanced, and transportation is fast, more and more people seem to be able to join the ranks of this leisure class. From Canada and the United States, flocks of people retired from middle-class professions or individual entrepreneurships migrate to tropical resorts in Mexico for a long getaway from their winter home. Some even resettle in sunshine states in the West or in the South. From Hong Kong, Macao, Singapore, Taiwan, and even Mainland China, throngs of families make efforts to purchase homes in Australia, Canada, the United States, and other advanced nations so that some of their members can enjoy and appreciate political freedom, cultural diversity, and the everyday life amenities afforded by well-developed economies and long-democratized social systems. Among those families that can afford to make such a cross-border attempt, some are wealthy, powerful, and connected, and some are plainly reliant upon common business operations, ordinary professional practices, and other regular income-generating endeavors. The leisure class is clearly no longer exclusive in the contemporary era. It draws people more and more from different ranks in society under the expanding material affluence across the globe.

In contrast to the migratory movement by an emergent leisure class, exile and refuge have risen to salience as a form of individual move made by commoners, even have-nots. Exile used to be a reserved option for deposed heads of state, prominent political, religious, or cultural dissidents or critics, or notorious criminal group leaders. Refuge was once limited to a specific number of people dislocated by a widely known natural or unnatural event in a particular region for a definite period of time. In today's increasingly globalized world, however, exile and refuge have both become a common avenue, if not a general excuse, for people to move from place to place. At the international level, a few factors seem to be responsible for the ever increasing flow of exiles and refugees from impoverished to advanced economies, from oppressed to democratized polities, and from one-sided to multifaceted socio-cultural systems. First, as it works to place and protect refugees, the United Nations plays an important role in creating the need for refuge as well as finding accommodations for refugees around the world. Second, as they monitor and criticize political, religious, cultural, and human rights practices in other countries, the United States and other advanced nations are obliged to offer exile or refuge for people who allegedly suffer from abuses in their home country. Third, as they help exiles and refugees, a number of lawyers, service workers, and other related professionals become not only specialized in but also dependent upon exile and refugee affairs for their employment and careers. Lastly, people in the contemporary era seem to care less and less about their attachment to a locale which they call home, birthplace, or place of origin. They tend to focus more and more on their relationship to a place where they can adapt, earn a living, and survive. Exile and refuge, therefore, are seen in frequent and wide use by ordinary people not just as last resorts in unexpected crises, but as personal options in unfavorable circumstances. For example, through careful planning and with professional assistance from lawyers, a Chinese couple can legitimately seek and secure asylum in the United States by reason of China's restrictive one-child policy.

Spouses, children, parents, and relatives of students, workers, owners of business ventures, members of the leisure class, exiles, and refugees join their loved ones in the migratory force sooner or later. Indeed, family reunion has been the most robust form of population movement on the face of the earth since ancient times. Social sentiment takes family for granted and gravitates naturally toward reunion of separated family members. When an illegal alien tells her relatives, friends, neighbors, congregational fellows, and co-workers that she has two young children back in Mexico, people around her often automatically offer her advice or tangible assistance for bringing her children to the United States, sometimes even through illegal means. Work and employment organizations acknowledge family and make efforts to accommodate employees in their need for family relocation. When an employee intends to bring his or her spouse to the place where he or she lives, the employer usually feels obligated to sponsor or facilitate a petition for such a move with the appropriate authority. In China, even during the time of stringent control, individual work units still managed to assist numerous employees in relocating their families from rural areas to townships to cities to metropolises where a rigid household registration system used to be enforced to limit new entries (Shaw 1996). State authorities sanction family and provide the legal framework for people to move and reorganize their family from one locale to another across geographical demarcations as well as national borders. The United States has long recognized family and family reunion as the most natural and legitimate reason in its immigration policy. For every immigrant it intends to receive for artistic, educational, entertainment, scientific, military, political, diplomatic, and other purposes, it may have to receive another five to ten people because of family and family connection. It is possible that persons who enter the country initially by themselves may, after a time, bring spouse, children, parents, parents-in-law, brothers, sisters, brothers-in-law, and sisters-in-law, and nephews to areas all over the United States through personal effort. In some locales famous for emigration in Asia, people in a whole village or township have made their way to the United States because one of their natives was first able to open the door to the most prosperous country in the world.

TYPE, PATTERN, AND CHARACERISTICS

No matter what causes them to move—war, revolution, and natural disasters or study, job assignment, and family reunion—migrants face contrasts between home and an unfamiliar place, between rural villages and urban compounds, or between peaceful communities and disorganized neighborhoods. No matter how they make their move, in large flocks or by individual choice, migrants have to deal with language barriers, developmental gaps, and cultural differences between communities, cities, or countries of origin and resettlement. Social disorganization deviance and crimes, therefore, become not only inevitable due to the level of the change involved in every migratory movement, but also diversified because of the complexity of the change accompanied by migrant crossings over regional and national borders.

Among migrants, being away from home can result in mental and behavioral adjustments. First is a general state of loneliness, restlessness, and helplessness, which may lead to anxiety, depression, and the disposition to abuse alcohol and even illicit drugs. Ordinarily, bars, liquor stores, strippers' clubs, and other businesses associated with vice thrive in the areas around bus depots, train stations, and even airports. Local business owners and sex workers like dealing with aliens and strangers because these clients are anxious, needy, know little about the local situation, and can be easily exploited for profit. Second is a desire to emulate local people in some personal hobbies or customary lifestyles. Since this desire is often externally stimulated and not yet integrated culturally, it may put a newcomer in trouble. For example, a newly arrived young student who thinks Halloween is completely fun and play time may get killed in his or her first "trick or treat" trip in the United States when he or she is not able to properly interpret some critical situational cues or fails to understand some local conversational English terms such as "freeze" and "shush." Someone who used to hunt freely in his or her home country may take aim at people when he or she is scolded, threatened, or shamed by a group of local hunters for transgression into private property in a country where people take private ownership seriously. Third is a natural attempt to stick to past connections or to keep what they bring with them. Migrants may ease their homesickness by following some old routines. They may remember their relatives by observing some rituals. Collectively, they may preserve their home culture by constructing temples, mosques, and other establishments in an alien environment. All these attempts often raise eyebrows among local people. In the extreme, hate crimes even occur from time to time around ethnic or religious symbols, businesses, and constructions. Finally, habit is a force in a person's continuing familiar practices in a new environment. If immigrants used to discipline children by corporal punishment or to silence spouses by physical force, some of them may feel hamstrung in their family lives when they learn they are not allowed legally to do so. For instance, some Asian immigrants in Canada and the United States go back to their home countries simply because they fear they may lose the custody of their children to the state authority for practicing a familiar family disciplining. In a rare case, an immigrant worker fell into years of mental disability following his arrest for slapping his girlfriend in the United States. He began to recover only after his friends found him and put him on a plane back to Asia.

Most migrants leave home because they hope for a better life elsewhere. Except for a few members of the leisure class, most migrants have to work on a job or operate a business to support themselves. While some begin with a small family asset brought with them, some rely upon friends or relatives, and some capitalize on their unique talents and skills, the largest number of migrants simply bet on the future job market. They hang out at marketplaces, near home improvement stores, or around a publicly known location for maids, nannies, porters, handymen, or craft workers. Waiting for hours or days in anxiety and humility, migrants may follow any job offer to work under every imaginable condition, any exploitative possible term for compensation and any harmful possible condition to personal health. Watching personal savings disappear rapidly in the everyday cost of living, migrants may have to take extraordinary measures: abandoning children, becoming street beggars, offering sex for sale, or yielding to the term of slavery. Falling into prostitution and slavery is a common outcome for many desperate migrants. Across Asia and the Pacific, despite the often dramatized and misinformed media portrayal that Western blondes profit by way of prostitution or sex-centered work in major metropolises or that rural beauties benefit from the flesh-trade in big cities, most prostitutes take the age-old practice out of no choice, no alternative, or sheer desperation. Upon querying any prostitute, in a five-star hotel or on a litter-strewn street, rarely does the researcher find one who would say she does it because she likes doing it. Most would likely counter with this question: "What else can I do to survive in this strange place?" On the matter of slavery or near-slavery, although abuse of domestic workers remains mostly in the dark, there are still reports that nannies are severely beaten, maids are sexually exploited, or housekeepers are periodically denied monetary compensations, constantly put in long hours of daily work, unreasonably punished for damaged or lost family items, or inhumanely forced into living with pets. In Malaysia, the author read a case exposed in a local newspaper in which an Indonesian maid was burned on her face with boiling water by her employer after she was repeatedly raped by the employer's husband. The situation faced by the maid is not uncommon. Oftentimes, when a maid is raped by the host, she then has to face double punishments: from the hostess for ruining her marriage and from the host for failing to keep the affair secret.

Migrants move from place to place. They stand out as strangers or aliens in any community in which they work or settle. Local law enforcement officials question migrants, order them to leave, or take them into custody when they rest in the park, sleep overnight at the bus or train station, or have a dispute with residents. Local people look down upon migrants, treat them with suspicion, or just take advantage of them. From merchants who overcharge them, to bus drivers who drop them in the middle of nowhere, to employers who threaten them with little or no pay, and to youth hooligans who extort money or sex from them, migrants face pressures and perils at almost every step of their life away from home. In every booming town, every transportation hub, and every transnational metropolis across Asia and the Pacific, there is no lack of stories and reports about migrants being ripped off, robbed, assaulted, harassed, or mistreated. These reports indeed come and go in waves and tides. While most remains unnoticed, only a few dramatic incidents make it to the local, national, or international headline. Among some of the local headlines seen by the author throughout the region, a female migrant worker was gang raped in a nightly city bus on her way from work to where she lived, a high school graduate jumped off a high-rise building after losing his migrant girl friend to prostitution amid his own failure to secure a job, and a male migrant worker carrying his yearly earnings and all his belongings was stabbed to death by a group of robbers in a narrow alley leading to the bus station where he was scheduled to take an early morning bus home for a major holiday.

Migrants look for migrants in their search for reference, guidance, support, companionship, opportunities, and new ways of life. On transportation lines, migrants may feel close to each other by just learning that they are the same group of people: coming from a faraway place, being on the move for jobs, and having no roots in the local community. Out of a spontaneous trust developed in the natural attempt to identify with others, some migrants may leave their belongings in the care of their newly made acquaintances. However, by the time they return from the toilet, a ticket office, or an information booth, they may find everything gone, as if with the wind. There are, of course, more carefully planned individual operations or sophisticatedly orchestrated group schemes. For example, the author gathered a Chinese story in which two migrant brothers would look for men with a similar appearance to them at transit stations in Northwestern China. Once they have identified a target, they would approach him with a promise of job, treat him as another brother, and advise him to tell everyone that he is indeed their brother. They then would travel to a private coalmine operator for job applications as brothers. After working together at the coalmine for a month or so, the two real brothers would kill the migrant man in an underground worksite in such a way as to look as if he died from a job accident. The two brothers would then ask for a considerable amount of accidental death compensation from the private coalmine owner who would pay to settle to avoid any investigation by the government. Upon receipt of payment, the two migrant brothers would flee to another place to plot yet another crime against an unguarded innocent migrant looking for a job.

In a locale where they stay, migrants turn to those who come from the same place, speak the same language or dialect, or belong to the same ethnic or racial group. Relationship differentiates along with variables of connectedness, from the most general, such as race, ethnicity, or country of origin, to the most specific as sharing the same surname or attending the same school. For instance, Chinese in the United States identify with each other first because they are Chinese. They then distinguish themselves by social system, country, dialect, province, county, township, village, and even family name. Chinese from Hong Kong, Taiwan, and Singapore often feel some degree of separateness from the Chinese of Mainland China because they grew up in a different social system with a different level of economic affluence. As for manipulation, exploitation, and criminal offense, older migrants tend to prey on their newly arrived counterparts knowing that newcomers are inexperienced, fearful, and dependent upon external assistance. Most commonly, the former misinforms the latter, overcharges the latter on goods, loans, rental properties, and services, keeps the latter on low-paying jobs or even in servitude, and prevents the latter from mingling with and assimilating into the larger society. As elsewhere, applicable to migrants is a general law that the more people are similar to one another, the more they interact with each other; and the more they interact, the more they experience conflict, including exploitation and criminal victimization.

While they are targeted most of the time, migrants also take advantage of their transient status and prey on local residents in the community. The most common crimes committed by migrants are thefts, burglaries, shoplifting, swindling, vandalism, and other property offenses. But there are also assaults, robberies, rapes, and other violent crimes. In some migration corridors and destinations, migrants even pose a general threat to public order and social morality. First, there is widespread distrust among people. Local residents become suspicious of migrants when they read headlines about nannies abusing children, maids misusing family resources, handymen leaving in the middle of a home improvement project, or transients posing as messengers, porters, deliverymen, or collectors in order to commit crime in private homes. Migrants are on the defensive when they share stories about abusive housewives, exploitative employers, treacherous middlemen, and generally manipulative urban residents. Second, there is a massive security buildup across the city. Businesses put up walls and wires around their premises. Doors, even fire exits, are locked to prevent property damage or theft. Body searches and other aggressive procedures are conducted to deter employee stealing. Households become fortified behind layers of security devices and measures. Parallel to the original door is an iron and steel gate. Above the glass window are lined metal rails. Besides conventional locks is a security locking system. In some Chinese cities, for instance, seeing a family in an apartment building can be like visiting someone in a prison. One follows the host or hostess through a live guard's security at the main entrance, a live operator's security in the elevator, a first metal gate to a unit of a few households on the same flight, a second metal gate to the apartment, and finally the regular door into the house. It could take an extraordinary amount of warmth and hospitality from the host and hostess to defuse the eerie feeling a visitor would develop upon bearing the stares of suspicious humans and hearing the sound of brittle metal. Third, there is occasionally argument and fighting in public arenas. While local residents tend to pressure the government to limit access to jobs and social benefits by migrants, migrants can only gather in the streets to protest against unfair and inhumane treatment by employers, landlords, and other stakeholders in the community. Statistically, cities impacted by migration often attribute their social problems to migrants they greet and receive within their boundaries. Wuhan, an all-way transportation hub city in central China, used to blame migrants for much criminal activity since 51.5% of criminal suspects in custody were migrants and 60.5% of prostitution offenses handled by the municipal authority were committed by migrants in the late 1990s (Chen and Deng 1999). Shenzhen, a major migration destination city due to its well-known economic developmental zone across Hong Kong, once traced 97.0% of its crimes to migrants (Cao 1997). On the Eastern coast of the Pacific, various American local jurisdictions continually seek reimbursement from the federal government using the argument that they treat, educate, care for, and jail a significant number of migrants from foreign countries, especially Mexico, in their respective health, school, welfare, and correctional systems (Drucker 2004; Friedman 2005; Vitello 2006).

On the home front, migrants have left behind a whole familial and communal network. As home keepers long in worry and fear for the safe return of their loved ones, they themselves face both real dangers in their physical environment and potential ambivalences in their personal feelings and sentiments. The absence of male adults weakens defense in villages. Intruders step in. They prey on senile villagers for monetary and property gains. They target young, married women, lure them into inappropriate sexual relationships, and sexually assault them or forcibly rape them. Family farming plots are left idle. Raising children becomes problematic. Stressed wives and parents turn to alcohol to alleviate their loneliness and pain. In the hinterland of various Asian countries, an adult exodus to cities and coastal regions leaves children, women, and the elderly in emotional and economic struggles. Family ties are loosened. Community interdependence becomes shaky. Separation between married couples causes emotional tension and sexual stress. Husbands seek temporary sex relief with prostitutes while in migration. Wives commit adultery or are forcibly raped without their husbands' presence and protection. Returning adults bring venereal diseases back to their otherwise pristine homeland. They may even commit serious crimes to avenge their loved ones' betrayal and victimization. In a mountainous county of China, a returning husband killed his wife, her adulterer, and his mother-in-law who remained acquiescent to the affair because of the money received from her daughter's extramarital lover.

Coupled with the higher vulnerability of a male-adult-absent household is its increased material attractiveness. Migrants send home money, which is usually spent for a larger house, better house amenities, and more fashionable consumer goods. They bring home household electronics and other luxury consumer goods that are not commonly seen in use in rural areas. During the holidays or at a time when migrants are home and everyone is around, material possessions on display showcase the success of a migrant's adventure in the outside world. But when everything falls back to normal, a successful migrant's home exhibit can become a prime target for criminal victimization. Stories abound from place to place where newly built houses are set on fire by envious arsonists, homes are ransacked overnight when nobody is around, and where migrants' children, spouses, or parents are trapped into addictive behaviors, such as drug use and gambling, to bleed their family of the wealth that has been created and accumulated with so much difficult effort and struggle.

Besides physical dangers, migrant families have to deal with a tremendous amount of ambivalence in spiritual and sentimental dimensions. On the surface, children, spouses, and parents wonder whether their migrant father or mother, husband or wife, and son or daughter will ever be back home again. On another level, they wonder whether their loved ones on migration will come back as totally different persons, speaking a new language, taking on new manners, and perhaps looking down upon everything at home. On an even deeper level, they dream or fantasize that their migrant parent, spouse, or child will take them out of their home into a new world. Having one member of the family out on migration can alienate the family from the rest of the community to a large degree. Expecting them to leave sooner or later, neighbors, relatives, and friends tend to withdraw from migrant families. With half of the heart thinking about loved ones outside, migrant families indeed are no longer able to fully commit their spirit and their interest to the village or neighborhood in which they are based. A home visit by the migrant, whether the visitor is a success or failure, may further make the family stand out of the crowd. The final choice is often dictated by the principle of certainty or definiteness. That is, a family either follows its migrant member to leave once and forever or pulls its migrant member back to stay at its home community.

In all, social disorganization occurs as society changes rapidly by way of war, revolution, reform, development, modernization, or natural forces. A city falls or rises, creating ethnic ghettos, urban slums, makeshift shelters, littered streets, dilapidated apartment complexes, red light districts, deserted downtowns, or bustling business zones. Villages turn into boomtowns or lie in ruins, making farmlands disappear, industrial pollutions spread, and opportunist adventures appear. People move in flocks, running away from dangers, searching for ways of survival, or just following the crowd toward a commonly perceived destiny. Individuals embark on adventures, challenging a tradition, climbing a career ladder, or embracing an unknown future. In the new environment, people are likely to gather in problematic neighborhoods, facing various physical dangers while making subtle inner adjustments. Social disorganization manifests itself in deviance, delinquency, crime, and other social problems when people experience difficulty or are taken advantage of in their adaptation to a new or constantly changing environment. Although people may still deviate from the norm, violate the law, or commit criminal offenses when they settle in their familiar home community, they are more likely to run into trouble when they are on the move from one job, one organization, one community, one culture, one region, and even one country to another. Change alone is a significant factor in deviations. Migration itself accounts for much of social disorganization and many of its associated problems.

Across Asia and the Pacific, while developed countries remain relatively safe and stable from the gradual impact of a continuing advance in science, technology, material affluence, and social complexity, a large number of developing societies constantly bear the deep scars of war, revolution, development, and natural disasters. Social disorganization and its various symptoms run the whole gamut: adultery on job assignment, sex perversions among lonely professionals, while-collar deviance within institutional walls, pockets of homelessness and vagrancy, and isolated ethnic enclaves in developed countries; and masses of migrants, blocks of dilapidated houses, boroughs of trash-strewn streets, cities of ghettos and slums, widespread impoverishment, rampant crime, unchecked corruption, burning landfills, polluted waters, and skyrocketing social problems in developing societies.

5

Crimes of Opportunity

As the value of achievement is stressed and success is simplified as material gain, more and more people are drawn into tight competition and hence constant conflict for economic recognition and dominance. Some individuals are even willing to attempt everything, legal or illegal, to benefit from opportunities that arise from economic reform, dramatic events, and general social development but are oftentimes unequally distributed across the population.

BCKGROUND

Much of the discussion of crime and opportunity centers around the rational choice perspective, whose contemporary version grows out of the fertile intellectual soil provided by classical, neoclassical, and positivistic criminology (Cornish and Clarke 1986; Shaw 2002). The central tenets of this perspective are that people choose to commit or forgo crime in consideration of both personal and situational factors; the personal factors a reasoning criminal usually weighs include his or her needs for material gains, thrills, or revenge, his or her criminal skills, and his or her access to legitimate avenues for success; the situational factors a rational offender evaluates may range from the vulnerability of the target, the location of the operation, the reward of criminal undertaking, and the risk of apprehension, to the severity of punishment. In alignment with routine activities theory, rational choice theory further claims that crime is a product of criminal opportunity. Opportunity opens up when suitable targets, such as corner homes, secluded properties, unlocked cars, open doors, unattended luggage, and access streets into the neighborhood from traffic arteries, become available. It increases when capable guardians, including police officers, vigilant residents, security fences, and household alarms, are absent. Opportunity may also interact with criminal motivation to create various patterns of crime amid specific routine activities in a given environment. For example, urban environments make suitable victimization sites and attractive crime targets because they gather an enormous collection of consumer goods, commercial establishments, and material utilities. These environments continually produce motivated offenders because they support a highly fluid lifestyle through mass media, advanced means of transportation, and peer networking (Clarke 1995).

The assumption that criminals act rationally leads logically to the conclusion that strategies for dealing with criminals will reduce crime. Four main strategies are then proposed: situational crime prevention, general deterrence, specific deterrence, and incapacitation. Under situational crime prevention, Clarke and Homel (1997) identify four groups of effective techniques to reduce criminal incidents. Group I is to increase perceived effort through such techniques as target hardening, access control, deflecting offenders, and controlling facilitators. For example, restrictive gun control legislation may make it difficult for potential offenders to gain access to guns as crime facilitators. Group II includes entry/exit screening, formal surveillance by security devices or guards, surveillance by employees, and natural surveillance through street lighting. The general intent is to increase perceived risks by possible offenders. Group III involves a reduction of anticipated rewards by removing targets, identifying property, reducing temptation, and denying benefits. For instance, a gender-neutral telephone list may reduce temptation for telephone harassment of women victims. Finally, Group IV centers on inducing guilt or shame. It includes rule setting, strengthening moral condemnation, controlling disinhibitors, and facilitating compliance. To control or discourage drinking, for example, a drinking age law is put in place to prevent underage alcohol use. Signs like "bloody idiots drink and drive" are attached to the rear bumper of the car to deride and discourage potential violators.

General deterrence aims to make potential criminals fear the consequences of crime. If criminals are rational and if they know crime will be punished, they will choose not to commit crime. Specific deterrence is to punish known criminals so that they will not repeat their offenses. The reasoning is the same: A rational criminal learns from his or her painful experience with punishment. Three variables critically pertain to the effect of deterrence (Gibbs 1968). They are certainty, severity, and celerity. Certainty requires that criminals are caught and punished definitely for their lawbreaking behaviors. A potential offender with criminal friends may not fear punishment much if he or she learns from them how easy it is to get away with crime. Severity is about the level of pain, suffering, or threat inflicted or posed by punishment. The stiffer a sanction is, the more effective it is supposed to be in deterring crime. Celerity refers to the speed with which a sanction is applied to an offender or offense. The swifter it is imposed, the more effective it is in preventing future offense. The three variables are obviously interrelated. The death penalty, the most severe form of punishment, would lose its rigor if it took a considerable portion of an offender's lifetime for him or her to be executed for a capital offense. In addition to certainty, severity, and swiftness, studies also point to other variables, such as perception and informal sanctions, as important influences on penal effectiveness. For example, John Braithwaite (1989) argues that crime control should incorporate reintegrative shaming, by which criminal offenders are made to understand their wrongdoing and shame themselves before they are forgiven and reaccepted by society.

Incapacitation attempts to reduce crime by denying motivated offenders the opportunity to commit it. There are first critical ages during which people are more at risk for criminal offense. If offenders are placed behind bars in their prime crime-prone years, they would miss their lifetime opportunity to commit crime and develop a criminal career. There are, then, a core group of chronic offenders who are responsible for a large percentage of crime in society. Selective incarceration under a "three strikes and you're out" policy or similar measures would significantly shorten criminal careers and contribute fewer offenses to the whole inventory of crime (Greenwood 1982). While advocates claim that it leads to actual decline and overall stabilization in some crimes, incapacitation itself causes a number of problems as well. First, it results in a steep increase in prison population. Second, prison maintenance and management are costly. Third, some offenders are locked up for an unnecessarily long time. Fourth, crowdedness and deteriorating conditions make prisons a fertile ground for future criminality. Many inmates habitually relapse into crime and return to prison. Recidivism is a major problem in prison populations (Wallerstedt 1984). Lastly, there are always motivated people to take the place of incarcerated offenders as long as there are benefits from crime. For example, local gang members may take over a drug market when organized crime leaders are imprisoned.

CAUSE

While it is important to examine specific opportunities, such as lifestyles, routine activities, and material affluence, as potential factors in criminal offenses, it is insightful to follow large social processes, including change of environment, change of government, and change of interpersonal relations, as actual grounds or stages for deviance, crime, and other social problems, especially in a dynamic region at a fast-changing time.

Across Asia and the Pacific, opportunity is created and unleashed at the macro level when countries cope with natural disasters, embrace economic reform, or undergo other sweeping social changes. Crimes of opportunity take place when opportunity is perceived, grasped, and utilized by people within and outside a changing system. Among drastic events, there are wars, revolutions, change of government, epidemics, and natural disasters, such as hurricanes, tsunamis, and droughts. Although they vary in nature, scope, duration, and intensity, all these drastic occurrences share three fundamental characteristics in outcome for crimes of opportunity. First, they disrupt, threaten, or even uproot the existing social order. Second, they cause phenomenal losses of properties and massive dislocations of people. Third, they open the door for external influence, including foreign intervention, international peacekeeping, terrorism, religious missions, and humanitarian aid. For example, war creates social chaos. Whereas one part of a country is put under military control, another part may fall into total anarchy. National treasures in museums or archives are suddenly available to cross-border smuggling. Private properties are left unprotected, creating widespread looting from community to community. Parents are killed, exposing children to abduction, slavery, sexual exploitation, or illegal adoption. Husbands and sons are forced into the battlefield, leaving wives and elderly parents struggling for survival. Markets rise and fall overnight, sending valuable goods sky-high in price or necessities for daily living in chronic shortage. People live in fear, waiting to be manipulated, taken advantage of, and exploited in exchange for some sense of safety and security.

Countries in Asia and the Pacific constantly experience change of law, change of public policy, change of governmental procedure, change of foreign relations, change of social custom, and change of cultural practice as part of their quest for development, modernization, and integration into the world community. At the time of change, some sectors, properties, or goods may be ruthlessly devalued, dumped, or abandoned while others rise to unprecedented popularity, valuation, and dominance. Along the process of change, some groups gain power and influence instantly while others see themselves plunge in profit and status helplessly. Manipulation, speculation, and opportunism can reign. For instance, in expectation of a new tax on a luxury item, insiders may purchase the item in bulk at the expense of government revenue. Speculating on change in restrictions on travel or trade to a foreign country, bus, rail, ship, airline, and other transit companies may raise prices for passenger travel or transportation of goods across the border. As always, when new laws, policies, and procedures are phased in, they not only leave one group of people in misfortune to be exploited, but also present another group of people with opportunities to be envied.

Opportunity is generally spontaneous, specific to a locale, or pertinent to a particular line of events, even when it involves large social processes. From a historical point of view, opportunity is not equally distributed from time to time. More important, it is never widely available to every individual or every part within a social system. As for crime and deviance, the distribution of opportunity across a population is indeed more critical than whether there exists any opportunity at all. Multiple social implications and consequences emerge when opportunity is unequally distributed throughout society (Merton 1957). First, when opportunity takes the center stage of public attention, it creates an opportunity mentality that de-emphasizes diligence, honesty, law, and conventional practices. In many industrializing Asian and Pacific societies, although economic reform and general social development have systematically increased opportunities for wealth accumulation, power acquisition, and other material or nonmaterial gains, new opportunities come mainly into the hands of the connected, the established, the famous, the knowledgeable, and the otherwise privileged. However, since opportunity allows a few to build their economic fortunes and luxurious lifestyles in a short period of time, a social impression is created that opportunities are widely available for people to benefit quickly and easily. People actively look for opportunities within and outside the social system, circumstances which provide fertile social soil for deviations from conventional wisdom and normal ways of thinking and acting.

Second, people who are in advantaged positions to seize and benefit from opportunity can be drawn into deviance and illegal activities in two major ways. On the one hand, they may actually engage in a form of deviance or law violation as they avail themselves of an opportunity in their immediate surroundings. For example, when children of business executives, government officials, and social celebrities use their parents' fame, power, and influence to advance their own personal or professional pursuits, they make a *de facto* invasion upon social order and public interests. On the other hand, since they gain benefits easily, beneficiaries of opportunity are likely to dispose of their material or nonmaterial gains unconventionally or opportunistically. It is widely known that fops and dandies of wealthy business tycoons or powerful political families in Asia and the Pacific live extravagantly on their parents' wealth or benefit unscrupulously from their families' stake in local or national polity. They buy luxury goods, maintain followers, frequent brothels, entertain mistresses, gamble in exclusive resorts, use drugs, or directly engage in criminal activities. Taking on a fortune-driven lifestyle, these gainers sooner or later become real opportunists who have no regard for normative social order but take great enjoyment in living outside the rules of convention and sometime outside the law (Frisby 1998).

Third, people who fail repeatedly to obtain a share of their perceived social opportunity may become innovators, retreatists, dependents, critics, and rebels, or even commit suicide (Durkheim 1952; Merton 1957). In other words, crimes of opportunity occur both in the course of seeking opportunity and as a result of failure to grasp an opportunity. Across Asia and the Pacific, modernization in general, political reform and economic development in particular, have pushed many countries and their respective population into a race for wealth. The increased gap between a few upstarts and the majority makes local riots and robberies a major public safety hazard across vast rural areas. In a hinterland province of China, the motorcade of the Provincial Party Secretary was even attacked by local mobsters who prey on passing travelers and vehicles. In Hong Kong and Macao, residents no longer feel shocked when they watch the evening news about armed robberies against jewelry stores, banks, and other commercial establishments. In Taiwan, ransom has reached a plateau where only an "astronomical" figure seems to catch public attention as people are no longer impressed with news reports about abductions. The situation was especially serious at the turn of the century when a wave of crime made its way through greater China (Moore 1997; Faison 1998; Shaw 2003).

However, what makes this gap between the wealthy and the poor a regional problem is money laundering from developing to developed societies, from socialist to capitalist countries across Asia and the Pacific (Williams 1999). From the impoverished Philippines, millions of the national treasure were transferred to personal accounts in Western banks under the regime of Ferdinand Marcos. From China, billions of state investments into overseas businesses disappear in the name of operational loss, lawsuit, and bankruptcy. In Southern California, real estate agents are habituated to ask their Asian clients if they will pay cash for a luxury home. Among those cash-paying homebuyers, many are connected to high-ranking officials and large-scale state enterprises in China. One Russian scholar estimated that the so-publicized Western aid to Russia constitutes only a tiny tip compared to the huge amount of money transferred out of Russia.

The United States is a prime destination in this cross-border cash drainage from economically backward and politically troubled countries. The directional flow of cash is due to inequalities within the world political economy. Thus the poor become poorer and the rich richer. This sad, immoral, irrational process adds a new dimension to development and political democratization in developing countries. Obviously, political instability, economic poverty, cultural conflict, racial tension, and social chaos create opportunities for problematic behavior, including domination by localized tyrants, lawbreaking by experienced insiders, and criminal offending by organized gangsters. Conspicuous consumption by those who make fortunes through opportunity serves to motivate people to turn to socially illegitimate means to achieve their material success. Crimes of opportunity seem to feed back on themselves in the context of economic development and general modernization across Asia and the Pacific.

TYPE, PATTERN, AND CHARACTERISTICS

In a sense, every crime is an act of opportunity. However, this study will only focus on major cross-border social problems related conspicuously to opportunity.

Warmongers are probably the oldest of opportunity offenders. By advocating war, they gain power within a system, expand influence over public opinions, and accumulate wealth in the process of battle. In contemporary contexts, thanks to advanced means of transportation and communication, dramatic events can send shockwaves immediately across an impacted region or population. An epidemic creates a public scare. People trust hearsay to avoid risks, turn to folk suggestions to prevent infections, or count on preliminary diagnostics or unproven treatments to solve problems. The healthcare establishment and some of its practitioners may take advantage of the situation for monetary gains. A large-scale natural disaster, as demonstrated by the devastating tsunami across the Indian Ocean in the end of 2004, can put on display a variety of opportunity-prompted problems (Associated Press 2005). Looting occurs as property is exposed. Fighting and thefts happen in refugee camps and homeless shelters. Displaced adults take jobs unfairly underpaid out of dire need for survival. Orphaned children fall into the prey of child traffickers and sex predators. Even aid organizations may take advantage of a human tragedy to boost their collection of donations from governmental and private sources. Before disbursing donations to intended victims, some charitable organizations rush to raise salaries and benefits for their executives or allow their staff to travel on unnecessarily wasteful terms.

Aid workers in the field may also abuse their positions over a massive clientele in need of immediate help for day-to-day life. Stories of abuse by the United Nations peacekeeping forces and humanitarian operations in Asia and Africa point to the universally weak side of human beings in resisting the temptation of opportunities that exist in their environment for personal gain or individual pleasure (Farley 2004). Private organizations that are not put on the world stage, not placed under international scrutiny, or not charged with a noble mission of helping people in difficulty may have to deal with more serious infractions by staff or subsidiaries in their committed sphere of activities, whether it be cultural exchange, religious mission, academic research, medical treatment, child protection, or humanitarian assistance.

Specific change occurs from time to time in every jurisdiction across Asia and the Pacific. Opportunities arise when law is changed to allow for some activities while prohibiting others, when policy is revised to promote some practices while restricting others, or when the government is reformed to reinforce some commitments while downplaying others. Special interests are usually major forces for or against change. Some spend money, targeting public opinions, appealing to high authorities or manipulating political processes, for change. Others mobilize all their resources to resist change. In an open society, there are orchestrated influences, such as lobbying and campaign contributions for and against change. In a secret society, dealings may range from flattery, bribery, offering of sex, threat, and subjection, to sabotage. When change is set to take place, there are then contrasts between insiders and outsiders. Insiders act on the information they have at hand to protect their vested interest, to tip their friends and relatives, or even to make a profit for themselves. For example, a financial secretary in a special administrative region may advise his or her immediate family members to purchase some high-priced consumer goods before a new tariff or tax is levied on those items. Gains on the part of insiders and their personal networks are direct losses on governmental revenues. Unless it happens to be caught by the media, which is not likely in an authoritarian society, using or leaking information by insiders for personal gain will never be known or questioned by any party or source. So is any damage done to the public interest. Outsiders or the general populace can only guess or gossip about the unfairness they face in their work and life. Finally, in the beginning of a changed law, policy, or practice, enforcement agencies and officials may take advantage of public confusion or misunderstanding to raise fees, to expand influence, or just to scare people. The current massive buildup of policing, firefighting, border patrolling, customs inspecting, and other homeland security forces in the United States can be critically analyzed as an opportunity for those agencies to keep a stake higher than they normally deserve in public life. The general climate creates a greater potential for abuse of power and violations of civil liberties. It also brings about instances of blatant opportunistic behavior in the name of fighting crime, protecting people, or defending the homeland. For example, taxes may be raised for bigger paychecks, larger bonuses, or better benefits for law enforcement ranks and ratings in cities or counties around the country. Donations may be sought by a law enforcement officers' union or association to support programs that ease work, reduce workload, provide convenient work schedules, improve the quality of life, or increase the presence in media, politics, and other public domain for individual officers.

Social instability and contrast between political systems fuel opportunity deviance, crime, and problems as well. Knowing that their home country is unstable, people take every opportunity to rip off the existing system and transfer whatever they gain into a country that they perceive to be free, safe, and secure. Ordinary citizens attack or resist customary practices, accumulating credit for refuge application in a foreign country. Educated liberals, from reporters in the media to intellectuals on university campuses to actors or actresses in the entertainment industry, criticize or challenge the status quo, earning a reputation as a dissident to secure political exile or asylum in a nonnative land. Entrepreneurs and business executives squeeze profit from every dealing with employees or tax authorities so that they can send sufficient money to a bank account or maintain a backup operation overseas. Officials in local and national governments scramble to send their children to study or work in advanced societies so that they have someone to follow when they need to exit the system in time of political crisis. Even a head of state may prey on the country in his or her control or take advantage of the people under his or her leadership. Presidents and monarchs across Asia and the Pacific hold large assets in secret bank accounts in Western countries or send their confidants to scout out or even to maintain luxury home bases in foreign territories where these heads of state can take refuge in case they are driven from power.

Poverty and differences in economic development present another clear opportunity for problematic behaviors. Betting on the economic advantage their country has over others, people may explore a wide range of opportunities for profit and pleasure. Regular consumers travel to a foreign country to buy cheap goods in bulk, putting pressure on domestic retailers and wholesalers. Corporations set up operations in a low labor-cost territory, pushing native workers out of employment. Some less scrupulous adoption agencies profit from a boundless supply of displaced children in impoverished societies. Pimps, madams, and sex ringleaders recruit desperate women from poor countries, forcing them to work in bars, nightclubs, brothels, and other sex establishments. Even ordinary families move to sponsor relatives or acquaintances from developing countries, keeping those sponsored in servitude for housework or family-run business. The most notorious offense is the so-called sex tourism. Each year, hundreds of thousands of people from developed countries, including old-age retirees, savvy business travelers, and college students, travel to developing or undeveloped countries throughout Asia and the Pacific for the sole sake of sex simply because sex is cheap, widely available, unregulated, unprotected, and often offered by children in those places. Cases abound where people in their fifties, sixties, or even eighties bring home for marriage or partnership girls or boys in their late teens or early twenties from poor countries. At Los Angeles International Airport, an 85-year-old man was arrested by United States Customs inspectors when he boarded a flight to the Philippines. He was found carrying 100 pounds of chocolate and pistachios in his luggage, along with sexual aids and letters from girls who were only nine and eleven (Reza 2004).

Still another area for opportunistic behaviors is international trade. Taking advantage of language barriers, geographical distances, developmental gaps, technological contrasts, and other differentials, companies in one nation may dictate business dealings with or force unfavorable terms upon their counterparts in another. There are blatantly fraudulent practices, such as overcharging, delivery of substandard products, or underpayment. For example, a company on the West coast of the Pacific may have to treat tons of industrial waste after making a nearly complete payment for recyclable metals to its contracted partner on the other side of the ocean. More generally, established corporations in developed societies often benefit enormously from their advanced technology as well as poor or less developed countries' steady need for hard currency. A few shiploads of apparel, shoes, toys, and other daily articles from China, Indonesia, or Thailand is often not enough for any of these countries to buy an aircraft from an American company or feed an embassy for a few months in the United States. From a critical point of view, cheap labor is not an offer made by but rather a condition imposed upon poor or developing nations by multinational corporations in developed countries. Suppose that there is no overcharge on advanced equipment by developed economies or undercharge of ordinary consumer goods from poor countries. Even when the charge is generally honest and fair, international trade still undergirds the global inequality that massive consumption by middle class citizens in a few rich, developed nations builds upon low wage and material scarcity for working-class people in most poor, developing societies. The reasoning is simple and direct: (a) advanced equipment from developed economies is sold at a high price because middle-class citizens who work to produce it are paid high salaries for an affluent lifestyle; (b) ordinary consumer goods from developing countries are low priced so that middle-class citizens in developed societies can buy and enjoy amenities considered necessary in their lives; and (c) because the ordinary consumer goods they produce are sold at a low price, working class people in developing countries have to be paid low wages with no or minimal fringe benefits.

Similar to international trade is international exchange. Whereas people from Third World countries are fascinated with technological advance, material affluence, and everyday amenities in developed societies, citizens from First World nations are eager to explore pristine landscapes, enjoy untainted natural beauty, and appreciate undisturbed cultural tradition in undeveloped territories. With improved transportation and a higher standard of living, cultural exchange accelerates among national or territorial entities. Tourism booms around the world, especially throughout Asia and the Pacific. Along with cross-border cultural and tourist activities, however, there follow various problem behaviors, including criminal dealings. For example, foreign tourists are scheduled for unnecessarily costly travel packages, bused to factories or specialty stores where they have to make certain purchases, or hustled into sex-centered establishments where they are pressured to pay for various categories of service. Occasionally, governmental and industrial spies pose as ordinary tourists on their espionage missions. In order to enter or exit a country, some tourists use documentary proofs from purely nominal programs, such as language studies and training seminars in service, communications, and other apparently substantive skills. International records reveal a wide variety of document frauds, from doctored school transcripts, falsified certifications of birth, death, marriage, or inheritance, and unsubstantiated letters of recommendation, to forged passports and identification cards. A sometime related troubling cross-border problem is the selling and buying of pseudo degrees among individuals or institutions between Western and non-Western countries across the Pacific. The author learned that people in some Asian countries spend thousands of American dollars for a nicely printed M.B.A., M.P.A., or Ph.D. degree sent by a nominal or nonexistent university in Australia, Canada, or the United States.

In general, deviance and crimes of opportunity take place both in large social processes and in small situational encounters. While situational opportunists, such as street criminals, target specific individuals or properties for a small profit, social process opportunists eye the general social system and its sweeping changes for huge fortunes. However, since most social process opportunists are stakeholders in legal, political, economic, and cultural arenas, they are often neither caught nor punished for the big benefits they harvest from their adventures that may in fact have caused widespread damage to society.

As in the case of social disorganization, deviance and crimes of opportunity are caused by overall change in social dynamics. They both tend to be unreported or underreported, yet for different reasons. Among problems relating to social disorganization, offenses by migrants against migrants are often not serious concerns for a defined authority that is charged with keeping order for local residents. Large social opportunities, on the other hand, are often seen and seized by power holders. Who in the social system is to question stakeholders or bring them to court when they break the law? With respect to other variables, deviance and crimes resulting from social disorganization are internally mediated because they arise from moral confusion or emotional maladjustments experienced by individuals in a changed or changing social environment. Opportunistic behaviors, in contrast, are externally prompted because they take place in response to the opportunities unleashed from a social system that either undergoes a fundamental transformation or changes from one mode of operation to another.

6

Corporate and Entrepreneurial Crime

Corporate deviance, entrepreneurial crimes, organizational infractions, and other business problems increase as domestic enterprises proliferate, foreign investments grow, and multinational corporations expand across the vast landscape of Asia and the Pacific (Braithwaite 1984; Geis, Meier, and Salinger 1995; Ermann and Lundman 2002; Simpson 2002; Rosoff, Pontell, and Tillman 2004).

BACKGROUND

Corporate crime involves both individuals and an organizational entity. Individuals are usually organizational personnel who choose, execute, cover up, or defend a criminal act on behalf of the corporation. Since a corporation itself as an artificial person created by state charter is not able to do anything without individuals who run it, corporate crime has been considered essentially criminal acts committed by individuals.

Unlike street crimes that cause obviously observable injuries to victims or directly measurable damages to properties, crime by organizational personnel can easily go unnoticed under the cloak of organization, occupation, or profession. Although it dates back to ancient Greece, where public officials violated the law by purchasing land slated for government acquisition, crime by respectable people in established or recognized organizations remained off limits to public questioning as well as scholarly inquiry until the end of the nineteenth century (Renfrew 1980). In 1907, Edward Ross identified the "criminaloid," when he witnessed what he called a nationwide "devastation of the adulterator, the rebater, the commercial freebooter, the fraud promoter, and the law-defying monopolist" (1965: 54). According to Ross, criminaloids seek personal gains through any means beneath the veneer of their public image as a person of respectability, a paragon of virtue, or even a pillar of the community. In 1939, Edwin Sutherland first coined the term "white-collar crime" in his presidential address to the American Sociological Association. He used the term to refer to those criminal acts "committed by a person of respectability and high social status in the course of his occupation" (1983: 7). With the concept and its formal definition, Sutherland connected the social status of an offender to the occupational mechanism or organizational apparatus by which an offense is committed.

Following his call for study of white-collar criminality, Sutherland (1983) himself examined criminal convictions, civil judgments, and other adverse decisions taken by various criminal justice systems, civil courts, and administrative agencies against the seventy biggest American manufacturing, mining, and mercantile corporations over a seventy-year period up to 1945. He found that of the seventy corporations included, forty-one (60%) had been convicted of criminal charges. Averaging four convictions for each, those major corporations would qualify as "habitual criminals," a label that is customarily applied to common street criminals in many states. Marshall Clinard and Peter Yeager (1980) followed 477 large corporations charged with various offenses by twenty-five federal agencies in 1975 and 1976, ranging from administrative, financial, labor, and manufacturing violations to illegal trade practices. They found that certain sectors, such as the oil, pharmaceutical, and automobile industries, experience a higher level of criminal wrongdoing than other sectors and that larger corporations are more likely to engage in violations of the law than small firms.

The investigation of white-collar crime has seen a shift from a focus on the persons or occupations involved to the nature of the crime, specifically, the type of offenses committed and the variety of methods utilized (Schlegel and Weisburd 1993). Herbert Edelhertz (1970) defined white-collar crime as any "illegal act or series of illegal acts committed by nonphysical means and by concealment or guile, to obtain money or property, to avoid the payment or loss of money or property, or to obtain business or personal advantages." Gilbert Geis (1974) focused on "upperworld crime" to call attention to "the violation of a variety of criminal statutes by persons who at the moment are generally not considered, in connection with such violations, to be the 'usual' kind of underworld and/or psychologically aberrant offenders." Gary Green (1990) moved further to a general term, "occupational crime." He used it to refer to "any act punishable by law that is committed through opportunity created in the course of an occupation which is legal." According to Green, occupational crime can be committed by an employing organization as "organizational occupational crime," by officials in public office as "state authority occupational crime," by trained or licensed professionals as "professional occupational crime," and by any working individuals as "individual occupational crime." Obviously, there is blue-collar crime on the other side of white-collar crime under the "catch-all" term of occupational crime. In contrast to white-collar crime, blue-collar crime involves law-violating behaviors by less-prestigious occupational groups, such as workers and small business owners in automobile repairs, gardening, house cleaning, household moving, and general installation services.

With generations of research and refinement, white-collar crime now generally refers to a violation of the law committed by a person or group of persons in the course of an otherwise legitimate and respected occupation or business enterprise. White-collar crime committed by individuals ranges from bribery, corruption, political fraud, tax fraud, fraud against the government, insider-related fraud, insurance fraud, bankruptcy fraud, and consumer fraud, to securities-related fraud. For example, churning, trading on insider information, stock manipulation, and boiler-room operations are the four most prevalent offenses under securities-related fraud. Insider-related fraud commonly includes embezzlement, employee thefts, and sale of confidential information. Consumer fraud may manifest variously in business opportunity fraud, deceptive advertising, land fraud, home-improvement fraud, and telemarketing fraud.

Corporate crime falls under white-collar crime in the latter's broad definition. While a white-collar classification highlights the fact that it is committed by white-collar personnel, such as managers, professionals, and executives, in a business organization, corporate crime is essentially attributed to the organization itself. A corporation or business enterprise is chartered to engage in business activities, from making products, dealing in consumer goods, and running transportation or communication lines, to providing client services. It may and can cause harm to people and properties in its surroundings while conducting a chartered business. Although it does not have a soul, a corporation normally has a board of directors or a team of managerial agents who know what is right and what is wrong. Although a business enterprise by its nature cannot be incarcerated for its criminal wrongdoing, it can be held accountable by way of fines, business restraints, structural reforms, operational specifications, and general industrial or trade standards.

For example, tobacco companies are ordered to compensate victims, contribute to state healthcare funds, or provide anti-smoking educational programs for youths. Industrial polluters are required to pay for cleaning-up projects, install high-tech equipment for pollution monitoring or treatment, reduce emission of noxious waste into the environment, comply with specific rulings rendered by administrative authority, or set up funds for general environment protection purposes.

Corporate crime varies by business, organizational size, level of economic development, and society. There are general corporate crimes that apply to all types of business entities. For example, bribery, tax law violations, and obstruction of justice can be committed by any enterprise, large or small, in any line of business, manufacturing, trading, retailing, or servicing. There are corporate crimes that are specific to particular types of business. For instance, chemical plants may be charged with environmental pollution, financial institutions may be convicted of money laundering, and knowledge-based corporations may be found in violation of patent, copyright, or trademark laws. With respect to size, smaller businesses may be more likely to engage in illegal activities as they are under less public scrutiny. Fortunately, since they are small in their scope of business, they usually have only a limited impact on the general public. On the other hand, although larger corporations are generally less likely to commit crimes due to their public visibility, they can cause large-scale, long-term damages or injuries to consumers or the environment when they do make serious mistakes. In the United States, official statistics show that the vast majority of corporate offenders are small to medium-size privately held corporations with fewer than 100 employees (United States Sentencing Commission 2002). However, a few scandals involving large American corporations, from the General Electric Corporation, Westinghouse Electric Corporation, Lincoln Savings and Loans, and Enron Corporation, to the WorldCom Corporation, often impact a whole industry, shock the entire economy, or even shake the general public and its opinion about law, business, government, and social morality (Ermann and Lundman 2002; Rosoff, Pontell, and Tillman 2004).

From a global point of view, level of development can give corporate crime drastically different scenes among developed, developing, and undeveloped economies. In developed economies, corporate crime is corporate crime by mega-corporations, medium-sized enterprises, and small businesses in all areas of agriculture, industry, commerce, and service. In developing countries, corporate crime may vary as regular yet minor infractions by numerous household-based businesses, occasional yet significant violations by several state-operated or old-and-well-known-family-owned monopolies, and incidental yet symbolic lawbreaking by a few multinational corporations. On undeveloped lands, corporate crime may only involve conflicts among families, villages, and townships in agricultural production, crafts, bartering, and simple trade, domination over a locale or a line of business by landlords or tribal chiefs, or mishandling of vital economic affairs by the state. Eastern cultures seem to spawn family enterprises and individual entrepreneurship whereas Western cultures have evidently provided space for growth of formal, sized, scaled, and bureaucratized corporate entities. Corporate crime thus is more an entrepreneurial violation in the East, with each incident's impact limited to a particular entrepreneur, business, or locale. On the other hand, a corporate crime in the West, although it generally does not occur in high frequency, may cause widespread damage or injury when it happens. With the spread of Western-style business models and the dispersion of multinational corporations across the globe, it is important to conceptualize and punish corporate crime in its various territorial or cultural contexts and forms (Gilbert and Russell 2002; Mon 2002; Vining 2003; Swedberg 2005).

CAUSE

Greed lies at the core of most, if not all, corporate and entrepreneurial deviance and crime. From a philosophical point of view, self-interest is part of human nature. Greed is the desire for wealth, far more than one needs. Every human being is born to pursue self-interest. Business, in the larger human context, is a socially legitimated means or instrument to change raw materials into final products, translate labor into value, or turn self-interest—and greed—into calculable profit. But large corporations are often perceived to be greedy in their desire to control access to natural resources, to guard their technology, to dominate market, and to drive up the price of their stock.

In the past, business has been owned and operated by individual entrepreneurs. Profit has been squeezed from landless laborers to benefit business owners and their households, family networks, kinships, or tribes. Although there is not much regulation from external sources or upper authorities, community relatedness often serves as a check on the potentially limitless desire for profit from locally based business operators. In contemporary society, many businesses grow into sizable corporations. There are boards of directors, executives, middle-level management, professional staff, and floor workers. The board of directors, as policy setters, are interested in investment returns in the form of dividends or stock values. Executives are driven by their desire for large compensation packages involving bonuses, housing and travel benefits, and salaries. Middle-level managerial and professional staffers are concerned with job stability, upward mobility, and monthly paychecks. Floor workers may be represented by a union to fight for best possible wages and fringe benefits. Self-interest or individual greed, diversified, objectified, and kept in check, though, can nevertheless converge or balloon into an overall larger and more powerful drive for performance and profit. A corporation, under various internal demands, may indeed have to engage in extraordinary adventures, legal or illegal, just to stay afloat. The market, the public, and specifically consumers may have to bear the cost left by such internally stressed companies.

Despite the fact that there are business laws, consumer protection acts, watchdog groups, and regulatory agencies in corporate arenas, the market remains a relatively free place for most businesses to conduct production, trade, or service in a self-regulated manner. A manufacturing company chooses its own terms for raw materials, processing procedures, quality control, final products, packaging, marketing, pricing, and employee hiring. Unless it is caught in serious environmental pollution, employee abuse, or product degradation, it feels free to do whatever it takes to reach its profit-making goal. Specifically, no one would follow the company to see whether it buys raw materials from a problematic source at an under-market price, whether it includes some health-hazardous ingredients in its product formula, whether it discriminates against one group of employees due to their race or gender, whether it sets an unreasonably high price for its products. Although market competition might help keep a particular company from making a usurious profit at the expense of consumers, similar individual companies set market conditions and determine competition dynamics. There is always monopoly or quasi-monopoly by product, industry, or sector in various pockets of a generally free market. Although government might help hold some manufacturing companies to certain regulations, often health, environmental, and other standards are put in place long after a series of violations and damages have occurred. When they are written into law, standards are up to individual corporations to implement. No governmental body would police a company at every step of its operation or on every product out of its mass production line. The best possible enforcement is a random check, done once in a period of time, on a few samples among millions of pieces. Obviously, a lack of monitoring is the rule of the business world. The questions then is this: To what degree can the public trust a corporate entity that is set up to make a profit?

Most corporate and entrepreneurial problems occur in the process of exchange. Exchange is spontaneous. Buyers normally do not carry scales, rulers, abacuses, or calculators with them when they enter the marketplace. They pay whatever amount sellers figure out for them. Exchange is fluid. Merchants come and go in the marketplace. Price, quality, and brand name rise and fall from time to time. Supply fails to meet demand for some goods while exceeding consumer needs for other products. Although victimization takes place then and there, there is not much one can do to prevent it. For instance, consumers may never see an original seller when they find problems with their purchases from an open flea market or a farmers' market. Even when dealing with long-term retailers or large corporations in established markets, consumers may still find that they are left with a loss and with only such explanation as a phased-out product, a discontinued brand, an untraceable transaction, or a bankrupt producer. From a human interaction point of view, exchange is public presentation. Ordinary consumers, when caught unprepared for an offer of product or service in the marketplace, often take the offer for fear of not looking economically sufficient. For the same reason, they are not so likely to confront a merchant for a loss they think they have suffered in a transaction. In all, the nature of exchange puts regular consumers in a natural yet vulnerable situation for economic loss, emotional stress, and even criminal victimization.

Another common observation is that consumer goods are priced by the principle of indispensability. That is, producers and merchants seem to reckon with the fact that a product or merchandise is some essential item consumers have to have in their daily life or cannot live without. The more people depend on an item, especially in a market of under-supply or in a situation of difficulty or crisis, the more likely the item is overpriced at the expense of the consuming public. With a similar logic, consumer goods or services can be set at a high price if people do not have to have the goods or services but choose to have them as a way of enriching their lives or for the purpose of status display. This kind of consumer demand can be called the principle of luxury. In other words, consumers are made to pay a premium for the luxury they are privileged to enjoy over necessity. For instance, a few upper class consumers are seduced or pressured to pay millions for collectible items. Airline or train passengers in the first-class cabin receive a few VIP services at a price several times higher than what their counterparts in the coach section pay. More commonly yet often beyond public notice, toys and games are overpriced under the assumption that children do not need those items to grow up well and healthy. One step further, children's daily life articles, including diapers, clothes, shoes, and foods, are pricey, seemingly because of a widespread assumption that adults tend to indulge children in contemporary society.

Migrants, tourists, transients, and foreigners are likely targets by corporate and business entities for cross-border crime. Employers hire migrants or transients to work long hours in hazardous conditions for low wages as they reason that migrants are rootless, unorganized, and unprotected by local authorities. They may even reason that they extend a favor to migrants, for without employment migrants would suffer even more on the street or in transit. Merchants sell outdated or low-quality foods, products, and daily articles to transients and tourists because they bet that tourists will never return and that transients are rough enough to deal with whatever merchandise they have paid for. At the bottom line, it is better for transients to have a not-so-good meal, an expired or not-so-potent medication than nothing at all. Foreigners suffer from similar discrimination or mistreatment in another country when various business establishments taken advantage of the fact that these people do not know enough about the local society or that they fear for their lives far away from home. In international transactions, foreigners can become targets for victimization simply because they are not "us" and do not deserve what "we" have in "our" land. From poor to rich countries, foods and other daily articles may be carelessly prepared or even tainted when some individuals or businesses act upon their general sentiment that people in rich countries are so wealthy and happy that they deserve something not so good once in a while in their life. From advanced to backward nations, expired drugs and defective consumer goods are dumped or delivered because some corporate executives and business enterprises believe that people in deprived economic conditions are not entitled to the same high standards of living they enjoy in their blessed social environments.

TYPE, PATTERN, AND CHARACTERISTICS

Corporate enterprises, professional organizations, and other business entities may sometimes engage in problem behaviors, including legal violations and criminal offenses, in a form that fits the type of business they conduct, the scale of operation they maintain, and the kind of social environment they face.

With regard to the type of business, industrial companies may use low-quality materials, ignore manufacturing standards, dump untreated wastes, or ship defective products to the market. For example, manufacturers substitute raw materials from a secondary source for those of the primary origin they claim in public announcements. Producers do not seriously follow national or international standards in the routine mass production process once they selectively use those standards to win approval or entitlement for their products. Factories release questionable waste to the environment until they are exposed by an accident, a disaster, or an inquiry. Defective or poor-quality products are dumped in the marketplace, victimizing consumers. Product defects or low quality are not always noticeable for small-item consumer goods as people do not usually bother to take them back to a merchant for refund or the merchant is likely to sell them as one-time dealings. Who would return a dysfunctional nail cutter that was made in China to a Wal-Mart store where he or she bought the item for less than a dollar? Where would one find the vendor for return of the broken Mexican-made leather belt he or she bought from a street vendor in downtown Los Angeles two weeks before?

In a similar fashion, farmers, fishermen, and other agricultural entrepreneurs may not always be honest and careful in the use of pesticides, fertilizers, and other chemicals or in the application of so-called organic growing, natural feeding, or healthy processing methods. For example, they may keep only a small amount of hand-harvested natural crops for their own use while delivering mass-processed products to the market. In the aftermath of the Asian tsunami in the end of 2004, the author received warnings that some fishermen in the disaster region may have used dead fishes by the killer wave to prepare fish balls and other fish meat products they routinely ship to international markets, including those in Hong Kong, Japan, and North America. How does it feel when a consumer is told that the fish balls, the sausages, and other dried, salted, or canned foods he or she just ate might have been made from dead fishes or sick animals in a foreign land?

Service, professional, and knowledge-based enterprises or organizations are by no means outdone in their involvement in problem behaviors. They have their own versions of various kinds as well. For example, travel agencies work with universities, medical institutions, governmental bureaucracies, and production companies on nominal seminars, workshops, business expeditions, and cultural exchanges. Year after year since it was opened to the outside in 1978, China has paid billions for governmental officials and business executives of public enterprises who travel, one group after another, to Hong Kong, Macao, Singapore, South Korea, Japan, Europe, Oceania, North America, and other popular destinations worldwide for personal leisure in the name of learning, business visits, and official dealings. In these destinations, universities collect fees by issuing certificates or diplomas; governmental agencies record deeds of friendly exchanges with China by hosting Chinese visitors; travel operators profit by overcharging the Chinese government several times more than they pay for the actual cost; Chinese travelers enjoy the visits because they may not have to pay a dime from their own pockets for all those places they visit, all those shows they see, or all the merchandises they purchase; and in fact, they may even receive some pocket money from their tour operators for their daily expenses. Another interesting scam is that people in some Asian countries are persuaded to own a piece of land in the United States out of their love or hate for this most powerful and prosperous country in the world. The land they own is not real but purely symbolic. The only thing that is real is that they pay a certain amount of money for a piece of paper, a pseudo deed of trust that they can somehow .cherish in their treasure box.

As far as the size of operation is concerned, small businesses are likely to engage in problem behaviors in the areas of taxes, insurance, employee safety, health, and product. In the matter of taxes, small businesses may not keep a consistent record of sales and revenues when they make transactions by cash. For example, an immigrant who teaches classes in arts, sports, or music in his or her private home in the United States may only report a certain amount of income to claim for his or her earned income credit on the federal tax return. Small businesses may fail to buy any insurance or pay for a sufficient coverage for their facilities, operations, or employee liabilities. To keep their profit margin, small entrepreneurs may use their relatives for no formal compensation or hire migrants or undocumented aliens for below-market pay and benefits. For example, an operator of a small elderly home-care facility in California may rely upon some of his or her distant relatives from Mexico to run the business. While the operator provides the relatives with food, shelter, and daily life articles, the operator may pay little or nothing for their around-the-clock labor and contributions. Safety is a known common problem for many small businesses. Unfortunately, serious attention is drawn only when fires break out, trauma is caused, or life is lost. Health standards are often disregarded in the territory of small businesses as well. Local residents shop at their own risk. Tourists may only blame their personal maladjustment when they fall sick upon visits to street eateries. In Los Angeles people can use local governmental ratings as a reference to decide what restaurant to dine in; in Jakarta or Manila tourists will have either to use their common sense or pray to the almighty when they choose to swallow something from a street food peddler. Finally, consumers need to be aware when they buy things from small businesses. There are unique client-tailored services or special custom-designed goods from these establishments. However, there are also outdated, defective products and merchandise in stock.

Self-monitoring, mutual surveillance, and internal deterrence increase when companies grow in size and operation. Medium-sized companies, compared to their small business counterparts, are less likely to engage in problem behaviors perhaps because the need for profit or the need to survive as a business enterprise is no longer fueled simply by the need for profit of one owner or one household operator but often must be synchronized among joint interests of partners or stakeholders. However, when medium-sized companies commit something wrong or unlawful, they can cause much larger impacts upon their local economies. There are also specific types of crimes, violations, or problem behaviors that are more likely to involve medium-sized enterprises. For example, employees in medium-sized companies can be treated unfairly with low wages and minimal benefits because they are neither close to the employer as in the case of many small businesses nor able to unionize as in the case of large corporations. Medium-sized manufacturing businesses are sometimes equipped with necessary tools and technologies to produce patented products illegally or bootleg branded consumer goods on a scale of operation that usually does not cause attention from the public or regulatory agencies. In the retailing business, medium-sized stores may attract buyers with competitive prices. However, they are likely to turn their back on the consumers should the latter find problems with their purchases.

Across Asia and the Pacific, common offenses by medium-sized businesses include tax frauds, patent thefts, safety violations, environment pollution, defective and counterfeit products, bribery, and labor abuses. There are underground factories in almost every country in the region that churn out fake name-brand consumer goods into local, national, and international markets. Some fake audio/video products are dumped into the market even before their real versions are officially released in the country of origin. Foreign investments, especially small-scale whole-owned ventures by overseas nationals, tend to take advantage of local governments' intent to attract foreign capitals. These businesses are sometimes run to the detriment of environment and at the expense of workers' welfare. For example, they produce a product they would not be allowed to produce under a stringent environmental protection law in their home country. Or they engage in a production that would bring them only a marginal profit should they make the product under the minimum wage and labor rights legislation in their home territory. In the fast growing Pearl Delta area of Southern China, overseas Chinese investors from Hong Kong, Macao, Taiwan, and Singapore build their medium-sized factories like fortresses. Children and school-age youth are employed at a discount labor rate. Workers are required to surrender their ID card and make a deposit at the time of hiring. They are forced to labor long hours, without freedom of movement on and off work. Salaries are not paid on time, sometimes not for months. Harsh punishment is used. In some cases, workers are forced by their boss to kneel for hours under the scorching sunlight. As they make money, some of these medium-sized business owners or executives attempt to apply their influence in local politics, others scramble to transfer profit out of the country by a pseudo business set up elsewhere in the world.

Large corporations normally have a relatively long and rich history behind their growth and expansion. Over time, they may have developed a management structure or an operational procedure that serves to insulate them from problem behaviors, especially criminal wrongdoings. Moreover, large corporations, since they are large and important to various socioeconomic interests, are in the public eye, receiving constant scrutiny from the mass media, watchdog groups, and regulatory agencies. Compared to small businesses and medium-sized enterprises, large corporations are thus less likely to engage in problem behaviors. However, when they are involved in deviant or criminal acts, large corporations can cause widespread damage to society or serious harm upon the public. Some common deeds by corporate giants include market manipulation, territorial domination, contract exploitation, political leverage, and stock fraud. For example, a few conglomerates implicitly or explicitly conspire to keep bank interest, labor cost, product price, and other vital economic indicators at a premium level ideal to their profit-making goals. A major corporation uses scare, suspicion, and suppression to eliminate competition in order to attain total domination over a country or a regional market with its products or services. Multinational companies take advantage of their market position to force exploitative business terms upon selected subcontractors within a large competitive pool. Some regional executives of multinational corporations may even fill their own pockets by demanding bribes from the subcontractors to whom they have awarded contracts. As for political leverage, large corporations are known to spend heavily on lobbying and political campaigns in and around city halls, state capitals, and the national government in democratic societies. In nondemocratic systems, corporate giants may even exert direct influences upon various levels of public office by bribes, threats, or installation of their preferred representatives. Finally, stock frauds are featured in a series of recent corporate debacles inside and outside the United States. From Enron to WorldCom, large companies are found to falsify numbers, doctor records, or cook financial books to keep their stocks hot and high in security exchange markets. Hundreds of investors become penniless overnight and thousands of pensioners and retirees see their safety net broken and gone suddenly when such scams are exposed one after another.

Across Asia and the Pacific, there is a growing presence of huge multinational business entities. Multinational corporations expand to developing countries in Asia and the Pacific not only because they want to cover that part of the world with their businesses, but rather because they face tough regulation, business maturation, profit stagnation in their developed base countries and because they want to take advantage of a lax legal system, a vast consumer population, and cheap labor in developing countries. The underlying motive or the business bottom line provides fertile soil or a natural reason for problem behaviors. Among irresponsible and unethical or illegal conducts by multinational corporations in Asia and the Pacific are price fixing, price gouging, market domination, contract exploitations of small businesses, use of child labor, inaction regarding unsafe working conditions, shipments of industrial wastes, dumping of expired products, environment pollution, funneling of profits back to their home country, and inappropriate influence on local and even national politics. Regarding contract exploitation, for example, a former vice-president of Vans Inc. who headed the company's procurement from international manufacturers pleaded guilty recently to charges of conspiracy, conspiracy to launder money, foreign travel to promote commercial bribery, and wire fraud in a federal court in the United States. According to American authorities, the former corporate officer demanded and received more than $4.7 million in kickbacks from Chinese factories that made shoes for the company in just about three years (Editorial Staff 2005).

Finally, the social environment provides the critical conditions in which business entities form, grow, operate, and dissolve. Those critical conditions may involve the stage of development, the skills of labor force, the complexity of legal regulation, the efficiency of management, the level of technology, and the adequacy of infrastructure. While all of those critical conditions affect whether business enterprises deviate or offend, they may also shed light on the criminal intent of actual entrepreneurial and corporate troublemakers, violators, or perpetrators. For example, in a developed economy where the labor force is skilled, the legal system is sophisticated, management is effective, technology is advanced, and infrastructure is systemized, there normally ought to be fewer abuses of labor, better compliance with the law, more open, flexible, and responsible management teams, higher production standards, more effective quality control, and less delay, friction, filtering, or confusion due to transportation and communication problems. However, when crimes take place, they can suggest that there might be a higher level of wrongdoing involved, especially on the part of management. In other words, a higher level of blame should be assigned to a corporate person who has knowledge and resources to do what is right yet chooses to do what is wrong at the expense of employees or consumers.

In a developing or undeveloped economy, individual entrepreneurs as well as scaled business entities may fail to follow some manufacturing standards, implement certain quality control procedures, or fulfill some employee obligations simply because they suffer from a lack of information, resources, or opportunities. A case gathered by the author in his fieldwork in Asia may help illustrate the point. A pig raised by a farming household died of an unknown disease. Instead of burying the dead pig underground, the family handled it as if it were killed live and fresh. That is, they sold the meat in the local farmers' market and kept the dead pig's fat, internal organs, and miscellanies, the parts that are most likely to carry disease, for their own consumption, as they always do with their family animals. Obviously, there is not much evil involved in selling a dead animal's meat to stranger consumers. At issue is a matter of ignorance in the first place. Some farmers simply do not think it a heath risk to eat meat from a dead animal. Besides ignorance is the matter of economy. In a poor or deprived community, people simply cannot afford to discard a feast by burying it in the mud. They may not feel good to eat meat from a dead animal. But having meat to eat is still much better than having no meat to eat at all.

7

Governmental and Bureaucratic Crime

The government makes, enforces, and interprets the law concerning many aspects of life in society. The enormous power it holds makes it a source of problems. For example, when it reflects the interests of one dominant group without much public scrutiny and accountability, the government may commit crimes—crimes of social class—against other subordinate segments of the population. When it staffs its gigantic bureaucracy with unscrupulous individuals who follow only self-interest, the government may become a breeding ground for bribery, nepotism, and favoritism. Across Asia and the Pacific, the government and bureaucrats play a phenomenally prominent role in various legal, economic, cultural, and social activities. Thus abuse of power, corruption, and other political wrongdoings become inevitable elements in the dynamics of development, modernization, and historical change.

BACKGROUND

Deviance, crime, and problem behavior by the government and government office holders occurred as early as there were governments and governmental officials in human history. An emperor or king in a society of monogamy violated a basic social norm regarding marriage when he maintained a whole court of concubines and maids for himself. The empire or kingdom was guilty of discriminations and genocide when it targeted a minority group for containment or total elimination through oppression or violence. The reason why such acts by the emperor or the king were not considered deviance or crime is simple. For generations, people took it for granted that the empire or kingdom decided what was right and what was wrong and that the emperor or king himself was above what had been determined as the law for the common citizens of the empire or kingdom.

The idea of deviance, crime, and problem behavior by the government and public officials came to light when philosophers began to treat churches, governments, and other entities of sanctity the same as secular groups in their depiction of social reality. If ordinary systems can fail, royal families, state apparatuses, and religious hierarchies may sometimes not live up to expectations. If commoners can make mistakes, kings, queens, priests, and popes may occasionally falter and fail in their duties as well. Most important, when states and heads of state err, they can spread error and encourage lawbreaking across society.

While it takes intellectual awakening or a cultural renaissance to recognize the fallibility of holy and imperial entities, it takes rebellion, revolution, and evolutionary change to introduce institutional checks in the state machinery or implement realistically effective measures against those in power. The American Constitution, drafted by revolutionary settlers in the New World, separated lawmaking from law enforcement and created an independent judiciary to interpret the law. Power is therefore shared and balanced among three branches of government. The president or the head of state, "on impeachment for, and conviction of, treason, bribery, or other high crimes and misdemeanors," can be removed from the office. Under the United States Constitution, governmental agencies and public officials are subject to the law just as are all nongovernmental organizations and private citizens.

Because of intergovernmental check, media vigilance, and civil alertness, the United States has become a leading voice in the world in the exposure of deviance, crime, and other misconduct by public offices and office-holders. Ironically, the United States government itself has been found guilty of a variety of illegal activities against American citizens, foreign countries, and the general public, domestically or around the world. For example, despite its apparent acceptance of the Nuremberg Code of 1947 that sets informed consent as an absolutely inviolable requirement for human experimentation, the United States government has sponsored various experiments using prisoners, soldiers, and unsuspecting civilians as subjects. The former Atomic Energy Commission funded studies by Harvard University and the Massachusetts Institute of Technology in which mentally retarded teenage boys were fed radioactive milk and breakfast cereal to study the body's digestive ability as part of their membership activities in a "science club" (Editorial Staff 1993). The Department of Defense supported research at the University of Cincinnati in which cancer patients were exposed to intense levels of radiation to test how much radiation a soldier could endure before becoming disoriented (Schneider 1994). The Central Intelligence Agency (CIA) conducted various experiments using knockout drugs and incapacitating substances on unwitting subjects to develop essential mind-control techniques for its espionage operations around the world (Thomas 1989). The three branches of the United States military all used their own members as human guinea pigs in developmental research on offensive weapons and defensive strategies. Of all the military experiments, the most horrendous was the use of young Navy men for "man break tests" of chemical agents. In those tests, sailors were ordered into the gas chambers to endure a continuing exposure to chemical agents, such as mustard gas, until they broke down (Jones 1993). The American Civil Liberties Union estimated that approximately ten percent of the American prison population participates in medical and drug experiments (Mitford 1973). Although they all sign consent forms and waivers, some prisoners may have been forced into these experiments out of fear, ignorance, material deprivation, and psychological defenselessness.

Besides unlawful use of citizens in intelligence, military, and scientific research, the United States government has targeted specific segments of the population for surveillance, control, and persecution. During World War II, over 100,000 Japanese Americans were gathered from around the country and herded into barbed wire enclosures under military guard (Daniels 1972). In decades of the Cold War, hundreds of liberal organizations, civil rights groups, peace movements, and professional coalitions were penetrated; thousands of ordinary citizens were monitored, questioned, followed, or restrained for possible procommunist activities or communist sympathies; organizational penetration and surveillance were orchestrated not only by the CIA, the Federal Bureau of Investigation (FBI), and the military, but also by the Internal Revenue Service (IRS) and other federal agencies (Vankin and Whalen 1997). For example, the IRS created a Special Service Staff (SSS) in 1969 just to "gather information on political groups and individuals" and to "stimulate audits by local and district IRS offices based upon this information." Of the thousands of surveillance files kept by the SSS are those over individual American citizens, even popular and internationally renowned, such as New York Mayor John Lindsay and Nobel Prize-winning scientist Linus Pauling. There are also files on well-known American organizations, such as Americans for Democratic Action and the California Migrant Ministry (Halperin, Berman, Borosage, and Marwick 1977). Public surveillance, especially electronic monitoring, has intensified with the advance of technology and under the name of the war against terrorism.

Outside its national territory, the United States government has long been known to take advantage of its military strength, economic power, and technological advancement to interfere in the internal affairs of other sovereign nations for its favored political order in a region and across the world. In Asia, the CIA engineered the restoration of the dictatorial Shah to the throne in the 1950s, when the Iranian government aspired to nationalize American oil companies in the country; the CIA had a heavy hand in the bloody Indonesian revolution in the 1960s, wherein about a half million people were killed; and the CIA unlawfully recruited ethnic minorities from Laos and Thailand into a secret army to fight along the borders of North and South Vietnam in the 1970s. In Africa, the CIA participated in the overthrow or attempted overthrow of various national governments, from Angola, Ghana, Somalia, and the Sudan, to Zaire; and the intrusion has caused social chaos, reinforced political oppression, and sent masses of people into poverty. In Central and Latin America, the CIA has played a pivotal role in regime change for Brazil, Chile, Ecuador, El Salvador, Guatemala, Guyana, Nicaragua, and Panama; and in the case of Chile, the CIA worked to destabilize the socialist government led by Salvador Allende, prompting his assassination and replacement by General Augusto Pinochet, who was friendly to American corporate and political interests while torturing and murdering thousands of his own countrymen in crackdowns on labor leaders and the political left (Agee 1975; Blum 1995).

Although most of them are elected into office by public votes, officials in various levels of government in the United States are not immune from deviance and criminal wrongdoings. From city halls to state capitals, there is no lack of elected officials who are investigated for or found guilty of bribery, corruption, abuse of power, dereliction of duty, violation of election laws, fraud, and other offenses. Between 1970 and 1985, for example, nearly fifty mayors, more than sixty state legislators, and seven current or former governors were indicted on various criminal charges (Maas 1987; Editorial Staff 1991). Even in the forefront of a governmental offensive against crime, police officers from jurisdiction to jurisdiction are known to sometimes engage in illegal activities they are sworn to oppose. Among most common law enforcement misconduct, a police officer may take free or discounted merchandises from business establishments within his or her beat; receive goods, services, or money for referring business to taxi drivers, towing companies, ambulances, repair shops, lawyers, doctors, and bail bondsmen; accept payoffs for not making an arrest; steal money and valuable belongings from arrestees or unconscious accident victims; dispose of traffic tickets, control an investigation, or "sell the case" in exchange for material rewards; and demand contributions from drug dealers, prostitution ring operators, and other illegal business owners for protection money (Barker and Roebuck 1973; Weitzer and Tuch 2006).

In the federal government, President Richard Nixon resigned from office amid the Watergate scandal; President Bill Clinton went through a formal impeachment proceeding for the Monica Lewinsky affair; and President George W. Bush faces questions about his own service in the National Guard, his vice-president's former company's dealings with the United States government, his administration's justification for war against Iraq, and his military's involvement in possible tortures at Guantanamo Bay and in the Abu Ghraib scandals. In the legislative branch, members of Congress are implicated in bribery, payroll fraud, violation of election laws, and various other wrongdoings from time to time. An illustrative case is that of Dan Rostenkowski, who had for years chaired the powerful Ways and Means Committee in the House of Representatives. In 1996, Rostenkowski was sentenced to a seventeen-month prison term in federal court upon conviction of two criminal felonies amid a pattern of corrupt activities spanning three decades of his political career (Editorial Staff 1996; Merriner 1999). The judiciary fares better in comparison to its executive and legislative counterparts. Still, there are federal judges who are stripped of their judicial positions following conviction of high crimes and misdemeanors (Borkin 1962). In 1991, for example, Federal District Judge Robert Collins of Louisiana was convicted of bribery, conspiracy, and obstruction of justice after a convicted drug smuggler acting as an FBI informant paid Collins $100,000 in return for a lenient sentence (Marcus 1991).

If officials in the most open and watched democratic government in the world can engage in a variety of illegal behaviors, it is not difficult to imagine how much more widespread and serious deviance and crimes by government officials and power holders are in many not-so-open and not-so-watched, less democratic societies, especially in those where an authoritarian regime maintains tight control over the population and its access to information, resources, and opportunities. Transparency International, an international non-governmental organization, ranks countries in corruption by the Corruption Perception Index that measures the degree of corruption as seen by business people and country analysts in a range between ten (highly clean) and zero (highly corrupt). According to its most recent findings for 2004, corruption is rampant in more than sixty countries, with Haiti, Bangladesh, Nigeria, Myanmar, Chad, Paraguay, Azerbaijan, Turkmenistan, Tajikistan, and Indonesia topping the list of ten. The greatest victims of corruption are the world's poorest nations, where bribery remains key to scarce yet essential resources controlled at every level of public office. Even in civil sectors, under-funded, understaffed healthcare, education, and professional services provide a breeding ground for corruption. It is not uncommon in many poor countries for parents to bribe underpaid teachers to secure an education for their children. The world's rich fare better in governmental integrity but are by no means free from corruption. In fact, corruption in developed countries often involves huge sums of money in scandals ranging from secret payments to finance political campaigns to the complicity of banks in money laundering to bribery by corporate conglomerates. For example, in 2001, former Foreign Minister Roland Dumas of France was convicted of receiving large amounts of illegal funds from oil giant Elf Aquitaine between 1989 and 1992 (Daley 2001); in the same year in Germany, a loans and campaign contributions scandal at Bankgesellschaft Berlin brought down the whole Berlin city-state government (Editorial Staff 2001).

Besides domestic corruption, some deviance, crime, and problem behaviors committed by national governments have international repercussions. For example, human rights abuses are usually committed by repressive regimes against political dissidents, civilian prisoners, liberal intellectuals, non-orthodox religious believers, and social activists (Fernandez 2004). Theoretically, human rights abuses are considered as crimes against humanity because all human beings are supposedly entitled to some inalienable rights, and violations of those rights threaten the very existence of human civilization. Practically, some democratic countries in the world are particularly sensitive to human rights violations. They penalize perpetrators by trade embargos, diplomatic isolation, and other tangible pressures while providing victims with political asylum, media exposure, and various practical accommodations. Human rights abuses have therefore become a matter of global attention and significance. Another issue of international origin and fame is the so-called donor-promoted corruption (Hanlon 2004). The United Nations, the World Bank, the International Monetary Fund, the Group-8, and other forums or consortiums led by developed countries make plans for the world, prescribing treatment regimens for undeveloped or developing nations across the globe. In implementing their ideas or aid packages for a country, they often rely upon a Western-oriented, reform-minded, or dominant political group in the country. Once the group is chosen, it is left to do what it proposed to do on its own. While the chosen group may appear to follow the will of the donors, in actuality it may do more in funneling money into the pockets of its own members than in disbursing funds honestly and fairly to aid the general population. Still another phenomenon of global scale and consequence is bribery by multinational corporations. In developing or undeveloped countries, some multinational corporations are known to take advantage of the corrupt nature of national and local host governments to gain business entry, obtain tax favors, and expand market share. Among developed countries, although it is used less blatantly and more tactically, corruption is still touted as a common and effective strategy for large corporate gains. For example, corporate giants, such as Mobil Oil, Lockheed, and Litton Industries, were found to have paid millions of dollars to governmental officials, royal family members, and political parties in Italy, Japan, and the Netherlands in bribes for sales and businesses (Roebuck and Weeber 1978; Editorial Staff 1999).

CAUSE

From a democratic point of view, it may seem difficult to understand why officials of a government elected by the people would engage in activities against the people they are entrusted to defend, protect, and represent. A class conflict argument, that government always falls into the hands of the rich, the powerful, and the educated, who automatically place their own individual, group, and class interests over the poor, the powerless, the uneducated, and all others in society, helps in exploring the quandary. But concrete understanding lies in specific examination of various realistic forces surrounding public offices and office holders.

First, in the structure of government itself, checks and balances are either inadequate or simply lacking. A model democratic government may have a constitutional division of power among the legislative, the executive, and the judiciary. But each branch itself can be an authoritarian, sometimes even totalitarian, system. For example, the head of the executive branch may appoint classmates, aides, friends, or relatives to key cabinet posts to run a country as a personal clique, a family business, a kinship network, or a tribal enterprise. In non-democratic governments, the head of state controls all. The parliament serves as a rubber stamp. The court makes judgment according to the will of the supreme leader. And the administration becomes simply a tool to implement whatever policies the king, the president, or the party secretary general wants to pursue. As power is concentrated in the hands of a few without effective checks and viable challenges, it is likely to be misused or abused. In the worst scenario, a hawkish leader may take a country into war, causing thousands of people to die; an authoritarian head of state may hijack a nation under a radical policy, allowing millions of people to starve or otherwise suffer; and a dictator may use one segment of the population to oppress another, creating a general state of fear across society. Most commonly when there is a lack of counterbalance, leaders in various levels of government will take advantage of the power they hold, filling their own pockets before serving the people in the constituency.

Second, in the larger society, there is a phenomenal level of passiveness in the minds of people toward government and governmental misconducts. The most salient sentiments are that government is powerful, that government is the business of the powerful, and that as ordinary citizens it is wise to stay as far away from government as possible. These general feelings are most evident in traditional and undemocratic societies where government has for generations been focusing on keeping people quiet and submissive. In nontraditional and democratic countries, people may find other reasons for silence and complacency while taking a participatory approach. For example, people may blindly trust those elected officials whom they send to office. Or people may feel that political parties take turns in running government; thus political parties not in office should stay on the sideline while they wait for their opportunity; and they must cash the political capital they think they have won when they have their turn in government. Government is thus perceived and utilized as an instrument to advance interests and realize goals. Knowing the limits of term they have in office, officials may count each minute in using power, benefiting their own social class, political party, family, and themselves.

Third, between government and the public, there is a general lack of scrutiny on government and governmental officials. In closed societies, the civil society and the mass media are either rudimentary, fragile, and immature or censored, controlled, and suppressed. The communist government in socialist countries unequivocally defines the mass media as the ruling party's mouthpiece. No civil society is ever recognized or allowed beyond a general mass led by and rallied behind government. In open societies, although the mass media spread news, expose evils, and stir debates, they are by no means free from governmental manipulation. For example, as the center of interest of the media, the government leads the media with its powerful ideology and active policy agenda. In times of emergency, troops, police officers, firefighters, and other defense personnel automatically take center stage, dominating news coverage, feature stories, and public debate. Critics and opposition forces are sidelined or simply silenced. As a civil society becomes less vocal in a society facing a crisis, the government seemingly does what it wants to do, just or unjust, fair or unfair, legitimate or illegitimate. Officials seemingly get whatever they desire, deserved or undeserved, warranted or unwarranted, legal or illegal.

Finally, with regard to cross-border crime, contrasts between developing and developed countries, safe deposits offered by some Western financial institutions, protection of private properties in capitalist countries, and opportunities for exile serve as sources of reference, motivation, defense, and justification for deviations by government and governmental officials. Contrasts in development may prompt private companies from a rich country to buy access to business opportunities in a poor nation. Knowing that public officials live on a meager salary or that a local government wrestles with limited revenues, some foreign investors may find it cost-effective to set aside a small amount of their operational budget for bribery or public relations spending. Governmental officials in poor countries, on the other hand, may not necessarily feel much moral shame at taking gifts or contributions from foreign businesses, believing that foreign businesses are rich in the first place and that these businesses will make a considerable profit under the favorable terms given to them. Safe bank accounts offered by financial institutions in the West, especially the world-renowned Swiss banks, are known depositories of funds by many heads of state, royal families, political dynasties, and even brutal dictators around the globe. It is no fantasy that a dictator holds billions of dollars in a Swiss bank while watching millions of his countrymen starve, suffer, and die in famine, epidemic, or social chaos. Powerful officials in non-capitalist countries may also take advantage of solid property protection under capitalism to acquire real estate properties in the West. It is a great irony that officials in socialist countries embezzle money from the state to send their children and family members to study and live in the capitalist West while criticizing and attacking everything capitalist or Western in their official duty. The West, motivated at least partly by greed, seldom shows any hesitancy in taking powerful heads of state, wealthy royal families, or influential governmental officials for exile or political asylum no matter how corrupt, abusive, or incompetent these persons were in their home countries. The benefits to the West are obvious: Exiled foreign leaders bring in wealth for the good of economy; they can be used as a critical force to influence foreign governments; and they may be reinstated in their home nations in the future. However, to many poor countries in the world, this appeasement by the West in the form of safe deposits, property protection, and political exile are destructive forces in their path toward political stability, economic independence, and social sufficiency.

Without doubt, lack of checks and balances, public passivity, lack of scrutiny, contrast in development, and appeasement by the West are major structural causes for crime and deviance by government and governmental officials. Regarding structural factors, an important development to take notice of is collective leadership. Collective leadership may seemingly serve to balance power among different leaders and their factions. However, when problems arise, collective leadership can become a natural excuse for any individual leader to avoid responsibility. In other words, it can significantly reduce the level of accountability that is critically lacking in most governments in the world. With respect to contrast in development among countries, a domestic addition is that gaps in income between regions as well as across professions may make some underpaid officials vulnerable to corruptive practices in office.

TYPE, PATTERN, AND CHARACTERISTICS

Specific crime, deviance, and problem behaviors by government and governmental officials in Asia and the Pacific differ by social system, political structure, economic development, and cultural tradition.

With respect to social system, capitalist countries are likely to experience problematic business dealings between government and the corporate world or a secret alliance between corporate management and governmental officials. Local governments often bow to the overarching influence of key employers in the community while the national government may query major corporations over profitable manufacturing or service contracts. It is not uncommon that the mayor of a small city appeases a principal business by attending its ceremonial events, appearing in its commercials, or openly endorsing some of its products at the city hall. It is also no surprise that powerful procurement officials in the national government demand personal favors in the process of awarding lucrative defense and other business deals. A recent incident in the United States involved several multibillion-dollar contracts between Boeing and the Air Force. The disgraced former Air Force official admitted that she favored Boeing over other competitors because the company gave her daughter and son-in-law jobs at her request. The official even took a $250,000-a-year job later for herself at Boeing after leaving the Air Force (Wayne 2005).

A subtle yet common phenomenon is that noted government officials as well as successful business executives alternate between public service and positions in private industry. They eye the corporate world while holding powerful governmental positions. Or they seek public office on the basis of their experiences in corporate management. In Japan, boards of directors in various business entities seem to be a natural retirement or post-political career destination for powerful government officials (Xu 1996). American corporations and non-profit organizations are always fond of enlisting big-name celebrities, including lawmakers and political appointees, in their governing bodies. Although there is not always an identifiable connection, the expectation of a post-political career in business on the part of office-holders can profoundly influence overall decision-making processes and outcomes by the government. The issue of conflict of interest in this latent form can often appear and then evade notice beneath the radar of legal regulations.

In socialist countries, because major industries and services are still directly run by the government, public and private enterprises can be exploited and victimized at the hands of government officials. In China, where the government maintains a generally tight control over land, utilities, licensing, and business resources, there exists ample opportunity for stake-holding officials and their children or relatives to cash in their influence and power for economic benefits. As exposed by a number of high-profile cases, children of some high-ranking officials engage in large-scale smuggling operations, causing loss to the state revenue on automobiles, tobacco, and luxury consumer goods. Local governments pass their transportation, administrative, and other costs on to the business organizations under their jurisdiction. For example, they borrow-order (Jiediao) cars from local enterprises without any compensation; they hold banquets in local hotels or restaurants without any payment; and they directly ask businesses to support holiday bonus allocations for officials and staff. Individual officials also solicit and receive benefits from business owners. As a township head in central China honestly admits, he does not have to buy anything for his family and can comfortably support a few of his relatives' families for most of their general living needs if he just takes what is sent to him by local businesses in town. A professor in a provincial party school that trains ranking officials said she can have all the city bus coupons, all the tickets to parks and museums, and some vacation costs for her family reimbursed by her students.

Between capitalist and socialist countries, problematic dealings reflect their mutual contrasts and differences. In socialist countries, investing capitalist companies target meagerly salaried socialist officials, gaining business access and preferential treatment by bribery. Bribery may take the form of a personal payment, a deposit into a secret account, a giving of luxury goods, a sponsored trip to the capitalist world, or a study arrangement for a child in a developed society. In capitalist countries, an embassy or consular office of a socialist nation may give money to its carefully selected representatives from among expatriates who then make donations to some high-profile political campaigns or lobby the legislature or administration for a change of policy, an easing of trade restrictions, or approval of strategic sales in technology and military equipment to the socialist nation.

In political structure, democratic governments are relatively clean and transparent due to the fact that officials are voted into and out of office by the people in their constituency. Ironically, however, the election itself often becomes the center of political corruption. In established democracies such

as Australia, Canada, Japan, and the United States, illegal campaign financ-
ings gain public attention from political season to political season. Elected
officials bow to special interests that contribute heavily to their successful
ascendance to public office. Some local office holders may even misuse
campaign funds for personal or family purposes. Canada, whose rules on
lobbying were once touted as a model for the rest of the world, had to add an
amendment to its national election legislation in 2003 after a series of scandals involving political donations and misuse of public funds (Transparency
International 2004). In newly adopted democracies, from South Korea to
Taiwan, from the Philippines to Pakistan, political parties are immersed in
economic activities. National leaders emerge from or ally themselves with
military strongmen and business tycoons in the political landscape. Using
slush funds, coercing voters, buying votes, and making illegal campaign contributions are frequent stories on local and national news reports. Former
presidents are convicted, existing premiers are charged, and political hopefuls on campaign trails are investigated for abuse of power, misuse of election funds, and various inappropriate or illegal behaviors. In Taiwan, twenty-
seven percent of a random sample of eligible voters from the third largest
city and its surrounding areas acknowledged receipt of cash from various
political campaigns. The Nakhon Ratchasima Rajabhat Institute of Thailand
estimates that candidates disbursed a total of $460 million to voters in the
country's legislative elections in 2001. The Philippines sees its share of vote-
buying problems in both national and local scenes. In the 2002 community-
level elections, an estimated three million people received some form of
payment for their votes (Transparency International 2004).

Unlike democratic countries, where the corruption of public officials is
often exposed, in non-democratic nations, corrupt political leaders do not
usually face public scrutiny. Living extravagantly on state treasuries, embez-
zling money from national coffers, receiving contributions from lower level
officials, and making lucrative deals with foreign interests may be considered part of the privilege of office for these leaders, who conduct most of
their business back stage. Indeed, it is difficult to estimate how much a dictator in a country has in his personal wealth because he almost literally owns
the whole country. Similarly, it is impossible to judge whether a dictator advances or sacrifices a nation and its fundamental interests when he runs the
nation as his personal fiefdom. In the former Iraq, Saddam Hussein built
grand palaces and presidential resorts around the country. Was this extravagance legitimate or illegitimate in the eyes of the Iraqis under his dictatorship? In North Korea, Kim Jong-Il inherited national leadership from his
father. Are there people in North Korea who dare to think that transfer of
power from father to son is a scandal in their political system? In Cuba, Fidel

Castro puts his younger brother in charge of the armed forces and publicly confirms that Raul Castro is in line to become his successor. Are there many people in the island nation who consider Castro's effort in passing power to his brother a historical example of corruption in the Communist movement? At lower levels, bribe-taking and abuse of power by public officials in authoritarian polities can be more conveniently accommodated or forgiven than noncompliance with or defiance or opposition to the policies or demands made by the leader in the center. Thus repressing political dissidents, mistreating ethnic minorities, and violating civil liberties can only be raised against a non-democratic country from a democratic, Western, or international point of view. In fact, human rights violations may be taken for granted as part of life in the national and local politics of a non-democratic system.

Between democratic and non-democratic systems, the best known international allegation has been that the United States and its democratic allies select, train, and support authoritarian regimes in various countries as part of their geopolitical strategies to contain Communist movements, establish regional controls, and solidify dominance around the globe. Thus the democratic bloc led by the United States sends economic aid and humanitarian donations to a non-democratic nation, knowing that this aid may well be misused in the hands of corrupt officials in the nation's government. The United States trains troops, delivers military equipment, and entertains the national leaders of a non-democratic country, knowing that people in that country are mistreated, brutalized, and generally oppressed by their military, police force, and whole state machinery (Blum 1995). With backing or acquiescence from the United States and other leading democracies in the world, authoritarian regimes can become more corrupt, abusive, and coercive in their conduct of governmental affairs. Thus the world becomes more divided between democracy and its opposites, including dictatorship and military juntas.

Another key dimension at issue is economic development. In developed economies, the government at times bows to special interests, failing in its function to regulate industry, to protect consumers, and to manage social conflict. At times, it may yield to conservative blocks, corporate giants, and social elites. Elements of the population are monitored with intrusive surveillance measures. The environment is threatened with aggressive business practices. Corporate misconduct is left unchecked, leading to society-wide scandals in security exchanges, banking, and various other areas. At another time, the government may side with liberals, workers' unions, professional associations, or some radical activism. Wages and benefits for government employees, police officers, firefighters, and public school teachers are unwarrantedly raised at the expense of ordinary taxpayers. Reasonable performance standards are brushed aside, leaving public school students ill-prepared in basic knowledge and academic skills. Radical or socially marginal elements dominate public debates, drawing attention as well as draining resources from essentially vital mainstream social interests. In a similar fashion, public officials of a developed economy are likely to abuse the power they hold in government to secure and solidify a position in the general socioeconomic hierarchy. Knowing that wealth is likely to be the ultimate determinant of status and privileges in their social environment, they may execute their duties only in the expectation of a continuing alliance with business interests or a post-political career in the corporate world.

In developing societies, the government generally attends to business regulation only sporadically. It is available in granting access, issuing permits, approving entry, or determining what can be done but less available in offering guidance, lending support, providing service, or deciding how something can be done. It is strong in control, containment, or saying "no" while being weak in regulation, direction, or specifying "yes." People may find it difficult to open a business but once the business is opened they may feel free to do whatever they like. A business may see various obstacles, sometimes seemingly insurmountable, in its normal dealings with the government, but once a critical relationship with a governmental agency and its stakeholders is secured, the business may embrace everything that comes its way. Consistent with the conduct of government in these societies, officials here may exhibit an unbelievable level of sharpness, alertness, and greed in extorting contributions from businesses and private interests while displaying a shocking degree of unhelpfulness, cold-bloodedness, and apathy toward losses or suffering on the part of people, the environment, the state, and the whole society. Where is the government when trashes pile up rotting in the streets, when children work in hazardous conditions for long hours, and when large, established, or connected enterprises bully new, small, or independent businesses? Where are public officials when people lose properties, become jobless, contract contagious diseases, or starve to death? As far as the environment, the state, or the whole society is concerned, both government officials and common citizens may inflict harm upon each of these entities for the sake of their own interests. For example, private businesses may strike a deal with rural governments to keep their air-polluting or water-polluting factories running on farmlands. They may even bribe government officials to muddle legitimate production procedures or bypass necessary quality standards at the expense of the environment, workers, or the consuming public.

Between developing and developed economies, private citizens, professional organizations, and business entities in the former may have to spend a
fortune just to apply for visas or permits to visit family members, to travel as
ordinary tourists, or to enter into a business relationship or cultural exchange
with legitimate partners in the latter. In the United States embassies or con-
sulates around the world, people line up for entry visas to the United States.
Some spend their lifetime savings to pay fees and other costs in one failed
application after another. Imagine an elderly couple in rural China who
wants to visit their son studying in the United States. The couple has to walk
a day from their village to the nearest town where they can take a bus to the
county seat or even farther to the provincial capital. From the provincial
capital they take a train to Beijing, where they have to stay a few days to
prepare and submit their application. If they are lucky, they will have to wait
a few days to receive their visas. But in most cases, they are denied visas and
have to return home in sadness. However, with some incomprehensible
hope, some keep trying, trying, trying. Then a conscientious observer would
naturally ask: Why is the United States government so inconsiderate of foreign citizens when it takes exorbitant fees on denied visa applications, one
after another? Do the United States embassy or consulate officials know that
they are robbing foreign citizens, not only of their trust but also of their
safety net, given that average people in developing countries may have to
work a whole year just to pay for an application fee for the American visa?
On the other hand, people from developed nations may need only to use their
name, position, or passport to receive benefits from developing societies.
Business corporations in the affluent West may need only to give small tips
to concerned officials in poor countries to gain enormous economic advantages. For example, many developing countries in Asia and the Pacific, in
their effort to attract foreign investments, have implemented various preferential treatments for joint ventures. The system of preferential treatment provides an opportunity for abuse by both domestic and foreign businesses.
Businesspersons in Australia, Canada, Japan, or the United States may sit in
comfort to collect profit just by allowing their names or business licenses to
be listed in officially filed documents with a known company in a developing country. In China, joint ventures are sometimes approved by bribe-taking
government officials for nominal establishments with no actual investment
from abroad. Tax breaks are given to bogus joint enterprises while the state
loses its supposed sources of revenue.

Finally, cultural tradition affects how government and officials perceive
and are perceived by citizenry and society. In Western tradition, government
is most commonly seen as a third party overseeing contractual relationships
among members of society. Thus government steps out of bounds when it

meddles into the private affairs of individuals and individual contractors, for example in the case of excessive regulation. Officials fail to perform their duties if they do not communicate information in a timely fashion from one contractor to another or if they without any legitimate reason do not attend agreements among willing parties. Pitting one contractor against another, spying one for another, or acting unfairly toward some parties in a contract can only be dealt with as abuse of power, compromise of contract, and disruption of social order. However, also in Western culture, government is sometimes seen as an instrument used by a dominant social group to exploit and control other groups. The group in power exercises authority to issue orders, impose mandates, implement programs, categorize people, marginalize minorities, and persecute dissidents to the benefit of the ruling class. Officials assume their normal responsibilities when they hear from one individual while ignoring another, speak for one program while condemning another, or discriminate against one group while protecting another. Consolidating power, cashing in wealth for power, and translating power into wealth are all touted as part of political gamesmanship.

In Eastern civilizations, on the other hand, there seems to be a widely taken-for-granted assumption that government is an authority sanctified by God or nature to govern people. Government can be as demanding or undemanding, restrictive or permissive, and tolerant or intolerant as it likes toward people, their attitudes and behaviors. An official, while on duty, can be as manipulative, exploitative, and abusive as a ruthless dictator or as considerate, consultative, and accommodative as a parent. In the best scenario, a government protects people as a family although it mistreats them in various aspects of life. Officials take the role of parents in caring for people although these officials make unreasonable demands and solicit undue contributions. However, just as in some families members cause pain to each other, a government may inflict on its citizens suffering, both physical and emotional. Just as some parents raise their children only to sell them later for profit, some officials may target people under their rule for pleasure or material gain. The vain hope for benevolence from the government and officials in folktales only reflects harsh reality faced by the majority of the population in society.

Between Western and Eastern cultures, a government in the West may force unfavorable trade terms or diplomatic deals upon a government in the East, knowing that the recipient government is able to keep its people quiet to conform to any stipulations imposed by foreign powers. In the meantime, a government in the East may have to target specific groups or forces to influence general contractual dynamics or to support one party, one candidate, or one governmental policy over another in Western politics. Obviously, official behaviors within and between cultural contexts can be problematic and illegal in terms of specific laws as well as general principles of human freedom, decency, and dignity. Isn't it a serious crime against the environment, native people, their culture and tradition, and ultimately human liberty when a multinational corporation, backed by a Western government, builds a massive industrial complex with miles of pipelines on and through pristine tribal land in a secret deal with a local or national government in the East?

8

Substance Smuggling and the Drug Trade

Drug smuggling is a salient problem in Asia and the Pacific (United Nations Office for Drug Control and Crime Prevention 2000; Schiray 2001). In fact, the region bears most of the global drug bruises and wounds as it holds the three major drug production bases and the largest drug consumer market in the world.

BACKGROUND

The human being is a body of substances constituted and maintained by other substances in nature. It is due to a long, gradual, evolutionary process that human beings use one substance as food, another as medicine, and yet another as psychodelic drug.

Use of substances to alter physical functioning and psychological states began as early as the Old Stone Age (Merlin 1984). Egyptians incorporated opium in the performance of religious rituals in 3500 B.C. Amerindians chewed coca leaves in their daily life and as part of their Andean culture several thousand years ago. Cannabis, the hemp plant from which marijuana and hashish are derived, also has a history of thousands of years (Schultes and Hofmann 1979; Abadinsky 1989; Inciardi and McElrath 1995).

The modern era of drug abuse emerged when effective elements were separated from natural substances through chemical procedures and were then used on a large scale for medicinal purposes. Morphine and codeine were found in the sap of the opium poppy in the early nineteenth century. Unaware of their addictive properties, physicians prescribed them for treatment of a variety of human illnesses. Cocaine was separated from the coca leaf in 1859. It soon gained popularity when it was used to unblock the sinuses, suppress fatigue, and alleviate neurotic symptoms in medical treatments, as well as to give its consumers a sense of well-being in commercial tonics, such as Peruvian Wine of Coca and the famous Coca-Cola. Even cannabis, which later fell into medical disfavor because of its water insolubility and potency variability, was once marketed by such well-known pharmaceutical companies as Parke-Davis and Squibb as a cure for depression, convulsions, insanity, mental retardation, and impotence (Inciardi 1992).

The initial uses of marijuana, cocaine, and opium products in medicine somehow seemed to provide a legitimate background for their use and abuse by the general populace. In the 1900s, federal authorities in the United States estimated that there were already 200,000 cocaine and narcotic addicts, in addition to many marijuana users among petty criminals, jazz musicians, bohemians, and, in the Southwest, Mexicans (Abadinsky 1989). The extent of drug abuse grew continually over the course of the twentieth century. Not only was there a sharp increase in the number of users from thousands to hundreds of thousands to millions, there was also a wide expansion in the variety of substances abused, from alcohol, tobacco, and caffeine to marijuana, cocaine, and heroin to glue, Valium and Librium, and LSD and then to dietary supplements, prescription medications, and over-the-counter drugs (Shaw 2002). In the United States, the national household survey presents a clear, systematic picture of how drug abuse changes from year to year by the type of substances, the route of administration, and the characteristics of users such as age, gender, and race. For example, in the most recent survey of 2003, about 19.5 million Americans, or 8.2 percent of the population aged twelve or older, said they used an illicit drug during the month prior to the survey interview (Office of Applied Studies 2004). Specifically, about 14.6 million people (6.2%) identified themselves as current marijuana users, 2.3 million (1.0%) as current cocaine users, 1.0 million (0.4%) as current users of hallucinogens, and 119,000 (0.05%) as current heroin users. Aside from legally controlled substances, about 6.3 million Americans, or 2.7 percent of the population aged twelve or older, acknowledged that they take psychotherapeutic drugs nonmedically, with an estimated 4.7 million using pain relievers, 1.8 million using tranquilizers, 1.2 million using stimulants, and 0.3 million using sedatives (Office of Applied Studies 2004). Across the globe, to a much lesser degree though, substance use and abuse exhibit a current pattern as well as a historical trend similar to what has been witnessed in the United States.

As substance use and abuse spread and worsen, calls for tighter control and tougher punishment intensify. In the United States, the Harrison Act was passed in 1914 to regulate the domestic use, sale, and transfer of opium and coca products. With respect to marijuana and its growing popularity, Congress first responded with the Marijuana Tax Act in 1937. Fourteen years later, in 1951, the Boggs Act was made to add increased penalties for possession and trafficking in marijuana and other controlled substances. The most systematic reaction to drug use and abuse, however, is epitomized in the passage of the Comprehensive Drug Abuse Prevention and Control Act, or the Controlled Substance Act, in 1970. The Act places controlled substances in five different schedules according to their abuse potential. It also requires that state legislation be brought into conformity with federal law. Now, the Uniform Controlled Substances Act has become the law in fifty states, the District of Columbia, Puerto Rico, the Virgin Islands, and Guam. And Title Twenty-One of the United States Code includes all the federal anti-drug legislation, including many amendments passed since 1970, especially the Anti-Drug Abuse Act of 1988, which states: "It is the declared policy of the United States Government to create a drug-free America by 1995."

On the international stage, the first control efforts were instituted following the Opium Commission in Shanghai in 1909. Over the years, various United Nations Conventions had hammered out restrictive clauses on the sale and use of different substances for medical purposes. A synthesis was reached in the 1961 Single Convention on Narcotic Drugs, which in turn was supplemented by a 1972 Protocol that stressed the need for treatment and rehabilitation services. In 1971, the Convention on Psychotropic Substances established an international control system for a list of mind-affecting pharmaceutical drugs and other substances. The term "drug abuse" was adopted to refer to the illicit, or nonmedical, use of any of the substances listed in the previous conventions. Drug trafficking was first addressed at a 1988 Convention in which specific provisions were meted out against money laundering and the diversion of precursor chemicals used in the manufacture of illicit drugs. In 1998, the Global Assessment Programme on Drug Abuse (GAP) was launched to collect reliable internationally comparable drug abuse data and to assess the magnitude and patterns of drug abuse at country, regional, and global levels. With GAP, the United Nations and national governments around the world can now access one global and nine regional systems for up-to-date statistics on who was taking drugs and why.

While attempts to control drugs do not necessarily stem drug abuse or even reduce drug use, they fuel an underground drug market. The drug market, as it goes underground, not only drives up the cost for users but also increases the profit potential for dealers. Inherent in the drug-crime relationship, drug abusers are arrested primarily for property offenses, and drug dealers often use violence in the drug trade. In the United States, cities divide into distinct turfs. Rival drug dealers settle disputes with guns. Within each individual drug enterprise, power struggles often lead to assaults and homicides. Innocent bystanders, including children, often become caught in the crossfire of drug dealings. On the global market, the drug trade has been one of the largest types of economic transaction across national borders. Warlords, guerrillas, terrorist groups, rogue governments, Mafias, triads, and cartels are main players in the business. They deal four major drugs, three naturally grown: marijuana, cocaine, and heroin, and one synthetically made, ecstasy or MDMA. Farmers, scientists, engineers, pilots, boat owners, and truckers are involved in the production, processing, and transportation of drugs. Politicians, judges, lawyers, and diplomats are bribed for their silence, complacency, or even support. Banks and other economic institutions are brought on board in the financing of trade and the transfer of profit. Colombian drug cartels, for example, continue to grow and thrive in their home country to supply the world with marijuana, heroin, and cocaine (as high as eighty percent of the cocaine market) because of a corrupt government, ample funding, and heavy arms. Even in the United States, these cartels are able to coordinate the trade with some estimated 100,000 illegal Colombian aliens to maintain their massive distribution apparatus across North America.

CAUSE

Causes for substance abuse and drug trafficking range from forces general to the human species and its evolution to factors specific to particular individuals, groups, cultures, and territories. Asia and the Pacific is an important area of the world in the production and consumption of illicit drugs.

Production of the main controlled substances, including marijuana, cocaine, and heroin, is all based in Asia and the Pacific. Poppies, opium, and heroin are grown, processed, and produced in the Golden Triangle, a border region that includes Upper Myanmar, Upper Laos, and Northern Thailand long controlled by the militarized Kunsha Group. Shipment of various narcotic products from the area travels through Southeast China or directly to such relay stations as Hong Kong, Macao, Bombay, Calcutta, and Madagascar toward their final destinations in Europe and North America (Renard

1996; Zhao 1997). The Golden Crescent within Afghanistan, Iran, and Pakistan constitutes another major production base for narcotics. Through Turkey, Cyprus, Albania, Bulgaria, Yugoslavia, and Greece, opium, heroin, and other narcotic drugs from the Crescent area are transported to Western Europe and North America. In the mid-1980s, about half of the heroin supply to the United States came from Southwest Asia (Ray and Ksir 1996). Coca plants grow only in Central and South Americas on the Eastern side of the Pacific Ocean. Cocaine produced in the Silver Triangle within Bolivia, Peru, and Colombia reaches Florida and other parts of the United States through Mexico, the Caribbean Sea, and Central American nations, such as Guatemala and Panama. Besides cocaine productions, Colombia is also the largest producer of marijuana, followed by Mexico, Jamaica, and the United States. The notorious Cali and Medellin cartels both operate in Colombia.

Consumption of both natural and synthetic drugs combined in the world takes place in many prosperous nations associated with Asia and the Pacific. These include such free, open, and affluent societies as Australia, Canada, Hong Kong, Japan, Macao, New Zealand, and the United States. The United States alone represents the largest drug consumer market in the world. More than half of the illicit substances produced across the globe are sold to the United States. It is already widely known, by years of the National Household Survey on Drug Abuse, that millions of Americans use illicit drugs, including millions of current cocaine or marijuana users and millions of lifetime heroin users (Office of Applied Studies 1998). Besides use statistics, seizure of illicit drugs at the national border shows at least the tip of the iceberg, the bulk of illicit substances that are poured into the market in the United States. In 1996, for example, the Federal-wide Drug Seizure System registered a total seizure of 115.3 metric tons of cocaine, 1,532.3 kilograms of heroin, and 663.6 metric tons of cannabis (Office of National Drug Control Policy 1998). A report prepared by Abt Associates for the Office of National Drug Control Policy reveals that American drug users, in 1988, spent a total of 91.4 billion dollars on illicit drugs, including 61.2 billion on cocaine, 17.7 billion on heroin, and 9.1 billion on marijuana. Although drug user expenditures had continuously decreased over time, they were still as high as 7.0 billion dollars for marijuana, 9.6 billion for heroin, 38.0 billion for cocaine, and 57.3 billion for all illicit drugs in 1995 (Office of National Drug Control Policy 1998). The general social cost caused by illicit drug use is obviously much higher. For instance, drug offenders accounted for about sixty percent of inmates in federal prisons over most of the 1990s (Bureau of Justice Statistics 1999). Each year, the federal government spends billions of dollars on drug interdiction, drug abuse research, and drug abuse treatment. From Washington, D.C., to state capitals, to city halls, officials witness the large sums spent for various drug-related welfare services and law enforcement tasks.

There are significant differences across societies in Asia and the Pacific in the matter of substances and their use. Knowledge, perceptions, and attitudes vary, from ignorance, sympathy, and complacency, to endorsement. Regulation, control, and legal sanctions fluctuate, from protection to prohibition, from inadequacy to excessiveness, and from leniency to severity. In the United States and other Western countries, people speak about illicit drugs freely in the mass media as well as in their everyday lives. Although there are laws prescribing specific punishments for possession, dealing, and use of controlled substances, there are numerous subculture groups that openly condone, glamorize, or even advocate drug use within and outside their respective constituency. In Singapore and other Southeast Asian societies, controlled substances are seemingly viewed as menaces to national existence. Individuals caught in possession of certain amounts of illicit drugs can be hanged. In China and other more moderate countries, although drugs and addiction are not yet vilified as sin or evil, people still dislike talking about them openly. Legal sanctions against drug use and dealings are as severe as penalties for heinous crimes, such as murder, rape, and treason. With differences in law, control, and public opinion from country to country, it is not difficult to imagine that drugs would move from place to place to maximize utility, users would migrate from season to season to optimize use, and dealers would change from market to market to minimize costs. Cross-border transactions can therefore increase systematically. Even in similarly affluent societies, people may cross borders to take advantage of a small convenience that would be less available in their native country. For instance, some American customers may travel to Canada or Mexico for marijuana and even attempt to smuggle some of it for future use at home if they reason that they can obtain the drug a little more easily from their Northern or Southern neighbor.

Differences in development among countries in Asia and the Pacific are huge, providing economic rationales for readjustment in drug growing, processing, and trade. Gaps in wealth among societies across the region are tremendous and thus supply mercenary motives for redistribution in the drug trade. Developed countries possess educated managers, trained workers, advanced technologies, and scaled infrastructure. They manufacture equipment, produce consumer goods, and harvest the majority of profits in the world economy. People from rich countries, especially those who enjoy power, wealth, and celebrity, can harbor so much disposable income that sometimes they feel no guilt in spending much of it on drugs. In developing and undeveloped societies, on the other hand, people often have strictly limited access to education, information, resources, and opportunity. Growing crops and selling raw materials may be the only means of survival available in their harsh environments. In remote mountainous villages from Afghanistan to Colombia and from Myanmar to Peru, farmers or peasants grow poppies or harvest coca leaves because those products bring tangible economic rewards. They respond to crop substitution programs sponsored by the United States, the United Nations, and/or their native government only when these programs prove to be beneficial and effective. At the national level, drug production and trafficking, no matter how much they take place underground, may still constitute a significant part of the overall economy for a small, poor country. Drugs bring not only attention but also needed resources from the international community. Even when the government of a poor country is willing to combat the drug trade, it may simply not be able to fight a decisive battle due to its own dependence upon the drug economy. Drugs, drug production, and drug trafficking may to some degree seem to serve as a necessary or inevitable evil to keep disadvantaged groups and impoverished nations in balance, both physically and psychologically, with their more privileged counterparts across the globe.

Political instability in drug production and transit countries across Asia and the Pacific offers prime conditions for drug traffickers to optimize their regional and global operations. Drug profits corrupt public officials, hamstring law enforcement agents, silence private citizens, and lessen the credibility of governmental agencies. Drug control invites foreign influences and international interventions. As a result, a country often divides into polarizing camps separating those who are for and those who are against external interference. At the extreme, an opposing group may take its ideological and political arguments to the mountains or countryside in the form of guerilla warfare with the government. The guerilla group keeps its following as long as the government remains weak, tainted by drug dealing networks, or influenced by foreign powers or if the government itself engages in drug activities for self-support. In Colombia, Pablo Escabar of the Medellin drug cartel and other drug traffickers once became so powerful that they arrogantly declared a "war" against the state. Now major insurgent groups, including the Revolutionary Armed Forces of Colombia (FARC), the Libertadores Bloc of the United Self-Defense Forces of Columbia (AUC), and the Army for National Liberation (ELN), are all involved in drug dealing. These groups not only offer protection of drug cultivation areas and laboratories, but also engage in transportation of drugs and chemical precursors, and in some cases, maintain direct control of cocaine processing facilities. FARC leaders acknowledge openly that they will continue to use income from cocaine, heroin, and marijuana to finance their escalating war with the government (Rabasa and Chalk 2001; Forero 2005; Molinski 2005). In Myanmar, Laos, and Thailand, while there is seemingly a relatively stable government in place, there are always areas that never fall under the reach of state control. Mountainous tribes, regional warlords, and local bandits coordinate drug producing, processing, and transporting in various isolated pockets across the region. The same holds true for Iran and Pakistan. In war-torn Afghanistan, the ruling Taliban used to ban poppy growing with a religious edict of Islam. The United States-led invasion in 2001 created a new period of chaos, spurring a drastic increase in opium output from the country. It will take years for the new democratically elected government to grow strong enough to tackle drug production and distribution in and out of Afghanistan. Generally, although it is difficult to identify which comes first, there is no doubt that drug dealers capitalize on political instability and try to perpetuate the latter to the benefit of their operational activities.

TYPE, PATTERN, AND CHARACTERISTICS

Drug trafficking, by its scale, value, and impact, stands alone as a major sector in the global economy. It is unimaginably difficult to identify all types of substances and their producing, processing, transporting, trading, and using activities or operations within and outside national borders.

Five principal features of substance smuggling in the world, especially across Asia and the Pacific, offer insights into the drug trade that has resisted efforts to control it. Most notably, the drug trade involves both national effort and international coordination. Cultivation of poppy, coca, and marijuana plants takes place in individual countries. Each drug production country has its own groups that motivate farmers to grow crops, that keep chemists, guards, or formal troops, that run laboratories and airfields, that oversee transit operations, and that harvest profits. Colombia even hosts incorporated drug cartels that dare to challenge the formal state apparatus. The same holds true for distribution of drugs in consuming countries. For example, drug dealing in the United States used to be dominated by Mafias. It now falls more and more into the hands of urban gangs in sprawling metropolises across much of the Union.

While a localized network may emphasize a drug's national brand or a group's business reputation, the drug trade overall is truly international. The natural plants that produce heroin, cocaine, and marijuana are grown primarily in poor countries where combined consumption by local growers, porters, dealers, and social elites is limited. The majority of drugs produced in countries across the so-called Golden Triangle, the Silver Triangle, and the

Golden Crescent are shipped far away to Europe, North America, and other economically developed markets in the world. International coordination is obviously necessary to ensure safe passage of drugs from production sites to processing facilities to relay stations to destinations of consumption. There are well-known routes by established organizations in the international drug trade. Throughout Asia and the Pacific, famous drug trafficking corridors include these: the narcotic products of the Golden Triangle from Bangkok via Hong Kong, Japan, or the Philippines to Europe or the United States, or from Bangkok via Malaysia or Singapore to Europe or the United States; the cocaine of the Silver Triangle from Colombia via the Caribbean to Florida, or from Colombia via major cities in Brazil to Madrid or Lisbon; and the marijuana of Mexico and Colombia from Mexico to the United States via vast border areas. Transportation involves air, water, land, or a combination of all three in most drug trafficking routes.

Another notable feature is that the drug trade is both individualized and organized. There are various reasons for individual transactions in drug operations. On the side of consumption, users are individuals. They may travel to a source country or a foreign market to buy their favorite brands that represent the quality they like at the price they can afford. Some users may even cultivate marijuana plants in their backyard for self-use. Growers in many remote areas are also individual farmers. While they are often coerced to sell their harvest to organized interests or enterprises, they can always pass some of their products to individual collectors who then distribute to individual dealers, retailers, or users. Most important, individual transactions are easy to sneak through custom inspection, border monitoring, and other official scrutiny. Even organized groups prefer to individualize their already scaled global drug trafficking operation by way of individual carriers who travel as ordinary passengers through international aviation, maritime, and land transporting systems. Among candidates for drug carriers, there are debtors, gamblers, victims of extortion, and sometimes just unsuspecting travelers. In Hong Kong, the author was even approached by an ordinary-looking woman at the train station who asked whether the author could help carry and deliver something over the border into Mainland China for an attractive payment.

While individual transactions can easily pass through official controls without confrontation, organized operations muster strength and advantage in finance, equipment, and personnel when it is necessary to confront state and international authorities. Drug growing competes with drug elimination and crop substitution programs funded by developed economies, the United Nations, and individual state governments. Drug processing calls for large amounts of chemical precursors and trained personnel. Drug transporting involves airfields, aircrafts, sea boats, and other high-tech equipment. Obviously, no single individual is able to mobilize all the resources or run all the activities throughout the whole process for a final drug product he or she wants. Only organized enterprises can gather sufficient funds to purchase expensive equipment, smuggle firearms, maintain transit routes, and train special agents necessary for drug trafficking. Only scaled organizations can provide both powerful economic incentives and coercive institutional restraints for growers, porters, pilots, boat operators, truckers, and guards who put their lives in danger in the operation. Among the notorious organized drug operations, the Medellin Cartel once employed about 20,000 members throughout its drug growing, processing, and trafficking enterprise. It even had its own airports, aircrafts, seaports, ships, and trucks. The Cali Cartel used to control sixty percent of the cocaine production in Colombia. In greater New York, it laundered millions of dollars a month for its drug distribution endeavor (Chepesiuk 2003). The Kunsha Group maintained a well-equipped force of about 7,000 members. For years, it supplied nearly fifty percent of narcotic products in the world (Zhao 1997). Even in Japan, thousands of drug dealers belong to organized crime groups rather than work alone. The high risk involved also explains why some guerrilla groups fit well in the drug venture. By insulating a specific area of their control from outside attacks, they can significantly reduce the cost of operation. With an increased and sustained profit, they can survive and even thrive in the drug business.

Still another marked feature is that the drug trade invokes both violence and innovation. Violence permeates the drug venture in all its aspects or phases. With their enormous profits, organized drug groups are able to purchase advanced weapons, hire and train daring killers, and pay for the trade's brutal operations. In the face of ruthless competition, drug-ring leaders feel safe only when they have eliminated those who vie for the same business. Under intensifying attacks by the state and other formal authorities, drug traffickers turn to the ultimate terrorist measure for possible relief. The Medellin Cartel, in its violent response to the country's drug control policy, assassinated many governmental officials and social celebrities. Among the victims of their murderous campaigns were reporters, editors, judges, police chiefs, prosecutors, the minister of justice, and even a presidential candidate. At one time, the cartel leadership openly vowed that they would kill ten judges for each one of their members extradited to the United States. Indeed, waves of bombings, assassinations, and other violent incidents break out all over the country every time the government attempts to mount assaults on drug operations (Chepesiuk 2003).

To solve problems of transportation, the drug trade has been resourceful and innovative. To pass customs inspections at international crossings, traffickers have invented four modes of cross-border drug transporting. The first is through shipment of goods. Traffickers sew wrapped drugs in fishes, mingle drug capsules with frozen items, or put drugs in canned foods. The second is use of the human body. A non-harmful method is to hide drugs inside an artificial limb or insert drugs into the vagina. In the most inhumane procedure, however, drugs have been inserted into the stomach, the uterus, and other parts of the body. Sometimes the drug carrier's life can be saved only through surgery. The third is reconfiguration of luggage, shoes, and other travel items. For example, drugs are buried inside the heel or sole of a shoe, sandwiched between hidden layers of a suitcase, or even concealed in the pages of a book. The fourth is by chemical reaction. Drugs are first soaked in liquid and then made to permeate some cotton materials or changed into clays to make ordinary artifacts. They are then recovered through chemical procedures. Some smugglers even exploit religion in their drug transportation knowing that people in many countries around the world would not blaspheme their gods by opening sacred objects known for use in religious rituals or ceremonies.

The drug trade responds to both market and control. Market forces lie in the difference between supply and demand. Demand stimulates supply. When supply lags, an unabated demand not only keeps the price high but also fosters speculation. Across Asia and the Pacific, drugs pour into affluent nations, open societies, and free-market economies where people are able to make free choices in their lives and possess sufficient resources for their chosen lifestyles, including a drug-using habit. In poor, non-democratic, and non-market countries where people neither have much choice nor much disposable income, there is little demand for drugs. As the drug trade seemingly connects agrarian to industrial economies, an interesting question to ponder is this: Does it serve to redistribute wealth or sustain the gap between haves and have-nots across the globe?

Although they are separate forces, the market is intertwined with control. A drug market does not normally form and sustain itself where comprehensive, restrictive control exists to disrupt drug flow and undercut drug profits. Throughout Asia and the Pacific, drug plants grow primarily in remote areas that are out of reach for the government. Drug processing occurs often in places that lie beyond the purview of official surveillance. Drug transporting routes begin with unknown hideouts or deserted airstrips, traverse secret trails, high seas, and open borders, or wind through bustling airports, harbors, or land crossings where control is nonexistent, sparse, or overwhelmed by smuggling problems. On the other hand, drug dealers do not necessarily retreat from places where they face tough, well-coordinated control. Nor does the drug trade necessarily decline or disappear in a time of fierce, systematic crackdowns. In fact, drug operations have become either organized or individualized, either violent or innovative, and therefore more efficient and profitable as control intensifies within and among nations in the world. The reaction by the drug trade to efforts to control it may be explained only by the fact that it is after all an underground economy operating on nothing close to conventional logic.

The drug trade differentiates drugs and drug handlers. The physical features of a particular drug include whether it can be chemically refined or restored, where it is grown or where most of its consumers are located, what route it has to take from origin to destination, and what means of transportation is amenable to its shipment. For example, refined heroin or cocaine can travel with individual carriers in small amounts by commercial airlines from one continent to another, either from Asia to North America or from South America to Asia. Raw marijuana may only move from one country to another on land by commercial train or truck freight or over water in container ships. Distance and routes of passage between a drug's origin and destination can be critical in determining what means of transportation is viable. Over the Caribbean, cocaine traffickers make effective use of various waterborne vehicles, such as steamships, motorboats, airships, and merchant ships. The airship is especially popular because it can move quickly past radar and other detections with a manageable load of cocaine. As traffickers become proficient in their specific operations, they may also find it most efficient to stick to a particular way of collecting, transporting, and delivering the drug.

Drug handlers include growers, collectors, porters, processing technicians, smugglers, distributors, sellers, and users. As human forces, they shape and reshape the drug trade. For example, a trade route would connect a particular drug originating in one part of the world to a consumer market on the other part when a considerable number of drug users in that market prefer the drug that is produced only in that place of origin. From an international point of view, drug handlers live under different cultures, political structures, and economic environments in different countries. While most drug handlers ask for hard currencies, especially American dollars and Euros, some may demand payment in a specific currency. While many deal with each other indiscriminately for profit, some may engage only in serious transactions with people of certain nationalities. While individual choices may look trivial in specific situations, these choices eventually determine who enters, dominates, and profits in regional as well as global drug trades. Overall, suspicion, distrust, and reservation exist in varying degrees among drug handlers of different backgrounds throughout Asia and the Pacific. Indeed, disagreement, dispute, conflict, and even confrontation with regard to terms of contract or sharing of the profit remain as conspicuous features in the drug venture.

One more aspect of the drug trade is that drug profits have corrupted many people, including the wealthy, the powerful, and the knowledgeable, in many countries around the world. Despite the stereotypical generalization that people in undeveloped economies, undemocratic polities, or unmodernized cultures are more susceptible to the seductive force of material incentives, cases abound in free, affluent, Western societies where police officers, court personnel, and other public figures are implicated in the drug trade. An account of a recent drug trade exposed in the United States reveals that scores of law enforcement officers and soldiers from a variety of agencies, including the United States Army, the Arizona Army National Guard, the United States Bureau of Prisons, the United States Bureau of Citizenship and Immigration Services, the Arizona Department of Corrections, and a local police department, were found to have aided and benefited from the drug trade along the United States-Mexico border. In one operation, a group of uniformed soldiers and other officials drove Army National Guard humvees to transport 132 pounds of cocaine from a desert landing strip to a resort hotel in Phoenix, where they took cash for payment (Vartabedian 2005). The case, in a sense, illustrates how much the drug trade has differentiated drug handlers. In other words, drug handlers know that the most effective way to bypass control is to utilize control itself. Is there a better means of transportation to transport drugs than to use a military or law enforcement vehicle manned by soldiers or officers in uniforms?

9

Human Trafficking and Illegal Immigration

Uneven economic development, natural disasters, political volatility, military uprising, cultural clashes, and social instability are all part of life at times among countries in Asia and the Pacific. They each or in combination make human trafficking and illegal immigration not only an issue for serious social attention but also a matter of urgent policy response throughout the region (Hodgson 1995; Leuchtag 1995; Kyle and Koslowski 2001; Schiray 2001; United Nations Economic and Social Commission for Asia and the Pacific 2003).

BACKGROUND

Human trafficking involves forcibly transporting people from one place where they live freely or feel at home to another where they are subjected to servitude or are identified as aliens. The earliest and the longest form of human trafficking in history is the slave trade. In ancient Greece and Rome, slaves were chained during labor or caged in transit like animals. There were even marketplaces where slaves were publicly traded among owners (MacMunn 1974).

The modern era began with great explorations across the globe by land and by sea. However, the discovery and colonizing of the New World did not just usher in a golden age of opportunity and prosperity for all. Its development also brought about the infamous slave trade across the Atlantic Ocean. From 1502 when first African slaves were reported in the New World, the Atlantic slave trade supplied various rice, sugar, and tobacco plantations for hundreds of years with hundreds of slaves taken often violently from African heartlands (MacMunn 1974). In the United States, slavery became so entrenched in the system that it took a civil war to abolish officially the institution. Although the civil rights movement and various legislated measures such as affirmative action work to expand opportunities for the descendants of former slaves, it will take many more years for various disfranchised minority groups, including latecomers, to share freely and equally in the American dream with the majority population of the country (Portes and Rumbaut 1996).

In the contemporary capitalist world system, the widening gap between a few industrialized countries and many developing and undeveloped nations provides an increasing impetus for trafficking in persons across territorial or jurisdictional borders (Wallerstein 1979). Besides the age-old sex trade in which attractive women are transported from one location to another for prostitution regardless of economic and geopolitical differences, flocks of people are now herded by organized crime groups or individual business interests from their politically repressive, economically backward, and often socially chaotic home environments to work under unfavorable, sometimes slave-like, conditions in supposedly free, open, affluent societies (Kyle and Koslowski 2001; Zhang and Chin 2002). Specifically, migratory laborers are transported from rural villages or small townships in one territory to cities or large metropolises in another to work under exploitive terms. Maids, nannies, and other domestic workers are transported from poor families in one society to rich households in another to work in a subservient capacity. Abandoned, orphaned, or otherwise displaced children are transferred from one jurisdiction to another for adoption not sanctioned by law. Women and young children are transported across international borders for the purpose of commercialized sex. Or illegal immigrants are secretly transported from their home country to face involuntary servitude in a foreign country in order to pay off a usurious border-crossing fee. The most brutal of all, however, is the trafficking of human beings for their body parts. To meet high demands for transplantable human organs from affluent countries, people, including children, in some poor nations are sold, smuggled, or even murdered for the life of organ recipients who fly in for instantly procured organs (Editorial Staff 1999; Agence France-Presse 2000; Deutsche Presse-Agentur 2003).

Human trafficking spawns lawbreaking and organized criminal activities in the process. It also plants seeds for deviance, legal violations, welfare dependency, and social unrest as its long-term consequence. Illegal immigrants, often unassimilated and marginalized, can become sources of crime and various other social problems in the hosting societies (Nadig 2002; Ku 2004).

CAUSE

Human trafficking is symptomatic of larger social dynamics in a region or across the globe. There are many forces behind its development into a challenging social problem in the contemporary era.

At the outset is the force of globalization. The world has become a global village, a common marketplace, an international community due to the advancement of science and technology. With the mass media, people know instantly what happens in almost every corner of the world. With advanced means of communication, people constantly stay in touch with one another. By modern transportation networks, people leave after breakfast from one continent in the morning and arrive in another continent for dinner in the evening. Through internet and other electronic connections, people conduct negotiations, make deals, and forge business relations without face-to-face interaction. Global interconnectedness supplies critical information about different peoples from place to place and about their various wants. Knowing that people in industrialized nations are more likely to be preoccupied with professional pursuits rather than marital, childbearing, and family affairs, agencies can bring in women and young children from Third World countries for marriage or adoption. Global connections also provide multiple channels for traffickers dealing with other kinds of human traffic, for example the sex trade and forced labor. With no reliance upon any single mode of transportation, traffickers can smuggle people on land, by air, and over water amid a border-crossing human crowd or in the regular international flow of consumer goods.

The causes for human trafficking can be summed up as essential and emergent. Essential causes are those that manifest themselves in normal times. What does the world look like in normal times? The world is dominated by a capitalist system (Wallerstein 1979). It is unequal, divided between the core and the peripheral, the poor and the rich, the powerful and the powerless, as well as the knowledgeable and the illiterate. A few rich countries in the core of the world economy dominate the global market. They make rules, control investments, own and run most production, distribution, and trading facilities and activities, and harvest the bulk of profit directly or through their multinational corporations. Poor nations at the periphery may have no choice but to surrender their natural resources, such as land and fossil fuels, in order to make enough hard currency for necessary diplomatic functions in or with foreign countries. Even some developing countries in the semi-periphery can only tap into their cheap labor or, plainly speaking, exploit their own citizens, to gain a competitive edge in the world economy. Across Asia and the Pacific, in contrast to people in the United States, who are legally guaranteed a minimum wage for every hour they work, a high-school dropout in China, many of whom contribute to the conspicuous prosperity in the Chinese coastal areas, may labor hard during a sixteen-hour day for little, only a small fraction of his or her American counterpart's hourly minimum pay. While many Canadians can count on a state-sponsored safety net when they are unemployed, ill, or retired, most Filipinos may expect nothing from government when they are out of work. While ordinary Americans can afford to shun low-paying hard labor in agricultural and home-service sectors, thousands of Mexicans would risk their lives just to take those jobs in the United States. Indeed, as normal human beings acting rationally for their self-interests, who would not cross borders, legally or illegally, if they knew they could make more money, have better welfare protection, and leave a better future for their family on the other side of the border? Human traffickers, knowing the gap between developed and developing societies in labor, welfare, and other substantive matters, obviously gamble when they transport willing or unwilling people across national borders for profit. But the gamble can pay off richly.

Emergent factors are those that manifest themselves in unusual times: wars, domestic turbulence, famine, epidemics, and natural disasters. Wars take place sporadically throughout the world. In Asia and the Pacific, there is large-scale warfare that engulfs whole nations, such as the wars in Iraq and Afghanistan. There are long-term wars between sovereign states, such as those in the Middle East or between governmental and rebel forces within a country, including those in India, Indonesia, the Philippines, Sri Lanka, and Colombia. Domestic turbulence arrives in a country when the government changes, the market collapses, or the populace decries some kind of injustice. Natural disasters occur seasonally from place to place. Epidemics and famines often follow when large-scale natural disasters strike Third World countries where a lack of social infrastructure coexists with a scarcity of material resources to leave people in vulnerable situations. People instinctively strive to survive. They seek safety and security. Illegal immigration follows when people leave their homelands for survival and safety that are not provided at home or by their native government. Human trafficking will unavoidably continue, may even flourish occasionally, as long as there are critical situations of dislocation in societies around the world as well as dire needs for relocation among people within or outside jurisdictional borders. From a global point of view, it is no coincidence that poor countries bear most of the wounds of social conflicts and natural calamities. In the end, everything boils down to the strength of a government, the capability of an economy, and the resilience of a society in protecting people from any man-made harm or a relentless onslaught of nature.

At a micro level, more and more people in developed societies are educated and trained to work in bureaucratized organizations for professional attainments. Focusing on their careers, many working professionals defer marriage, give birth to fewer children, or just remain single. By the time they develop a desire for children, some are no longer able to produce their own. Adoption then becomes the only option for them to form a family with children. Financially, most middle-class professionals hold a respectable amount of disposable income. When they spend on cleaning and home services, they create needs for maids, nannies, or generally, domestic workers. When they spend on entertainment, they support liquor industries, travel services, and along with them, bars and commercial sex. Ironically, when they spend on foods, drinks, and substances, they often create obesity and the variety of diseases characteristic of personal affluence. As these micro forces converge, they create constant, powerful macro needs for children, women, and men as adoptees, entertainers, or manual laborers across developed societies.

In the meantime, in undeveloped and developing countries, a great many people still live in natural or traditional settings. Life follows seasonal changes. Marriage starts as early as the body matures for reproductive activities. Ideas for family planning or contraceptive practices are unheard of. Children are born to a family one after another. They grow or perish at the will of various natural and social forces without much external attention and protection. As a Philippine scholar said satirically, "What else can you do when you are poor, unskilled, and unemployed? The easiest thing you can do is to sleep, have sex, and make children." From a sociological point of view, having a considerable number of children in each family may fulfill some larger social functions: keeping a group of otherwise idle, unproductive, or unimportant people busy, useful, or feeling important; giving people a sense of power, control, and personal accomplishments they are not able to achieve in other arenas; creating a safety net for people who can count only on family for support when they are old; and preserving a society with a wide population margin in event of catastrophe. While all these general social functions sound valid, having more and more children by individual families creates overpopulation and various social problems in many developing countries. With limited resources, children suffer from widespread malnutrition and a variety of preventable diseases. When parents die, become ill or disabled, they leave not one child but a group of children uncared for or simply orphaned. As many of them grow up without inadequate education, people have difficulty competing for jobs in the labor market. The net result is that there is an ample supply of children, women, and men from undeveloped and developing societies who are willing to be transported from their home country for life on foreign lands.

Human trafficking obviously capitalizes on the general gap between increasingly polarized economies, polities, or cultures in the world system. However, in successfully planning and carrying out specific operations, smugglers, as well as illegal immigrants, must also know and understand micro individual choices or experiences as well as macro social needs or dynamics in countries of both their origin and destination.

TYPE, PATTERN, AND CHARACTERISTICS

People move up to higher places whereas water flows down stream. The age-old Chinese saying hits the mark as to why, how, or in what direction illegal immigration and human trafficking take place among nations around the world.

Beginning with a few widely known migrations within and outside national borders throughout Asia and the Pacific, Vietnamese "boat people" clustered in Hong Kong following the Vietnam War. They were not completely expatriated until the former British colony's return to China in 1997. Filipino maids, legal and illegal, suffer abuses from their hosts and hostesses in foreign lands hundreds of miles away from home, as far as Saudi Arabia. Wealthy men from oil-rich countries in the Middle East buy under-age brides from poor villages in Bangladesh, India, Pakistan, and Sri Lanka. Young women from Thailand, Australia, and the Philippines are recruited, coerced, or tricked into entering the sex trade. They are then sold to brothel-keepers in various Japanese provinces to become the main income earners of these businesses (Tokyo Correspondent 1989). Russian prostitutes are active in hotels, beauty saloons, and saunas in Northeastern China. Thousands of North Korea refugees flock to the same Chinese territory. As expatriation of refugees back to North Korea often causes uproar and protest from Korean communities across Asia and the Pacific, China is beginning to use a third country in its handling of some of the most dramatic defections by North Koreans (Demick and Chu 2002).

On the Eastern side of the Pacific Rim, combined figures from the United States Departments of State, Justice, and Labor indicate that "more than 100,000 people, many of them smuggled into this country, are being forced to work in appalling conditions for little or no pay, often under threat of physical violence and death" in the United State (Gordy 2000: 4). Cases of abuse continually surface from United States courts: a 1993 guilty plea to conspiring to hold migrant workers in peonage; a 1998 conviction of reckless manslaughter involving a Filipino maid; a 1999 guilty plea to conspiring to enslave fourteen Mexican women as prostitutes; and a four-million dollar out-of-court settlement for Thai immigrants who were forced to work and live in an apartment complex surrounded by razor wire (Gordy 2000). More spectacularly as showed by pictures on national news, border-crossing Mexicans pose a challenge to motorists on American highways. The states of Arizona, California, and Texas have been complaining about the tremendous burden of caring for illegal immigrants and their children. In jail cost alone, for example, governments at state, county, and city levels spend an estimated one billion dollar each year to lock up undocumented immigrants who commit crimes on American soil (Friedman 2005). In California, state officials fear that the state can be financially drained by a continually growing charge for illegal immigrants.

The biggest potential threat in human trafficking across Asia and the Pacific, however, lies in China and the Chinese. China shares borders with a large number of countries by land. It also has the longest coastline in the region. The largest population in the world lives in China. As a socialist country, the communist government in China forcefully practices family planning and openly maintains various controls over different sectors of society. The economy is developing but is far from developed. The Chinese have a long tradition of emigration. Overseas Chinese live and prosper in almost every corner of the world. There is a worldwide Chinese network to receive emigrants from China. In many parts of the world, including the United States, Chinese immigrants have from time to time proved to be diligent, intelligent, and persistent, capable of bearing hardship and enduring hard labor. Thus human trafficking from China is often regarded as a great threat across Asia and the Pacific. In the past decades, thanks to tight border controls by the communist authority, millions of Chinese, eager to plunge into Western-style democracy and prosperity, are still kept at home. Now as China develops its own economy and opens up to the outside world, more and more people seem to be motivated by the prospect of a better life in other lands. Most important, more and more stowaways seem to be able to pay for the usurious passage fee, as high as 50,000 American dollars, charged by their "snakeheads." The Chinese government has been staging nationwide campaigns to "forcefully smash the human smuggling evil wind" (Ni 2000). Despite state campaigns, harsh punishment, repatriation by the foreign government, and numerous reports of death and abuse faced by stowaways overseas, many

Chinese in the coastal areas do not seem deterred from their attempt to sneak out of their motherland into a foreign territory to seek a higher living standard and a better economic future (Fried 1993; Tyler 2004; Lee 2006).

Beyond these migrations, however, there are three other kinds of human smuggling. First, women are transported from rural villages to small towns to large cities to international metropolises to work in sex-centered establishments or as prostitutes. International metropolises, such as Bangkok, Hong Kong, Istanbul, Kuala Lumpur, Los Angeles, Singapore, Sydney, and Tokyo, provide a wide range of commercial sex services for tourists, business people, and local residents. Major income-earners in sex establishments, from restaurants, bars, beauty salons, dancing halls, and gentlemen's clubs to brothels in the red-light district, come not only from the nation where they work, but also from various other countries. In Bangkok, for example, while clients can easily obtain services by native Thais, they have no problem gaining access to similar services by someone from Australia, Japan, or the United States. As a matter of fact, a small number of sex workers can always migrate voluntarily for monetary benefits. Posing as regular travelers, they stay wherever they feel comfortable and able to make a profit. For those who are not knowledgeable, who do not bother to adventure out by themselves, or who are forced by their circumstances to stay in the original destination, they either turn to a master or fall a prey to organized groups. No doubt there are still many coercive operations where women are abducted, swindled, or sold for sex (Engstrom, Minas, Espinoza, and Jones 2004; Goodey 2004; Hopper 2004). It is also no surprise that people interested in the sex trade willingly follow a guide, a leader, or a pimp to enter the society of destination to work for an amount of money promised by an oral or written contract or pledged by the organizer. For example, young women from Mainland China enter Hong Kong, Macao, Malaysia, or Singapore in regular tourist groups. With assistance from their group leader, they are able to work in and make a profit from various sex-related businesses during their traveler's sojourn.

Second, children are transported from impoverished, disaster-impacted, or overpopulated countries for adoption or sexual exploitation in industrial societies. Stories abound that children in one country are first rescued from manmade conflicts or natural disasters, then placed in orphanages, and eventually sent for adoption by families in other countries. There are also reports that grandparents, aunts, or uncles hand children to organized trafficking groups to join their parents on the other side of the border, especially from Mexico to the United States. Sponsorship and adoption are always ongoing between poor or developing and rich or developed economies. For example, organized adoption has placed numerous Chinese girls or orphaned children in Western families across Europe and North America. While official adoption can be carefully carried out by state agencies, it can sometimes be taken advantage of by various private interests. In the country of origin, children are taken from their birthplaces, gathered in collective shelters, and groomed for adoption, with some profit motive on the part of their handlers and temporary caretakers. In the country of destination, adoption agencies may exploit adoptive parents and their desire for children by charging a handsome fee for international communication, documentation, and transportation. Most important, are all adopted children well taken care of in their adoptive families? Are they marginalized when their adoptive parents are later able to give birth to their own children? If it is not made known by at least one celebrity case in Hollywood, who knows if any adopted children end up being married to one of their adoptive parents, why and how? Besides adoption, sponsorship and host family programs in many developed countries allow middle-class professionals, such as educators and artists, to sponsor and give support to foreign students who come to the United States to study in middle or high schools, to enter language or vocational programs, and to attend colleges or universities. While the arrangement paves the way for many teenagers and young people to learn science, technology, and a foreign culture, it also creates opportunities for individual manipulation or exploitation. For example, an American professor helps a youngster from Peru to come to his college as a foreign student. A few years later, the same youngster becomes his domestic partner. Does the case qualify as an example of human smuggling for the purpose of sex?

Third, manual and domestic workers are transported from labor-exporting countries to labor-importing societies. There are state-sponsored labor exports and imports. For example, China, Indonesia, and the Philippines all have official programs to recruit, train, and counsel people who go overseas to work in foreign households or on international projects. In labor-importing societies, there are also public and private agencies that handle placement, conflict resolution, and life-related emergencies for foreign laborers. While legally sanctioned labor exports and imports may appear to balance supply with demand, in actuality they often serve as reasons for illegal trafficking of laborers across national or territorial borders. Obviously, official labor exports do not offer incentives attractive enough for all persons willing to adventure overseas for a wage. For employers, state-regulated labor imports can never be as fast, cost-effective, and worry-free as these employers would like. As a result, there are always needs for illegal trafficking of human labor. Beginning with the least easily detected, families sponsor their relatives or friends, under false names when necessary, to work as maids or nannies at home or as critical aides in business. Ethnic groups use their legal or illegal resources, such as banks, law offices, travel agencies, medical practices, and welfare services, to advocate, certify, and protect labor imports from their native land. For example, businesses would state how much they need some types of employees even though they could easily find people with similar qualifications on the domestic market; travel agencies would bring in every tourist group they could assemble even though they knew some tourists join a tour simply for immigration; and lawyers would put all their talents on display in assisting those who are already in the host country to stay and those who are still out to come even though they know not everyone whom they assist is actually eligible or deserving. The most brazen violation of law is, of course, what appears in international headline news. Illegal emigrants pay an upfront fee to professional traffickers or organized crime groups to leave their homeland by air, over water, or by land. They fall into servitude or live under slave-like conditions when they arrive at their destination. Traffickers profit while migrants suffer or die in unsuccessful cross-border smuggling operations (Zhang and Chin 2002; Haynes 2004; Lee 2006).

With regard to the lives of migrants or illegal immigrants, sex workers make a decent income only when they are physically attractive. As they age, they have to look for other means of survival. If they have not contracted AIDS or other venereal diseases, sex workers may settle in foreign lands, marry someone, start a conventional business, or pursue a legitimate profession. After they have made sufficient money, they may return home to live comfortably the rest of their lives. The possible costs, however, are heavy: physical abuse, mental stress, disease, and even death. Children, either in adoption or under sponsorship, obviously must count on their adoptive or sponsoring families for their future. In the best scenario, they grow up with education and job opportunities they would never have access to in their homeland. In the worst scenario, they are abused, marginalized, or lost to youth gangs or criminal groups, outcomes which would not normally happen to them should they be raised in their native environment. Manual and domestic laborers differentiate markedly between men and women. Whereas maids and nannies can sometimes turn to marriage for a change of life pattern, male workers may forever face exploitative conditions until they return home. If they stay as aliens, they can only hope that their children will have a better life. Indeed, a considerable number of illegal immigrants would admit that it is this dream, this hope that helps them cope with the daily hardships they experience in an unfamiliar land. The dream is that they will earn enough money to bring their family into the new land so that their children will have easier lives.

Finally, illegal immigration and human trafficking occur as the world differentiates between rural and urban societies, between free and controlled political systems, between poor and rich countries, as well as between developed and developing regions. In closed societies where tradition holds strong or political control remains tight, the flow of traffic may be negligible. In poor economies where the government is weak and borders stay open, there may be heavy human traffic, especially of women and children, out of national or territorial boundaries. People in Mexico flock to the United States primarily because of the economy. Cubans who flee to the same destination may cite both economy and communist control as their reasons for resettlement. On the Western side of the Pacific, people in North Korea enter China, where they can seek better economic opportunities while experiencing all the communist symbolism of their native land. Chinese on Mainland China adventure into Hong Kong, Macao, Taiwan, and even Singapore, where they can make more money while feeling close to home in terms of culture and language. For Chinese who are able to pay the usurious passage fees to traffickers for trips to the West, there are three factors that seem to explain their move: a developing economy in China that creates more needs and buying power for consumers; a developing economy that raises people's awareness about jobs and pay; and a developing economy that makes people nervous about their future and that of their children as they feel that their way of life is threatened.

The United States has published an annual report that charts illegal trade for labor and sex across international frontiers since 2000. In its 2005 report, it accused fourteen countries of failing to do enough to stop the modern-day slave trade in prostitutes, child sex workers, and forced laborers. They include these nations: Bolivia, Cambodia, Cuba, Ecuador, Jamaica, Kuwait, Myanmar, Qatar, North Korea, Saudi Arabia, Sudan, Togo, United Arab Emirates, and Venezuela (United States Department of State 2005). As it vows to use its economic leverage, such as development assistance, funding for cultural and educational exchanges, and support from the World Bank and the International Monetary Fund, to penalize those countries on the list, one wonders whether the United States ever takes time to reflect upon its own role in human trafficking in which as many as 800,000 people are bought and sold across national borders annually or lured to other countries with false promises of work or other benefits. As the richest and the most powerful country in the world, the United States is able to take advantage of the natural resources, political opportunities, and human capital, both intellectual talent and cheap labor, afforded by the entire world, to build a society of affluence and wealth. To what extent does the United States bear responsibility for human trafficking when it creates a middle-class society, a long-living population, and a consumer culture that constantly call for childcare, care for the elderly, household work, manual labor, and other services to be furnished by these newcomers from foreign lands? More pointedly, what should the United States do when some of its corporate executives or managers habitually look for sex on overseas business trips, when some of its middle-class families anxiously await children for adoption or actively use illegal aliens for domestic work, or when some of its citizens, including affluent yet lonely retirees, routinely use their wealth or American citizenship to prey on children or young people in other countries for marriage, companionship, or profit?

10

Organized Crime

Drug smuggling, human trafficking, and illegal immigration are inherently related to organized criminal groups and gang activities around the world (Frisby 1998; Newman 1999). While the mass media draw attention to well-equipped, well-organized crime groups, such as the Medellin Cartel, the Cali Cartel, the Kunsha Group, and the Mafias, various ethnic and local gangs attract serious attention from law enforcement as well (Soothill 1996; Kraul, Connell, and Lopez 2005). In countries of origination, local gangs recruit prospective emigrants, gather and transport raw materials and drugs in small amounts, prepare equipment, offer information, and provide various services for the larger international crime group. In countries of destination, ethnic gangs, based in their ethnic enclaves, collect money from illegal immigrants who have jobs, sell drugs to users and street dealers, run prostitution rings, operate gambling houses, intervene in business disputes for economic gain, and extort business establishments in the name of protection. Taking advantage of modern communications and transportation, various gang groups are now able to broaden their network and diversify their operation across regional and national borders. In Asia and the Pacific, gang leaders in Hong Kong may dispatch their members to Mainland China or send word to their followers in San Francisco and Los Angeles.

BACKGROUND

Organized crime manifests in the organized nature of crime activities and groupings. There are highly structured criminal groups that recruit members, socialize recruits, select targets, plan activities, manage criminal undertakings, and strive for profit like business enterprises. Because they are organized, they are able to commit crimes of scale or international significance, such as drug trafficking and the sex trade, through extraordinary means, including conspiracy with corrupted officials, coercion of a localized community, public threat, and coordinated violence.

The most notorious organized crime group in the world is the Mafia. The term "Mafia" comes from a tale of revenge that allegedly took place on Easter Monday of 1282 in Sicily, Italy. On that day, a French soldier who was part of a band of marauding foreigners, raped a Sicilian woman at her wedding. The incident took bands of Sicilians to the streets of Palermo to slaughter hundreds of Frenchmen amid the screams of the young girl's mother "Ma fia, ma fia" (My daughter, my daughter). "Mafia" was later adopted as a concept that emphasizes family as a "place of refuge" for life and survival (Lewis 1964; Inciardi 1975). Indeed, on the island that was invaded by successive foreign invaders—Romans, Byzantines, Arabs, Normans, Germans, Spaniards, Austrians, and French—Sicilians learned to survive on the strength of their families. When they emigrated to the United States, they found that it was again family that helped them cope with their new hostile environment. Ironically, family and its extended yet united structure for securing trust, loyalty, and dedication also became an effective and reliable vehicle for some Sicilians to establish dominance and gain prominence in the criminal enterprise. Following World War II, Sicilian crime families were so successful that they made the Sicilian Mafia a live legend in the world of crime. For a long time, "Mafia" has been virtually synonymous with organized crime in the mind of most people around the world.

Sensational news dispatches and some television series would have people believe that an "alien conspiracy" composed of dozens of Italian-dominated crime families known as La Cosa Nostra dominates organized crime in the United States, and perhaps, the world. The truth is that organized crime goes far beyond the Mafias on the international stage (Cressey 1969; Paoli 2003). Across the globe, there are territorial clusters, based in a country, in a racial or ethnic culture, or in a geographical region. There are enterprise groups, specializing in drug trafficking, human trade, counterfeiting, money laundering, or contrabands. There are also project-oriented bands that are assembled or disassembled in response to specific opportunities or pressures. Because of the transnational nature of their business dealings, organized crime groups often establish and maintain routine or contingent ties with each other. Among the most well-known, Chinese triads focus on activities ranging from drugs, gambling, illegal immigration, money laundering, prostitution, and racketeering to usury in native Chinese societies, including Hong Kong, Macao, and Taiwan, or oversea Chinese communities, such as Chinatowns, throughout Asia and the Pacific. The Japanese Yakuza has thousands of members in numerous clans that engage in extortion, prostitution, and drug traffic, especially amphetamines, in Japan and across Asia. Colombian cartels are incorporated business entities specializing in the management of all aspects of drugs from growing to processing to transporting to distributing. Russian Mafias gather millions of members through hundreds of gangs in the former Soviet Union and beyond. These Russian groups penetrate in the government at home and reach out to other organized crime groups, including Colombian cartels and Sicilian Cosa Nostra. Around the world, Russian Mafias profit from a variety of crimes: the drug trade, dealing of weapons and firearms, trafficking in women and children, prostitution, extortion, money laundering, stolen automobiles, counterfeiting, and even shipment of nuclear materials (Finckenauer and Voronin 2001; Shelley 2003).

Diverse and varied though it is in both organizing and operating, all of organized crime shares several salient features. First, organized crime is a conspiratorial activity. It involves the coordination of a considerable number of people in the planning and execution of illegal acts or sometimes in the pursuit of a legitimate business by unlawful means. Second, organized crime requires serious commitment by its primary members as well as some close associates who provide specialized skills or services as needed. Rules are clearly specified. Violations are promptly responded to. Retributive punishment may include harsh measures, such as substantive loss, dramatic injury, a death threat, and sometimes even a death sentence, to the violator and his family. Third, organized crime builds upon a hierarchical structure. A chieftain leads his close advisors or confidants who in turn direct their trusted followers or subordinates to carry out specific activities. The chain of command is maintained with differential rank, status, and share of profit. It can only be successful because of personal trust, relational closeness, and shared risk at work. Fourth, organized crime aims at economic gain as its primary goal. Power and status may come along with profit but remain secondary in overall importance. To achieve or maximize economic gain, organized crime groups tend to maintain a monopoly on the illegal goods or services in which they specialize. Fifth, organized crime groups exploit people and their fear or greed with various predatory strategies or tactics. Government officials they corrupt; to legitimate businesses and the general populace they often employ abduction, intimidation, arson, and violence. Sixth, organized crime does not exist only in the illegal business arena. Sometimes it uses legitimate businesses for illegal activities. For example, money is laundered through commercial banks or drug profits are transferred to licensed enterprises. Sometimes it engages in legitimate activities for unlawful gains. For instance, it processes dues for labor unions or manages small capitalization stock transactions on behalf of elderly or inexperienced investors. Finally, organized crime evolves with time in selecting and using modes of communication, means of transportation, weaponry for defense and offense, ways of responding to social pressures, lines of business, and even styles of management. In the information age, various organized groups have actively explored and employed computers and the internet for multiple purposes, especially sales of illegal materials, such as pornography (President's Commission on Organized Crime 2001; United Nations Office on Drugs and Crime 2005).

Reaction to organized crime often begins with sensational coverage of mob wars and their victims by the mass media. Following news reports, there are then academic studies, governmental investigations, enactment of laws, and prosecution of criminal cases. In the United States, major investigations conducted at the federal level include those by the Committee on Mercenary Crimes in 1932, the Special Senate Committee to Investigate Organized Crime in Interstate Commerce from 1950 to 1951, the Senate Permanent Subcommittee on Investigations from 1956 to 1963, President Lyndon Johnson's Commission on Law Enforcement and Administration of Justice from 1964 to 1967, and the President's Commission on Organized Crime from 1986 to 1987. In 1963, the Senate Permanent Subcommittee on Investigations secured testimony by Joseph Valachi, a disenchanted soldier in New York's Genovese crime family. The testimony, as the first account by an insider, provided critical information on the inner workings of a secret quasi-military criminal syndicate by Italian organized crime known as La Cosa Nostra (United States Senate Committee on Governmental Affairs 1990).

Most important, governmental investigations pave the way for formal lawmaking and institutionalized reaction. Among the first legislative measures aimed directly at organized crime was the Interstate and Foreign Travel or Transportation in Aid of Racketeering Enterprise Act in 1952. The Act prohibits travel in interstate commerce or use of interstate facilities with the intent to promote, manage, establish, carry on, or facilitate unlawful activities, such as gambling, bribery, extortion, arson, and liquor law violations. In 1970, Congress passed the Organized Crime Control Act. Title IX of the act, known as the Racketeer Influenced and Corrupt Organization Act (RICO), attacks racketeering activities by prohibiting the use of racketeering as a means of making income, collecting loans, or conducting business and prohibiting the investment of funds derived from racketeering in any enterprise involved in interstate commerce. To aid in prosecution, the Act even authorizes the establishment of a Federal Witness Protection Program under which witnesses who testify in court are guaranteed new identities and other forms of protection against revenge. RICO and its successful implementation also prompted the adoption of an enterprise theory of investigation by the Federal Bureau of Investigation. Instead of focusing on criminal acts as isolated incidents, the FBI now turns more and more to the criminal enterprise, its subsystems and their operational processes, such as day-to-day communication, transportation, and finance, to build a case against organized crime (McFeely 2001).

On the international front, debates on a United Nations response to transnational organized crime and its threat to the political, economic, and social fabric of member societies began in the mid-1990s. An International Convention against Transnational Organized Crime was subsequently formulated, representing a historic step in the global fight against illegitimate activities by criminal groups and enterprises. The Global Programme against Transnational Organized Crime, established under the Convention in the United Nations Office on Drugs and Crime, has since worked on the ratification of the Convention by individual national governments. To promote the ratification of the Convention, regional meetings were held in Algeria for African countries, in Ecuador for Latin American and Caribbean countries, in Guatemala for Central America, in Latvia for Eastern European countries, and in Japan for Asian countries. In addition, there were expert group meetings held to prepare legislative guides to the Convention and its three protocols and national level meetings held in cooperation with member states, such as Cape Verde, Guinea Bissau, Haiti, Indonesia, Nigeria, and Romania (United Nations Office on Drugs and Crime 2005).

Central to the Convention and its mission, the Global Programme against Transnational Organized Crime has made specific efforts in the assessment of prevailing patterns and trends, the training of criminal justice practitioners, the development of tools and technical assistance, and the sharing of information among member states on transnational organized crime. With respect to assessment, a database on organized crime groups across a variety of countries is now available for public review; a manual on investigating and countering organized crime is ready for official reference; and a few regional assessment surveys are conducted, covering such dynamic regions as Central Asia and West Africa. On the matter of training, a multimedia seminar is in shape to help police investigators, prosecutors and judges, intelligence analysts, and customs officials learn best practices in the fight against transnational organized crime. Pilot seminars were first held in Colombia, Croatia, Peru, and Slovakia. Since 2002, formal training has taken place in many other countries, including Chile, Ecuador, Guatemala, Mexico, Mongolia, Nigeria, Romania, Ukraine, and a number of Southern African countries. Finally, regarding information sharing, the Programme envisions a special "helpdesk" in the future on transnational organized crime, in addition to the data it gathers from and presents about individual countries and the whole world community on such common issues as the nature of active organized crime groups and their salient characteristics, national legislative systems and their institutional establishments, and international cooperation and its procedural arrangements (United Nations Office on Drugs and Crime 2005).

CAUSE

Causes for organized crime across national borders are multiple. While some are obvious and well known, others take meticulous research to uncover and understand.

One hypothesis argues that the failure of the state to deliver essential political goods such as security, justice, and stability encourages criminal groups to perform state functions (Sung 2004). In Asia and the Pacific, weak states exist in different countries, from those still in the shadow of colonialism to those strongly under the influence of foreign interests, from those caught between tradition and modernity to those mired in either autocratic recklessness or democratic indecision, and from those divided by civil wars to those united as a loose sovereign polity. For example, how much security can a government provide for its citizens, especially those in and around the war zones, when it engages in a war with guerrillas? In fact, civil or regional wars in Afghanistan, Cambodia, India, Indonesia, Myanmar, Pakistan, the Philippines, and Sri Lanka all create ideal milieus in which both domestic and international organized crime groups rule and prosper on matters ranging from business protection, local justice, shipments of arms, supplies of contrabands, and production of drugs to human trade in sex and slavery. Moreover, a general weakness of the state manifests itself in various contexts, from the rigidity of bureaucracy to a lack of trained personnel, from massive waste to rampant corruption, and from decision-making mistakes to carelessness in policy implementation. For instance, Russian Mafias may target corrupt officials and their greed in routine operations in the territory of the former Soviet Union whereas in the West, such as the United States and

Canada, such crime groups may take advantage of legal formalities and procedural loopholes for strategic survival.

Parallel to the state failure hypothesis is an economic failure hypothesis on predatory organized crime (Sung 2004). This hypothesis holds that poor economic outcomes such as high unemployment, a low standard of living, and reliance on an underground economy stimulate the growth of criminal syndicates as suppliers of goods in demand, services, and jobs. Throughout Asia and the Pacific, economic gaps between rural and urban areas, developing and developed regions, and poor and rich societies are staggeringly wide. The rural-urban divide alone, for example, may account for much of organized crime. In major cities, such as transportation hubs, political capitals, and international centers of commerce, there is not only a sizable middle class living in self-sufficiency but also a small leisure or elite class disposing of wealth through conspicuous consumption. By contrast, the majority of people in the countryside do not have much to gain in their day-to-day struggle for survival with nature. A farmer who tills the land laboriously from sunrise to sunset may still not able to earn as much as someone who digs in the waste discarded by city residents or even a small portion of what a porter would earn at a municipal seaport or a maid in an urban household. As a result, most youths flee their villages to become migrant laborers in cities. Some rebel against their customary way of life by forming gangs, joining organized bandits, or participating in an ongoing insurgency or an existing guerrilla force. Massive migrant labor provides both target and source for organized crime. As targets, rootless migrants are lured or forced into prostitution, servitude, or slavery. As sources, they supply aides, guards, associates, members, and even core leaders for various organized crime groups. When connection between rural areas and urban centers are needed, gangs, bandits, and insurgent groups originating from the countryside can be brought on board for larger organized crime operations, such as human trafficking and the drug trade.

Another noticeable explanation for organized crime is an advance in communication and transportation experienced even in the remote areas of Asia and the Pacific. In almost every communiqué issued by national and international organizations, transnational organized crime is viewed as an inevitable side product of increasing commercial, political, and social interactions across the globe brought about by modern technology, communication networks, and means of transportation. Indeed, advances in communication and transportation reduce distances, render state frontiers porous, and aid criminal groups in both planning and execution. Information shared over the internet and by cellular phones is instant, prompting new ideas and plans for special operations for emergent groups. Flights, ships, rails, and buses provide common schedules and vehicles for routine transactions for established groups. Despite tremendous differences in economic development, most countries in Asia and the Pacific are accessible by radio networks, satellite news, and commercial communication, such as airline, shipping, rail, and bus services. Like their legitimate counterparts in multinational corporations, transnational organized crime leaders can ride in sleek limousines, fly luxury business jets, carry advanced communication devices, stay at five-star resorts, and watch live satellite news from Bangkok to Los Angeles, from Hong Kong to Manila, from Phnom Penh to Singapore, or from Lima to Tokyo. Like any legitimate participant in international diplomacy, organized charity, or tourism, a member of an organized crime group can use a computer, take a bus, ride a train, fly a commercial airliner, and check into a hotel when he or she works on an assigned job anywhere across Asia and the Pacific, whether it is in Ulan Bator, Mongolia or in Sydney, Australia.

Besides those recognized factors, there are forces that need to be explored in the quest of causes for transnational organized crime. One is the contrast between human nature and social structure, between human needs and social supply, and between human desires and social constraints. Specifically, human beings, driven by their natural instincts and desires, tend to make unlimited demands for certain goods and services. Society, patterned in a traditional established order, tends to place limiting conditions on what goods and services are allowed, how they are delivered, and whether they are rationed by age, gender, race, or socioeconomic status. For example, sex is socially regulated and can be legitimately gratified only in legislated institutions such as marriage, the family, and domestic partnership. It becomes socially problematic when individuals follow their natural instincts to engage in sex at a time or in a situation appropriate to their mutual desires. Organized crime, in essence, fills in, capitalizes on, or profits from the gap between universal human demands and legitimized social supplies of goods and services. In Asia and the Pacific, the gap becomes widened when people in developed countries can spend so little of their disposable income to buy an illicit service or illicit goods from their counterparts in developing or undeveloped countries.

Another force is globalization. It is well known that globalization brings different countries closer, making the world a smaller and easier place for trade, cultural exchange, and social cooperation. It is, however, not completely understood that globalization does not necessarily equalize the world. In fact, while it pushes less developed societies closer to their more developed counterparts in the supply of labor, space, and raw materials, globalization pulls the former further from the latter in the share of profit, power, and prosperity. With globalization, people see each other and their differences more closely and frequently, and therefore can develop a sharper realization of inequality and injustice. For instance, many Mexicans who struggle hard in their native land can only enter the United States illegally to perform hard labor for Americans. Because they enter illegally, these immigrants are not able to claim or enjoy many social benefits in the country that sees them as illegal aliens. The situation creates an opportunity for organized crime: Organized crime groups recruit Mexicans nationals, transport them across the border, and place them in American households, farms, and other receiving institutions needing labor; organized crime groups aid illegal immigrants who are not allowed to open bank accounts nor allowed to drive by granting false identity cards, false driver licenses or issuing false insurance policies. In general, organized crime can act upon the public sentiment of deprivation, alienation, and injustice shared by people in the Third World. For example, some organized crime groups target only citizens from affluent societies or operate in the First World with a clear intent to create social disruption or spread fear among the general public. The drug trade seems to serve as a more indirect vehicle for social revenge. As some Third World scholars point out, drugs are fairy evils that help bleed rich countries for the wealth they have garnered, legitimately and illegitimately, from around the world. The reasoning is mischievous yet logical: "You have made so much from us. There must be some ways for you to lose or for us to get back."

At a practical level, profit enables the formation and maintenance of an institutional structure and network required for organized crime. Profit from organized crime can be potentially almost unlimited given the fact that organized crime groups do not pay tariffs or taxes, may unilaterally set prices for their goods and services, and have the leisure to decide how they will compensate their members. Also, by conventional logic, for the high risk involved, organized crime members deserve a high payoff. With profit, organized crime groups are able to keep members by attractive material incentives, train new recruits with advanced technology, enforce rules effectively, apply penalties in a timely fashion, and glorify leaders through all possible luxuries. In operation, economic muscle enables organized crime groups to increase sales, broaden services, expand territories, solidify monopolies, take up new businesses, or boost their reputation or status in relation to the conventional business, the government, or the general populace. Throughout Asia and the Pacific, organized crime specializes mainly in the drug trade, human trafficking, and arms smuggling. Profit makes some organized crime groups not only grow stronger and more stable inside their institutional boundary, but also become bold and aggressive in dealing with law enforcement, business rivalry, and membership betrayal. While small-grouped entrepreneurial snakeheads tend to use many means, including bribery, to buy their ways in and out of the system for a human trafficking operation, large-scaled corporate syndicates often show no hesitation in engaging in personal assassinations, public bombings, and even military-style skirmishes or battles in their drug growing, processing, transporting, and distributing businesses.

On the other side of profit is cost. Organized crime incurs high cost compared to conventional business ventures. Bribing corrupt officials, paying trained or skilled operatives, eliciting membership dedication and loyalty, supporting leaders and their risk-taking or status-demanding lifestyle means that an organized crime group may have to bear costs several times more than what a legitimate business need spend on the operation of a project or the delivery of a client-oriented service. The criminal organization must be able to control and absorb this high cost. Organized crime is an underground enterprise. Secrecy demands the power and protection of an institutional structure. It is only through an organized network that information can be gathered with a certain amount of independence, the core of command can be relatively sheltered from the team of operation, or on-field task execution can to some degree be buffered from post-incident evaluation. In Asia and the Pacific, there is a general observation that all organized crime groups take advantage of institutional setups in their illegal business undertakings. There are, however, specific developments. While a few groups capitalize on a large scale, an established reputation, or a familiar business for domination in a locale or region, many more organized crime enterprises appeal to small-business models to manage cost, keep secrecy, and bypass scrutiny from law enforcement, media, and the general public. For example, most Chinese smuggling groups operate as ad hoc task forces with limited hierarchical structure. Using familial networks as well as fortuitous social contacts, Chinese smugglers assemble, disassemble, and reassemble groups strategically or tactically in response to business opportunities, market conditions, and social control reactions (Zhang and Chin 2002).

Finally, organized crime exists and thrives simply because some criminal activities, such as the drug trade, human trafficking, arms dealing, and other cross-border transactions, lie beyond individuals and their individual capacities. A single individual, no matter how ambitious, adventurous, smart, or strong, cannot carry out certain complex criminal tasks all on his or her own. Even for many criminal acts that individuals perform well, an organization can show its advantage by doing them in scale, by a set procedure, for a known feared reputation, and with effectiveness and efficiency.

TYPE, PATTERN, AND CHRACTERISTICS

For profit, power, or status, organized crime is a conspiratorial enterprise. It involves a group of people in the planning and execution of illegal activities or in the pursuit of a legal business venture by unlawful means.

Beginning with the way people are brought together for a task, organized crime groups divide into four categories. The first is family-based. The most well known is the Mafia. A family-based crime group, however, is not necessarily built on blood relationships. Members may come from a particular locale or organization, sharing a unique memory of a hometown or some stage-of-life deeds. They call each other brothers and sisters. They look up to senior folk or an emergent leader as their guide or head. For example, some alumni groups and hometown associations in Chinatowns on the Pacific Rim may fall into this category when they engage in the recruitment and placement of illegal aliens who belong to them by family or community. The second is age-graded. An age-graded crime organization attracts people from a specific age group. Members in the age range share a similar level of experience, education, or energy. The most prevalent is the youth gang. For instance, Mara Salvatrucha or MS-13 and its rival, Mara 18, include members from early teens to early adulthood. Active in the United States, Central America, Mexico, and Canada, MS-13 is responsible for waves of violence and crimes, from making firearms, transporting drugs, exporting stolen cars, and murder, to various street offenses, on the Eastern shoreline of the Pacific Ocean (Kraul, Connell, and Lopez 2005). The third is race or ethnicity-based. This category is characteristic of almost all organized crime groups, from Italian Cosa Nostra to Japanese Yakuza, from Chinese triads to Latino gangs, and from Colombian cartels to Russian mafias. Race or ethnicity-based organized crime groups build upon a membership of the same race or ethnicity for greater mutual understanding, solidarity, and security. People of other races or ethnicities may be used only as sponsored associates or paid specialists. The fourth is language-connected. This category relates to the third type as people of the same race or ethnicity are likely to speak one common language. It, however, goes beyond the third because people who speak one common language do not necessarily belong to one race or ethnicity. For instance, Latino gangs spread across different countries in Americas mainly due to the fact that members of those gangs speak Spanish. Russian Mafias expand to Eastern Europe and Central Asia because people in those regions can conveniently communicate with each other in Russian. As English becomes a worldwide means of communication, there will be more and more crimes committed among tourists, migrants, students, diplomats, multinational corporate workers in the actual world or over cyberspace by groups organized around or connected by the English language.

In terms of the activities involved, organized crime lives mainly on two types of business enterprises. The first is illegal business for big profit. Certain drugs are totally prohibited by almost every country in the world. The Colombian drug cartels have grown into regional and global business empires that challenge established national governments and legitimized international forces. These cartels produce, process, transport, and distribute cocaine, marijuana, and other drugs. Immigration is controlled across national borders, especially between affluent and impoverished societies. Chinese triads eye this reality as an opportunity to profit by recruiting, transporting, placing, and managing migrant laborers from Mainland China to Hong Kong, Macao, Singapore, and Taiwan, and even to advanced economies in Europe, Oceania, and North America. Prostitution is illegal and socially stigmatized. Russian mafias send women from Russia and Eastern European countries to major Asian and Pacific metropolises to work as prostitutes. Gambling is banned in most places by government. Japanese Yakuza niches in to develop and maintain a monopoly on gambling throughout Japan. Murder for hire is seen as one of the most heinous crimes by law enforcement. Latino gangs market it in response to needs from both criminal undergrounds and the conventional world. Although none of the aforementioned activities belongs solely to the groups cited above, these illegal activities altogether offer a wide range of business opportunities.

The other type of business adventure for organized crime remains relatively unnoticed. It is the conduct of legal business through illegal means, such as harassment, threat, and violence. Involvement in legal business is critically important to organized crime. It provides a business front to hide underground operations, transfer illegal gains, legitimize problematic transactions, and establish market influence. Japanese Yakuza offers an illustrative example of how some organized crime groups can grow into their respective social environment, developing a kind of symbiosis with law enforcement, political establishments, business communities, and the general public (Kaplan and Dubro 1986). In the community and with local residents, Japanese Yakuza controls turfs, settles disputes, engages in personal protection, and provides general security. When "A" suffers a loss with at-fault "B" in a traffic accident, "A" can receive a fast and reasonable compensation from "B" through the assistance of Yakuza without the tedious process of legal formalities. In the corporate world and with various businesses, Yakuza recruits day laborers and stevedores to work for Japanese shipping and construction companies to evade Japan's strict immigration law, dispatches so-called "land-raising" specialists to evict stubborn land owners or tenants to make way for new projects, or sends so-called "sokaiya" specialists to attend a company's annual meeting sometimes for the company's protection, sometimes for the company's harm. In the political world and with governmental officials, Japanese Yakuza provides services ranging from drumming up election campaigns, delivering sensitive messages, and blocking media releases of embarrassing information, to making connections to business and other vital interests. Even with law enforcement, Japanese Yakuza seems to enjoy a kind of respect from the police for its adherence to a feudal-era code of chivalry. From time to time, Yakuza turns in some of its members to help the police break a case. Most important, the police to some degree count on the existence of Yakuza for dealing with street crime. When some hooligans come into a neighborhood and start making trouble, chances are Yakuza will take care of them before the police are needed.

At the core of its business, organized crime seems to take on two different models. One is the multinational corporate model. The other is the small business model. The multinational corporate model is used in the drug trade, human trafficking, smuggling of weapons and military equipment, pornography in cyberspace, and sex tourism. In business, it connects suppliers or producers with transporters or distributors, with wholesalers or retailers, and eventually with consumers. By division of labor, it has a clear distinction between management and operation, between planning and production, and between finance and security. Its organizational structure is hierarchical, with the corporate headquarter and branch facilities or offices, with core members and sponsored or hired associates, and with a CEO-like head and frontline workers or handlers. An organized crime group under the multinational corporate model can use scale, risk, international reach, media exposure, law enforcement attention, and public fear in its pursuit of high profit and success. With an established reputation, it can easily pick up a business, take over a market, or silence a group of competitors or adversaries, sometimes even without actually taking any action at all. Colombian cartels, Italian Cosa Nostra, and Russian mafias, with their respective overarching dominance in major transnational crime ventures, exemplify well organized crime using the multinational corporate model.

On the other hand, the small business model thrives on migrant labor, civil disputes, gambling, smuggling of contrabands, and prostitution. An organized crime group following the small business model targets specific opportunities that arise from interpersonal or inter-group interactions or cross-border transactions. In operation, it uses small teams with each of the team members assuming multiple roles for different tasks. The group leader performs multiple duties as well: initiation, planning, financial management, facilitation, or field supervision. Differing from its counterpart corporate model, a small organized crime group resorts to portability or manageable size to minimize cost, reduce complexity in organization and operation, keep a low profile, avoid media attention, and ward off any possible law enforcement attack. Many Chinese organized crime groups, which are historically highly localized individual organizations, seem to fit into the small business model. In recent years, due to dramatic changes in their home territories, Chinese crime groups, including secret societies, self-help associations, and street gangs, have begun to spread prolifically across Asia and the Pacific. The most feared secret societies or triads are actively involved in a wide range of illegal activities, including human trafficking, drug smuggling, money laundering, loansharking, prostitution, gambling, and extortion within and across Mainland China, Hong Kong, Macao, Taiwan, and the United States (Chin 1999). In alien smuggling and heroin trafficking destinations, they work with self-help associations among Chinese immigrants or tongs and street gangs in Chinatown, forming a self-protection shield often impermeable to law enforcement. Although they are not as scaled, coordinated, and threatening as international Mafias, Chinese crime groups are each well-organized with clear objectives of profit and well-thought plans for operation. They persist as individual entrepreneurship flourishing in Hong Kong, Taiwan, Mainland China, and various Chinese enclaves in North America.

On a general level, organized crime thrives on war, political transition, economic development, cultural change, and social transformation. War gives rise to social anarchy. It also creates gaps between demand and supply in labor, consumer goods, and military materials. For example, wars in Afghanistan, Iraq, and many other parts of the world not only fan insurgency and terrorism, but also fuel organized crime and underground activities. Political transition weakens the state and its ability to keep social order and provide vital services. It also changes the distribution of power and the allocation of social resources. For instance, at the time of the breakdown of the former Soviet Union, when individual republics reemerged with a Western model, organized crime groups used violence, corruption, and other means to challenge or influence state authority in the redistribution of public properties, specifically in the regulations the state had to make regarding the processes and outcomes of privatization (Juska, Johnstone, and Pozzuto 2004). Russian mafias were especially aggressive. They purchased valuable state properties through insider deals and then resold them for lucrative profits; they recruited officials as their "silent partners" so that they could use the governmental apparatus to control businesses they required to have their "protection"; some of their trusted members attained public office; they bought other public officials so that they could influence the state's domestic as well as foreign policies to the benefit of their criminal enterprise (Shelley

2003; Finckenauer 2004). Thus, economic development, cultural change, and social transformation bring about opportunities for both legitimate and illegitimate business undertakings. Rapid change can alter the way people relate to the outside world, perceive different ideas and ideologies that come to their attention, and approach various practical issues in life. Throughout Asia and the Pacific, human trafficking, drug dealing, gambling, prostitution, and sex tourism rise as the flow of people, materials, and information increases within and outside national and territorial boundaries. Whether it is Japanese Yakuza or Chinese triad, whether it is Colombia cartel or Latino gang, no organized crime group will hesitate to seize for profit any opportunity that becomes available in an ever-changing era.

Finally, a troubling trend in organized crime is that it features more and more violence in developing countries. Partly because of the stark economic contrast between the rich and the poor, partly out of a reaction to police brutality, oppression by the regime, or corruption by public officials, and partly because of a general state of cultural disorientation or social maladjustment, organized and individual crime offenders in some emerging economies and democratizing societies often engage in kidnapping, assassination, murder for hire, and other violence for gain. In severely affected countries, most notably in Latin America, organized crime groups conduct hundreds of kidnappings each year, from expressive kidnapping to political kidnapping to kidnapping for money (United Nations Office on Drugs and Crime 2005). Besides inflicting enormous pain on innocent victims, kidnapping spreads fear among the public, threatens social stability, and discourages business investments that are so vital to societies struggling in the early stage of economic development. In developed countries, on the other hand, organized crime seems to become tactically lodged in high-tech and other institutionalized complexities just as society as a whole is enveloped in political democracy, middle-class affluence, cultural sophistication, public correctness, lifestyle diversity, and racial or ethnic tolerance. For example, some organized crime groups begin to penetrate unions, the corporate world, the governmental bureaucracy, or the stock market for hidden yet greater gain in their business ventures.

11

Crimes of Terror

Crimes of terror take place from country to country, in the time of peace or tension, and on issues of material or nonmaterial nature. The September 11 terrorist attack on the United States in 2001, however, has made crimes of terror a focal concern throughout the international community. Hosting Osama bin Laden and his al Qaeda network, featuring Middle East conflicts, and serving as United States battlefronts against terrorism, Asia and the Pacific is currently experiencing more fear of terrorist attacks, witnessing more incidents of terrorist activities, and therefore is making more effort to counteract crimes of terror than any other part of the world.

BACKGROUND

Crimes of terror began with the emergence of the state in human civilization. The assassination of Julius Caesar on March 15, 44 B.C. serves as a classical example. The word "assassin" originates from the old Arab world where members of a drug-using Muslim organization carried out terrorist plots against Christians and other religious enemies (Friedlander 1979). Acts of terrorism were instrumental to the Zealots, a Jewish sect, in their resistance against the Roman occupation in the first century. Toward the end of the

Middle Ages when terrorism became widespread, many political leaders died at the hands of assassins, some of whom could be armed.

In the era following the Renaissance, terrorism became a known weapon against state repression or foreign invasion in the political arena. Indeed, terrorist acts were sometimes viewed as the only means to gain political rights when rulers held absolute power. In Europe, the French Revolution brought down the Bastille in 1789, ushering in an age of the common citizenry within and beyond France. In North America, privateers attacked the British Navy during the Revolutionary War and the War of 1812, contributing to the rise of the United States in the New World.

In the twentieth century, terrorism became more popular as it worked itself into movements seeking liberation, self-rule, and independence across the globe. The Union of Death Society assassinated Archduke Franz Ferdinand in its resistance against the Austro-Hungarian Empire and its control of Serbia, triggering World War I. The Irish Republican Army battled the British army from 1919 to 1923, and was a major force in the formation of the Republic of Ireland as an independent nation. In Russia, left-wing revolutionaries killed the Czar in 1917 and replaced the Czarist government with a Marxist state, the Soviet Union. In India, the Hur Brotherhood attracted religious fanatics to its rank and file as it carried out various extreme acts against the ruling class of the country. In Palestine, Jewish terrorist groups, such as Haganah, Irgun, and the Stern Gang, waged war against the British and attempted to resettle Jews in what they believed to be their traditional homeland. Because many of these terrorist groups were viewed as patriotic or symbolic of self-determination, some of their prominent members later became national heroes or heads of the state. For example, Menachem Begin, who assumed the command of the Irgun Zvati Leumi (National Military Organization) since 1943, remained a major stakeholder in national politics after the establishment of Israel as a state. In 1978, he, as the Prime Minister of Israel, shared the Nobel Peace Prize with the Egyptian President Mohamed Anwar al-Sadat (Gervassi 1979).

Despite the historical fact that some terrorist groups gain social acceptance and some terrorist leaders become national heroes or heads of state, terrorism involves the illegal use of force against innocent people to achieve a political goal or aid a social cause. The political goal may be noble. The social cause may be just. But the means the group resorts to are often secretive, violent, and illegal under the existing political system. Instead of fighting their enemy in the battlefield, terrorists plot to assassinate the commander of the enemy force or kill the leader of the enemy party or the enemy state. Instead of protesting against corruption, abuse, or oppression by the established power in political arenas, terrorists may carry out bombings against the general populace to make a statement, to gain attention, or to cause social turbulence for the ruling class they actually target. The consequence is brutal, loss of life for innocent people. While terrorists themselves may view the deaths of innocent people as unavoidable collateral damage, people in the mainstream tend to reject terrorism in the same way they condemn crime. In fact, the United Nations used to endorse a definition of terrorism as a war crime in peacetime.

At the core of terrorism, there are three subtle yet clear distinctions. First, terrorists inflict pain and humiliation on direct targets in front of a large audience or indirect target. Direct targets of terrorism are usually political leaders, public policies, or international organizations. Because it is difficult to aim at a direct target, terrorism frequently diverts its attacks to people or properties under the guardianship of the direct target. The audience who observes terrorist acts is important as it serves to measure how much pain and humiliation a direct target is to bear. It is nonetheless indirect because the audience is present and will either condemn or cheer a terrorist act as it witnesses the shock of the act. For example, al-Qaeda's direct targets, by its ideological claims, should be the Western domination around the world in general and Western powers, political leaders, military installations, or corporate establishments in particular. Instead of assassinating individual Western heads of state, al-Qaeda targets masses of civilians for maximum horror and trauma in the eyes of the whole world. While it addresses an outer crowd with fear that al-Qaeda is powerful and unbeatable, it keeps an inner mass of people in awe that they can count on al-Qaeda "to do the right thing regarding world affairs" (Richter 2005). While it evokes fear from most people across the globe, al-Qaeda holds considerable respect and following among various parts of the world audience as well.

The audience functions in a number of important ways for the terrorists. Terrorists address direct audiences by way of an indirect target. In most terrorist attacks, innocent civilians killed or injured and public properties destroyed or damaged are not direct targets. However, by bombing indirect targets, terrorists shake the nerve central of their direct audiences. In the case of al-Qaeda and its operatives, their primary goal is to let their direct outer audience, the West and its allies, know that they fight a holy war against crusaders, imperialists, and dominators. To the same degree, they also want their direct inner audience, the world of Muslim and its sympathizers, to understand that they redress an injustice on behalf of the deprived and the oppressed. Second, terrorists deliver direct messages through an indirect medium. Direct messages of terrorism may include adherence to a tradition, promulgation of an ideology, denunciation of a policy, or resistance to a government. With no access or limited access to mainstream media, terrorists choose to engage in extremist acts to spread their messages. These acts witnessed and reported in the mass media can be a thousand times clearer and louder than words. Thus, terrorists cause pain to direct victims for the sake of an indirect gain. Terrorists may bypass direct targets but never miss direct victims. In many known terrorist attacks, hundreds of innocent civilians suffer pain, mutilation, or loss of life. However, despite the trauma it brings to the general public, terrorism gains only indirectly in the form of publicity about its existence or sympathy with its cause or version of reality.

The United States as a leading force in global domination serves as both a direct target and an indirect audience. Terrorists seem to want the United States not only to pay directly for its alleged aggression, exploitation, and imperialism around the world, but also to feel, at least indirectly, shamed, responsible, and sorry for the regimes, national policies, or international practices it has sponsored or supported on the face of the earth. In response, the United States is waging a war against terror at home to defend its homeland and abroad to protect many of its vital interests. According to the United States Department of State, terrorism refers to premeditated, politically motivated violence against noncombatant targets perpetrated by subnational groups or clandestine agents to influence an audience. The USA Patriot Act, enacted in the aftermath of the World Trade Center attack in 2001, provides sweeping new powers to domestic law enforcement and international intelligence agencies in their efforts to fight terrorism. The definition of terrorist activities is broadened. The government is now able to monitor closely anyone who is suspected of "harboring" or giving "material support" to terrorists. Traditional tools of surveillance, from wiretaps, search warrants, and "pen/trap" orders, to subpoenas, are expanded. The Federal Bureau of Investigation can now check telephone, internet, cable, and computer records without first demonstrating that they were being used by a suspect for terrorist planning or action. Sanctions for violent terrorism are tightened. To keep out any illegal alien who is a representative, member, or supporter of terrorist organizations, the Attorney General launched a Foreign Terrorist Tracking Task Force in 2001. To freeze terrorist assets, the Department of Treasury established a Foreign Terrorist Asset Tracking Center in 2002. To increase its effectiveness in protecting the country from terrorist attack, the FBI reformulated its priorities and set out to reorganize itself beginning 2004. Most important, a gigantic Department of Homeland Security came into being in 2002, with its key mission to reduce America's vulnerability to terrorism. The Homeland Security spending bill, focusing on biological, nuclear, and chemical antiterrorism while putting other critical areas, noticeably mass transit, in the back seat, totals more than thirty billion dollars for the fiscal year 2005-2006 (Gaouette and Curtius 2005).

At the United Nations, efforts to aid in the international campaign against terrorism have also intensified since the World Trade Center attack. The Security Council adopted Resolution 1373 on September 28, 2001, calling upon member states to "become parties as soon as possible to the relevant international conventions and protocols," especially the twelve universal legal instruments against international terrorism developed by the United Nations and its specialized agencies from 1963 to 1999. A Counter-Terrorism Committee (CTC) was established to monitor the implementation of the resolution by all states as well as to increase member capabilities to fight terrorism within and beyond the boundaries of national sovereignty. The CTC, along with the United Nations Office on Drugs and Crime, has since provided various forms of technical assistance to countries around the world. For example, between 2002 and 2004, lawmakers, law enforcement officials, and other criminal justice professionals from over eighty member states were familiarized with antiterrorism instruments and international cooperation arrangements. Direct country-specific assistance, including development of a national action plan, was delivered to forty-three countries. A number of regional workshops were held to allow countries in a same region to compare progress, to harmonize legislative acts, or just to learn from each other in their experience with terrorism. The Eleventh United Nations Crime Congress in 2005 reaffirmed the international body's commitment to a global fight against terrorism. Overall, as declared by Secretary-General Kofi Annan, "terrorism is an assault on the fundamental principles of law, order, human rights, and the peaceful settlement of disputes upon which the United Nations is established." The United Nations therefore "has an indispensable role to play in providing the legal and organizational framework within which the international campaign against terrorism can unfold" (United Nations Office on Drugs and Crime 2005).

CAUSE

It is no easy task to identify common causes for crimes of terror as these crimes take place in many different forms in many different countries. Individual personalities, group characteristics, and institutional functions and purposes affect a terrorist organization and its success and impact. Public sentiments, culture, religion, the economy, politics, and the mass media each play a part in fueling terrorism or containing it. In Iraq, insurgency may be due to the American occupation and the fundamental damage the American invasion has done to the country's political, military, and economic infrastructures. In the Middle East, suicide bombings may respond to both the massive economic impoverishment suffered by Palestinians and territorial or military advances made by Israelis. Around the world, terrorism on-the-rise may to some degree reflect the fact that Osama bin Laden has been deified as martyr or god and his al Qaeda network has been sanctified as legend or myth by a worldwide exposure contributed by the mass media and the global war against terror led by the United States.

At a general level, however, a number of forces can be examined in relation to the international spread of terrorism in the twenty-first century. Foremost is the ideology of cultural clashes and religious fanaticism. In an increasingly connected world, elements of different cultures, religions, and societies will converge to form a new dynamic system of beliefs, norms, values, practices, and lifestyles. For each individual culture, religion, and society, how much it gains or loses in the emerging dynamics depends upon the selectivity of the system as well as its own utility and adaptability. While most cultures, religions, and societies embrace global diversification and transformation with their positive contributions, some attempt to avoid, resist, or manipulate change by all possible forces. The most salient is the dramatization of cultural clashes and religious fanaticism. For example, Western cultures, religions, and societies, for fear of a loss of domination in the global dynamics, have intensified an ideological debate against the menace of a rising Eastern culture, a spreading non-Christian religion, and any newly emerging economy. In reaction, especially in the religious arena, non-Christian religions may indeed seek spiritual inspiration from historical differences, developing radical interpretations of reality and sometimes, extreme plans for action. In the court of public opinion or in ideological debates shaped or dominated by the United States in particular and the West in general, Eastern culture featuring a mixture of Buddhism, Confucianism, Taoism, and Communism is considered as incompatible to civil liberty, political democracy, and a market economy; Iran and North Korea are categorized as part of an axis of evil; Islam is related to violence and radicalism; China is viewed as a threat because of its economic development; and Muslim societies are suspect as breeding grounds for suicide bombers and terrorist acts. The general atmosphere may fuel religious fanaticism or ideological radicalism, making the disliked, the maligned, and the marginalized organize, join, and support each other throughout the region.

Another important cause of terrorist crime is state repression, a widespread phenomenon over time. State repression not only exists under authoritarian and totalitarian regimes in the barbarous form of genocide and torture, but also occurs in democratic and free political systems, often implicitly and subtly, through discrimination and mistreatment. Racial and ethnic minorities are discriminated against on jobs and in mainstream activities.

They are segregated, forced into war, and even cleansed if they aspire to be independent or just assertive. Political dissidents are stigmatized in the media and in public opinion. They are silenced, put in jail, or made to disappear if they dare to organize and rebel. Social deviants are harassed in life and routine exchanges. They are distanced, shamed, or arrested when they make noise or cause disruption. Throughout Asia and the Pacific, there are wars launched by the government against what it views as separatist racial or ethnic minorities in different countries, from India, Indonesia, and Sri Lanka to the Philippines; there are persecutions orchestrated by the government against what it considers as inciting, challenging, or simply dangerous religious sects, political groups, mass movements, and social activism in different countries, from China, Mexico, and Peru to South Korea; there are campaigns organized by the government against those whom it labels as criminals, deviants, terrorists, drug addicts, homosexuals, or vagrants in different nations, from Australia, Canada, and Japan to the United States. Systematic action by the state driven by some established ideology, policy, practice or tradition generates tension between the majority and the minority, the politically correct and the politically incorrect, as well as the socially dominating and the socially marginalized. The response of the socially marginalized may be acts of terror arising from hatred and the desire for revenge.

Still another cause of terrorist crime is foreign invasion, a devastating experience for the invaded. Invaders may feel a sense of triumph in the country they conquer, its land and natural resources, its tradition and cultural heritage. Or they may feel that they are aiding these people in forming a new, more representative government. The invaded, however, see conquerors as ruthless enemies who deserve no mercy but only destruction. In resistance, the invaded may find they have no other means to retaliate other than acts of terror. For example, suicide bombing reflects ultimate desperation or a complete loss of hope on the part of suicide bombers who might otherwise just want to make a statement about perceived injustice or take action to call attention to the misery of their lives. In Asia and the Pacific, there are continuing as well as ongoing cases of invasion that fuel crimes of terror over the region. Palestinians who have lost their homeland can only blame Israelis and Israel's friends in the West for their endless dislocation and sufferings. Until they have their own national state on the land they have lived for generations, Palestinians will continue their acts of terror in their ongoing uprising against Israel. Iraq is still an open wound, not only for Iraqis, but also for many people in the world. The American-led invasion has intensified hatred against the West, its people and material interests. But most important, it has opened the borders to domestic and foreign terrorists who have taken up residence there. Over the Pacific, Indonesia's twenty-four-year-long occupation of East Timor was resolved only recently when the latter became an independent nation in 2002. There are also spots where a central government's control of a region evokes feelings of alienation among the people in the region. Indonesia faces armed resistance in Aceh, one of its provinces. Australia and New Zealand have yet to close the gap between indigenous and non-indigenous peoples in their respective effort to manage the tension between mainstream and aboriginal societies. Even in Hawaii, the United States still needs to negotiate with the Nation of Hawaii on sovereignty over the fiftieth state in the Union (Editorial Staff 2005). In all, foreign invasion is at the root of crimes of terror, historically and in current times.

A fourth cause of terrorist crime is media exposure. Terrorists are eager to gain publicity. The more they are known to a locale, a nation, or the whole world as an organization with an ideology, the more they feel they have achieved their goals. The mass media, on the other hand, are hungry for news. The more secretive, dramatic, or even traumatic news or events they report to the public, the higher the number of recipients in their audience and the greater profit for them. The combination is not just ironic. It is injurious. The mass media have become a tool for terrorists to post their messages, highlight their deeds, keep their records, and most important, spread fear in the minds of both their direct targets, power-holders, and their indirect audiences, oftentimes innocent victims and unguarded ordinary people. Osama bin Laden was originally only an ordinary person. Because of massive media attention, he has become an international icon of terror, of defiance and opposition to the Western world. Al-Qaeda was originally only a regular terrorist group. Now due to a worldwide mass media frenzy, it has turned into a mighty symbol of terror, menace, and destruction. Acts of terror, regardless of where, when, and how they take place, are presumptively credited to bin Laden and his al Qaeda network. Individual and group terrorists, no matter where they are, what cause they fight for, or what means they resort to, are ostensibly showing direct allegiance to bin Laden as a source of inspiration and al Qaeda as an example of organizational planning and success in the pursuit of terrorism.

A fifth cause is public sentiment. People in the innocent public are not only the first to feel the fear of terror and bear the bruises of terrorist acts, but they are also the first to provide opportunities, resources, and sentiments for terrorism. The general population is always divided. Across the globe, there are people who take pride in, who remain silent about, and who oppose Western domination. In Asia and the Pacific, there are people who embrace, who remain neutral to, and who hate Islam and Muslims. Even in a particular country, it is normal that some support, some condemn, and the majority do not care about their government and its policy initiatives. The general population is often unduly influenced by its extreme elements and their performances on the public stage. In a country where a few terrorists are hunted down by a large, powerful state, some people will show sympathy for terrorists. At a time when the state moves toward extremism in ideology, policy, and social practice, people tend to accept arguments or actions for avoidance, resistance, and rebellion. Most cynically, although people do not like directly experiencing extremist behavior from either the government or the anti-government quarter, as the audience they seem to enjoy watching dramatic shows by both sides. To a large degree, the public's obsessive excitement over, fascination with terrorist activities provide a strong background of support for a global war against terror by the United States and its allies. Terrorists, on the other hand, plan ever larger and more destructive attacks because they reason that people are likely to dismiss smaller acts of terror as insignificant. The government presents a war against terror as it calculates that only a war can generate a sufficient amount of attention from the public.

Finally, the war against terror, more than anything else, has brought about what terrorists intended to achieve but were not able to achieve on their own: attention to terrorist ideologies, anxiety on the part of the government and its stakeholders, and a general hysteria throughout society. Terrorists are secretive agents. Terrorist organizations are clandestine networks. Remaining in the dark, terrorists can choose any target without the target's attention. Being small, they can make a plan at any time. Staying mobile, they may carry out an act of terror anywhere. The best way to counter terrorism is obviously the use of same or similar strategies and tactics employed by the terrorists and their organizations. In other words, a government in charge need only assemble a small task force that is shrewd in intelligence gathering, quick in planning action, and mobile in task execution. War is by no means a wise and effective countermeasure to terrorism. If it has to be called a war, antiterrorism must be a quiet war, an intelligence operation that involves neither loads of troops in the battlefield nor lines of police officers on the street, neither media extravaganza nor public panic. The global war against terror fashioned by the United States and its allies, inasmuch as it spreads fear, intensifies hatred, showcases state repression and terrorist brutality, and creates new waves of followers to terrorism, can only be seen as another cause in itself for crimes of terror.

TYPE, PATTERN, AND CHRACTERISTICS

Crimes of terror involve different forms of acts for the sake of different goals. In the contemporary era, eight types of terrorism can be identified as most common: impulsive terrorism, criminal terrorism, repressive terrorism, rebellious terrorism, separatist terrorism, revolutionary terrorism, ideological terrorism, and moralist terrorism.

Impulsive terrorism features isolated individuals. Perpetrators do not necessarily have a clear frame of reference or follow a known system of ideology. They can live a normal life or may face some negative currents, such as boredom, tiredness, loneliness, lack of attention, a change of schools, and loss of a job, in their everyday experience. However, a salient characteristic shared by all individual actors of terror seems to be that they stay tuned to current events and know what it takes to break silence, gain attention from immediate surroundings or the general public, or satisfy their own malice or personal obsession. Amid the tidal wave of high-tech glamorization, an impulsive terrorist can create a feeling of worry and vulnerability or just a general unease among the populace by breaking into a computer network, spreading a virus over the internet, or vandalizing a corporate or governmental data system. In the time of a worldwide hysteria toward terrorism, an impulsive actor can easily send an organization, a community, and even a nation into a state of emergency or cause a panic by running over security checkpoints, setting up pipe bombs in schools and other gathering places, sending suspicious powders through the mails, transporting truckloads of chemical precursors or bomb-related materials, or simply making a call about some nonexistent imminent danger aboard a passenger jet, train, or bus.

Criminal terrorism manifests itself in the commission of an officially defined or publicly recognized crime. Thus, a serial rapist or killer who terrorizes a community for a considerable period of time may be seen as a criminal terrorist. A youth gang that jars people's nerves repeatedly with car racing, freeway shooting, or street hooliganism in a city may qualify as a criminal terrorist group. There is usually no discernible political motive behind such direct criminal acts. If there is one, it is simply to disturb people and lower their quality of life. Within established terrorist groups, an insurgent group that specializes in cultivating, refining, and trafficking controlled substances for profit may have, to a large degree, degenerated into a criminal terrorist entity. So may a guerrilla force that actively engages in kidnapping foreign tourists, corporate personnel, or wealthy civilians for ransom. For example, insurgents in Myanmar have for years played a vital role in the heroin trade throughout the Golden Triangle of Asia, and the Revolutionary Armed Forces of Colombia (FARC) is known to maintain a heavy hand in the cocaine business across the Silver Triangle in Latin America. Following the connection by some trained individuals or organized groups to a terrorist cause, a nuclear expert who provides critical knowledge to governments that secretly acquire weapons of mass destruction may be viewed as a criminal terrorist. An organized group that sells nuclear materials and biochemical agents to rogue states and terrorist networks for profit may itself be considered a criminal terrorist organization. Since the downfall of the Soviet Union, there have been dozens of cases involving theft and transportation of nuclear materials around the world (Zaitseva and Hand 2003). In 2001, for example, Russian security forces arrested several members of the Balashikha gang when they were making a deal on top-grade uranium for weapons (Associated Press 2001). Finally, any criminal syndicate that employs assassination, kidnapping, public bombing, and other means of terror makes itself an out-and-out criminal terrorist apparatus. No one would dispute that Colombian drug cartels, Italian La Cosa Nostras, and Russian mafias qualify as criminal terrorist groups because each of them engages in acts of terror to defeat law enforcement.

Repressive terrorism takes place when the government of a country resorts to threat, unusual punishment, assassination, or war to suppress minorities, stifle political dissidents, and force the general populace into obedience. Throughout Asia and the Pacific, there are governments that launch bloody wars against minorities and minority movements toward autonomy or independence; there are governments that maintain secret police forces to monitor, follow, and harass people in their everyday lives; there are governments that keep death squads and other extra-judicial groups to assassinate social activists and destroy political opposition parties; there are governments that unjustifiably detain, brutally torture, and secretly execute prisoners of conscience; and there are governments that explicitly or implicitly motivate or encourage hate crimes by one segment of the population against another in an attempt to benefit overall social control. According to London-based Amnesty International (2005), dozens of countries in the world have government-sponsored death squads in operation that are responsible for systematic torture, murder, and disappearances of common citizens who are deemed by the authority as undesirable or dangerous. Among them, a number of Pacific Rim countries, such as Guatemala, El Salvador, Honduras, Peru, and Chile, have gained particular notoriety for their political terrorism against dissidence. Related to yet categorically different from repressive terrorism is state-sponsored terrorism where the government of a country provides safe haven and support to terrorist groups that run much of their operation outside its national borders. For example, North Korea harbored several hijackers of a Japanese airliner's flight to North Korea in the 1970s. Iran has been a source of support for various terrorist groups, including the Lebanese Hezbollah, HAMAS, and the Palestine Islamic Jihad, that seek to undermine the Middle East peace negotiations through waves of terror (Office of the Coordinator for Counterterrorism 2005). Along with Iran, Syria is now believed to be providing critical rear bases for insurgents that mount unabated attacks against American troops, Iraqi security forces, and noncombatant civilians in Iraq (Gertz 2005).

Rebellious terrorism aims at the government. Terrorists or terrorist groups in rebellion do not necessarily intend to replace the existing government. In fact, they may just want to avenge an atrocity they allege that has been committed by the government. For example, the Oklahoma City bombing, staged on the second anniversary of the Waco incident, was designed to be a tit-for-tat revenge against the federal government for the deaths of Branch Dividians near Waco, Texas in 1993. In a broader sense, rebellious terrorists may attempt to affect the government in its policies over certain issues, such as taxation, immigration, and church-state separation. They may also scramble to shape the government in its effort to integrate into the mainstream society some segments of the population, oftentimes minorities and immigrants, whom they define and hate as "inferiors" or "outsiders." In the United States, for instance, rebellious terrorists tend to organize themselves around such themes as militant tax resistance, religious revisionism, and white supremacy. Some known and armed groups include the Aryan Nation, the Aryan Republican Army, the Ku Klux Klan, and the Posse Comitatus.

Separatist terrorism challenges the central government of a country for its control over a specific region or a particular minority population. The ultimate goal of separatism is to carve out its own independent homeland. To achieve its goal, separatists organize insurgency and guerrilla war against the majority rule. They carry out terrorist attacks not only in the marginal territory where they fight for independence, but also in the heartland where the majority live. The capital of the central government is often a chosen target for series of acts of terror. Across Asia and the Pacific, separatist terrorism appeals either ideologically to communism or religiously to Islamism. It acts either politically upon state oppression or historically upon geographical isolation. Many states seem to encounter the problems of dealing with separatist movements on their land. Some even face multiple groups of separatism on different frontiers of their territory (Dunn and Dunn 1997; Hanzich 2003). China, while staying vigilant on any political development in Taiwan, an island it considers as a renegade province of its own, has been diligently fighting Uyghur separatists who engage in crimes of terror for a Muslim state called Eastern Turkistan in the Northwestern Xinjiang Autonomous Region (Magnier 2005). India, while remaining aware of various terrorist skirmishes between majority Hindus and minority Muslims, has openly launched military operations against separatist movements and their terrorist campaigns in Assam, Punjab, and Kashmir. Indonesia, while continuing its spiritual search for national identity, faces strong resistance to an overarching state government in several regions of its multi-island territory, from Aceh, Irian Jaya, and Sulawesi, to the Moluccas Islands. Besides the three most populous countries in the world, Myanmar has yet to resolve its conflict, either militarily or politically, with Karen rebels, the Philippines with communist insurgents, Sri Lanka with Tamil fighters, and Thailand with Muslim separatists. The Middle East is particularly conspicuous for separatist terrorism. As witnessed by the whole world, generations of terrorist activities in the region have centered on the Palestinians' desire to wrest their former homeland from Israel.

Revolutionary terrorism targets the existing government of a country for attack with systematic terror and violence. As goal, revolution is to replace a dictatorship, a totalitarian regime, or even a liberal democracy with a preferred form of government. As means, revolutionary terrorism motivates revolutionaries to use political assassination, public execution, and other extreme tactics to get rid of former rulers, keep in check reactionary elements, or stay in power. As justification, revolution appeals to the propaganda of the deed, specifically the use of spectacular acts, such as political assassination and massive violence, to ignite revolutionary fervor among the oppressed. Revolutionary terrorism is best illustrated by the two famous historical cases against an indigenous autocracy, one in France, where revolution and a subsequent Reign of Terror sent to the guillotine thousands of alleged representatives of tradition and the autocratic state, and the other in Russia, where a revolutionary state emerged in the aftermath of armed revolution against the imperial order. Throughout Asia and the Pacific, revolutionary terrorism has figured in the political processes of different countries in varying contexts, scales, and consequences. In China, besides a definite presence in Xinhe Revolution against the Qing Dynasty and the Communist Revolution against feudalism, imperialism, and colonialism, revolutionary terrorism also left its traces in the Great Cultural Revolution when urban youth were agitated to mount exposing and shaming attacks upon old revolutionaries and the state bureaucracy they symbolized. In Malaya, revolutionary terrorism stimulated violence against British rule, bringing independence to Malaysia and Singapore. In Turkey, revolutionary terrorism challenged parliamentary democracy with armed violence from both left and right, keeping the country in political turbulence for decades from 1960 to 1980 (Bal and Laciner 2001). Recently, Jemaah Islamiyah, a fundamentalist Islamic group aligned with al-Qaeda, has plotted or carried out series of bomb attacks against Western interests and governmental targets in Indonesia and neighboring countries. The group is believed to be intent on driving away foreign tourists, ruining national economies, and disrupting political processes so that this group can transform individual governments into a pan-

Islamic state across the bulk of Southeast Asia (Mapes 2002; Desker and Acharya 2004).

Ideological terrorism is driven by a system of beliefs or ideologies, either religious or political. Terrorists under this category are not necessarily interested in terminating a government or establishing their own homeland. Instead, they are primarily concerned with an ideological mission they undertake for themselves: to stop the spread of an ideology they are fearful of, to impose a social or religious code they espouse, or to keep their voice or presence in an interest group or political party they cannot afford to lose. During the Cold War, the Communist block, led by the former Soviet Union, made every effort to implement and sustain Marxism and Leninism. The capitalist world, championed by the United States, did not spare any attempts to abolish communism. The capitalist world used spying, clandestine operations, and acts of terror to sabotage labor, penetrate civil rights movements, topple communist governments, and salvage an infant or fragile democracy in countries around the world. In the name of freedom, the Central Intelligence Agency of the United States even worked with the right-wing group of a country to overthrow a popularly elected government for the benefit of American interests. Covert strategies and tactics used by the CIA often included propaganda, false stories about opponents in the local media, infiltration and disruption of opposing political parties, stuffed ballot boxes, purchased elections, sexual intrigue, blackmail, extortion, intimidation, economic sabotage, kidnapping, beating, torture, death squads, and even assassination (McCarthy 1987; Blum 1995).

Now in the new world where the threat of communism seems to be nonexistent, the West finds itself in a cultural clash with many non-Western beliefs or a hot war with public disenchantment, resentment, and resistance across the globe. On the side of the West, leading ideologues argue that there are "other" people in the world who abhor liberty and fear democracy and who, out of this hatred, would not hesitate to engage in acts of terror to destroy "our" way of life. To defend Western values and protect the "democratic" way of life, it is necessary to fight a global war against terrorists and the terrorist philosophy. The United States has even gone further in the debate by proposing "preemptive attack" and pledging to "fight a war against terror on other lands while keeping intact its own homeland." On the other side of the clash, non-Western ideologists believe that the West has ruined so many indigenous cultures, exploited so many traditional economies, and botched so many national polities through colonialism, imperialism, technological advance, and global domination that it needs to pay the rest of the world, not only voluntarily in the form of humanitarian aid, debt forgiveness, and development assistance, but also involuntarily in the form of crime, social problems, and even terrorist attacks.

The most radical ideologue of all is Osama bin Laden and his al-Qaeda terrorist organization. Epitomized in bin Laden's ideological terrorism is an argument that the world has been divided by the United States and its Western allies into two regions, "one of faith, where there is no hypocrisy, and another of infidelity, from which we hope God will protect us." More pointedly, the world of Muslims, according to bin Laden, faces an aggressive intervention from the West. To defend a sacred tradition, that no Muslim shall ever render the land of Islam to outsiders, it is necessary to fight blasphemers, nonbelievers, and their idol worship by all necessary means, even a martyr's death. Bin Laden has developed a sizable following through these references: a reference to distant history when Muslims had to fight Christian crusaders in their heartland; a reference to present-day reality where Palestinians have lost their homeland to a Western state, Israel; and a reference to individual national governments, including the big two, Egypt and Saudi Arabia, that have chosen to seek alliance with the West. While the spectacular attack on the United States on September 11, 2001 gave a tremendous boost to the reputation of al-Qaeda in the core of its followers, the subsequent media exposure of American-led Western killings of innocent civilians in Afghanistan and Iraq as collateral damage in wartime has opened a sharp chasm between the *umma*, or universal Islamic community, and the West. Now, bin Laden and his terrorist network represent the apex of Muslim terrorist resistance, non-state resistance to the West and Western ideology of freedom, open markets, democracy, and armed defense. An innocent populace on both sides of the ideological divide will have to bear more and greater sacrifice involving economic insecurity, maiming, and loss of life.

Finally, moralist terrorism exemplifies itself in the radical practice of pro-life and pro-environment movements. Moralists of terror seek higher morality in what they do. While some act out of their belief that life is precious, eternal, and beyond the temporality of every individual person here and now, others take to task an assumption that the environment is sacred, not to be exploited, polluted, or destroyed. Specifically, antiabortionists believe that life begins at conception and that the right to life is absolute. They therefore argue that every unborn child must be regarded as a human person with all the rights of a person from the moment of conception onward. To defend the right to life on behalf of the innocent unborn, antiabortion groups have spent enormous amounts of time, energy, and resources on multiple fronts, from the political, to the religious, and to the medical. Some antiabortionists have attacked clients, bombed abortion clinics, and even killed doctors who perform abortions, in ironic contrast to their own professed belief in the value of individual lives. North American antiabortion terrorism features almost every drama, from individualized sniper attacks, unprecedented anthrax hoaxes, and randomized clinic bombings, to systemized brazen campaigns of terror by some media-made-sensational fugitives such as Eric Rudolph and Clayton Waagner (Clines 2001; Dewan 2005).

Similarly, environmental moralists believe that nature exists for a larger purpose than human civilizations. They contend that while humans have a higher level of intelligence, they are not automatically entitled to dominion over nature. Humans, bestowed with reasoning, should instead bond themselves with nature, accepting nature as intrinsically sacred. To defend nature and its sanctity amid waste dumping, pollution, deforestation, species extinction, and various other degradations, environmentalists have staged a far-reaching social movement that seeks to influence the political arena and guard nature and natural resources by lobbying, education, and activism. Into the foray of terrorism, some radical elements of environmentalism have engaged in a considerable number of arsons, bombings, animal releases, crop destructions, thefts of chemical agents, and other acts of terror or crime, sometimes to the harm of the animals they claim to rescue or to the damage of the environment they vow to protect. The most known extremist environmental groups include Earth Liberation Front, Earth First!, and Animal Liberation Front. They are responsible for such high-profile attacks as a 1998 arson atop Vail Mountain in Colorado that caused twelve-million dollar in damages to a luxury ski resort, a 2001 fire at the University of Washington in Seattle that resulted in a 5.6-million estimated damage to its Center for Urban Horticulture, and a 2003 burning of dozens of sport utility vehicles at a Chevrolet dealership in California (Sullivan 1998; Madigan 2003; Egan 2005).

In all, terrorism varies by cause. But the consequences of terrorist crimes on society are the same: destruction of property, loss of life, public fear, higher business overhead, lower quality of living, and most precariously, the buildup of a police state that looms large to threaten civil liberty and individual freedom in democracies. Although no specific concessions should ever be extended to particular terrorists and terrorist groups, political wisdom and commonsense understanding are critically needed to rethink prevailing ideologies, examine dominant practices, in order to identify and moderate those cultural and geopolitical forces that lie deep beneath the outgrowth of terrorism in the contemporary era.

Part III

SOCIAL CONTROL:
PROBLEMS, PROGRESS, AND PROMISE

Increasing deviance, crime, and social problems amid growing economic development and sweeping social change pose serious challenges to social control systems in countries across Asia and the Pacific. It is obviously not enough to expand the old social control system. It is more important to modernize the whole system so that it is able to deal with new situations more effectively and efficiently (Xu 1995; Shaw 1996; Marx 1997; Newman 1999; Du Guerny and Hsu 2002; Nagel 2003; Terrill 2003).

12

Change of Control Ideologies

While it remains an open question whether control arrangements determine control ideas, or vice versa, it takes courage and a change of ideology to reform any existing social control system.

CONTEXT

The idea of social control appears as early as the time of Aristotle when scholars begin to reflect upon the nature of human social life (Roucek 1978). In sociology, Emile Durkheim, Karl Marx, Max Weber, and other great social figures who are considered founders of the social sciences generated a wealth of ideas on social control as they studied authority, power, and order in society. However, it is Edward Ross (1901) who first elaborated social control as a formal sociological concept. According to Ross, belief systems, as reflected in law, public opinion, education, religion, custom, ceremony, art, enlightenment, illusion, and morality, guide what people do and therefore serve to control behavior.

After Ross, social control took on a variety of interpretations in the sociological literature (Janowitz 1975). Macrosociological perspectives direct attention to formal systems, including laws, the criminal justice system, and powerful social groups. They examine how formal control agents and actions inhibit rule-breaking behavior as well as foster oppression, fear, and alienation in society (Davis and Anderson 1983; Cohen and Scull 1983). Microsociological perspectives, on the other hand, concentrate on informal systems, such as self-esteem, family, school, and peer groups. They attempt to explain how people conform by internalizing the external source of control through an individual socialization process.

Reiss (1951) was one of the first sociologists to study the relationship between personal and social controls. Reiss felt that social control began with individuals. He argued that juvenile delinquency results from (a) a lack of social rules that prescribe behavior in the family, the school, and other group settings; (b) a failure to internalize socially prescribed norms of behavior; and (c) a breakdown of internal controls. Toby (1957) observed that only a few among many youths in socially disorganized neighborhoods committed crimes. He attributed the difference as to why one particular individual becomes a delinquent while another does not to the individual's own stake in conformity to society's norms or standards. Reckless (1961) presented an even broader analysis of how personal factors interact with social control in his containment theory. According to Reckless, for every individual there exists a containing external structure and a protective internal structure, both of which provide defense, protection, and insulation against deviant behavior. Included in the outer containment are a social role that guides daily activities, a set of reasonable limits, an opportunity for status attainment, association with a group, a sense of belonging, and alternative ways of satisfaction. Inherent in the inner containment are a positive self-concept, self-control, a strong ego, a well-developed conscience, tolerance for frustration, and a clear sense of responsibility. Deviance occurs when inner containment fails to control internal pushes, such as a need for immediate gratification, restlessness, and hostility, when outer containment fails to deal with external pulls, such as poverty, unemployment, and blocked opportunities, or most likely when both internal and external controls remain ineffective in addressing pressures from within and without.

Matza (1964) assumed that adolescents normally sense a moral obligation to abide by the conventional "bind" between a person and the law. They drift into delinquency not because of an involuntary failure of their inner and/or outer containment, but rather because of a voluntary development of defense mechanisms that release them from the constraints of convention. For example, they use denial of responsibility, denial of injury, denial of the victim, condemnation of the condemner, and appeal to higher loyalties as defenses to neutralize their inner sense of guilt, to ward off possible social attacks, and to rationalize particular delinquent acts (Sykes and Matza 1957).

Hirschi (1969) shifted focus from individual motivations to commit delinquent acts to individual determinations to conform to social norms in his work on the cause of delinquency. To explain why people adhere to rules, Hirschi identified four social bonds. First is attachment: how closely a juvenile is tied to his or her parents, school, and peers. Second is commitment: whether a juvenile aspires to educational excellence, vocational success, and other attainments. Third is involvement: how much time and energy a youth invests in activities that promote the interests of society. The last bond is belief: whether a youth share mainstream social beliefs and values that entail respect for law and order. As a dominant paradigm in the literature, Hirschi's social bonds theory has made social control theorizing more of an exploration into conformity rather than into crime and its causation.

Outside the somewhat functionalist tradition that centers on socialization, personal control, social bonds, and conformity, Gibbs (1981) defined social control as an attempt by one or more individuals to manipulate the behavior of another individual or individuals. In an interactionist perspective, he identified five types of social control: referential, allegative, vicarious, modulative, and prelusive. Black explained social control as "all of the practices by which people define and respond to deviant behavior" (1984: xi). Horwitz (1990) developed a systematic typology of social control in terms of style, form, and effectiveness.

More recently and in a systematic fashion, Shaw (1996, 2002) views social control as any mechanism or practice for securing individual compliance, maintaining collective order and normative consistency, or dealing with problematic or deviant situations. Analyzing the Chinese work unit as an agent of social control, he explores the West versus the Third World, formal versus informal, primary versus secondary group, social versus organizational, regulative versus suggestive, and external versus internal dimensions of social control (Shaw 1996). He also examines control with regard to its source, dimension, degree, substitution, and restoration when he applies the concept of social control to the field of substance use and abuse (Shaw 2002).

BOTH SIDES

The ideology of social control centers on such fundamental issues as to whom control is applied, how it is exercised, and what purpose it serves. In the contemporary era social control ideology manifests formally in the organization of a state, its policies and practices toward deviance and deviants, crime and criminal offenders, or social problems and troublemakers. Informally it takes root in public opinion, social sentiment, and cultural activities.

In Asia and the Pacific, there exist three major contradictions in social control ideology. The first contradiction is between traditional and contemporary forces. The traditional force emphasizes conscience, self-discipline, family, patriarchal power, kinship, tribe, and community as primary sources or agents in socialization, order keeping, conflict resolution, and justice administration. The contemporary force, in contrast, stresses the importance of legal codes, justice systems, social organizations, and governmental apparatuses in educating the young, correcting the wayward, and maintaining order, justice, and peace in society. Almost every developing country in the region, whether it is India, Indonesia, Papua New Guinea, or Peru, experiences a certain degree of tension, sometimes open struggle, between existing authorities embedded in tradition and the emerging forces of modernization.

The second contradiction is between socialist and capitalist systems. The socialist system advocates collectivism, a unified national ideology, one-party control, an organized social deterrence system, repentance through thought reform, and correction by way of productive labor, whereas the capitalist system embraces individualism, open media, multi-party rule, specific reactions by specialized professionals, freedom of belief, doing-time imprisonment, and just-deserts punishment (Shaw 1996; Barlow 2000). Conflict between social systems constantly figures in international dynamics and occasionally escalates into ideological warfare across territorial borders, when capitalist nations, mainly the United States and its allies, criticize socialist states for power abuse, political repression, and human rights violations, and when socialist countries, including China, North Korea, Vietnam, and Cuba, counteractively admonish capitalist societies for drug epidemics, racial tensions, and rampant criminality on the streets and in organizational settings.

The third contradiction is between Eastern and Western civilizations. In the Eastern civilization, people are cultivated to observe the unity between mind and body, between individuals and society, and between society and nature. Individuals who strive for inner peace do not expect to be forgiven for their wrongs. Instead they remain ready to admit guilt, to receive punishment, and to change themselves through serious struggle in both mind and body. In the Western civilization, on the other hand, people are warned of the essentially adversarial relationships they have with their fellow human beings, social institutions, and natural environments. Individuals who aspire for self-actualization would mobilize every possible resource they have to defend and protect themselves against a charge. They will not admit guilt even they are indeed guilty of crimes until they fully explore and exploit procedural technicalities in the court of law.

Besides the three major contradictions general to the whole region, there are other important clashes specific to some nations or territories throughout Asia and the Pacific. For instance, just as Muslim countries tackle the task of balancing the dictates of Islamism with the needs of a secular social order, societies with a history of colonialism face the challenge of reconciling the influence of colonizers with the mandate of independence and self-rule. Most critically, societies and countries that are in a systematic transition from traditional to contemporary, socialist to capitalist, and/or Eastern to Western forms of social control often experience an inevitable state of ideological ambivalence and practical disorganization. On the one hand, they question older social control philosophy and lament the declining influence of past or existing social control measures. On the other hand, they remain suspicious about new ideas and techniques for social control and have yet to see the full effect of any new approach or initiative in practice. In socialist countries, for example, the social control system wrestles with various contradictions between communist ideology and social reality. The long-held explanation that deviance and crimes are historical residues of feudalism, capitalism, and imperialism from an older society no longer seems plausible and convincing to the general public. There is also a reluctance or even resistance to apply Western theories to the new social situation of socioeconomic development. The result is a weakening and contradictory ideological system. Under it, socialization of children becomes problematic. Mobilization of public support and social forces for preventing and fighting crimes is in limbo (Xu 1995; Shaw 1996; Liu, Zhang, and Messner 2001).

SYNTHESIS

Social control ideology obviously not only influences individual thought and behavior, but also impacts national strategies and policies on deviance, crime, social problems, and social control. While there is a general movement from traditional, socialist, and Eastern to contemporary, capitalist, and Western forms of social control among countries in Asia and the Pacific, there exist both ideological bases and practical needs to bring seemingly opposing forces and developments into a synthesis for the greater social good of peace, justice, cohesion, and stability (Lotspeich 1995; Xu 1995; White 1996; Marx 1997; Inglehart and Baker 2000).

Change begins with a bottom line agreement that no one side, one source, or one force should be ever singled out to bear the whole blame of deviance, crime, and social problems in a society and beyond. Tradition sanctions the force of inhibition but fosters ignorance, neglect, and negligence. Modernity unleashes the energy of freedom but spreads arrogance, extravagance, and exploitation. Socialism engenders individual laziness, managerial ineffectiveness, and political corruption while emphasizing collective unity. Capitalism brings about egoistic selfishness, organizational manipulation, and economic cruelty while stressing entrepreneurial prosperity. Eastern culture experiences favoritism, nepotism, and different conflicts of interest as it emphasizes strength of family, balance of groupings, and harmony of community. Western civilization witnesses the exploitative aspect of individualism, the inflexibility and slowness of bureaucratism, and various symptoms of apathy when it commits to trying new procedures, testing their effectiveness, and assessing the productivity, the possible gains, of the new system. Each side, source, or force has its innate advantages and drawbacks. It creates symptomatic problems in some areas while it generates unique defense mechanisms against deviations and disruptions in other dimensions. Most important, deviance, crime, and social problems arrive on the scene in response to the dynamics of multiple factors in contemporary society when one side meets the other, when one source mingles with the other, and, more accurately, when different forces converge into a general social process. Social control, therefore, must stop assigning blames to individual sources but move forward to developing comprehensive solutions for the whole system and its overall integration.

With a no-blame clause in sight on the cause of deviance, crime, and social problems, there then can be a no-incompatibility view of social control and its measures. Specifically, are measures inherited from history, socialism, Eastern civilizations, or communal settings compatible with those that have emerged in modernization, capitalist development, Western culture, or the process of institutionalization? There used to be hostility and absolute rejection of the other side's ideas, especially in the time of the Cold War. For example, socialist countries attacked due process, court proceedings, and other justice procedures in capitalist societies as political ploys or public shows for the rich, the powerful, and the educated to manipulate or mock the poor, the powerless, and the illiterate. Capitalist nations condemned collective surveillance, thought reform, and correctional labor in socialist states as grave violations of civil liberties by government against the citizenry. Within socialist camps, patriarchal order, kinship-based restraints, and other traditional social control forces were criticized as backward, reactionary, or outright hazardous to social progress. Between the East and the West, there was the infamous "clashes of civilization" debate ignited by Samuel Huntington (1993), who speculated that an imaginative infusion of Confucianism with Islam was the realistic threat to the dominant Western civilization. Now with the Cold War as history, ideological barriers have begun to come down. It is time for one side to look into the other in social control practice openly and honestly. Although there is increasing mutual understanding, still suspicion, reluctance, and reservation make it difficult for one side to borrow and adopt from the other critical social control policies and procedures. However, for any nation state to tackle deviance, crime, and social problems effectively within and outside its borders in the era of globalization, it must reexamine many ideological biases it might have within its own tradition. Instead, it must incorporate every useful element from both tradition and modernity, both socialism and capitalism, or both Eastern and Western cultures, into its overall social control system as it deals with a more nearly global reality of social forces.

A recognition that social control measures from previously opposing sources can be brought to work side by side further entails that no workable control approach shall ever be sanctified as a panacea for any single or set of social problems. In fact, each control practice develops and works with specific people within their general environment. When it is stretched beyond normal capacity, it will lose effect and may even pose a danger to what it is supposed to serve: the general social order. For example, communal surveillance among people serves as a natural, customary measure of neighbor reminding neighbor, relative correcting relative, colleague motivating colleague, or friend helping friend when it takes place informally in traditional, socialist, or Eastern cultural settings. However, it can easily lead to mutual suspicion, distrust, and distancing if it is forcibly imposed upon the community by governmental authority as a formal form of social control. Similarly, due process ensures openness, fairness, and soundness in law and its application in modern, capitalist, Western social conditions. But it may cause bureaucratic stalemate, legal impasse, and ultimately control failure, and much worse, may even let loose serious criminals when it is superficially pursued as sheer formality rather than substantive safeguard. The "no panacea" clause is especially important for developing societies as they eagerly look for sets of preventive measures or a system of interventional control that would ideally take care of all their problems once and forever.

At a global level, there should be an ideological consensus that no country, no matter how strong, successful, or dominant it is in comparison to others, can legitimately serve as a center, an example, or a leader for the rest of the world to follow. There used to be stereotypical views of particular countries in the world. One country is viewed as mired in traditional forces, plagued with some ideological fever, or burdened by a culture that does not facilitate social progress whereas another is celebrated as an almighty supermodel or superpower possessing everything that is key to order, justice, and prosperity. Now as traditional, socialist, and Eastern forces mingle with contemporary, capitalist, and Western factors across the globe, it is time to develop a new world outlook. Indeed, no country symbolizes only one side of the contrast. In Asia and the Pacific, China is no longer an undisputable representative of tradition, socialism, or Eastern culture. Nor is the United States an identifiable model of the best of modern capitalism or Western civilization. With a no-model clause, developing societies can then learn specific and useful lessons from many of their developed counterparts, not just one dominating player such as the United States. Similarly, developed nations can turn to different developing countries, not just China or India, for critical insight.

On the new ideological basis of no blame, no incompatibility, no panacea, and no model, there seems to be one natural outcome. That is, a synthesis of thesis and antithesis. Specifically, social control must build upon and move beyond opposing forces, whether tradition or modernity, socialism or capitalism, and Eastern or Western culture, to face an increasingly dynamic reality. Population in the vast majority of national states is no longer homogenous in terms of race, ethnicity, education, occupation, ideological orientation, and political affiliation. In developing countries, highly trained managerial or technical personnel from multinational corporations mingle with illiterate migrant workers from aboriginal tribes or isolated villages on the hinterlands. In developed societies, refugees, legal and illegal immigrants from the Third World disperse in affluent middle- or upper-class households as nannies, gardeners, maids, and other types of domestic workers. The community is no longer closely knit. People come and go. In their sojourn, they leave for work before dawn and return home at dusk. There is not much opportunity to interact with one's neighbors. Nor is any community a sheer disarray of unrelated people and events. Residents still share common concerns and often come together to comfort one another in times of crisis or mutual difficulties. Social control, therefore, needs to be more flexible, specific enough to attend the needs of individual groups but general enough to maintain universal standards, quick enough to bring under control a particular troubled situation but gradual enough to gain understanding from the community, or informal enough to connect to the prevailing sentiment of its clientele but formal enough to demonstrate the soundness of the whole system.

Given the fact that tradition, socialism, and Eastern culture are losing ground to modernity, capitalism, and Western ways of life around the world, it is critically important in the synthesis that contemporary, capitalist, and Western forms of social control conscientiously learn from their traditional, socialist, Eastern counterparts in both general philosophy and specific approaches. In the United States, for example, leaders in both political parties have advocated social equality and universal justice, a cause that has much in common with socialism. Recently, conservative politicians have joined religious groups to emphasize the value of family and community in rearing the young. Community policing is gaining attention and popularity in cities and counties across the country (Barlow 2000; Shaw 2003). The Office of National Drug Control Policy is working on a unified message and a concerted effort through the mass media against drug use among the populace. In dealing with immigrants from Asian societies and former socialist countries within and outside their ethnic enclaves, American law enforcement agents and court officials are learning to become more sensitive to the concept of cultural, religious, and social system congruence. Hopefully in the end, most of them will be able to apply the law in a way that is not simply professional but clearly humanistic, not just procedurally formal but somehow familiar, to immigrants who come from different cultural, economic, and political systems.

13

Transfer of Control Technologies

Social control builds increasingly upon technology in the contemporary era. Technology changes rapidly across the globe. While many developing countries in Asia and the Pacific have yet to modernize their antiquated social control system with modern technology, developed nations need to overcome self-satisfaction, break away from the overuse of equipment, and look for continuing innovation and progress in technology useful in social control.

CONTEXT

Social control technology involves two essential dimensions: hardware and software. Hardware includes weapons, vehicles, communication devices, surveillance systems, test instruments, laboratory facilities, and other high-tech equipment used in crime control, both in detection and investigation. Software, on the other hand, involves ideas for issues that may range from organization of a police force, recruitment of law enforcement officers, training of correctional personnel, institutionalization of a legal procedure, and adoption of certain prosecuting strategies, to implementation of new prevention or rehabilitation programs.

Focusing on its hardware dimension, social control grows in technical complexity as forensic science expands its application of science and technology to criminal and civil laws enforced throughout the whole justice system. Forensic science begins literally with fiction. Arthur Doyle, through his fictional detective Sherlock Holmes, uncannily described how various principles and techniques of serology, fingerprinting, firearm identification, and questioned-document examination could be applied to criminal investigations (Berg 1970). In real life, Mathieu Orfila established forensic toxicology with his scientific treatise on the detection of poisons and their effects on animals in 1814. Alphonse Bertillon devised a systematic procedure of body measurements, known as anthropometry, to distinguish one individual from another in 1879. Francis Galton laid a foundation for criminal identification when he published *Finger Prints* in 1892. Albert Osborn, in 1910, formulated fundamental principles of document examination in his classical book *Questioned Documents*. Leone Lattes, in 1915, developed a simple procedure by which the blood type of a dried bloodstain can be determined for the purpose of criminal investigation. Calvin Goddard, in the 1920s, refined the techniques of firearm examination by the use of the comparison microscope (Inman and Rudin 2000).

As specific techniques and procedures developed and proliferated, Hans Gross coined the word *Criminalistics* and, for the first time, systematically detailed the assistance that criminal investigators could draw from various scientific disciplines, such as anthropometry, fingerprinting, microscopy, botany, chemistry, physics, mineralogy, and zoology. On the practical side, Edmond Locard worked diligently to build a crime laboratory in the police force so that all newly developed scientific methods could be timely used in aid of real world crime detection. With his phenomenal success in France, crime laboratories sprang up in various countries across Europe, from Austria, Finland, Germany, and Holland, to Sweden, following World War I (Thorwald 1967; Inman and Rudin 2000).

In the United States, the first forensic laboratory was created in the Los Angeles Police Department in 1924 by August Vollmer. About eight years later, the Federal Bureau of Investigation made an ambitious commitment to crime analysis when it organized a comprehensive national laboratory that aimed to offer a full spectrum of forensic services to all law enforcement agencies in the country (Inman and Rudin 2000). The FBI Laboratory has since served as a model for many later forensic facilities to be established at local or state levels within the United States as well as by foreign governments and international organizations around the world. Nowadays, a full-service crime laboratory typically includes such basic departments as those for physical science, biology, photography, firearms, and document examination. In addition, it normally has special units ranging from toxicology, latent fingerprint, polygraph, and voice print analysis, to evidence collection. In

1981, the FBI opened its Forensic Science Research and Training Center to develop cutting-edge technologies in forensic science and provide crime laboratory personnel with state-of-the-art training in forensic methods and techniques (Inman and Rudin 2000; Theoharis 2004).

Another important development to take notice of control hardware is the National Law Enforcement and Corrections Technology Center, a program sponsored by the National Institute of Justice since 1994. Based on the information posted on its official website, the Center provides five critical services, bridging science and technology with law enforcement and correctional practice. The first is to offer technological assistance in technology identification, communications system, corrections, evidence analysis, information-led policing, sensors and surveillance, and school safety. The second is to develop performance standards and testing methods for public safety equipment, such as ballistic- and stab-resistant body armor, double-locking metallic handcuffs, and semiautomatic pistols. The third is to introduce new and emerging technologies, in the form of technical assistance, to those who can use them through special events, conferences, and demonstrations such as the Mock Prison Riot. The fourth is to address equipment needs by making Federal excess and surplus property available to local law enforcement agencies and correctional facilities for little or no cost. Finally, in the area of technological innovation and application, the Center brings the research community and private industry together to put affordable, market-driven technologies into the hands of public safety officials. For that purpose, the Center, through its Office of Law Enforcement Technology Commercialization, keeps a pool of law enforcement and corrections professionals, product managers, engineers, and market research specialists who identify, develop, manufacture, and distribute new products for the ever-changing needs of public safety practices.

BOTH SIDES

In the matter of technology, social control is faced with four major contrasts: lack of technology versus a plethora of technology, low-level technology versus high-level technology, commonsensical wisdom versus artificial intelligence, and developing context versus developed environment. Throughout Asia and the Pacific, as societies vary widely in socioeconomic development, the advancement of social control exhibits the full spectrum of technological dimensions.

First, a social control situation or network lacking technology exposes its weaknesses or demonstrates its strengths in comparison with a social control scene or system full of technology. The advantages of the system that has all necessary technology over the other's lack of technology are obvious: when police officers have to walk on foot to patrol a limited area while traffickers use land vehicles, sea boats, or even airplanes to transport hostages, stowaways, or contrabands over a long distance; and when social control agents in one country have to use the naked eye and other natural senses to check people and materials for entry from another country with advanced technology, where outflow of human and nonhuman cargos is automatically processed by electronic devices. There are also apparent disadvantages for the side that has a great deal of technology compared to its counterpart that lacks technology. For example, in the country lacking modern technology a diligent investigator works with a criminal suspect to make the suspect confess while in the country possessing advanced technology a polygraph machine may let go a lying offender; in the former country a responsible correctional officer keeps every inmate under his or her watchful eyes while in the latter country an electronic surveillance system may fail to detect an inflow of controlled substances or even the escape of a convict until the incident is noticed by human agents. At a general level, technology brings about swiftness, effectiveness, and efficiency to social control, all of which makes it natural for people to apply technology as fully as possible. However, since technology is not always dependable and use of technology tends to cultivate a state of dependency, no technology or little technology does not necessarily represent a complete loss of social control.

Second, the contrast of low-level technology versus high-level technology is probably more prevalent that that of a complete lack of technology versus an abundance of technology because the use of technology has expanded to almost every corner of the world. At centers of technological innovation there is a greater presence of technology and its higher-end products. But there are remnants of older technology and its lower-end relics in various backwater regions of modernization. For example, in rural areas police officers ride bicycles, use flashlights, carry old-style hunting rifles, or depend on traditional wired telephone services when they are on duty in crime prevention, intervention, and investigation, whereas in cities law enforcement agents bear high-precision firearms, wear bulletproof vests, patrol in well-equipped vehicles, and benefit from wireless communication devices when they assume their responsibilities of containing criminal elements, ensuring public safety, and maintaining general social order. Similarly, some international organized crime groups often outperform local law enforcement agencies in transportation and communications because they have mobilized sufficient resources to outspend their opposition on high-tech equipment. Low-level technology usually builds on mechanics. It aids human agents in their natural bodily and mental abilities but does not necessarily replace them all in critical areas of substantive functions. With low-level technology, social control agents may still be able to call upon their natural abilities or activate their commonsensical responses whenever necessary. On the other hand, high technology typically develops from electronics. It sometimes assists but much of the time tends to replace humans and human capabilities altogether in major aspects of job performance. In a high-tech environment, agents of social control may end up depending solely upon external devices in their work.

Third, the contrast of commonsensical wisdom versus artificial intelligence figures in the debate because an absolute absence or a differential presence of technology not only defines the setting in which crime takes place but also determines the way by which social control reacts to crime. Technology is a human creation. Technological products reflect human intelligence and wisdom. However, in the sense that intelligence contained in technological equipment is external to and feeds back on any live agent who acts out of his or her natural intelligence, the former can be considered artificial. Obviously, artificial intelligence represents shared, crystallized, and externalized human knowledge and wisdom. It frees people from hard labor, inspires people in intellectual activities, and makes people effective on job functions. Commonsensical wisdom, on the other hand, is what individuals possess and exercise in life. Although it is limited in scope, it connects people to their environment with all necessary sensitivity. As far as social control is concerned, commonsensical wisdom is indispensable because it reminds agents of the human, communal, and social aspects of their work. Despite all the technological devices they may have in hand, they still need to make active use of their everyday insights, sharpness, or even shrewdness while working with people, dealing with criminal elements, and securing public trust and support. Most important, in social settings where technology has yet to take root, artificial intelligence may not only scare off people but also alienate people from participation in crime prevention, community solidarity, and other first line defense programs. Commonsensical wisdom may, therefore, serve as an image builder. Thus law enforcement officials do not just hide in armored vehicles; instead they walk among, talk to, and stay in tune with the populace as fellow guardians. They do not just monitor people by high-tech devices; instead they join with common citizens eye to eye and hand in hand on day-to-day social interactions.

Finally, the contrast of developing context versus developed environment is critical because to a large degree it affects the first three comparisons. In a developing society, technology is likely to be either nonexistent or at a low level. There can be acute needs for technology in general and its higher-end products in particular. Or there can be no need for technology at all. Resources for the acquisition of technology are likely to be lacking while infrastructure for the use of technology remains inadequate. For example, in many emerging urban centers across Asia and the Pacific, resources often lag behind the need for social control technology, especially high-tech devices and equipment. The developed environment, in contrast, serves as the center for technological innovation in the first place. Infrastructure supports the general application as well as a continuing upgrade of technology. Cost for technology is integrated in the budgetary process. Social control agents and agencies are tuned to the operation by way of technology. In fact, as technology is widely available and criminal elements are often savvy in the application of most recent scientific inventions, law enforcement functions properly only with adequate aid from technology and its higher-end products. But in the United States and other developed countries drug smugglers, human traffickers, and other organized crime figures sometimes outrun, outperform, or outsmart coast guards, customs agents, or border patrols who are often well equipped with advanced technology.

Obviously, it is most problematic when a social control system of no or low-level technology is overwhelmed by criminal groups who have access to higher-end technology. It is no less problematic, however, when law enforcement agents who use high-end technology in developed environments are caught off guard by perpetrators who, as complete strangers to technology and artificial intelligence, appeal only to commonsensical wisdom in their criminal undertakings. For instance, a police force that is highly dependent upon automobiles may suddenly lose its ability to pursue a suspect who abandons his or her vehicle and runs on foot into a forest. Or what aid can a surveillance system offer when offenders wear veils or whisper in each other's ear? Mismatches between various contrasting forces call for a synthesis of both sides.

SYNTHESIS

A change of technology in most social control contexts involves an increase in hardware and an upgrade of software. Across Asia and the Pacific, a large number of developing societies are in urgent need of importing from developed economies such hardware as weapons, vehicles, communications devices, surveillance systems, laboratory instruments, and other high-tech products used in crime control, detection, and investigation (Pawar and Goyal 1994; Inman and Rudin 2000). Regarding software, both developing and developed countries need to explore new control technologies, develop new training methods, apply new codes of conduct, institute new legal procedures, adopt new prosecuting strategies, and implement new prevention or rehabilitation programs for a social control system of high efficiency, standard, and integrity (Theoharis 2004; Benekos and Merlo 2005; Welsh and Harris 2005).

The importance of technology is most apparent in emerging societies. The reasons are simple: (a) emerging societies are faced with rising deviance, crime, and social problems; (b) they do not have much technology to begin with; and (c) technology is at the center of their socioeconomic emergence. For instance, to interdict organized crime groups from smuggling aliens, drugs, contraband, and luxury consumer goods, law enforcement needs trained coast guards, customs officials, and border patrols who can make use of high-speed sea boats, specially trained animals, four-wheel-drive vehicles, and high-tech surveillance devices. Watching with the naked eye and chasing on foot, procedures that worked before, simply become inadequate to handle the increasing flow of people and materials in and out of border crossings, and to respond to well-equipped criminal operations. To contain growing social unrest following rising unemployment and widening social gaps, law enforcement needs to develop special riot squads that specialize in using rubber bullets, high-pressure water, tear-gas grenades, and other deterrence measures. Thus law enforcement officers can disperse an unruly crowd, avoiding substantial injuries to civilians. Most important, police officers, prison guards, counselors, and social workers need to be educated about human rights, civil liberties, and enacted laws so that they treat subjects professionally while staging a necessary intervention. In China, more and more police stations are switching from foot patrolling and bicycle policing, procedures which are still used in many well-established urban neighborhoods in industrialized Japan, to American-style automobile patrols for more effective crime control in sprawling industrializing metropolises (Bayley 1991). In prisons, reeducation shifts from thought reform and ideological propaganda to academic learning and vocational training. The correctional system as a whole is becoming more open to successful rehabilitation programs around the world (Shaw 1998; Terrill 2003).

Borrowing, importing, and learning obviously bring closer different sides, making social control systems more similar across the world. To achieve a true synthesis, however, both sides must remain committed to each other's learning with a totally open attitude. First, the terms "borrowers," "lenders," "importers," "exporters," "learners," and "teachers" become relative. Countries that borrow technology offer sites or lend space for technological application. Nations that import technology provide funds or export capital for technological replication, and further, technological innovation. Societies that learn technology contribute feedback or teach how technological products can be modified for different users or improved for different operational conditions or social environments.

Specifically, borrowers, importers, or learners in law enforcement need to explore the past, understand the present, and look to the future when they decide what technology and how much technology they can incorporate into their social control system. They ought to remember that there were positive social mechanisms in place to keep crime low in older times when they contemplate a wholesale installation of technology. Indeed, sometimes in maintaining social order, law enforcement officers may benefit more from tradition than from technology, or from commonsensical wisdom than from technology or artificial intelligence. But on the other hand, they should recognize that there are inevitable social forces on the horizon to drive up crime in the new era when they lean toward rejecting or downplaying technology as a threat or a wasteful luxury. As a matter of fact, technology has become so intertwined with crime that it is impossible to fight crime without technology. Most important, learners must take an active role in the process of learning. In other words, they must learn to command, change, and invent in using technology rather than simply be commanded and be changed by technology in social control operations.

Lenders, exporters, or teachers, on the other hand, need to overcome a general sense of advantage they feel they have over their counterparts. Only when they hold a genuine respect for borrowers, importers, and learners, can they refrain from using technology as a weapon to break into a market for usurious profits, as an excuse to interfere in the internal affairs of a society, or as a bargaining chip to gain preferential treatments in bilateral dealings. Only when they take a neutral, objective view of technology can they develop a historical understanding of why a local society struggles between tradition and modernity, a sympathetic patience with how difficult it is for technology to take root in a changing society, and a contextual appreciation for what technology, high technology, or artificial intelligence may learn from no technology, low technology, or commonsensical wisdom. Only when they move beyond individual interests and toward the common welfare of mankind, can they willingly share breakthrough knowledge, unselfishly spread state-of-the-art technology, and generously donate their phased-out, yet still well functioning, equipment for use in undeveloped or developing environments. In the real world, it is often the lender, exporter, or teacher who stands in the way as the first, the biggest, and the last barrier to technology transfer. For instance, between developing socialist states and developed capitalist countries, the latter enforce a technological blockade from time to time so that the former do not benefit from most advanced technology in national defense and maintenance of social order. Between India and Japan, the latter may set the price of a technology so high that the former simply cannot afford to import it for use in social control or other areas. Between Mexico and the United States, if the latter is modest in its international manners, the former may feel comfortable in cooperating with the latter or may even receive excess technology and surplus equipment from the latter for use in joint patrols and other control operations along the border.

In all, a new synthesis in social control technology hinges upon a fusion between tradition and modernity, between commonsensical wisdom and artificial intelligence, and between the present and the future, as well as cooperation among different players, such as inventers, producers, distributors, and users, in the social construction of a new functioning international system of technology in law enforcement.

14

Professionalization of Control Forces

Professionalization of control forces seems inevitable when new control ideas are introduced and new technologies are applied in various phases of control operations. Throughout Asia and the Pacific, professionalization calls for a variety of tasks, approaches, and assessment standards in different social control settings.

CONTEXT

Professionalization involves both individual members and system components. On the part of individual members, it requires that they meet basic educational requirements, receive special career training, master essential knowledge and skills pertaining to their job, internalize professional codes of conduct, specialize in a line of duty, and handle their job responsibility with professional confidence and competency. Within the control system and among system components, professionalization means that a division of labor is clearly maintained, roles and ranks are rationally differentiated, practices are consistently guided by theoretically sound policies, and procedural restraints are properly instituted to ensure that control organizations and operations run with autonomy, sensitivity, effectiveness, efficiency, fairness, and integrity.

Professionalization of social control is evident primarily in the development of its software dimension, namely, the professionalization of the police, the formalization of the court, and the standardization of penal practices. In English history, the earliest system of policing was the "frankpledge" in the eleventh century, where members of a tithing joined hands to keep order in their community. The system gained strength later with the establishment of a king's representative, the *reeve*, in each shire or county. The shire reeve, or sheriff, drew assistance from a *posse comitatus* composed of able-bodied citizens as he performed his duties of presiding over the court, executing summonses, and enforcing the laws. As the population grew into larger towns and cities, more formal control titles such as constables, night watchmen, and justices of the peace gradually arrived in the law enforcement scene. However, it was not until the industrial revolution and the subsequent sweeping urban expansion that a system of professional police force came into being in England.

The New World followed a similar path. As in England, colonial America saw conditions of social order or disorder placed in the hands of county sheriffs, town marshals, constables, and *posses* composed of ordinary civilians. Uniformed police forces appeared late in American cities in the nineteenth century when migration, immigration, and industrialization fueled growing hostility toward minorities, resulting in mob violence and social unrest. For decades after the establishment of various formal municipal police forces, however, law enforcement in the United States was disappointedly mired in politics. Officers were admitted to the force without explicit standards. They received little training and supervision, and tended to be corrupt and abusive on the job (Walker 1980).

The chronic problem of untrained and corrupt police generated pressure for serious reform. Early in the twentieth century, progressive reformers started to work on the professionalization of the police force around the country. August Vollmer, a pioneer in the reform movement, developed a model of police organization and activity. Under his model, a professional police force takes crime fighting as its primary responsibility. To fulfill its professional duty, it has to be nonpolitical, well recruited, well trained, well disciplined, and equipped with modern technology. Vollmer's student, Orlando Wilson, also made significant contributions to modern policing in the area of management and administrative techniques (Cole 1989).

BOTH SIDES

The process of professionalization can be hindered by ideological dilemmas. In China, for example, the people's police, while being open to new control technology, is not able to make fundamental structural changes in its main force. Viewed as a tool of the communist political system, the people's police is not allowed to operate independently from party control. Police officers are evaluated not only in terms of the competency they demonstrate on their job, but also by the loyalty they show to the communist party. Similarly, police departments are judged not only by how they serve the needs of the general public, but also in terms of how they maintain social order under communist control. In recent years, the people's police has sent officials and students overseas to learn about police experiences in foreign lands, has invited foreign experts to train officers in riot control, drug interdiction, and antiterrorism operations, has imported advanced equipment, and has instituted various standards and procedures in recruitment, operation, and evaluation. Despite all these efforts, the people's police overall is still a communist controlled apparatus embedded in Mao's "mass lines" ideology that essentially favors mass campaigns over institutional professionalism.

The case of China represents a specific real world problem of professionalization in social control. At a general level, contrasting or opposing forces surrounding professionalization figure saliently in five arenas: professionalization versus secularization, professionalization in form versus professionalization in content, technological professionalization versus moral professionalization, organizational professionalization versus operational professionalization, and professionalization for impression versus professionalization for efficiency.

At the outset, professionalization is inherently connected to secularization. On the one hand, members of social control forces have a vested interest in gaining occupational prestige and social respect by becoming trained, disciplined, and equipped with systematic knowledge, comprehensive skills, sophisticated protocols, and advanced technology. Members of the populace have a desire to expect fair treatment and secure protection from a police force that looks neat, sharp, effective, and professional in their eyes. On the other hand, social control agents need to make proper connections to the community they serve to the extent that they feel they are part of rather than above the local society. People in the general public want to relate to social control personnel to a degree that they do not just revere them as crime fighters and legal-code-savvy professionals, but also can count on them as community watchpersons and social service agents. In Asia and the Pacific, there is polarization across the spectrum of professionalization and secularization. While in some developed contexts social control falls into the professional cage as an alien or alienating force to its serving public, in some developing or undeveloped environments social control is so mired in the masses and mass dynamics that it is often unable to distinguish itself for routine functions. For example, in the United States there is community uproar over excessive or unnecessary forces used by the police whereas in an economically depressed country there may be public lootings in which police officers join street mobs in taking others' properties for their own use or possession.

Within the sphere of professionalization, there exist four pairs of focal interests. Professionalization in form puts its emphasis on uniform, equipment, procedure, institution, and physical layout. Grounded ideologically in materialism, it seems to believe that a social control force automatically has a professional outlook when its individual members wear standard uniforms, bear advanced firearms, and are made to follow clearly set procedures or when it as a whole is housed in an awe-evoking building complex, is armed with state-of-the-art equipment, and operates with maximum institutional sanctity. For example, China has made a national effort to put all its police officers, prosecutors, judges, and correctional guards in standard uniforms so that they are no longer immersed in the masses as ordinary servants of people but stand out from the crowd as professionals in law and social control. Professionalization in content, on the other hand, places its focus on knowledge and skills, rules and regulations, as well as social customs and cultural norms. Drawing from idealism, it tends to argue that professionalism begins with brain and mind. In other words, a social control force becomes professional only if its members command expert knowledge, master specialist skills, and are competent in each specific area of their professional duty or if it overall is clearly tempered with institutional restraints, is relatively separated from partisan politics, and resonates well with the general public in their society. On the road in some Asian countries, motorists sometimes can buy their way out of a traffic violation by submitting to the examining officer their driver's license with cash inside or underneath it. The officer may look professional in every physical aspect. However, when he or she takes bribes on duty, people can only wonder what is left professionally, if there is anything at all, under his or her seemingly professional cloak. Indeed, form is empty without content.

The technological versus moral contrast points to another dimension to professionalization in social control. Technological professionalization emphasizes what and how much members of a social control force know about their profession, its most recent developments, fundamental skills, and essential techniques, or whether the entire force itself keeps pace with scientific process. The test of its technological capacity is the speed and readiness with which it can react to change and changing dynamics in crime, deviance, and social problems. Moral professionalization, in comparison, stresses what principles, philosophy, or ideology a social control force upholds, which party, side, or interest it protects, and how loyal it is to its cause. As far as members of the social control force are concerned, moral professionalization requires that they follow an ethical code of conduct, resist corruptive influences, and serve as role models for the general public. For example, in capitalist countries members of a law enforcement agency typically pledge to be loyal defenders of democracy rather than of partisan politics whereas in socialist states social control professionals normally vow to be people's humble servants rather than part of an abusive officialdom. In both capitalist and socialist contexts in Asia and the Pacific, it is also common that technological professionalization procceds often after moral professionalization is well on track. Obviously, police officers would not explore far into a technology that shields them from ordinary people if they are taught to be of the people and for the people on their professional duty. By a similar logic, they would learn ways of connecting to the people when community policing is touted as a moral guideline.

Still another dimension is organizational versus operational professionalization. The former eyes the way the social control force is set up, its recruitment procedure, training protocols, evaluation processes, disciplining policies, and even buildings, facilities, or equipment, especially as to whether some of their physical features combine to give the public a sense of organizational efficiency and authority. The latter, in contrast, points to the importance of the responsiveness, sharpness, and effectiveness with which the social control force is able to operate amid its various professional tasks, from fighting crime, containing social disorder, and dealing with an emergency or crisis, to addressing people's immediate needs. Throughout Asia and the Pacific, while some social control forces are so bureaucratized or fortified that they often fail miserably in face of a large-scale attack or disaster, some police forces as order-keeping units are so overly agitated to respond to social contingencies, one after another, that they rarely rest and settle into their everyday duties.

Finally, what is the goal of professionalization? Is it for public impression or for organizational efficiency? Obviously, professionalization for impression is outwardly oriented to the public and public image of the social control force. When individual members behave professionally on job duties as well as in dealings with the community, they earn a favorable reputation of competency, dependability, trustworthiness, and respectability for their force as a whole. Professionalization for efficiency, in contrast, is tied to the administration and its handling of the social control operation. Are there mechanisms in place to keep one branch of power in balance with another? Are there watchdogs on site to minimize waste and expose corruptive practices? Is the social control force overall effective, efficient, and worthwhile in terms of operational performance, managerial process, and taxpayer accountability? In Asia and the Pacific, there are closed states where the authority sometimes spares no effort, even at an unnecessary cost of the government, in putting a positive face on its social control force in the public eye, especially on the eve of a national event that is a spectacle to the outside world. There are also open societies where a social control force is routinely scrutinized by different interest groups for its cost effectiveness or administrative integrity, so much so that it often wonders if it can afford to spend enough on any image-building campaign in public arenas.

SYNTHESIS

It takes a full developmental path of each side to arrive at a true synthesis of both sides. Progress, in a sense, is made when each side sizes up itself and challenges any unwarranted overgrowth of the other.

Within a domestic context, professionalization of social control may begin with different dimensions, move in opposing directions, and attain varying levels of equilibrium. A country that already has a formal social control force in place benefits most when it fashions its professionalization in the direction of secularization, furthering or deepening substance, morality, operation, and efficiency to balance its well developed, installed, or routinized formality, technology, organization, and public image. In the United States and other developed economies, social control is fully integrated into the mainstream political system. There are law schools to prepare lawyers, prosecutors, and judges, police academies to train law enforcement agents, and other formal procedures to screen people for correctional staffs. Social control personnel move up or down along a long-instituted civil service system or through a democratic mechanism. The social control force as a whole is well equipped, organized, and scrutinized, giving the populace a general image that it is up to the challenge of its task. Now the general question is how it is connected to the people and their changing social life? Specifically, does it spend taxpayer's money wisely? Does it put people first in all its operational activities? Do all its members take to their heart the fundamental rights and interests of people? Do social control personnel resonate well with prevailing customs, practices, and sentiments in their community?

In countries where social control remains immersed in civil vigilance, political manipulation, and economic domination, establishment of an independent police force is the first step toward professionalization. Members of an emerging force may not necessarily master or understand all the knowledge, skills, rules, and procedures pertaining to their job. However, as long as they patrol the street or handle cases in uniform, they create an impetus for progress, from moral disciplining to technological learning and from operational proficiency to impression management. As long as they function on institutional tracks and within organizational constraints, they build pressure for procedural clarification, structural improvement, and systemic advancement. In fact, only when they have moved enough in the direction of technological, organizational, or physical professionalization, can they determine how much secularity, community connectedness, or cultural embeddedness they want to keep and savor in their overall professional outlook.

Japan, Singapore, Hong Kong, and a few other developed societies across Asia have each kept much of their fine tradition in social control, especially communal embedment and social connection, while making significant strides in technology, bureaucratization, and formalization. For both developed and developing societies, the systems in these societies serve as models in blending tradition with modernity, more generally, in achieving a genuine synthesis of various seemingly opposing developments in the sphere of social control professionalization.

On the international stage, social control systems in developed economies, democratic polities, Western societies, or capitalist countries are generally high on professionalization, not only in terms of form, technology, organization, and public impression, but also in terms of content, morality, operation, and managerial efficiency. In developing contexts, undemocratic systems, Eastern cultures, and socialist states, however, most social control forces still struggle to overcome their own technological simplicity, operational irregularity, and organizational inefficiency for a better professional image in the eyes of the public and greater independence from the dominant structure of power. Given the large gap in reality, what does it take to move beyond traditional divides so that different social control forces can learn from each other? In Asia and the Pacific, an encouraging development first arrived on the scene when China sent some of its would-be social control personnel to study law, technology, and professional protocols in the United States and other Western societies. Now as terrorism and organized crime emerge to become a common threat to international order, individual countries seem to be more and more willing to look to each other for insightful ideas and effective measures in social control. Only by mutual learning, can true professionalization take place, as well as some kind of real synthesis of control systems for the world as a whole.

15

Modernization of Control Systems

Ideology, technology, and professionalization are critical dimensions in social control. When they change separately or simultaneously, they may not only influence individual members and units but also shake up the entire force. At the system level, however, social control faces a general challenge of modernization that is above and beyond change of ideology, installation of technology, professionalization, or any combination thereof.

CONTEXT

The social control system divides into three major branches: law enforcement, the courts, and corrections. Lawmaking as the beginning and the end of social control ironically falls in the hands of partisan politicians as part of the political process.

In previous centuries, law enforcement was simply a matter of order maintenance when all males over a certain age were bound to keep the peace, watch out for strangers, or track down deviators or outliers. The first professional police force came into existence in England in the early nineteenth century after the Industrial Revolution brought about a phenomenal expansion of towns and cities as working and living environments for the bulk of the population. Since then, law enforcement throughout the Western world has pursued its own modernization on many different fronts. Externally in relation to power and the government, it sought to become independent from politics. With regard to people and the community, police officers and police departments initially emphasized fighting crime and enforcing the law as their fundamental duties to achieve public safety and security. However, when they realized that crime fighting and law enforcement functions had alienated them from the community, they began to experiment with various innovative methods to change their public image. Internally on the matter of membership, efforts were made from time to time to raise the quality of recruits and to improve procedures for recruitment, training, performance, evaluation, and disciplining. With regard to organization, attempts to streamline structural establishments, standardize procedural protocols, sharpen operational responses, and improve managerial cost-effectiveness surfaced from place to place as goals on various police reform agendas. The United States served as a prime example of police modernization in the Western social context. From establishment of a formal force, separation from politics, and professionalization of the rank and file to bureaucratization of the force itself, United States policing has now evolved into three major categories of functions: law enforcement, order maintenance, and community service. The community service function engages many local American police forces in foot patrols, bicycle patrols, team policing, problem-oriented policing, and community policing, all of which help police departments overcome public distrust, defuse social tension, and build cooperative relations with the general populace (Walker 1992; Peak 2006).

The court, meaning in Latin "together" at the "garden" or "yard," was initially used by the king, the queen, and nobles to refer to the castles or estates they owned and occupied. Since it was also the place where important business was conducted, the court was later equated with power and its massive apparatus and following. For example, the court of the King of England symbolized the authority and influence he held over all of England and beyond. Justice, as part of power, was determined in the court. The guilt or innocence of a person accused of crime was adjudicated through a trial procedure. The trial was a time for opposing sides, adversaries, to confront each other in open court. The judge ensured that written court procedures were followed. He pronounced judgment when the trial was over. The British common law model took root in the New World. Over the years in its drive for modernization in the court system, the United States has made serious efforts to specify a division of labor or jurisdictional interfaces between state and federal courts, to clarify the roles of prosecutors, defense counsels, civilian jurists, and trial judges through criminal proceedings, and to standardize penal dispositions in the aftermath of a conviction. Guiding all these efforts are four principles: due process, fundamental fairness, judicial impartiality, and sentencing comparability (Meador 2000; Segal, Spaeth, and Benesh 2005). To some extent, it is the same principles that have permeated court reforms of various countries around the world.

Corrections take place in the process that executes and implements sentences imposed by the court. The terms "corrections," "correctional specialists," and a "correctional system" replace "penology," "penologists," and the "penal process" used in the nineteenth century and the first half of the twentieth. The replacement of the terms themselves is the result of a modernization effort that changes the administration of court dispositions from punishment for retributive or utilitarian purposes to correction to emphasize rehabilitation or restitution. Besides the once-in-time change of name, outlook, and approach, the penal-to-correctional system has undergone a history of continuing reform and improvement to overcome abuse, corruption, and failure. In the Old World, major penal inventions included use of spectacular executions, experimentation with galley slavery, establishment of Bridewells, building of panopticons, and transportation of convicts to the colonies (Morris and Rothman 1995). In the New World, the first systematic efforts were to use the penitentiaries for separate confinement or congregate labor. A reformatory movement attempted to end the imposition of suffering on convicts and substitute it instead with treatment, moral regeneration, and reformation. From World War I to World War II, a medical treatment model gained popularity when psychiatrists and psychologists became involved in the treatment of inmates and the reform of the penal system. As the medical model developed into a more general therapeutic and rehabilitative approach, community involvement rose to prominence. Probation, parole, halfway houses, work release, and other community diversion projects were increasingly used in later years. Beginning in the 1960s, a prisoner's rights movement started to build momentum. Through legal battles, the movement has eventually won for prisoners all the rights guaranteed by the Constitution. Now in the face of overcrowding and various court-sanctioned reforms for the prisons, the American correctional system is more than ever in need of innovative ideas and practices. Some recent developments are encouragingly noticeable, especially intermediate corrections in the form of probation with intensive supervision, home confinement, restitution, community service, shock incarceration programs, and systems of fines (Morris and Rothman 1995; Clear, Cole, and Reisig 2005). These developments may represent a new direction in corrections.

Overall, modernization of the social control system attempts to synchronize law enforcement, the court system, and corrections as an integrated structure that is in tune with public needs. Indeed, social control must keep up with social change.

BOTH SIDES

In the matter of modernization, there exist five main sets of opposing arguments. One argument centers on system integration. Supporters of integration hold that law enforcement, the court, and corrections departments must coordinate with each other to save taxpayers' money, minimize organizational friction, keep power in balance, and, most essentially, serve the interest of social control. It is a waste of resources as well as a blow to social order when the police work diligently to catch criminal suspects, many of whom were those former inmates corrections departments sought for early release. System integration helps fight abuse, contain corruption, and improve efficiency when the court intervenes to order reform for the prison. But to what degree, does a court-imposed order become an unnecessary interference in a correctional system's independent functioning? Opponents of integration maintain that law enforcement, the court, and corrections are separate entities, each of which has its own tradition to continue, its own logic to follow, and its own mission to fulfill. Around Asia and the Pacific, individual social control components are yet to develop and differentiate in many undeveloped or developing societies. A premature push for integration can only cause harm to a much-needed growth of each component in an emerging social control system.

Another debate revolves around the role of politics in social control. Supporters of this stance call for independence from the political process. To them, crime is a general social challenge. Fighting crime is to the benefit of all. A modernized social control system distinguishes itself primarily by going beyond and staying above the interests of groups and social classes. It maintains social order for the common good of an entire society. Opponents of this stance aim at political integration. To them, crime is socially defined. Social control is part of political establishment. A modernized social control system is clear and sharp on what interest it stands for, what social order it defends, and what group it protects. In fact, only when it aligns well with the political process, can social control become purposeful, predictable, and effective. The alignment explains why social order tends to be definite, simple, and routine in traditional, authoritarian, or totalitarian societies where social control falls firmly and exclusively in the hands of the ruling class. In free, open, and democratic contexts, on the other hand, social order becomes complex, diverse, and changeable, often because social control agencies are out of alignment with political power.

Still another argument focuses on synchronization with the general public, their needs, sentiments, and attitudes. Supporters of synchronization point out that crime occurs among people. When citizens take actions to ensure their own safety and security, they can change the whole crime scene. Social control, similarly, is people's business. When social control professionals, notably the police, work with people in the community, they can function not only as a force of deterrence against crime, but also as a net of service for peace and justice. The more a social control system is modernized, the better it will resonate with people in the general social environment. Opponents of synchronization place faith in the neutrality and objectivity of social control. To ensure its integrity, social control needs to be exercised at some distance from the community. In fact, when people suffer from crime in their immediate environment, they often hope that they will be able to count on a third party for resolution. Across the developing world, it is not uncommon that social control forces fail in popular votes of confidence because they are so mired in communal affairs. For the same reason, some social control forces even lose the trust of the government under which they are supposed to operate. In a sense, a modernized social control system is one that transcends various group interests so that it can relate fairly and professionally to the public as a whole.

The fourth point of debate surrounds use of technology. The general consensus is that modernization goes side by side with technology. No social control system qualifies as modernized if it does not incorporate a sufficient amount of technology in its structure and operation. However, there are critical divides and divisions on the matter of technology. In developed societies, technology has penetrated so many aspects of social control that it creates a state of dependency for social control. Social control succeeds when technology is advanced. Social control professionals become stranded when equipment fails. In developing countries, on the other hand, technology is so lacking that social control personnel either wonder what technology could do for them routinely or fantasize how technology might revolutionize their job functioning miraculously. The use of technology is so sporadic that only some are able to see its promise while others are left with worry about its reliability. Between developed and developing nations, there is sometimes a dramatic struggle that involves the former's attempts to sell technology versus the latter's efforts to mobilize resources to acquire it, the former's desire to withhold sensitive high-tech patents or secrets versus the latter's willingness to duplicate common low-tech devices or instruments, or the former's interest to maintain technological control and supremacy versus the latter's motive to foster its own ability to invent, innovate, and produce. Thus, technology often serves as a common ground for contact and conversation in social control agencies in countries with drastically different cultures and political economies. For example, American law enforcement agents can engage in a meaningful exchange with their Chinese counterparts on technology and its use in social control despite their fundamental differences in ideological belief, political philosophy, and social morality.

Finally, the debate is about discipline. As with technology, there is basic agreement on the importance of discipline. The goal of modernization to a large extent is to introduce and implement discipline so that social control personnel do not abuse their positions and privileges while on duty and social control agencies do not sink into corruption and discrimination while in operation. However, differences exist as how discipline should be pursued. At the outset, some argue for discipline from outside whereas others advocate discipline from within. Supporters of the former looks beyond the control apparatus to find social mechanisms, such as mass media, public scrutiny, watchdog surveillance, and civilian involvement, that keep social control agents and agencies in check regarding use of power, performance of duty, disbursement of public funds, and other critical issues of accountability. Supporters of the latter, in contrast, delve into the social control system itself to identify institutional means—internal audit, performance evaluation, ethical panel, reward, and punishment—to make control personnel perform and control units operate within the bounds of cost effectiveness, ethics, and professionalism. As to the content of discipline, some emphasize proficiency, competency, and efficiency on the basis of knowledge, skills, technology, and organization whereas others stress commitment, loyalty, and accountability with respect to ideology, morality, political affiliation, and social integration. For example, to those who believe more in moral than technological input in the exercise of self-discipline, a modernized social control system is one in which control professionals serve honestly as role models for the common citizenry and control organizations commit fully to the protection of the general social establishment.

SYNTHESIS

Modernization of the social control system advances when one side gains an upper hand over the other. From a macro and dynamic point of view, synthesis is achieved only when thesis develops fully to reach antithesis and antithesis goes far enough to its own exhaustion or negation.

Throughout Asia and the Pacific, progress first has to be made by individual states in their respective pursuits of social control modernization. Regardless of social context, synthesis will inevitably manifest in some equilibrium in the areas of system integration, relation to political dynamics, synchronization with public needs, use of technology, and self-discipline. Specifically, a modernized social control system must have a clear, rational, and specialized division of labor among its essential components, namely law enforcement, the courts, and corrections, while allowing for mutual surveillance, supervision, cooperation, encouragement, and support between individual parts or units. A modern system of social control must maintain sufficient autonomy, neutrality, and objectivity while remaining current in political processes. Regarding synchronization with public needs, a modernized social control system must rise above group, community, or class interests while resonating well with general social sentiments. Technology is widely used to the extent that it is in line with institutional resources, personnel competency, communal assets, and traditional means of social control. Discipline is uniformly maintained in the sense that due process, equity, and justice procedures are in place to reconcile institutional requirements with individual performance, technological proficiency with moral conscience, and social demands with organizational reality.

Within individual societies, the movement toward synthesis is likely to take different focuses or directions. In developing countries, people may put system integration on the backburner when they struggle to expand and consolidate each social control component. To win support and secure resources from the government as well as the populace, an emerging or growing social control system may not be able to be as assertive as it would like on the issues of independence, objectivity, and impartiality. Use of technology can only be pursued slowly and in piecemeal as resources are lacking, staff personnel are ill prepared, and the general infrastructure remains poor. Discipline may hinge more upon individual conscience rather than institutional safeguards, more ideological brainstorming rather than technological learning, more external scrutiny rather than internal review. In developed nations, by comparison, greater system integration is in order since each social control component itself is well established, and sometimes, deeply entrenched. Better coordination with the political process is needed because claims for autonomy can push social control to a point where it serves more of its own interests than those of society. More synchronization with the general public rises to the forefront of the agenda as the interests and needs of people, tradition, and the community are often overlooked, sacrificed to the needs for equipment, modernity, and the support of the bureaucracy. Similarly, widespread use of technology can be compensated by focal application of human instincts, commonsensical wisdom, and communal heritages so that harmony is kept among people rather than imposed from the outside and order is maintained within a society rather than superimposed from above. Finally, in an era when people habitually count on external forces, such as technology and the media, to highlight desirable acts and conducts, the old forces of conscience, self-discipline, and internal corrections still appeal as forces that encourage positive behavior.

On a global scale, synthesis calls for dialogue, builds on confrontation, or will emerge from conference and compromise between modernizing and anti- or de-modernizing forces. Some such compromise will decide the utility of many tools of social control used in specific circumstances; it will also conserve worthwhile elements of police procedure from an earlier era. Among various forces of modernization, developed societies possess capital, manpower, and an infrastructure to continually produce, use, and export advanced consumer products, effective management protocols, and innovative technology in every arena of life, including social control. Developing countries are motivated or pressured to give up tradition, import technology, and undertake reform as they open up to the outside for opportunities toward material affluence and social prosperity. And criminal elements become increasingly organized to the extent that they are able to acquire technology and achieve operational efficiency from time to time at a level comparable to or even higher than some formal social control agencies. The situation challenges authorities to pursue further modernization. Anti- or de-modernizing forces, on the other hand, primarily feature postmodernization in developed nations where attention to details, work on specifics, harmonization with localities, and synchronization with temporalities make their way to fill blanks and gaps left by massive standardization, universal bureaucratization, and other large-scale modernization drives. Thus community policing, diversion, and restorative justice appear on the horizon as viable alternatives to crime fighting, imprisonment, and retributive penology. Throughout the developing world, anti-and de-modernizing forces often manifest in grassroots initiatives, conservative movements, patriotic fervor, citizen vigilance, or mass justice. On the part of criminal elements, there are still perpetrators who appeal to superstition, religion, and custom when they offend and victimize. The reality calls for more human-focused work rather than technology-centered intervention. For example, how much technology is needed to prevent, stop, and catch individual fortunetellers, religious cults, or miraculous healers who prey on local residents for money and sex from village to village?

As opposing forces confront each other in equilibrium, they create a collection of premodern, modern, and postmodern residues on the face of the earth. In social control, modern as well as postmodern residues may range from spy satellites in orbit, surveillance devices within organizational establishments, high-speed boats over the water, all-wheel drive vehicles on mountain terrains, and antiterrorist equipment throughout transit systems, to weapons, firearms, and protective gadgets carried by urban squad teams on public streets. Premodern, anti-modern, or postmodern residues, in contrast, may include both acts and artifacts. As for acts, uniformed police officers walk on foot from block to block in the heart of a downtown business district, giving residents and tourists a sense of protection. Undercover law enforcement agents mingle with ordinary people in everyday routines, spotting suspicious activities by target groups and individuals. Older, traditional means of social control outside the public system can include dogs raised by residents to scare off strangers around private homes, hidden traps installed by farmers to catch thieves in the crop field, and simple shooting devices made by villagers to deter transgressors on isolated land. In synthesis, a modernized social control system will incorporate the residue of traditional systems, what worked well down the years, as well as newer technologies.

Overall, to bring about a full modernization of social control in Asia and the Pacific, developed societies need to break down technological barriers, share advanced knowledge and effective practices, offer financial aid, provide professional training, and foster a spirit of co-security, co-safety, and co-prosperity. At the same time, these developed societies need to learn from developing or undeveloped experiences and preserve the best of their own tradition. Developing countries, on the other hand, need to overcome their own sense of disadvantage, recognize the value of their existing system, and face the challenge of their changing social reality while being open enough to embrace new and different ideas, methods, skills, protocols, and procedures in social control. A synthesis of modernization in social control throughout the region of Asia and the Pacific and around the world will inevitably lie in the fusion of science with common sense, technology with instinct, and modernity with tradition in the cooperative interface between developed and developing societies.

16

Cross-Border Collaboration and Cooperation

With the vast Pacific Ocean sitting in the center of the region, borders among nations in Asia and the Pacific can not be simply drawn on land by clear-cut lines and visible signs. Border crossings are, therefore, not limited to the common form of movements on land. They also heavily involve travel, trade, and communication by sea, by air, and through the airwaves (Marx 1997; Shaw 2003).

CONTEXT

Historically cooperation between neighboring territories in crime fighting and prevention could start as early as there was a division of control over land and might last as long as there was a consensus on acts deemed as threats to collective survivals. For example, when two settlements depended on the same body of water as their lifeline, they were most likely to take joint action against any possible or actual criminal sabotage at the origin, along the route, or on the water itself.

Learning and collaboration in crime control could take place for nation states in proximity or separated over sea and land. In the fifth century B.C., the Romans sent a delegation to Greece to learn more advanced techniques for dealing with crime when they faced it as a serious social problem within their burgeoning empire. Law, lawmaking, and promulgation of law were brought home as valuable lessons for maintenance of social order. In fact, the laws of the old Roman Empire were so comprehensive that they became a source of inspiration as well as a model of reference for various cities and principalities across continental Europe seeking to develop their own systems of law when these laws were rediscovered in the late Middle Ages and during the Renaissance.

Despite an enlightened interest in law, punishment remained repressively brutal in Europe until late in the eighteenth century. Besides forced labor on treadmills and secure incarceration in Bridewells and the Hulks, England invented a new method of penal treatment for convicted prisoners. Like galley slaves sold by one city-state to another in Italy and other parts of Europe at an earlier time, offenders were transported by England to its various colonies around the world. In North America, Virginia and other Southern colonies benefited notably from exiled convicts who labored in the service of plantations and towns. In Australia, prison labor even became an indispensable contribution to the founding of the entire country (Morris and Rothman 1995). From a historical point of view, export of prison inmates by England to its colonies represented a unique chapter of cooperation in country-to-country efforts in crime control.

Voluntary exchange of both ideas and methods of control accelerated as communications improved, trade increased, and transportation progressed. Through the nineteenth and the early twentieth century, the penitentiary, the reformatory, the juvenile court, probation, and parole arrived on the scene, gained acceptance or popularity, and retreated to the background when countries in the core of capitalism sought counsel from each other for rational yet effective crime control models (Clear, Cole, and Reisig 2005; Sheptycki, Wardak, and Hardie-Bick 2005). In the periphery, people looked to their counterparts in the West for ideas and inspiration. The Chinese, for example, traveled far to Europe and North America to study laws and law enforcement practices in their effort to develop a modern legal system. The Beijing Model Prison, built in the early twentieth century upon the Western panoptic idea of separate confinement for each inmate, set aside a special altar to honor the five great teachers who were said to have influenced Chinese prison reform. One of them was the Western prison reformer John Howard (Dutton 1992; Xu 1995).

Now as the world becomes a global village, collaboration is even more important among individuals, groups, and countries in every aspect of life. Across Asia and the Pacific, country-to-country coordination and cooperation in crime control and prevention take various forms (Hodgson 1995; Sheptycki, Wardak, and Hardie-Bick 2005). There are bilateral, trilateral, and multilateral agreements among nations on illegal immigration, slave labor, imports and exports of controlled goods, smuggling of illicit substances, international terrorism, transnational sex rings, and other cross-border crimes. Liaison stations or coordinating offices are usually opened and operated by each national government among countries bound by an agreement. To control the supply of illicit drugs to the Unites States, for example, American drug control agents travel to poppy, coca, and marijuana growing countries in Asia and Latin America to run various operations to aid these governments in their efforts at crop eradication, drug interdiction, and plant supplementation.

There are also many case-specific cooperative exchanges among nations and special jurisdictions in Asia and the Pacific. Cases may vary in type, seriousness, and technical complexity. For instance, Federal Bureau of Investigation agents in the United States sought assistance from their Mexican counterparts in their search for a railroad series killer (Ragavan 1999). A municipal police department in Hawaii, through the FBI, asked Japan to extradite a double-murder suspect for trial in the United States. Special police agents in Hong Kong and Macao joined their counterparts in Mainland China to break criminal rings that are active in the country's special economic zones and special administration districts. The Exchange-with-Taiwan Association on Mainland China communicates with the Taiwan-Strait Foundation in Taiwan on the handling of airplane hijackers, stowaways from Mainland China to Taiwan Island, and on criminally victimizing or victimized Taiwanese investors and tourists in Mainland China (Jiang and Wen 2000).

BOTH SIDES

On the matter of cross-border cooperation in social control, debate often centers on five major choices: national pride versus practical need, difference in ideology versus commonality in crime control, specific solution versus general agreement, border-to-border exchange versus state-to-state diplomacy, and bilateral dealing versus multilateral transaction.

Each country has its own heritage, character, and pride no matter how small, poor, or backward it is. In the world community, however, it is the law of the jungle that governs the relations among nations most of the time. Thus the weak fall prey to the strong in matters varying from trade, diplomacy, and civil exchange to almost every other cross-border dealing. In crime and social control, a strong country may fuel or export criminal activities to its less strong neighbors while criticizing these neighbors for lack of legal regulation or inadequacy of law enforcement. For example, the existence of the United States is a main reason for drug growing and transporting, migrant recruiting and smuggling, the sex trade, and other social problems in Mexico while Mexico often bears the blame for harboring criminal fugitives, attracting sex tourists, and failing to meet law enforcement demands from the United States. The irony is that one is hurt in its national pride at the same time that the other becomes even more demanding on the international scene. The contrast makes it difficult for countries to forge mutual collaboration on practical grounds. When one country lowers its guard to release political dissidents, criminal suspects, migrant laborers, and socially troublesome elements, the other will have to mobilize resources to either admit and assimilate or keep out whatever comes to its doorway. Between Canada and the United States, for instance, a liberal border policy by the former will inevitably cost a great amount of conservative energy from the latter. Only when practical needs become common, serious, and widespread enough across border areas, can two neighboring countries be expected to put aside their respective national sentiments and join in cooperative control operations. Canada allows United States customs agents to operate in its major airports, prescreening passengers bound to the United States. Canada's willing cooperation reflects the fact that terrorism has grown into a common threat to the free world. However, there is an undertone of national pride or identity as well. Canada definitely does not want to develop a reputation as a free corridor for terrorists or international criminals to enter in order to attack the most powerful democracy on the face of the earth.

Another dimension affecting control cooperation among nations lies in how difference in ideology is outweighed by commonality in crime control. It is widely known that countries in capitalist camps, with democratic forms of government, and in the West embrace totally different ideologies from those in socialist camps, with non-democratic forms of government, and in the East. The United States, in the eyes of China, is a country where democracy is the game of the powerful to fool the powerless and the market is the venue of the rich to exploit the poor. With money, the rich may get away with crimes they have committed against the poor in the United States. China, from the perspective of the United States, is a nation where communists use their authoritarian government to crush political dissidence, stifle religious freedom, and even persecute ordinary people who just want to have more than one child. With power, communist leaders can gain immunity from corruption, abuse, and other misconduct in which they engage routinely in China. Differences in ideology also exist among countries with similar political economies. For example, whereas Japan emphasizes ethnic, traditional, and social cohesiveness or sameness as ways to achieve peace and harmony, the United States draws upon racial, historical, and cultural diversity or differences in the maintenance of social order. Of course, commonality in crime control can sometimes overcome ideological gaps and forge collaboration among countries involved heavily or frequently in trade, diplomacy, and civil exchange. Indeed, despite their fundamental differences in ideology, China and the United States still feel a mutual urgency to work jointly on copyright violations, patent thefts, human trafficking, and other cross-border crimes as bilateral contacts increase exponentially. A regional example is between Mainland China and the island of Taiwan. Although the two ideologically opposing governments across the Taiwan Strait have yet to deal with each other directly, there are various common terms, coordination, and joint actions taken with regard to crime and crime control. The bottom line contention, however, is still valid that difference in ideology creates differences in attitude, definition, and reaction to crime, which in turn tend to pull countries or similar entities away from one another in actions to foster social control.

Still another dimension regarding country-to-country cooperation in social control is whether focus is put on developing specific solutions to concrete cases or reaching a general agreement on a wide range of issues. The two seemingly different efforts or outcomes are obviously interconnected. Specific solutions to similar incidents or events lay the foundations for a general agreement. A comprehensive treaty provides directions or guidelines for how individual cases are handled. However, the two orientations sometimes remain at odds, hampering each country's efforts to achieve functional utility. Specific solutions may never rise to the level of generality. In fact, two countries may use case-to-case dealings to avoid or dampen their historical feuds and ideological differences. Between Cuba and the United States, North and South Koreas, or the island of Taiwan and Mainland China, coast guards, frontier troops, border patrols, and customs agents on one side deal with those on the other side from time to time but would never attempt to move beyond the status quo in their routine operations. The frequency as well as the complexity of day-to-day transactions may also prevent any effort of generalization or standardization. Between Canada and the United States or Hong Kong and Mainland China, governments of both sides keep an eye on the tremendous flow of people and materials across the border but seek to maintain a hands-off stance. A general treaty may never materialize. Out of an impulsive enthusiasm by some powerful figures or a ceremonial contact between heads of state, a bilateral or multilateral agreement may sound achievable, but such an agreement remains at present impractical or unenforceable. As a matter of fact, such an agreement might divert attention, create problems, waste resources, and hence become a hindrance for two or more sides to work on immediate issues in crime control. For example, would a systematic treaty between China and the United States on intellectual property rights not provide legal loopholes or lawful excuses for theft of some specific patents or laxity of enforcement in certain areas? Similarly, would an all-inclusive agreement on immigration between Mexico and the United States not offer instant relief or new opportunities for criminal elements navigating through the border?

The fourth contrast relates border-to-border exchange to state-to-state diplomacy. Civil exchanges take place naturally between two countries with or without shared borderlines. In the scenario of a shared border, a robber who is seen robbing people on one side of the border is likely to be treated as a robber by the other side should he or she escape from the side where he or she is committing the crime. To show their good will, more importantly to maintain social stability at the border area, officials on the side to which the robber flees are likely to catch and return him or her to the original side. Even in the scenario of two remote countries without a shared land border, one may approach or respond to the other when criminal figures leave or enter its territory by air or over water. Border-to-border exchange may build up to state-to-state diplomacy. The latter often involves two sovereign states in a wide-ranging agreement, a far-reaching treaty, or some joint action programs. For example, the United States customarily employs military assistance, development aid, and other financial incentives to secure bilateral agreements with countries where drug production becomes a major source of supply for the American market. At the time when a diplomatic agreement is put into practice, the United States may send its anti-drug agents to work on plant eradication, crop substitution, drug interception, border inspection, and other control activities in the country with which the agreement is made. Implementation of a diplomatic agreement obviously impacts everyday dealings at the border. The contradiction is that state-to-state diplomacy does not necessarily reciprocate border-to-border exchange. From time to time, one even works to the detriment of the other. For instance, a murderer caught in running from one side to the other at the border may not be immediately released back to the side where he or she kills under an extradition treaty signed between two countries. Instead, it may take a whole diplomatic journey through two state bureaucracies to complete an otherwise simple return of a perpetrator to the original spot of his or her criminal offense.

Finally, cross-border cooperation hinges upon the comparison and contrast between bilateral dealing and multilateral transaction. Bilateral dealing revolves around issues that are common to two countries. It can be direct to the parties concerned, specific to the cases involved, and immediate to the situation where control collaboration is initiated. For instance, China can cooperate with Japan while Canada and the United States can work hand in hand on a variety of cross-border issues common to their respective interests. Multinational transactions, on the other hand, rise above specific dealings between nations. These transactions are likely to result from a state-to-state diplomacy whose intent is to provide a regional or international framework for tackling interests, problems, or threats common to the nations involved. An example is the Shanghai Cooperation Organization (SCO) forged among China, Kazakhstan, Kyrgyz, Russia, Tajikistan, and Uzbekistan in central Asia. Besides economic and military cooperation, the SCO pledges to work on a joint crackdown against terrorism, separatism, and extremism, more specifically, a multinational offensive against arms smuggling, drug trafficking, illegal migration, and other criminal activities throughout its member countries' massive border regions (Craig 2003). A multinational treaty or transactional agreement may give rise to or facilitate bilateral dealings. However, since bilateral dealings usually take place first, naturally, frequently, or on a day-to-day basis, multinational transactions may come in only as interfering dictation, disruption, or diversion. The North America Free Trade Agreement (NAFTA) signed among Canada, Mexico, and the United States has obviously brought about a whole new inventory of problems and challenges to cross-border transactions the United States has with its Northern and Southern neighbors (Warner and Gerbasi 2004; Olive 2005). To what extent does the NAFTA then negatively impact the United States' capacity to keep illegal immigrants, controlled substances, exploitive labor practices, and industrial pollutants out of its long borderlines?

SYNTHESIS

A synthesis of cross-border collaboration and cooperation in social control requires that opposing factors or forces be incorporated in a systemic dynamic to allow for effective problem solving under the guidance of a general agreement, smooth border-to-border dealings within the framework of state-to-state diplomacy, and productive bilateral exchanges in the spirit of a multilateral coexistence.

The three most obvious obstacles to cross-border work in social control are national character, difference in political economy, and gaps in development. In synthesizing, however, the goal is not to remove any of those obstacles. Instead, an immediate objective is to recognize, study, and face each one of them. Next is to see how any joint action may begin with, build upon, or rise above these seemingly negative elements or currents. From a nationalist point of view, national heritage, character, and pride may indeed provide motivation and determination for countries to seek alliance with one another or to fulfill mutual obligations with each other. Difference in ideology often invokes its opposite, that is, similarity in beliefs, norms, and values. Countries with similar social systems tend to deal more with each other. Gaps in development work in the same way as contacts among countries at a similar level of development. In addition, gaps may provide a powerful potential energy for the developed to explore or assist the undeveloped or for developing societies to borrow or learn from their developed counterparts. Most important, genuine collaboration between states takes place only when this collaboration reserves room for national pride and dignity. Arrogance is nonproductive. Thus a powerful country such as the United States would not casually enter into a cooperative arrangement if it cannot preserve its international overconfidence. Dignity represents the bottom line for country-to-country relations. A country, no matter how small, poor, or weak it is, would normally not subject itself to an agreement it feels will hurt its own sense of national dignity. Differences in political economy determine whether a cross-border cooperation in social control will last. Although it may practice socialism, China may still be able to forge long-term cooperation in crime control with Japan, Singapore, South Korea, the United States, and many other countries in the capitalist camp inasmuch as differences in ideology and social systems are fully acknowledged, understood, and factored into such cooperation. Development must be given its due weight when a cross-border agreement is hammered out. For instance, between Mexico and the United States, a fruitful collaboration occurs only when the former acknowledges its relative disadvantages in control hardware, when the latter recognizes its relative weakness in moral development and social cohesion, and when they both know they need to learn from each other and work with each other in keeping their common borders safe and secure.

In contrast to obstacles, there are also three apparent forces pushing for cross-border cooperation in social control: the universality of the challenge of crime, the commonality already present in control of crime, and the inevitability of cross-border exchange. Crime is part of social life. It increases as population grows in size, density, and mobility. In contemporary society, advanced medicine reduces infant mortality and extends the age of seniors. Urbanization gathers people in crowded towns, cities, and metropolises. Industrialization and development sweep people from border to border, frontier to frontier, and opportunity to opportunity. All countries in the world face mounting deviance, crime, and social problems not only at home but also abroad. To control crime, authority has to recruit and train personnel, acquire technology and equipment, build an operational infrastructure or system, and draw upon both domestic and foreign, both traditional and modern, or both communal and institutional forces or experiences. There is already a great deal of commonality in crime control from society to society, a circumstance that augurs well for border-to-border collaboration and cooperation. At a general level, contact and exchange between and among countries become inevitable in a globalized world where advanced means of communication and transportation bring one next to another regardless of time and distance. In social control, what can a national government do other than reach out to its counterparts in other countries when criminal elements follow the forces of social change to commit crimes, seek hideouts, or bribe law enforcement or justice officials in and out of its sovereign territories?

By building upon forces for contact and dialogue, countries in Asia and the Pacific can undoubtedly overcome obstacles and build bilateral as well as multilateral cooperative arrangements in crime control and prevention. In this kind of synthesis, individual states would look eye to eye into each other's history, social system, and reality. Common ground would be identified. Shared threats and challenges would be specified. In everyday dealings, focus would be put on issues and their immediate solutions. When similar cases would converge to a considerable level of generality, higher levels of contact would begin, opening the door for general agreements in a larger area. Since agreements are based upon realistic forces and factors, they provide useful guidance for routine transactions along the border and its major checkpoints rather than unnecessary restraints. For example, between Mainland China and its special administrative districts, Hong Kong and Macao, frequent border crossings and transactions generate an ample wealth of experience for forging and modifying general agreements. Face-to-face interactions connect concrete dealings to common understandings or specific solutions to joint communiqués, thus bringing both sides into close cooperation in social control and other operations.

Rapport among control agents on both sides at the border, of course, depends on the good will held by the top leadership or general populace of one country toward the other. In the case of China and its relations with Hong Kong or Macao, border-to-border exchange serves as a barometer of the conspicuous support the communist government in Beijing intends to show for each of its two small yet eye-catching capitalist enclaves. At the level of international relations, state-to-state diplomacy reaches full synthesis with citizen-to-citizen exchange when the former draws from and feeds positively on the latter at the borderline. In other words, when leaders of two countries convene in national capitals, they can toast the harmonious relationship their peoples have with each other. Bilateral understandings, communiqués, or treaties reached by high-level officials can hence build upon border-to-border exchanges while providing the latter with general spirits, sentiments, or guidance. For instance, between China and the United States, Chinese officials can always refer to the positive attitudes and feelings embraced by ordinary people toward the United States as the leader of Western capitalism. The Chinese send the brightest of their young people to the West to seek advanced knowledge. When the Chinese greet people from the United States and other Western countries, they show the best of their age-old hospitality. Once positive diplomatic relations take shape and a cooperative arrangement is in place between two countries, each can affect how social control agents of one side greet and treat people from the other side on the border. For example, mentioning the great friendship their national leaders have with each other may smooth a difficult dealing between Chinese and North Korean agents along their joint border in East Asia. To highlight the importance of state-to-state diplomacy, portraits or memorabilia of national leaders in friendly summit with each other are sometimes put up in the frontline offices of customs and immigration so that agents at border crossings can carry on their duty in the same collaborative spirit conveyed by the symbolic props or settings in which they work.

State-to-state diplomacy may also rise above individual nations to the level of a multilateral agreement on the basis of regional proximity or some other common grounds. Multilateral treaties, in general, have various potentials for bilateral transactions. Interference is one scenario. Facilitation is another. To arrive at a synthesis with bilateral dealings or independent national operation, however, multilateral agreements should first take into account individual countries and their mutual transactions over the border. Or once a multilateral treaty enters its phase of enforcement, efforts should be made to reconcile its postulates with those from bilateral agreements that may be involved. The good news is that most countries use a central office to scout, enter, enforce, and monitor all the treaties, bilateral, multilateral, or global, they have with other sovereign entities or international organizations. In China, for example, the Ministry of Public Security, the Supreme People's Procuratorate, and the Supreme People's Court each has an office of foreign affairs to deal with visits, exchange programs, or treaty obligations to or from other sovereign entities in the international community. The office can obviously check for and iron out any noticeable inconsistencies before passing on specific directives or operational protocols to concerned functional branches or local levels in its routine handlings of international agreements and treaties.

In all, cross-border collaboration in fighting crime and keeping social order faces both challenges and opportunities. As the world becomes increasingly interconnected and globally integrated, a promising prospect is on the horizon for a genuine synthesis of social control of different, even opposing, forces. The realization of this prospect can lead to a multifaceted cooperation among countries with or without common borders.

17

International Organization and Coordination

Since the establishment of the United Nations in the aftermath of World War II, there has been a global proliferation of international organizations, some out of ideals and ideas, some out of practical needs and urgencies. Idealism and pragmatism indeed are two inseparable driving forces behind various international missions and endeavors. Transnational offenses, organized crime, and global terrorism are realistic threats that invite and inspire bold and comprehensive responses from the international community in controlling crime and deviance.

CONTEXT

International coordination emerges from mail, telegraph, telephone, transportation, and other civil contacts among sovereign entities. The oldest international organization, the International Telegraph Union, was founded in 1865, when technological inventions in telecommunications created immediate needs for interconnection codes and logistics among countries in Continental Europe and beyond. Message delivery services appeared far earlier in country-to-country exchanges. However, the Universal Postal Union (UPU) was established only later in 1874. As the second oldest international organization, the UPU allegedly maintains the largest physical distribution network involving nearly two hundred countries on the face of the earth.

The first international effort in social control took place in 1899 when the International Peace Conference was held in The Hague of Holland to elaborate rules and standards governing peace, diplomacy, and order in the world. The Convention of the Pacific Settlement of International Disputes was adopted, providing general instruments for settling crises peacefully, preventing wars, and codifying rules of warfare. Three years later, the Permanent Court of Arbitration established by the Conference began to work on cases within its jurisdiction.

The International Criminal Police Commission, founded in 1923 in Austria, had as its purposes the detection, the control, and the prevention of crime. Known widely by its telegraphic address, Interpol, the now officially named International Criminal Police Organization, is the second largest international organization, after the United Nations, in the world. To maintain political neutrality and technical objectivity, Interpol refrains from involvement not only in religious, racial, military, and political crimes, but also in crimes that do not concern several member countries. As a result, it focuses only on organized crime, weapons smuggling, terrorism and public safety, drug production and transportation, money laundering, corruption, high-tech crime, human trafficking, and child pornography. To its more than one hundred eighty member states, Interpol offers a unique global police communication system, a wide range of criminal databases and analytic services, and proactive support for criminal detection, search, and investigation throughout the world (Anderson 1989).

In Asia and the Pacific, Interpol has established an extensive governmental network against cross-border crimes from one member country to another. Interpol member states are required to appoint a permanent police department to serve as its country's Interpol national central bureau (NCB) and act as the focal point for international cooperation in crime control. Major countries in the region, including Australia, Canada, China, Japan, and the United States, maintain a scaled NCB operation in response to Interpol. In addition, Interpol has set up two special bureaus, including a drug liaison bureau in Bangkok and a sub-regional bureau in Buenos Aires, and a general Asia and South Pacific sub-directorate in the region. Individual NCBs, special bureaus, and the regional sub-directorate are connected to each other as well as to the Interpol Headquarter in Europe. They share information about major criminal activities across national borders, provide staff training and data access, heighten interests and challenges common to the region, and promote multilateral cooperation in the investigation and prosecution of important criminal cases involving different member states across Asia and the Pacific.

At the United Nations, the Commission on Narcotic Drugs (CND) was established in 1946 to monitor drug abuse situations and develop control strategies around the world. The Committee on Crime Prevention and Control (CCPC) was formed in 1971 to provide expert advice on international criminal justice policies. In 1991, the CND expanded its general policymaking mandates to include a specially funded United Nations International Drug Control Programme (UNDCP). One year later, the CCPC developed into the Commission on Crime Prevention and Criminal Justice, becoming a subsidiary of the Economic and Social Council of the United Nations for policy formulation and action recommendation in the field of crime control. In 1997, the United Nations Office on Drugs and Crime (UNODC) was founded. With UNDCP incorporated in its major function in 2002 and various other crime-related commissions, conventions, or mandates translated into its primary task on a routine basis, the UNODC now serves as a focal agency of planning, programming, and action coordination for global crime control. Targeting corruption, human trafficking, terrorism, drug production and distribution, money laundering, and organized crime, the UNODC is committed to spreading knowledge, forming, implementing, and monitoring international treaties, promoting legislative work by member states in response to international obligations, and facilitating technical cooperation for an effective and efficient global offense against drugs and crime. In Asia and the Pacific, the UNODC maintains field offices in Afghanistan, India, Iran, Laos, Mexico, Myanmar, Pakistan, Peru, Thailand, Uzbekistan, and Vietnam to work with individual national governments to carry out various specific duties within its general mission.

Besides Interpol and the UNODC, other international organizations, at general levels such as the Association of Southeast Asian Nations and Organization of American States as well as in specific areas including the United Nations Children's Funds and the Office of the United Nations High Commissioner for Human Rights, have either joined in the battle against crime or participated directly in the task of social control.

BOTH SIDES

Multilateral treaties reached by a considerable number of sovereign entities on equal footing are more likely to be considered as carrying an acceptable level of legitimacy than bilateral agreements by domestic interest groups. However, national resistance against international interference in social control can be mounted on a valid ideological basis as well as on sound pragmatic reasoning.

Ideologically, international organization can be viewed as an institutional vehicle to expand domination by a core of large, strong, or active countries over a group of small, weak, peripheral, sometimes inactive nations. International coordination can become a legitimizing façade for developed, Westernized states to interfere in the domestic affairs of yet-to-be developed, democratized, or Westernized governments. The supposedly most representative organization, the United Nations, lends its governance to the Security Council where sits the world's large, powerful, dominant players—Britain, China, France, Russia, and the United States. The General Assembly involves a few small, developing, and non-Western countries whose presence serves more to legitimize others' wants or desires rather than represent their own needs or interests. In social control, major international organizations, including Interpol, the UNODC, the International Criminal Court, and the International Court of Justice, are funded primarily by member states that are developed or advanced, staffed by professionals who have received education and training in the West, equipped by products that come from major industrial powers, and bureaucratized by rules that lie at the core of modern capitalism. International coordination, from general planning, special programs, and specific actions, to field assistance, is often designed for the social reality shared by leading industrial member nations, initiated at the urging of a few active players in a region or on international stage, and implemented by the will of a minority of economic or military powers over the majority of other countries in the world community. For instance, who can effectively rebut or mute the argument that the UNODC sets up its field offices in poor drug production countries for the sake of drug reduction in affluent drug consumption societies? While it does not necessarily enhance domestic agendas on behalf of individual national interests, international effort largely serves to maintain a global social order in favor of Western domination.

Pragmatically speaking, international organizations show their functionality by the ideas they spread, the products they promote, the staff they employ, the programs they implement, and the problems they tackle. On the part of Third World countries, democracy, free trade, open media, and other Western ideas or ideals are not necessarily appropriate to or workable in their prevailing social conditions. Western consumer goods corrupt the rich while alienating the poor. Most devastatingly, they exist to disable and destroy domestic production. Employment at international organizations is first reserved for the trained surplus labor of the First World. When people from the Third World are hired, they are likely to be placed at the bottom of the bureaucracy. For a small, poor country, sending a few of its brightest people to the lower echelon of the hierarchy at various international organizations may present a serious enough drain of intelligence from its already limited pool of intellectual capital. Interpol, the UNODC, and other international organizations are seemingly preoccupied with terrorism, drug trafficking, arms dealing, human smuggling, and organized crime, offenses that primarily impact the First World. For the Third World, when they open offices, send agents, or operate programs, international organizations seldom pay attention to nor make any effort to stem rampant corruption, widespread property offenses, chronic human abuse or neglect, or entrenched poverty within a host country. In fact, to fulfill international obligation, many undeveloped as well as developing countries have to divert personnel and material resources from their domestic social control responsibilities. Moreover, to the credit of nationalistic critics, international coordination brings in foreign agents to spy on or interfere in domestic affairs, putting public safety and national security in danger. Isn't it a serious challenge to the maintenance of domestic order when international observers criticize a police crackdown on a mass riot as a violation of universal human rights?

Forces for international endeavor in social control are real and strong as the world becomes more and more global and unidirectional. Since the end of the Cold War, the whole world has turned into a vast testing ground for Western-style capitalism. Democracy, civil liberty, and human rights are now international slogans. The subjects of free trade, open markets, and private enterprise dominate economic debates. The United Nations is no longer caught unwilling or undecided between confronting or balancing superpowers. Instead, it serves conspicuously as a forum or a vehicle to spread and solidify Western ideas, standards, and the rule of law across the globe. For example, the UNODC draws upon prevailing practices in Western Europe, North America, and other developed capitalist economies when it develops training protocols for legislators, court personnel, and law enforcement agents in developing countries. It would sound awkward if the UNODC, Interpol, or any other international organization were to consider any models from non-Western contexts, such as socialist North Korea, Buddhist Nepal, or Confucian China, as possible prototypes of social control for international emulation or popularization. Indeed, through the United Nations and various other global forums, many Western ideals and standards have directly developed into international customary practices or conventions. Individual countries, like it or not, have to abide by these so-established international conventions should they want to be included as members in good standing of the international community. In social control, which country would not rather heed Interpol or the UNODC regarding an international pursuit of criminals or a global call for crackdown on terrorism, drug smuggling, arms dealings, or human trafficking than face economic embargo, political isolation, or general ostracism?

Another realistic force for international coordination in social control is the internationalization of crime, deviance, and social problems. No matter what national conditions a country may have, it seems to provide for some outsiders an attractive milieu for crime. A developed economy draws illicit drugs and illegal migrants while a developing country offers opportunities for investment fraud and intellectual property rights violations. A democratic system attracts social radicals while an authoritarian regime may sponsor terrorists or political extremists. A land of industrial affluence fuels money laundering and organized crime while a land of natural beauty encourages tourism and interest in commercial sex. An open society offers easy hideouts for free-lance fugitives while a closed state provides safe havens for special crime figures or perhaps terrorists. International cooperation is obviously in order when crime takes place across national borders. Interpol, the UNODC, and other international organizations hereto find solid reasons for their routine operations when the need for cooperation among nations in crime control rises to the level of international coordination.

In response to external pressures or international needs, domestic forces hosting multinational organizations or benefiting from foreign contacts are likely to call for opening to the outside, adopting international standards, or aligning with global dynamics. For example, law enforcement agents and justice officials who have received training from the UNODC may see a clear advantage of some international measures over their similar national practices. From a Western point of view, UNODC protocols are not based solely upon familiar Western ideas. They are seasoned with non-Western experiences. From the perspective of non-Western societies, UNODC suggestions or standards do not draw just from dominant Western models. They have incorporated non-Western reality. As a result, the United States may find it easier to reach out to other nations with its advanced technology through an international forum. China may feel more comfortable to learn state-of-the-art practices around the world under the sponsorship of a United Nations program. An individual NCB may see a response to Interpol as a national obligation to the world when it comes to breaking criminal cases, apprehending criminal offenders, pursuing justice, and maintaining peace.

Specifically, participation in international endeavors brings about practical benefits to national efforts. At the outset, a country and its problems in crime and social control are made known to the international community. In a world governed by what might be termed the rule of presence, a small country receives attention just for being on board while a large country may find itself passed over, missing an important opportunity only because it is absent. With attention and recognition come sympathy, understanding, assistance, resources, and sometimes support. For example, training is offered, giving social control personnel up-to-date information, knowledge, skills, and perspectives needed to do their jobs effectively and in accordance with international conventions. Equipment may be donated or provided with a discount, rendering social control apparatus greater power, mobility, and overall capacity to fight and prevent crime. Field office, liaison, and national contact are established or maintained, connecting the country and its operation to a worldwide network. Most important, for both Western and non-Western, developed and developing, or open and closed societies, response to or participation in upholding international law, justice, and order serves as an opportunity to take a broader perspective (historical and comparative), a more comprehensive approach (professional and communal), and a more systematic measure (hardware and software) in dealing with deviance, crime, and social problems on the domestic front.

SYNTHESIS

Obviously, much progress remains to be made regarding the legitimacy of international organization as well as the effectiveness of international coordination. In social control, what national concerns, interests, or reservations have to be addressed before an international synthesis can be reached?

An immediate concern is representation. Does an international organization represent its assumed constituency, not only by membership, but also in terms of staff, standards, preferences, and practices? Membership is a surface issue. It can be satisfied easily either by the desire of a country to be recognized internationally or by the need of an international agency to be all-inclusive. The United Nations boasts of a 191-nation-strong membership. Interpol claims to be representative of 184 countries in the world. More substantive than membership, however, is how an international agency is staffed and organized. In the history of Interpol, the presidency of its executive committee has been filled all, except for three out of twenty four times, by countries in Europe and North America. The position of its Secretary General has even been reserved exclusively for career officials in Western industrial countries. Since it is headquartered in France, staff personnel of its various functional departments are mainly French citizens and other Europeans. When citizens of non-Western countries are employed, they are more than likely educated and trained in Western social experiences. Most important, Interpol, the United Nations, and other international organizations serve to spread and implement Western standards, preferences, and practices. Developing, non-Western countries are given seats of representation to take in external influences and often yield control while developed, Western states are granted membership privileges to expand markets, establish dominance, and exercise international leverage.

Synthesis in the dimension of representation hence hinges on the extent to which standards and practices of social control in non-Western, non-capitalist, developing, and even undeveloped contexts are properly recognized and utilized in international programming and protocol development. Once there is a balance in content or substance, there then is a need for hiring organizational staff and drawing leadership personnel from diverse national sources. Only when leadership rotates from country to country and staff are recruited from different national backgrounds, can state membership in Interpol, the United Nations, and other international agencies achieve its full meaning in terms of fair representation, equal participation, and common progress.

Another critical issue in moving toward synthesis is incorporation of deviance, problems, and criminal offenses symptomatic of non-capitalist, non-Western social reality in the target issues, tasks, or agendas of major international law enforcement and justice agencies. Currently, Interpol, the UNODC, and other international organizations follow what Western powers or industrial nations see as problems or threats. Drugs are attacked because they disrupt social order and threaten the public health of affluent nations. Piracies, intellectual property rights violations, or patent thefts are addressed because these offenses thwart trade and cause the loss of profit for developed economies. Corruption, human rights abuses, and political repression are addressed because they weaken democratic values and challenge norms in Western ideology. Pollution, deforestation, and land erosion matter greatly because they cross national borders and affect overall human survival. Money laundering, the sex trade, human trafficking, and organized crime are targeted because they cause moral decay and lead to financial and social disorder in industrial countries. Most saliently, terrorism is battled because it takes aim at Western powers. The United States has a selfish interest in keeping terrorists, drug dealers, human traffickers, organized crime leaders, and other offenders out of its national borders. This nation has waged wars, campaigns, and conducted various nonmilitary programs around the world. Poor, non-capitalist, non-Western, developing, or undeveloped countries become battlegrounds, bearing the wounds for the sake of public safety and security in the United States or in the lands of its Western allies. International organizations often serve as fronts for the United States and Western powers. Throughout Asia and the Pacific, from poppy-growing fields to al-Queda hideouts, from guerilla bases to insurgent strongholds, wherever there are American troops, American-led allied forces, and agents of international control, are any local safety interests served? For example, does Iraq now exist only as a pawn on the chessboard to ensure that there will not be another September 11 attack on American soil? What about hundreds of thousands of Iraqis who have perished in the preemptive war and dozens more who are losing their life to terrorist insurgency from day to day?

Obviously, for any international organization's coordination in social control to be legitimate, there is an urgent need for the organization to include deviance, crime, and social problems typical of developing or undeveloped societies in the general agenda or specific action programs. At any time, an effort at international control in any particular country must first produce tangible benefits in maintaining order in that country before that nation contributes to peace and justice in other nations or around the world.

Realistically, representation, access to opportunities, and sharing of benefits are inherently connected to contribution, assumption of responsibilities, and fulfilling of obligations. Developed countries are eager to translate their bountiful material and human resources into power and influence around the world. International organizations become an ideal forum in which individual countries may cloak their national interests and gain worldwide legitimacy for general leadership or in specific causes. Developing nations, on the other hand, may have to be drawn into international efforts with monetary, material, and personnel assistance. Because of the incentives received, they are often coerced into giving their votes or consensus to some international initiatives or action programs they themselves do not necessarily understand, care about, or benefit from. Sadly though, a complete international synthesis in social control obviously can never become a reality so long as countries in the world remain varied and different in size, level of development, and volume of economic output. China may someday become as powerful as or even stronger than the United States. However, could it ever happen at any time that Brunei might exert the same clout or as great leverage as the United States at Interpol, the United Nations, any international organization in social control, or in a multinational campaign against deviance and crime across Asia and the Pacific?

18

Civil Penetration and Global Synchronization

Along with the increase in cross-border criminality as well as the expanding international cooperation in criminal justice responses, there is a growing reciprocity in ideas about social control among countries around the world. Civil penetration in Asia and the Pacific benefits not only from the internationalization of trade, labor, and media, but also the localization of race, ethnicity, and nationality.

CONTEXT

Civil penetration began as early as traders, explorers, diplomats, messengers, and religious missionaries cross national borders to pursue their dreams or goals or to carry out their duties or missions in foreign lands. They first spread their native ideas, customs, and practices among the people with whom they came in contact. They then brought home what they had learned in other lands. For example, Special Envoy Zhang Qian of Emperor Wudi in the Chinese Han Dynasty traveled to Central Asia first in 138 B.C. and then in 119 B.C., opening the historical Silk Road from China to Persia, and then farther to Europe.

In contemporary society, civil penetration takes place when people travel for business and leisure, giving rise to a tourist industry; when people study and research within and outside national borders, creating a knowledge enterprise; and when people search for news and headlines, fueling a worldwide web in cyberspace as well as an international medium through radio wave (Shaw 2004). With respect to information access, the internet carries current news, historical data, and every imaginable record, making this information available for anyone to view at any time in any place where there is a computer, a laptop, a cellular phone, or other transmitting/receiving device in the world. The cable network provides instant news or constant programs from continent to continent. So does the satellite system in spreading information in both audio and video forms throughout the globe. In addition to Cable Network News (CNN) and other international media organizations that cater to the general needs of multinational corporations, diplomatic missions, and an educated or otherwise privileged worldwide audience, ethnic information services follow migrants and immigrants to every country, every community, or every local corner, churning out newspapers, radio talk shows, and television programs in various native languages or ethnic flavors. With a combination of all these different channels for information, what happens here and now can be made known to there and then in the other parts of the world.

In social control, the acquittal of an American homeowner who killed a Japanese exchange student at his doorway caused nationwide surprise and anger in Japan. The Japanese reaction may have had a bearing on the civil lawsuit in which the parents of the slain student were awarded monetary compensations (Nossiter 1994). The media blitz in Taiwan on the killings of a Taiwanese businessman's mistress and illegitimate child in the United States by his wife may affect many Taiwanese in their perceptions of social order, public safety, and criminal justice on American soil. So may the extensive coverage by ethnic Chinese media in the United States of the abduction and murder of a famous actress's daughter in Taiwan influence the attitude of many Chinese Americans toward crime and social control on their home island. The sentencing of an American teenager to caning in Singapore brought about the intervention of the United States President (Shenon 1994). United States pressures on China have to some extent changed the handling of political dissidents by Chinese communists. Beginning in the late 1990s, the Chinese government seems more willing to release them from prisons for exile overseas (Broder 1998). The capture of General Manuel Noriega by United States forces and his later imprisonment in the United States may have served as a warning for authoritarian leaders in Central and Latin America countries who directly or indirectly engage in human trafficking, drug smuggling, and other activities against American interests (Arrarte 1992). Recently, the worldwide media exposure of Michael Jackson and his trial for child molestation may have fed the curiosity of people of many different countries interested in law and justice in the United States. The hanging of an Australian drug smuggler in Singapore in spite of numerous appeals for clemency, including those by Australian leaders, has undoubtedly left the world the impression that Singapore is seriously and unwaveringly determined to eradicate drugs as an ultimate evil with the ultimate punishment (Times Wire Reports 2005). Most interestingly, Saddam Hussein and his ongoing court proceedings on charges of genocide and crime against humanity in Iraq can show the world how far Western ideas, norms, and practices in social control may be incorporated in the context of the Middle East.

Comparative research in crime and criminal justice has gained worldwide interest and phenomenal growth since the 1970s (Beirne and Hill 1991). With the realization that criminological theories become more credible and applicable when they are tested under diverse cultural conditions, scholars, especially those from the West, embarked on a wide range of comparative research to gather data, validate theories, and develop pragmatic measures. Under the expectation that one nation can learn from the experience of another in crime and social control, researchers and policy analysts in individual countries as well as in international organizations look into the practices of different legal systems in the world, from the civil law system to the common law system to the other systems, such as Islamic law, customary law, and socialist law. At present, a considerable number of United Nations and affiliated agencies engage in the task of developing international measurements, maintaining regional or global databases, and providing country-specific or world-general trends, analyses, and reports on crime and criminal justice. For example, Interpol has continuously published the world crime statistics supplied to it by the majority of its member states since 1951. The United Nations, beginning in 1970, sponsors three major surveys on the basis of member states' participatory contributions, covering prevalence of crime, operation of criminal justice systems, and crime prevention strategies for more than 100 countries around the world. The World Health Organization maintains a systematic homicide dataset in its annual publication *World Health Statistics*. To obtain a more accurate picture of crime across the globe, researchers from various nations have even attempted to launch a few self-study surveys. Among them, the International Crime Victim Survey has conducted several rounds of interviews in more than forty different languages, reaching hundreds of thousands of people concerning their household experience of crime, policing, and crime prevention in both developed and developing countries (Kury 2002). This knowledge sharing can open the way to needed change in crime prevention.

Without doubt, the knowledge enterprise commands power and influence in civil penetration and global synchronization (Shaw 2004). Thus people learn and may, consciously or unconsciously, borrow from different legal systems and their various approaches to crime and crime prevention through education, training, research, media reporting, policy consultation, and statistical referencing. For instance, students, officials, and the general public may change their attitudes and behavior when they come into contact with institutes and universities that conduct research and spread their research findings in academic publications, classroom instruction, training sessions, conference presentations, media briefing, governmental testimonies, and data services. Throughout Asia and the Pacific, the United Nations Asia and Far East Institute for the Prevention of Crime and the Treatment of Offenders in Tokyo, the United Nations Latin American Institute for the Prevention of Crime and the Treatment of Offenders in San Jose, Costa Rica, the Arab Security Studies and Training Center in Riyadh, the Australian Institute of Criminology in Canberra, the International Center for Criminal Law Reform and Criminal Justice Policy in Vancouver, and various other international organizations in consultative status or by special agreement with the United Nations can be particularly important for pushing civil penetration in social control to an ever higher level as they each serve the region with training, technical assistance, research, and publications across national borders.

While the media transmit information worldwide and the knowledge enterprise spreads knowledge across lands, the tourist industry takes people physically and directly to where they want to be. Visitors bear witness to law and social order in a foreign country when they walk through immigration and customs, see uniformed officers carrying out their duties on the streets or at major tourist sights, ask information from the police, or report problems to the local authorities. For example, ordinary travelers are bound to take notice of the overwhelming presence of military and police forces in public places throughout the Middle East. Some activists make special trips to foreign countries to register their support for or opposition to a particular social cause. Participating in public protest, they often run into direct confrontation with local law enforcement authorities.

Travelers' impressions and witness reports can shape public opinions about crime and social control in one country by another country. When these impressions and reports repeat themselves from group to group, a simple issue-specific opinion may surface in the form of alerts or warnings in travel guidebooks, on websites, or in newspapers. A general perception, such as that of police corruption, brutality, and incompetence that so often develops and spreads about some Third World countries, may then follow, triggering negative advisories or boycotts. As public pressure mounts, there are, hopefully, movements toward self-reform. On a subtle note, court personnel, law enforcement officers, and justice professionals are often also business or leisure travelers around the world. Different from laypersons, they are likely to pay particular attention to the way members of a foreign social control force behave, their manner, their level of professionalism. In their own duties in their home country, they may try to emulate or avoid what they have perceived in the work of their counterparts in other lands.

BOTH SIDES

Civil penetration is a natural process. As long as there are people traveling across national borders, cables lying on the ocean floor, satellites orbiting in outer space, and printed material circulating around the planet, ideas and practices in one place will influence ideas and practices elsewhere.

Revolving exactly around the nature of civil penetration, however, arise four contrasting contentions. Despite the common assumption that civil penetration takes place naturally, there are too many manmade barriers that stand in its way. Ideologically, while people in capitalist countries tend to view any socialist approaches to deviance, crimes, and social problems as repressive and revolutionary, communist enthusiasts automatically disregard any social control measures by a capitalist government as corrupt and reactionary. Politically, whereas authoritarian regimes often use censorship and terror to keep out foreign ideas in law and order, democratic governments criticize undemocratic social control practices as inhumane and backward. Technologically, while people with no access to advanced law enforcement equipment or tools are fearful of technology, people who own and command technological inventions tend to keep the newest or the most effective for their own functional operations in social control. In terms of development, while developed countries often seem too arrogant to learn any effective social control methods from sources they deem less developed, developing nations have enough ego and pride to just remain self-sufficient or self-reliant in maintenance of public order. With these considerations, it is natural to see various unnatural barriers being erected to prevent, disrupt, or stop beneficial civil penetration in social control from ever taking place naturally and smoothly across national borders.

Another argument is that civil penetration does not necessarily give way to what is reasonable and workable. Against the commonsensical proposition that what is rational, effective, and useful gets spread in civil penetration, it can be argued that it is often the popular, the superficial, and the idealistic that becomes dispersed. Wearing uniforms, bearing firearms, using heavy equipment, following organizational protocols, patrolling public arenas, and keeping distance from private space are considered modern and professional in policing. No matter how superficial or impractical any of these elements is in any particular social context, it is still promoted as a principle or standard. Nobody, professional or nonprofessional, would risk reputation to propose anything different yet workable. By similar logic, dueling, group revenge, collective shaming, ostracism, vigilantism, communal surveillance, justice by elders, and kinship disciplining are viewed as outdated, backward, and dangerous. Even though some of these forces still work to socialize youth, manage conflict, and keep peace in the community, they are automatically discarded as undesirable residues of an older social order. Neither officials in an agency of social control nor members of the general public would advocate any of these practices.

Across Asia and the Pacific, or around the world in general, some social control measures used in particular countries or under special circumstances are not likely to spread although they serve as effective deterrents in their original contexts. For example, Singapore employs caning as an effective discipline for children and hanging as a powerful deterrent for drug smugglers. A political or military regime under which ordinary people already experience considerable economic difficulty and psychological pain in their ordinary lives may take torture and terror as necessary procedures for criminal offenders or prisoners of war. However, neither caning nor hanging, neither torture nor terror would obviously move much beyond individual national or territorial borders due to their complete rejection in the court of world opinion.

Still another argument is that civil penetration often falls prey to the powerful, the rich, and the knowledgeable. Civil penetration is, to a large extent, influenced by power, wealth, and knowledge. People normally look up to the powerful, the rich, and the knowledgeable for inspiration or guidance. They sometimes look down upon the powerless, the poor, and the ignorant. Moreover, the powerful, the rich, and the knowledgeable have a built-in interest in utilizing their power, wealth, and knowledge to spread their ideas and establish their influence. For example, while a great many countries listen to the United States on various matters, they are aware that the United States uses its economic, military, and technological prowess to expand its presence in strategic regions and to increase its clout in international organizations. Whatever becomes fashionable in the United States, no matter how problematic it is, enters the currents of the media and the popular culture.

The powerful, affluent, knowledgeable West now favors an economy where regulation gives way to the rules of a relatively free market, a form of government where the power of governance lies in public suffrage, and a type of society where life builds upon freedom of association, enterprise, and expression. Specifically, press censorship, suppression of political dissidence, unwarranted search, torture, forced confessions, and often the death penalty are viewed as cruel and unusual forms of punishment. Open media, public monitoring or supervision, due process, trial by jury, and the right to appeal in the court system are legislated as institutional safeguards against abuse of power and dereliction of duty. Most important, the West faces the direct menace of drug abuse, human trafficking, sex exploitation, technological pirating, organized crime, and international terrorism, singly and in combination. As a result, media reports, training programs, technological inventions, and other civil exchanges around the world are focused on these concerns. Needs by the vast Third World in social control are automatically pushed to the sideline.

The fourth argument concerns the frequency, intensity, duration, and periodicity of civil penetration. On the matter of frequency, some believe that civil penetration is gradual, continuous, and frequent while others think it is eruptive, discrete, and event-specific or climate-contingent. For example, people could reasonably argue that there was not much civil penetration in social control between capitalist and communist countries during the Cold War or that a good deal of infiltration from capitalism to socialism, and vice versa, went on at the civil level when both sides were in serious conflict. Regarding intensity, some argue that people learn from each other unconsciously, naturally, and without any obvious internal effort or external pressure; others contend that countries draw upon one another's practices in social control, largely because of extraordinary experiences. Learning, whether self-motivated or superimposed, can be intense. Another important point is that civil penetration often takes place when an idea or practice becomes trendy and fashionable. The intensity with which a trend or fashion spreads is usually high. Duration is related directly to intensity. The more intense a civil exchange is, the less likely it is to last for a considerable length of time. For those who believe in the natural permeability of all human languages, institutions, and practices across any manmade barriers including national borders, civil penetration is a process that has no beginning nor ending. On the other hand, people may so emphasize the uniqueness of a spiritual idea, a cultural artifact, or a social custom that they believe the permeation or migration of such an idea, artifact, or custom from its origin to other places can only be caused by force or fashion. The duration of any forced or fashionable movement is not likely to be long.

Finally, looking at the rise and fall of different polities, economies, cultures, or civilizations over human history, some assume that there is a hidden hand behind the periodicity of major social forces, such as those contrasting forces between capitalism and socialism, democracy and totalitarianism, a free market and state planning, individualism and control, or cultural pluralism and ethnocentrism. As one side dominates public arenas, spreading in the form of civil penetration, it creates social conditions that lead to its own replacement by the other. There are certainly people who downplay such cyclical assumptions, arguing instead that it is always the strong, the rational, the good, or the right that gets its way in civil permeation. In social control, as in everything else in the human sphere, there is no law of periodicity that inevitably calls back slavery, dictatorship, terror, torture, and any other unusual punishment against humanity. In the future, there will only be things that are better than what is currently available in democracy, self-discipline, institutional transparency, procedural fairness, and other forms of humane treatment coming for global learning, transmission, and synchronization.

SYNTHESIS

Although it is somewhat against intuition and common sense, a synthesis in civil penetration indeed hinges on whether the little, the quiet, and the negligible are given their due attention under the spotlight of the mass media, are heard in the court of world opinion, and are afforded a fair opportunity to leave their impact on human evolution.

To that end, a few new ways of thinking and acting ought to be invoked to moderate or balance the long-established forces of contrast. First, cultural skepticism is a necessary tool to use in harnessing natural tendency. By their evolutionary experience with survival of the fittest, people learned to look up to the powerful, the rich, and the knowledgeable as sources of inspiration or models of success while looking down upon the powerless, the poor, and the ignorant as references of mistakes. It has become a natural tendency for tourists to flock to developed nations while avoiding backward countries. Reporters eulogize human achievements in the West while exposing only social ills in the rest of the world. Scholars provide justification for capitalism while casting doubts on other alternatives of political economy. In social control, whereas there are developing or undeveloped countries that are willing to empty their coffers to purchase advanced equipment, take training courses, use professional consultancies, and hire retired law enforcement or justice officials from developed nations, there is not much borrowing of ideas or practices by the industrial West from other parts of the world. Only when a spirit of cultural skepticism questions the rationality of what happens as well as the utility of what is transmitted in civil penetration, can there then be a reasonable level of synthesis or synchronization among various opposing forces in the world dynamics of social control.

Second, multiculturalism offers a needed counterbalance to ethnocentrism. To preserve what proves to be useful and effective for survival in their local environment, people sometimes sanctify what they have created in both material and nonmaterial aspects. With an ethnocentric attitude, they overvalue native conventions and customs while downplaying anything alien to their familiar ways of thinking and acting. Across Asia and the Pacific, differences in every possible dimension, from geography, history, population, religion, and culture, to political economy, are so huge that ethnocentrism can literally hold people from going beyond whatever natural boundaries they set around themselves. If villagers in India or China find civil mediation effective in resolving their disputes, why do they have to learn about formal procedures to pit one against another in a court of law? If a professional law enforcement force works to provide public safety and security for rights-conscious citizens in Canada and the United States, are there any strong reasons for it to borrow from China or Japan social control practices that might raise the eyebrows of those who advocate individual privacy and civil liberty? On the other hand, people do engage in self-examination, self-reflection, and self-criticism, laying ground for learning from other cultures or countries. In the contemporary era, multiculturalism has actually risen to prominence not only as a domestic movement to integrate various ethnic or subcultural groups within individual territorial sovereignties, but also as a global trend to engage different countries in dialogue on the horizon of a united world. Multiculturalism emphasizes the unique value of each culture while pointing to its relative contribution to other cultures in an overall social dynamic. As for social control, a multicultural orientation can obviously prevent people from ever falling into the trap of ethnocentrism. More important, it helps people to respect other ideas or practices, and when necessary, to learn or to borrow from those other ideas or practices. A synthesis in the form of civil penetration can therefore be realized around the world.

Third, diversification is a critical force needed to overcome domination so that diversity can reign over dominance as a standard state of affairs in human sphere. Ever since the beginning and over the course of human civilizations, people have developed and reinforced their belief in the rights of the truthful, the righteous, the orthodox, or the efficient to question, conquer, and replace the questionable, the problematic, or the wasteful in ideological debates and policy practices. A powerful social force or group, when it deems something is true or right, would not cease mobilizing all its assets or resources to spread and promote that something until an acceptable dominance is established. Alternatives, different approaches, the dissenting, or the rebellious are rarely allowed. Even in today's world where the value of diversity seems to be duly recognized, the West, led by the United States, still takes as its inalienable responsibility the task of expanding democracy, free markets, and the rule of law to every corner of the globe. With respect to social control, however, a synthesis of civil penetration will obviously not come to the fore when there is only one-way traffic of ideas or practices, such as professionalization of staff and personnel, formalization of equipment and logistics, and institutionalization of rules and procedures, developed or favored by the West and dispatched to non-Western destinations. Beginning with the elimination of dominance by any particular philosophy or model of crime prevention and intervention, synthetic synchronization must involve a total integration of all different social control inventions and creations from diverse political, economic, cultural, and territorial sources. In fact, only in a world of diversity can people across Asia and the Pacific in particular, and around the world in general, willingly learn and borrow ideas and practices in social control from one another, not because an idea or practice is dominant or popular but because it offers a different perspective or a desired operational alternative.

Finally, as people perceive, witness, study, and make comments on social control in different places through travel, education, research, the internet, and the mass media, they need to keep an awareness of the relativity of each particular idea or practice. Something is rational, effective, and beneficial where it finds its home environment. Something becomes unreasonable, costly, and dysfunctional when it is out of fashion. In a vulgar world where people automatically follow what is popular, fashionable, or trendy, it is important to know and understand that trends change while fashion ebbs and flows (Shaw 2004). More pointedly as the world is divided between the core and the periphery with countries in the core dominating the court of world opinions and leading the way of human evolution, it is vital to recognize that the core can be fallible in some of its prevailing practices while places in the periphery can be promising with respect to many of their ideas. In other words, seeing the fallibility of the famous and the fashionable as well as the potential of the unknown, the unpopular, or the negligible is key to achieving a synthesis of civil learning and influence among nation states and other sovereign entities around the world. For example, the United Nations, Interpol, and other international agencies can make a positive contribution to such synthesizing efforts or movements when they fully disclose both the advantages and disadvantages of each of the social control modules or protocols they intend to promote through their training, research, and demonstration programs in vast developing regions.

Overall, cooperation and penetration in the field of crime, deviance, and social control are on the rise among countries around the world. In Asia and the Pacific, however, given the tremendous diversity in cultural tradition, social custom, and political ideology throughout the region, conflicts will be unavoidable in the process of either voluntary cooperation or involuntary penetration.

Part IV

CRIME AND SOCIAL CONTROL: LARGER SOCIAL INSTITUTIONS, PROCESSES, AND CONTEXTS

As trade, the mass media, and advanced means of communication and transportation bring people and nations closer to one another, crime and social control become more and more an issue that intertwines with important economic, political, cultural, and social forces within and outside national borders (Marx 1997; Newman 1999; Andersson and Gunnarsson 2003; Shamir 2005). Across Asia and the Pacific, there are capitalist versus socialist confrontations in political economy, East versus West clashes in culture and civilizations, individualistic versus collectivistic conflicts in social organization, and various other dimensional contrasts or contradictions. All have critical impacts upon crime, deviance, social problems, and social control in the region (Shaw 1996; Garland 2001; Terrill 2003; Beiras 2005).

19

Capitalism and Socialism

As a system of political economy, capitalism encourages, maintains, and protects private investment in and ownership of natural resources, factories, machinery, and other material means for the production, distribution, and exchange of goods and services under market conditions. Socialism, on the other hand, insists that the means of production as well as the necessities of survival be owned and controlled by the state for the collective good of a whole society. In view of the fact that the two rival systems of political economy have been zeroing in on each other since Karl Marx envisioned a socialist transition to the ultimate human paradise, communism, Asia and the Pacific provide a fascinating stage for competition, conflict, and confrontation in the capitalist versus socialist quest for influence, domination, and control over every country in the world (Lee 1966; Josey 1973; Marx and Engels 1979; McCormick and Unger 1995; Shaw 2000; Busky 2002; Paton 2005).

THE PAST

The struggle between capitalism and socialism fermented long before socialism arose as a rival system. As early as in 1845, Friedrich Engels systematically documented the dire social conditions under which various members of the working class lived in capitalist England. In the same year, he met Karl Marx. Joining hands, they developed comprehensive ideas, theories, and strategies to criticize, condemn, and counteract capitalism. *The Communist Manifesto*, which Marx and Engels jointly presented to the world in 1848, was not just a shocking declaration of opposition to capitalist ideology and practices. It has since become a blueprint, an action plan, for the proletariat to organize itself to establish a new society in the revolutionary ruins of the whole capitalist system.

Marx's critiques, calls for action, and their general appeal to revolutionary aspirants as well as to ordinary working people around the world paralleled the rough and tough reality of capitalism. From the very beginning, capitalism exhibited its ruthless nature by forcing flocks of farmers off land, keeping a constant army of unemployed laborers in the market, and usurping from the state its power in regulation, welfare delivery, and maintenance of social order. From the British Isles to Continental Europe, capitalism brought about rapid industrialization and widespread urbanization, transforming society from mechanical to organic solidarities. While self-interest, self-organization, and profit made some private enterprises into corporate conglomerates or business empires, a mass of individuals became rootless, counting on the sale of their labor for survival. Across rural areas, there were newly constructed roads, quarries, mines, or factories amid deserted villages, abandoned farms, polluted rivers, or deforested hillsides. Throughout cities, there were beggars, homeless vagrants, drug addicts, pickpockets, prostitutes, and gangsters roaming in litter-strewn streets. Graffiti-filled transit depots, ghettos or slums, red-light districts, and dilapidated apartments or warehouses became familiar urban scenes. With their profits, capitalists entered politics, invested in the media, and engaged in philanthropy, ensuring that capitalism and its exploitation of labor and nature were legitimized and sustained in the name of freedom, democracy, individualism, and universal human rights. Crime, deviance, and social problems came in waves and spread as the capitalist state savored its lofty yet near merciless policy and practice of no or minimum intervention in the markets (Garland 2001; Muller 2002; Case and Fair 2004).

Beyond Europe, capitalism made sweeping advances all over the world. Across the Atlantic, capitalist explorers found the New World, leading to the slaughter of Native Americans and the settlement of European farmers, traders, laborers, and proprietors. In the Pacific, capitalist expeditions made their way to Australia and New Zealand, resulting in the marginalization of aboriginals and the inclusion of Oceania in the British Commonwealth. To the North as well as to the South of the Sahara, colonialists took over various kingdoms or territories, creating pockets of capitalist or quasi-capitalist operations throughout Africa. In the heartland of Asia, imperialists took over India, broke into the Chinese Empire, and shook up other traditional societies, extracting tons of cotton, silk, rubber, silver, gold, and other raw materials for capitalist production while disposing of loads of consumer goods and industrial products from the same system of capitalist production. The capitalist expansion showed little regard for sovereignty, native rights, the rule of law, or the etiquettes of civil transaction. Around the globe, people were killed, communities were ruined, traditional ways of life were uprooted, and countries were thrown into war, chaos, or helpless dependency.

In Asia and the Pacific, while a few settler societies, such as Australia and the United States, successfully replicated capitalism, the majority struggled in new uncertainties: capitalist versus feudalist, nationalist versus colonialist, modern versus traditional, or Western versus Eastern organizations of production, trade, and social life. China provided a unique yet somehow representative example. Upon being forced open by imperialist capitalism, China, once a proud self-sufficient empire, had to give up coastal territories for capitalist trade and commerce, let in the foreign interests and influence of various capitalist powers throughout its heartland, and stay indulgent toward a small unscrupulous national bourgeoisie on all of its domestic fronts. For about one hundred years between the Opium War and the founding of socialist China, the Chinese saw, experienced, and suffered it all: the brutal aggression of capitalist powers against weak nations, the merciless exploitation of poor laborers by capitalist enterprises, and the coldhearted attitude of capitalist governments toward those in need. With the division of the nation, the suffering of common citizens, the spread of disease, the skyrocketing of crime, the incapacitation of justice, and the disorganization of social life, capitalism did not seem to offer China much hope but instead, mounting frustration, delusion, and resentment.

Exploitative accumulation of capital at home and expansionist pillaging overseas made capitalists look like the fiercest predators on the face of the earth. While there were depressions, protests, riots, and social disarray in the heartlands of capitalism, there were revolutions, uprisings, and wars secretly or openly waged in other parts of the world against capitalist colonization, domination, and advance. The October Revolution of Russia in 1917 fired the first and most critical shot. It ushered in a new era of socialism. But most important, it laid the ground for a division of the world into capitalist and socialist competition, confrontation, and mutual destruction over much of the twentieth century. Following the lead of Russia, Eastern Europe soon fell into the socialist camp. Chinese communists, through years of struggle, established China as a shining socialist star when it came into power in 1949. With revolutionary inspiration from the Soviet Union and China, various independence movements in Africa, Asia, and Latin America also looked to socialism as their model toward national self-sufficiency, self-reliance, or self-determination. By the 1960s, socialism had indeed taken a considerable part of the world in a head-on rivalry with capitalism.

Having emerged in the revolutionary bloodshed, socialism, notably in China, never slacked off in its attention to social order. As revolutionary heroes turned into national leaders, they first attempted to wipe out elements of resistance. Landlords, capitalists, enemy soldiers, former government officials, and other known reactionaries were put under the proletarian dictatorship. Addicts were forced onto the road to recovery. Prostitutes were reformed as productive citizens. Working-class people were organized as the core of political support. Villages, work units, neighborhoods, and communities were networked as webs of social surveillance. The whole country was charged not only with a heightened level of alertness against wayward thoughts but also with a uniform standard of conformity to general norms. Sabotage as a form of crime was dealt maximum punishment. Deviance, even in matters of different opinions, was countered by revolutionary intolerance. It was a disciplined way of life, which, in the beginning, held a great deal of appeal for many people, especially those who were tired of the social disarray under capitalism.

Control, discipline, and organization supposedly brought about spiritual purity, behavioral simplicity, and social orderliness. However, along with suppressed impulses for deviance, crime, and social nonconformity, there also seemed to be a phenomenal loss of motivation for productive imagination, innovation, and creativity under socialism. Most critically, as a minority of state managers took charge to plan and design work and life for the majority of working people, a social cleavage soon developed across the socialist landscape. In China, Mao Zedong attempted to address the problem by staging a grass-roots response to ever arrogant, abusive, corrupt state bureaucrats in the Great Cultural Revolution. Unfortunately, instead of uprooting individual selfishness and overcoming governmental bureaucratism, Mao's new revolution only threw China into productive paralysis, leaving the majority of the populace with a stronger sense of betrayal, disenchantment, and alienation.

About the time when socialist states experienced difficulty in feeding their populations, continuing their bureaucratic operations, and producing their favored versions of social order, capitalist countries made dramatic strides on both domestic and international fronts. Domestically, almost as if by natural occurrence, unions, interest groups, labor movements, the mass media, the middle class, and civil society developed as free market forces to counter capitalists and their expansive presence in politics, culture, and other social affairs. With increasing contributions from private sectors, the capitalist state grew larger and stronger, moving gradually to the center as more of a representative entity for a broad variety of social interests. Laws were enacted and enforced not only to control the poor, but also to regulate the rich. Workers were extended protection on and off the job while capitalists were warned of their essential social obligations. Internationally, capitalist nations were able to use the wealth they had created and the technology they had developed to first form a line of resistance against communist expansion and then a net of containment around socialist presence across the globe. At the height of the Cold War, most capitalist countries still seemed able to enjoy and draw from a dynamic infusion of multiple social elements while they watched their socialist counterparts struggling and exhausting themselves in one dimension or another of state planning and control.

THE PRESENT

Socialism did not last long in its confrontation with capitalism. As at the inception, the Soviet Union was the first in line to step into an era of socialist collapse and change. Along with its demise, the East European block disappeared from the socialist map as well. In Asia and the Pacific, China has led a path of socialist reform while North Korea still enjoys its status as the last bastion of old-fashioned socialist practice.

Now as a system of political economy, capitalism is advancing and socialism is retreating at both national and international levels. At the international level, Russia and all the former Soviet socialist republics have changed into market or quasi-market economies (Shlapentokh 1997; Ware and Kisriev 2001; Sievers 2003). Reforming socialist countries, including China and Vietnam, have taken systematic measures to adapt to the world political and economic order dominated by capitalism. Multinational corporations and individual investors from advanced capitalist societies, such as Japan and the United States, have invaded developing countries, spreading capitalist modes of production, consumer goods, lifestyles, and symbols to almost every corner of the world, especially in Asia and the Pacific. At the national level, countries that still adhere to socialism are witnessing a growing private sector led by small businesses and foreign investments and a declining public economy represented by state and collective enterprises. Even the seemingly staunchest socialist North Korea has started to receive economic aid from capitalist sources in its search for relief from natural disasters. In capitalist economies, socialist or quasi-socialist elements, such as public enterprises and state intervention, have also diminished in response to domestic calls for market rationality and international pressures for trade liberalization.

Despite its general decline, socialism is still a significant force across the globe. In Asia and the Pacific where the majority of socialist countries on the earth are located, socialism offers a particularly salient dimension for contrast and comparison. China, the largest developing economy in the world, continues to be a socialist state. The Chinese government maintains essential control over land, natural resources, and major means of production. State corporations dominate key economic sectors, overshadowing business operations for almost all other players with no affiliation with the government. Private and foreign enterprises, while representing most dynamic segments in recent years, are not yet leading elements in the whole socialist economy. In capitalist countries, including Canada and the United States, legal regulations, small business grants, tax incentives, interest rate adjustments, and state interventions have become recurring topics of concern in economic activities. In Japan, Singapore, South Korea, and Taiwan, the government has long been accustomed to playing an interventionist role in economic processes (Xu 1996). Overall, the counterbalance between capitalist and socialist elements or forces remains clear, strong, and critical in the world economy.

As to crime and social control, the capitalist advance seems to go hand in hand with socialist retreat, leading to a broadened social gap between social classes, weakened control by the state and tradition, increased mobility for individuals, heightened public attention to material gain, and an increased flow of consumer goods across society. People's properties fall into the hands of a few stakeholders and opportunists when former socialist countries switch overnight from public to market economies. Public funds and resources funnel into the coffers of a minority of upstart private businesses when existing socialist countries loosen state control over economic sectors (Lotspeich 1995; Frisby 1998; Ware and Kisriev 2001). As private enterprises and foreign investments grow and expand, some of these businesses engage in unethical or illegal practices: bullying local residents and small businesses, bribing public officials for preferential treatments, avoiding taxes, exploiting workers, polluting the environment, and transferring unreported profits overseas or into personal accounts. To a degree, social disorganization, symptomatic of the early stage of capitalist development, seems to be making a noticeable reappearance in all former socialist countries as they are changing into capitalism or reforming themselves toward a better integration in the capitalist-dominated world economy.

At the individual level, urban residents who become unemployed from many a defunct state enterprise join peasants who leave an increasingly marginalized rural community. They form a large army of migrants or transit populations in search of economic opportunities for a better life. Since opportunities are limited and competition is keen, some turn to illegal activities: pickpocketing in public places, burglarizing private houses, robbing banks and commercial establishments, disrupting public order, looting, swindling, dealing drugs, gambling, or offering sex for sale. Some take on an unproductive lifestyle, becoming drug addicts, alcoholics, homeless people, or vagrants. Since it persists as a social system in openly proclaimed socialist states and as economic elements in capitalist nations, socialism will continue to produce the same social problems associated with its very existence: corruption, abuse of power, wasting of public resources, excessive state intervention, and unwarranted intrusion into private life.

THE FUTURE

As the world has borne the wounds of exploitative capitalism, authoritarian socialism, invading capitalist economies, and changing socialist states, the question arises whether people would benefit from a possible integration of capitalist and socialist ideologies and practices.

Apart from an allegiance to a particular political economy, a socialist government can free itself from total control of economic resources and activities while a capitalist state can take an active role in the regulation of private businesses, the protection of social welfare, and the maintenance of public order. With a national economy growing, civil society advancing, social activities diversifying, and international transactions becoming global, any state government, no matter whether of capitalist or socialist orientation, must retreat from direct involvement in some substantive matters so that it has enough time and energy to monitor and ensure overall effective social functioning. Socialist experimentation has revealed that state ownership of means of production, control of economic operations, and distribution of goods or services have some degree of success only when the economy is of limited scale, with a limited level of technology, and with limited output. In an economy of scale and global reach, a socialist model will not only result in corruption, dereliction of duty, abuse of power, waste, and inefficiency as it so often does in a simple economy, but will also lead to breakdown, stagnation, and systemic crisis. Capitalist experience has shown that when the economy develops its scope and complexity, various groups and interests—unions, the media, a middle class, and overall civil society—can benefit from it enormously and can advance to a new maturity, to social prominence, and to political assertiveness. In a society of diverse interests and multidimensional transactions, a noninterventionist state will exist only as an ideal. In actuality, there is a fundamental need for the state to take political leadership, provide legal guidance, enforce social contracts, monitor civil obligations, and maintain general order so that different productive sectors, interest groups, and population segments can deal with each other smoothly and effectively.

In Asia and the Pacific, as both capitalist and socialist states shape and reshape their role of governing on the basis of an expanded economy and in full view of a diversified society, there will be less likelihood that landlords, business owners, and other organizational operators will be free to abuse tenants, mistreat customers, discriminate against minorities, or exploit employees. The state, either a socialist government in China or a capitalist system in America, will have laws to prevent unscrupulous behavior, law enforcement to punish merciless predators, and social assistance to help those who have not fared well in the labor market or have not adapted well to recurring economic dynamics. Nor will there be much likelihood that the state keeps a heavy hand in controlling most social organizations, penetrates deeply into every corner of private life, and assumes more power without checks and balances from the civil society. Instead, the state will have to encourage self-discipline within the private sector, cultivate public trust throughout society, and aim more at the outcome and quality rather than the process and weight in the administration of social control for public safety, security, and order.

Regardless of how business, service, and other organizations are defined legally and seen publicly, either as collective representations of public ownership in socialist terms or as independent entities of private interests under the capitalist light, they will all have to accept a growing level of scrutiny in an increasingly open society. A socialist work unit needs to face its employees in groups such as the youth league, the association of retired employees, and the convention of employees at large just as a capitalist enterprise has to negotiate with a union and other employee representatives on matters of compensation, working conditions, and job security. In terms of production performance, profit realization, and goal attainment, a socialist work unit reports to the state whereas a capitalist corporation is held accountable by investors. To the state as well as to the general public, both capitalist and socialist organizations are required to follow the law, pay taxes, and fulfill specific social obligations. Indeed by design and normal operation, neither socialist work units nor capitalist corporations should create or shield deviance, criminality, or human degradation within their institutional walls. To a much lesser degree, they will spread resentment, hopelessness, and unrest to the larger society.

With socialist reform strengthening public enterprises to move toward independent operation, capitalist expansion seems to have increased state influence over private corporations in the form of regulations, administrative sanction, taxation, and even executive decrees. Moreover, globalization is placing similar requirements on governments, businesses, services, and all other social institutions so that they can deal with each other smoothly, effectively, and beneficially in the common world market. In the new era of cross-border infusion and integration, while it is safe to say that business organizations are less likely to become sources of grave social problems because of increasing self-discipline and preparedness for public scrutiny, it is also realistic to expect that they cannot serve as critical means for maintenance of social order. For many developing societies in Asia and the Pacific, a retreat by business, service, and community in social control poses an obvious challenge to the state. It will be a long journey before a middle point of compromise can be located where substantive social institutions specialize in their due business affairs while assuming some social responsibility for monitoring the state and caring for individuals.

Despite different conceptions of individuals and individuality, there can be a fusion between capitalism and socialism in the matter of citizens and citizen roles in social control. Under socialist ideology, people are masters of their society. They own the means of production, produce goods for self-consumption, and are responsible for overall public order and social prosperity. To emphasize collective cohesiveness, master citizens in socialist society are also expected to be willing and loyal servants of their neighbors, co-workers, working groups, communities, and government. Capitalism, on the other hand, views individuals as agents of self-interest and self-actualization. Individuals are independent, egoistic, and have essentially only their own labor as an ultimate asset for survival. To keep society whole, they nonetheless must avoid pursuing self-interest to the detriment of others. In other words, all individuals, no matter how much they pursue self-interest, are supposed to be law-abiding citizens. Here, then, is common ground for citizen behavior for both socialism and capitalism. By collective conscience, socialist masters of society attend to the needs of their fellow citizens; under legal mandate, capitalist individuals of private interest can effectively act only within the premises of law, contract, and order.

As people cross cultural, religious, ideological, and national divides to learn from each other as students, fieldwork researchers, correspondents on assignment, and technical or managerial staff in transfer, they combine and mix models and expectations developed for citizens under different social systems. In Asia and the Pacific, there are a growing number of individuals who abandon their socialist training and become instead strongly individualistic in pursuit of their own professional or business interests. There are also people who modify their capitalist affinity and engage in charitable, missionary, and humanitarian projects. Most important, while individualism may generally create greater challenge for social order than collectivism, collectivism can be more devastating to law and law enforcement when it is implanted in the working of organized crime. Indeed, criminal groups modeled after family, an authoritarian regime, or abstractly a socialist organization or a quasi-socialist state may last longer, perform more effectively, and profit faster than those built upon individualistic drives, motivations, and incentives.

All in all, deviance, crime, and social control are to a large degree defined and determined by the social system or political economy that exists in a society. In the past, capitalist states remained completely hands-off when private businesses felt free to exploit individual workers, pushing the latter to the brink as they experience unemployment, vagrancy, homelessness, addiction, and criminality. Socialism attempted to reverse this course of action. However, as socialist nations took a heavy-handed approach to every sphere of social life, they found they had created helpless bureaucratism, corruption, abuse of power, organizational ineffectiveness, and productive inefficiency. Now economic vibrancy in the capitalist camp seems to be at center stage internationally. A significant number of former socialist countries have formally switched to the capitalist mode of production. The remaining socialist states are undertaking systemic reforms to adapt to a world economy dominated by capitalism. While advanced capitalist economies have to some extent cured some of the social ills they suffered in their earlier stages of development, countries undergoing socialist-to-capitalist conversion or socialist-toward-capitalist reform are finding a multiplicity of social problems within and outside their national boundaries. Across Asia and the Pacific, there are crimes and violations rooted in socialism: transfer of public wealth into private ownership, formation of state-like organized crime groups, and favoritism in business licensing or taxation. But there are also problems symptomatic of primitive capitalism: unsafe business operations, use of child labor, withholding of worker's compensation, running of gambling houses or prostitution rings, and sometimes social chaos. In the future, although socialism is in retreat as a social system, socialist elements will inevitably continue to offer critical contrasts and countermeasures to capitalism in both national and international political economies. Deviance, crime, and social control will unavoidably reflect the shockwaves of continuing capitalist versus socialist conflict, confrontation, fusion, or integration in the new era.

20

Eastern Civilizations and Western Development

The core value system of Eastern civilizations is reflected in the existence and influence of Buddhism, Confucianism, and Taoism. Representatively, Confucianism features a profound admiration for nature, tradition, and authority and an exclusionary emphasis on family, community, education, diligence, conscience, and meritocracy. This age-old philosophy of life permeates Eastern cultures broadly and deeply, serving as a state ideology, a civil religion, and a people's behavioral guide in many Asian countries. Through immigration and even through academic exchanges, Confucianism has established a noticeable presence in the general culture of some Western societies such as Australia, Canada, New Zealand, and the United States. Western development, on the other hand, has long been characterized as a break from tradition, a conquest of nature, and a sweeping industrialization, urbanization, specialization, and differentiation throughout society. Beginning in Europe and North America, Western development has sent human beings into outer space and created an unprecedented presence of bureaucracy, transportation networks, communication devices, material artifacts, and consumer goods on and even above the surface of the earth. Armed with the power of capital and the lure of material affluence, Western development is now rapidly expanding to Asia and the Pacific, becoming a model for many developing and undeveloped countries in their drive for technological modernization, economic prosperity, and social progress (Evans and Rauch 1999;

Inglehart and Baker 2000; Goddard 2001; Schiray 2001; Elman, Duncan, and Ooms 2002; Andersson and Gunnarsson 2003; Rigg 2003).

THE PAST

In the East, Confucianism took root from empire to empire, dependency to dependency, and dynasty to dynasty when it provided spiritual inspiration as well as behavioral guidelines for both ruling and ruled classes. The head of a tributary state, the emperor, and the royal family drew from Confucianism because it enabled them to focus on wisdom, benevolence, and virtue to carry out the sacred charge of feeding people, keeping society prosperous, and maintaining order in their land. Under Confucian philosophy, for example, a benevolent king would love and take care of his people as his own sons and daughters. Court officials followed Confucianism since it turned them to competency, kindheartedness, and self-discipline in exercising their duty on behalf of the king or emperor. According to Confucian teachings, all court officials ought to earn their position or reward by competitive or meritorious performance. Even to ordinary people, Confucianism seemed to offer hope, encouragement, and tranquility as it advised them to fulfill reciprocally filial piety, humaneness, and loyalty to their spouses, siblings, children, parents, family, kinship, community, and state. Family, in particular, was everyone's whole purpose of effort and struggle as well as one's ultimate source of protection and comfort (Yao 2000; Elman, Duncan, and Ooms 2002).

Along with Confucianism yet with a broader appeal to the general populace, Buddhism presented a worldview where people could end the cycle of rebirth by purifying their mind and acting in accord with the laws of *karma*, cause and effect. Specifically, Buddhism prescribed the *Noble Eightfold Path* so that people could effectively deal with change, impermanence, and suffering toward a state of no-selfness and a cycle of positive acts for positive results. Indeed by faithfully following the *Path* from right understanding, right thought, right speech, right action, right livelihood, right effort, and right mindfulness, to right concentration, people would to a large degree, if not automatically, refrain from killing (harming living creatures), stealing (taking what is not freely given), sexual misconduct, incorrect speech, (lying, harsh language, slander, and idle chit-chat), and use of intoxicants (Gethin 1998; Yin 1998).

With lesser public appeal and influence, Taoism alerted people to their critical relationships with nature, time, and space. In the dimension of time, various exercises, rituals, and substances were suggested for people to commemorate their genealogical ancestors and to pay homage to dynastic deities so that they could receive constant blessings and eternal protection from those who departed in history. Over the span of space, certain mental states, physical balances, and lifestyles seemed to be key to achieving a positive alignment with different cosmic forces and supernatural entities such as gods and ghosts. Besides issuing proscriptive warnings as well as offering prescriptive precepts to the general public in the form of a folk religion, Taoism as a school of thought also attracted an elite group of artists, scholars, and philosophers who would reach both their inner purity, peace, or emptiness and outer balance, harmony, or strength through study of Taoist classics, research into *yin* (negative), *yang* (positive), *wuxing* (five elements), and *qi* (air), or practice of calligraphy, medicine, music, painting, poetry, and other deeds (Robinet 1992; Ni 1998).

A common and consistent thread through Confucianism, Buddhism, and Taoism is the three doctrines' respective emphasis on humans, their interactions, and their relationships with nature, history, the future, and the universe. Individuals are taught to cultivate morality, strive for virtue, and maintain a harmonious coexistence with various human and nonhuman factors or forces in their environment. As for social control, society can keep peace and order naturally when people accept cosmically determined fates, follow god-granted mandates, fulfill socially generated obligations, perform survival-prompted duties, think about what is right, and do what is right and useful in their individual lives.

However, there are unavoidable side effects as well as inevitable drawbacks in Eastern ways of thinking and acting. First of all, individuals are locked into rigid positions in society and the universe. While they may live a quiet, peaceful, and satisfactory life if they accept, honor, and enjoy the status quo, people can hardly risk an adventure, explore something new, and hence leave a mark or impact because they seldom look beyond their harmonious coexistence with the environment. Second, individuals are forced into blind dedication and loyalty to their family, relatives and kinship, and home society. In the name of belonging to a group, people may feel free and at times even noble to follow greed, indulge in envy, seek revenge, engage in corrupt behavior, hide evildoers, or ignore justice. Third, individuals are focused heavily on human relations. With significant investment in interrelationships, people often fail to attend to the material aspects of life while using most of their time and energy on mutual referencing, comparing, contracting, competing, and conflict. Throughout the history of Eastern civilizations, there were indeed no lack of families, kinships, tribes, dependencies, kingdoms, and empires that fell into decline due to intense political maneuvering, fierce infighting, rampant corruption, or prolonged neglect of material welfare. Ironically, it often took another family-based, centered, or modeled organization, movement, or campaign to end a failing dynasty and begin a new one. As a result, Eastern civilizations overall featured more of an endless recycling of human entrenchment from harmony to conflict to breakdown to rebirth. On the matter of exploring the universe, harnessing nature, utilizing the environment, or improving the quality of life, the East seemingly had yet to make significant strides to be on a par with the more aggressive part of the world.

In the West, after the long dark period of the Middle Ages came a new epoch of spiritual awakening, intellectual enlightenment, and a Renaissance revival of art, literature, and learning. Inside themselves, individuals rediscovered not only their intellectual faculty, logical reasoning, and inquisitorial curiosity, but also their ego as well as their desire and drive for self-actualization. Outside themselves, people rediscovered both nature as a playing field destined for human triumph and society as a contractual network directed toward individual achievement. In the sphere of religious belief, there appeared a God who rose above all other gods or goddesses embedded in observable forces in nature or immersed in tangible factors in human affairs. In other words, with one almighty God, individuals freed themselves from any immediate concern or worry about disturbing or offending a particular god or goddess when they explored, exploited, or changed nature or the environment to their own benefits. Most important, God seemed open and accessible to all on the face of the earth. No matter what they did, people could always report to God directly and individually, seeking his ultimate forgiveness and acceptance. In fact, individual achievements, not excluding the accumulation of wealth, knowledge, and power, obtained by people in earthly undertakings or on the backdrop of nature, were all admissible deeds for redemption of sin, salvation from hell, and elevation to heaven (Weber 2001; Israel 2002).

Emancipation of people from secular and religious restraints led to the unleashing of individual creativity, productivity, and potential in every possible sphere or arena. To nature, people made a unilateral demand for knowledge, resources, and predictability. To the outside world, Westerners launched one expedition or exploration after another, expanding trade, influence, and control while bringing home valuable natural assets and priceless human artifacts. Landowners, business operators, and corporate capitalists spared nothing, except a rationally conceived social contract that kept society running, for tangible profit and imaginable progress. As for crime and social control, the early stage of Western development built mostly, if not solely, upon manipulation of nature, aggression against undeveloped societies around the world, and exploitation of the masses of propertyless commoners and rootless laborers on domestic markets. Thus, land was over-cultivated, rivers polluted, and some animals and plants pushed to the brink of extinction; foreign people were traded as slaves; foreign lands, assets, or resources were taken for illegal settlement, possession, or use, and some traditional societies were completely ruined; rural residents were driven off land; urban laborers were forced to work under exploitative contracts or unsafe conditions; and some sectors of cities became slums, ghettos, or hotbeds of gambling, prostitution, gang activities, and organized criminality.

Into Asia and the Pacific, Western-style development came initially as a predatory force. Australia was annexed as a destination for convicts and exiles. North America was seized as a settlement for a growing population of European laborers and proprietors. India was colonized as a gateway for trade and other missions to the Far East. China, the once powerful and mysterious Eastern Empire, was forced to cede Hong Kong and Macao as ports of entry for Western imports and influences. Even Japan experienced pressure, struggle, and pain in breaking away from its deeply rooted Eastern tradition for an apparently voluntary pursuit of capitalist modernization.

When Western development settled in various pockets throughout Asia and the Pacific, it generated similar scenes as it did in Europe: rural marginality, urban decay, communal dislocation, and social disorganization. With regard to crime, deviance, and social control, the rich only found more ways to exploit the poor under the rather rapid disappearance of traditional restraints and constraints; the powerful only found more means to suppress the powerless in the ever-growing absence of Eastern benevolence and conscience; and the knowledgeable only became cannier and slyer in deceiving the ignorant in the ever-expanding vacuum of religious faith and traditional values. In desperation, parents pawned their children, women sold their bodies, and migrants turned into beggars, pickpockets, or robbers. Without much intervention from government, urban gangsters, rural bandits, and warlords took control over streets, villages, and specific territories. Social order was at best a matter of corruptive power and at worst a state of disarray. Shanghai, for example, was once touted as the Paris of the East. However, the title was not so much a tribute to conspicuously materialistic prosperity. It was rather a comment on its reputation as a notorious haven of unlimited indulgence for the rich without any check and control from authority while being a hell of bottomless suffering for the poor, who lacked care and concern by society.

THE PRESENT

Western development now dominates much of the landscape around the world. It is no exception in Asia and the Pacific. In fact, there exist at least three classes or levels of societies throughout the region by measure of Westernization or Western-style modernization.

On the first level are leading industrial countries, including Australia, Canada, Japan, Singapore, and the United States. They produce consumer goods, display human artifacts, and maintain Western material affluence at home. They create norms, establish values, and pass on Western ideological symbolism to future generations. Most important, taking advantage of their domination over the global market as well as international relations, Western powers actively push and effectively spread Western ways of production, trade, government, organization, and life to every non-Western territory on the face of the earth. Industrializing societies or emergent economies constitute the second level. Counting on Western capital, technology, managerial measures, and market resources in their modernization drive, developing countries seem to be most susceptible to Western manipulation and influence. Engaging in active trade, technological transfer, and personnel exchange with developed economies, industrializing nations can be most receptive to Western beliefs, values, and norms. In the strong current of development, even China is not able to stick firmly to its Confucian roots, socialist ideology, and one-party authoritarian practices. The same holds true for India, with respect to its tradition, religion, and Eastern civilization base. The third level is made up of underdeveloped, undeveloped, and primitive societies. They are candidates for a Western makeover. Developed nations in the West have them in mind but have yet to place them on an active agenda due to those societies' geographical isolation, economic backwardness, and/or social instability. Internally, a small minority of elites in those societies are gaining access to Western consumer goods, education, and popular culture, a factor which may serve to overcome the majority's reservations about or resistance against full-blown Westernization.

Crime and social control in the trace of Western development revolve saliently around property, wealth, technology, and material means. Business enterprises, property owners, and private investors in highly industrialized nations count on law, governmental regulation, technology, institutional safeguards, and watchdog agencies to protect their vital economic interests from skilled, sophisticated, and occasionally scaled frauds, such as insurance frauds, insider trading, and price gouging. People in newly industrializing and urbanizing societies still rely mostly upon friends, hometown folks, their own common sense, or their physical strength to defend against crime in the forms that these societies know it: assaults, thefts, robberies, and other victimizations on the streets, at transit depots, and in other public places. There are obviously a wide range of societies lying between beginning industrialization and advanced economies on the track of Western development where either a small group of aristocratic, royal, political, corporate, educational, or foreign individuals, families, or organizations take advantage of legal laxities, policy loopholes, civil weaknesses, or media obtuseness to their own material benefit, or an overwhelming presence of military, public security, and private police forces serves to keep order and maintain the status quo at the expense of individual creativity, economic productivity, and overall social prosperity. From Indonesia to Peru, from Mexico to Pakistan, and from the Philippines to Turkey, an ordinary tourist scene will include lines of armed security personnel, besides less noticeable plainclothes operatives, in or around public squares, cultural or historical sights, foreign establishments, and other places of significance. People cannot help but wonder to what extent and at what cost social order is maintained for the sake of Western development. More pointedly, are developing countries in pursuit of Western modernization obliged to answer all the calls, such as those of fighting terrorism, from Western powers who lead the way of Western-style social progress, to protect interests of multinational corporations that sit at the center of Western materialistic capitalism, and to create a safe haven of recreations and indulgence for tourists who come from countries of Western affluence?

Cross-border exchange, internationalization, or globalization is another noticeable trend arising from Western development. On the surface, the importation of deviance, crime, and social problems ranges from transfer of wealth to the West by social elites in the East, sale of children to people within affluent countries by desperate parents in impoverished societies, transportation of drugs to advanced nations by organized crime groups in struggling economies, and dumping of industrial wastes in pristine environments of undeveloped countries by developed nations, to Western interference with domestic politics in weak nations. The Third World has also witnessed an influx of trainers, educators, corporate managers, technical staff, military service personnel, diplomats, religious missionaries, and ordinary tourists into its poorer societies by First World countries. There are, of course, migrant laborers who illegally cross national borders for work and better pay, on-the-loose fugitives who secretly live in foreign territories to avoid prosecution and punishment, and transient sex providers who openly pose as travelers to engage in the international flesh trade. Even terrorism seems to be a likely outcome under Western development where the rich exploit the poor, the knowledgeable fool the ignorant, and the powerful bully the powerless on the world stage, perpetuating misunderstanding, resentment, and hatred throughout a whole spectrum of cultural, religious, and political matters. With regard to social control, exportation often features training of legal personnel and law enforcement agents in developing societies with Western procedures and protocols through international agencies such as Interpol and the United Nations, selling or donation of vehicles, firearms, and other equipment to poor nations by more wealthy countries, and establishment of monitoring, enforcement, or legal aid agencies, including the United States Drug Enforcement Administration's overseas operations and Interpol's regional or national offices, by the West or First World countries in the East or Third World economies. There are, certainly, international students who come from the East to study in the West, global scholars who put forth suggestions for developing nations to learn from developed economies, and transnational consultants who promulgate Western ideas or practices in the non-Western part of the world. Their contributions support the expansion of Western forms of social control throughout the globe in general and across Asia and the Pacific in particular.

Eastern civilizations, on the other hand, are losing ground. Just as Western expansion has created three levels of development, the decline of Eastern civilizations is leaving behind three typical states of mind that indicate an uncritical acceptance of change, a nostalgia for the past, and an ambivalence about where change might take their society.

The first state of mind is uncritical acceptance of change. Youth, liberal elements, radical academics, and reformers in Eastern societies gather in political arenas and use the mass media as a forum. They attack history or tradition, blaming it for economic backwardness. They criticize convention or custom, holding it accountable for human corruption, political repression, and overall social stagnation. They rebel against Eastern civilization, charging it with inertia, hindrance, or negative attitudes toward development and modernization. At the height of their protest and debate, these groups may discard useful social control measures as oppressive human restraints against which they inveigh. They may even tout some deviant or criminal incidents as hopeful possible replacements for the status quo. For example, people see more of essential individual bravery than potential social disruptiveness when they sympathize with young couples who live together without marriage, support a career politician who breaks rules in order to salvage a communal organization, or cheer on a street demonstrator who throws stones at a governmental target. When a few take everything Eastern as wrong or backward, they embrace anything non-Eastern, especially Western, no matter how potentially harmful, as good and advanced. This mentality explains why a few developing countries or territories have already contracted some of the social problems the developed world has long worked out while they are far from gaining some of the more desirable amenities that Western-style development can offer.

The second state of mind is nostalgia for the past. The older generation, the conservatives, and national or restorative movements in the East converge and consolidate, permeating public opinion, cultural attitudes, and social sentiments with a longing for life as it once was in their memories. These people in their idealization of the past do not necessarily dump coffee, flush fertilizers or pesticides, burn Western consumer goods, or sabotage automated production lines. Instead, they drink tea, use animal wastes to grow crops, walk on foot, cultivate land with traditional tools, honor their ancestors, and often bless deities at home or in temples. Apparently harmless, this passive resistance to anything new nevertheless serves to divide the population and at times can even hold back society from any movement of change. In fact, it affirms an ideological belief that encroaching Western development is corrupting youth, destroying family and community, and taking society to a dangerous destination. It also fosters a social practice of resistance, that is, while people may feel powerless to do anything about trendy Westernization, they can do something important for their own good by sticking to their familiarly dear Eastern ways of life. Indeed, for every step it takes on a Western track, many an Eastern society pauses for reflection and sometimes repentance due to a deep concern for ancestry, history, and tradition.

The third state of mind is endless ambivalence. This sentiment can run widely among those who advocate Western-style reform, those who long for return of the good old days as they remember them, and those who just follow the crowd or remain simply undecided and uncommitted. People in the camp of Western development wonder whether they have gone too fast or too far or whether they have taken the right track at all as they see widening economic gaps, rising civil unrest, and the alarming social disorganization which accompany rapid reform, opening-up, and modernization. People who want to hold on to Eastern tradition ponder whether they should have been more open-minded, flexible, or creative regarding Western ideas and practices when they witness expansion of productive capacities, upgrade of basic infrastructures, and improvement of general livelihood. Even people who just follow the crowd also question whether they should have been more reserved or forthcoming in making choices or whether they have done anything wrong when they remained undecided on and uncommitted to either Westernization or Eastern tradition. The social implication of such a widespread ambivalence is obvious: More time, energy, and resources are wasted on useless bickering and blame than on carrying out productive actions. As a result, developing societies in the East often remain chronically mired in indecision. Seemingly, they cannot take an assertive role in choosing their own development strategies or model.

THE FUTURE

Looking beyond the present, the thoughtful observer must ask whether there will be an integrative fusion of the East with the West. How likely is it that Eastern beliefs and values will be important in an increasingly Westernized world? While adherence to tradition by the East may serve as a background of reference, incorporation of Eastern civilizations in the postmodern era ironically lies with the West, given the existing dominance of Western development around the globe.

There then comes a natural question: What complementary yet indispensable assistance can Eastern civilizations possibly offer to Western development, especially in the matter of deviance, crime, social problems, and social control (Bursik and Grasmick 1993; Xu 1994; White 1996; Shaw 1998; Rountree and Warner 1999)? First of all, Eastern concern over cosmic harmony can help relieve the tremendous strain Western industrialization has created on nature. While a simple cultural orientation does not serve to halt the continuing exploitation of land, water, air, flora and fauna, and even outer space in the search for fossil fuels, metals, foods, and other natural resources, Eastern ways of thinking remind people of the need to keep balance or to restore balance when it is disturbed. Alternatives can be explored to a particular line of action driven solely by development. Actions can be taken before damage ever occurs irreversibly amid technological advance. Most subtly, humans resonate with nature in Eastern reasoning. When nature is out of equilibrium, society will by no means have peace, order, and tranquility. Indeed, to what extent can deviant, criminal, and otherwise problematic behaviors by people in Westernized societies be ultimately attributed to the polluted air they breathe, the contaminated water they drink, the engineered or inorganically grown food they eat, or the generally manmade environment they live in?

Second, Eastern attention to human relationships can help counteract an overgrown egoism or individualism brought about by Western development. With focus on self-interest and self-development, individuals in Western societies are not able to invest enough in familial, relative, and communal networks. Acting on their own, they are more likely than their counterparts in Eastern cultures to engage in imaginative, creative, adventurous, and at times deviant pursuits. As revealed by governmental statistics as well as comparative studies, crime almost always takes place at a higher rate in modern Western economies than in traditional Eastern territories. While it is nearly impossible to restore the power of family, kinship, and tribe in the context of developed and developing nations, it is intellectually insightful and pragmatically useful to draw upon the spirit of family, community, and human interconnectedness inherent in Eastern civilizations to approach various social problems facing Western-style development. For example, to what degree can business enterprises, professional bureaucracies, employee unions, occupational associations, interest clubs, charitable organizations, volunteer groups, and other cause-initiated or location-based networks be expanded and strengthened to provide individuals with a similar kind of advice, direction, sense of belongings, opportunity, support, protection, and/or restraint that gradually loosen and disappear from declining family, kinship, and other traditional groupings under modern and postmodern social conditions?

Third, Eastern civilizations can serve as critical references for Western development in three other vital areas. To the unlimited pursuit of wealth and pleasure emphasized by Western materialism, Eastern cultivation of morality, virtue, and conscience offers regulation and moderation. In pursuit of material success, individuals may violate social rules or infringe on the rights of others. An active conscience not only leads to self-discipline in the conduct of everyday behavior but also prompts a sense of guilt and thus an assumption of social responsibility for misdeeds. To the overwhelming emphasis on conquest and domination under Western ideology, Eastern emphasis on inner peace and fulfillment provides the rationale for retreat and reflection. Indeed, social order can be less problematic when an individual's inner life provides resources for his or her outer life. Finally, to the overreaching goal of ultimate triumph there and then in Western worldview, Eastern attendance to happiness here and now renders choice and compromise. While lofty plans are likely to exert pressure and strain on individuals, a close-range, step-by-step approach to specific challenges may bring about truly favorable outcomes to life. After all, it is in existing earthly experience rather than in a dreamed of heavenly fantasy that the quality of life in particular and the prosperity of society in general are ultimately measured.

As Eastern ideas and ideals become integrated into Western development, they can be modified and enriched by the new experience of materialistic modernization. For example, between humans and society, it is important to acknowledge institutional constraints relative to individual endeavors. In a society where fundamental structural defects exist, abuse of power, corruption, and social disorganization may still run out of control in spite of serious efforts by conscientious individuals. Between mind and material means, it is critical to recognize benefits, tangible incentives, or realistic mechanism compared to beliefs, spiritual orientations, or habitual adherence. It is plainly simple that trash can be removed, graffiti prevented, and poverty eliminated only through effective policies in law, law enforcement, investment, and growth. Similarly, between routines, customs, or normal ways of life and extraordinary actions, exigent measures, or even wayward adventures, it is sometimes necessary to resort to the extreme in order to save the conventional. Malignant tissues or a decaying body part must be quickly contained or drastically removed by way of Western medicine before a person can live and live long enough to benefit from the idea and practice of Eastern medicine about balancing *yin* with *yang*, maintaining functions of *qi*, and healing through nature.

Overall, the critical emphasis on family, human relationship, and communal interdependence in Eastern civilizations serves as a collective surveillance over individuals and a public deterrence against deviant or criminal behaviors. When conflicts and victimization occur, people embedded in their closely-knit community tend to resolve disputes and carry out appropriate compensation plans by themselves. Toward offenders, there seems to be a clear public preference for reforming them by imparting positive thoughts and useful skills rather than casting them further into criminality by way of sheer punishment. Western development, in contrast, has led to a declining family and community, growing individualism and alienation, rising social tension and conflict, and increasing criminality and deviancy. The adversarial legal system pits offenders against morality, authority, and the social establishment. The prison network paradoxically serves as a school base for training career criminals rather than as a correctional facility for bringing inmates back to the mainstream population. Although professional groups and the middle class have emerged to bridge the remote state with a citizenry of self-interest, there are still many individuals caught in between, with neither adequate communal attachment nor proper social regulation.

While each faces and fosters specific deviances, crimes, and social problems, Eastern civilizations and Western development also share some common concerns and challenges. For instance, the Eastern emphasis on education combined with the Western standardization of the educational process may put young people under peer pressure for some group-favored but socially disapproved of behavior in school. A common teaching by Buddhist monks, masters of Taoism, or fortunetellers that urges people to give up worldly possessions they have earned through Western-style employment may direct wealth to abbeys, monasteries, temples, and even specific individuals who issue advice in the name of religion or virtue. After all, what lies ahead is a dynamic of mutual penetration, complementary supplementation, and joint fusion between Eastern civilizations and Western development. Across Asia and the Pacific where the dynamics take the center stage, it is most inspiring to see how developing societies in Eastern civilizations keep their cultural heritage to curb rising deviance and crime in their pursuit of a Western-style development, as well as how developed countries in Western traditions apply characteristic Eastern ideas and measures of social control to contain challenging social problems in their continuing drive toward material prosperity.

21

Democratic Forms of Government and Authoritarian Leadership

As widespread as the region itself, a broad variety of governments and leadership styles exist throughout Asia and the Pacific. There are long established democracies, such as Australia, Canada, Japan, and the United States. There are recently installed democratic forms of government, including those in Indonesia, the Philippines, South Korea, the former Soviet republics of Central Asia, and the island of Taiwan. China and Vietnam are one-party socialist states. North Korea and some small kingdoms in the Pacific may even qualify as family or tribe-based totalitarian regimes or dictatorships (Durutalo 1992). The style of leadership is even more diverse, crossing categorical lines between one-party dictatorship and multi-party democracy, socialist state and capitalist government, and traditional kingdom and modern administration. For instance, socialist China practices collective leadership within its one-party dictatorship whereas capitalist Singapore exhibits traces of patriarchal authoritarianism in its democratic form of government, especially under the rule of Lee Kuan-Yew (Seow 1990).

THE PAST

Forms of government and styles of leadership obviously affect societal reactions to criminality and deviancy. A hereditary dictator can by no means be more tolerant of public rebellion than an elected leader. Forms of government and styles of leadership both also influence the social conditions in which crime, deviance, and social problems occur. While democracy tends to leave room for individual deviation, dictatorship is often found at fault for civil repression.

Democracy derives from the Greek term "demokratia," meaning "the common people rule." As a form of government, democracy has taken various forms. The oldest and the most original form was Athenian democracy in which people gathered at one place to directly exercise the power of making decisions for their own city-state. However, because it is difficult to muster all the people of a certain territory in one place for the purpose of voting, direct democracy as it existed in ancient Athens and other small communities rarely expands to larger political entities. On the level of nation-states and above, an operationally feasible and a historically common mechanism is representative democracy, under which the people elect government members or representatives to handle political affairs in accordance with the people's fundamental interests. Representative democracy branches off into two sub-forms. Liberal democracy requires that a ruling government be subject to the rule of law whereas illiberal democracy does not place any effective limits on the power of elected officials during the term of office. As a result, governments elected by a democratic majority range from those that genuinely respect the people and their inviolable rights, to those that only cater to the interests of special groups, and to those that openly encroach on the liberty of individuals or minorities (Lijphart 1999; Birch 2001).

Despite an increasingly positive connotation associated with the term, there are fundamental problems or paradoxes inherent in democracy and a democratic form of government. The most noticeable is "the tyranny of the majority" in which a government reflecting the majority view may act without regard for the interests of the minority; or a politically active, shrewd, dominant minority may tyrannize another minority in the name of the majority (Mill 1974; De Tocqueville 2003). Another unsettling issue with democracy is that it leads to a so-called plutocracy. Indeed, the cost of election campaigning gives the rich, a small minority of the voters, a likely insurmountable advantage over all other population segments in political competitions. Overloading the bureaucracy is yet another drawback related to democracy. With a short-term focus, a newly elected government may unnecessarily change the law or spew out a flood of new laws, confusing the populace while causing error, slowdown, and overall ineffectiveness in law enforcement. Democracy may also merit some blame for political apathy by the general public, a lack of effective response during wartime, racial conflict, and ethnic hostility. While democratization in former Yugoslavia, the Caucasus, and Moldova resulted in ethnic cleansing or civil war, anti-immigrant populism has always had a following in established democracies across Asia, Europe, and North America.

The history of democracy is replete with unfortunate occurrences. Socrates was executed for impiety in ancient Athens, a direct democracy; Great Britain, a representative democracy, levied taxes on many of its colonies around the world from the eighteenth century to the nineteenth century; the United States maintained a system of slavery for decades; and in the 1930s the Weimar Republic elected the Nazi party to power. On various specific matters, abortion legislation or antiabortion legislation is passed in accordance with the religious attitudes of the majority, drug use is declared legal or illegal on the basis of public acceptance or tolerance, homosexuality is criminalized or accepted consistent with the sexual mores of the general population, pornography is prohibited in terms of a so-called community standard of decency, a wealthy minority is discriminatively taxed to the benefit of a democratically run welfare state, and a poor minority is often repressively cornered into criminality, poverty, or political disenfranchisement for the sake of an apparently prosperous society.

Authoritarianism, on the other hand, refers to a form of government where the state demands obedience from citizens through use of restrictive measures of social control. The term also describes individual leaders who seek dominance in their sphere of influence without much concern for building consensus. Just as authoritarian regimes range from absolute monarchies, dictatorships, and totalitarian states to one-party monopolies, authoritarian leaders or leaderships vary from coldhearted despots or ruthless warlords on the one extreme to caring familial patriarchs or benevolent tribal headsmen on the other.

While authoritarianism carries a generally negative overtone in political debates, it has aroused much hope and has achieved some notable success throughout the developing world. A number of economies have witnessed growth under authoritarian leadership. Malaysia, Singapore, South Korea, and Taiwan, all in Asia, scored phenomenal economic growth with comprehensive development plans adopted by their authoritarian governments. There then comes an argument that a developing country can benefit more from developmental authoritarianism than from parliamentary democracy because the developing country needs to concentrate all its attention, energy, and limited resources for a critical take-off from economic poverty and backwardness into development and social progress. Factional bickering, power struggle, and political indecisiveness typical of democracy only serve to scare off foreign investment, dampen inner motivation to learn technology and advanced management skills, and therefore keep a country in helpless paralysis. In Singapore, Lee Kuan Yew practiced his version of developmental authoritarianism not only in various domains of political economy, but also in a wide range of aspects for social conduct. He purportedly touted Singapore's restrictive social conduct laws as "a way to force civility onto a Third World country."

Social control indeed remains widespread, strong, and at times repressive even under some soft authoritarian states, such as China, Singapore, and South Korea. To justify a heavy-handed social control policy, most authoritarian regimes and their leaders say that they know what is right for the people and their overall welfare and that they do what is necessary for the country and its long-term interests. Just as a patriarchal household head disciplines his children while providing them with foods, shelter, care, and education, an authoritarian government or leader seems to feel no sorrow for the imposition of harsh measures, such as censorship, curfew, crackdown, and even outright violence, upon ordinary citizens as long as it preserves and protects the country, the homeland. Although a few developmentally oriented states can cite economic growth and overall social prosperity as their achievement, many authoritarian regimes ultimately find themselves in economic stagnation and poverty. Deviance, crime, and social problems among civilians may hover at a low level amid repressive control by the regime and a generally low volume of exchange, interaction, and productivity across society. Corruption, abuse of power, and dereliction of duty within the regime and among members of the ruling class, however, often become rampant. For example, the Philippines did not experience any rapid growth while losing much of its national treasury to the construction of luxury palaces, the collection of exotic items, and the balance of private bank accounts under the authoritarian rule of Ferdinand Marcos. North Korea might boast of itself as a haven where people did not worry much about being criminally victimized on the street under the partly patriarchal and partly totalitarian control of Kim and the Kim family. But ordinary Koreans in the North seemed to have struggled every day to provide food on the table at their own homes. Most critically, what other sufferings did North Koreans bear from time to time when their great then dear Leader acted unilaterally without public consent yet often erratically on the world stage?

THE PRESENT

Democracy is now a catchword for almost every possible category of people, both the rich and the poor, politicians and non-politicians, or conservative rightists and liberal leftists. Economically disadvantaged groups favor democracy as it allows them to wander, demonstrate, offend, or suffer in public streets. People of wealth savor democracy because it renders them opportunity and legitimacy to manipulate, co-opt, legislate, and rule the masses and public behavior in political arenas. On the world stage, leaders of established democracies advocate democratic ideas and practices in the hope of becoming some kind of avant-garde in human progress, while dictators, monarchists, and other authoritarian heads of state seem also willing to engage in pre-arranged show elections and other democratic ploys for the purpose of ensuring the stability and longevity of their regimes.

Statistically, democratic forms of government correlate positively with a wide range of socioeconomic indicators (Berggren 1999; Choi 2004; Siegle, Weinstein, and Halperin 2004). First of all, democratic countries score points lower on the human poverty index and higher on the per capita gross domestic product as well as on the human development index than their non-democratic counterparts. Secondly, democratic nations show a higher level of political stability and continuity because election provides an institutional procedure for shift of government and policies without violence, coup d'etat, and general social chaos that so commonly accompany political change under authoritarian rule. Thirdly, democratic societies tend to make more prudent and balanced policies as public consultation and parliamentary debates invite input from different population segments in a given time span. Fourthly, a democratic state seems to be able to render a higher level of happiness for its citizens since it fosters a civil society where people can feel free to express opinions and, develop and prosper among and for themselves. Even against the backdrop of escalating racial and ethnic conflicts in various parts of the world, the increase of democratic states upon the fall of communism has actually brought about a decline in warfare, including interstate wars, ethnic wars, and revolutionary wars, as well as in the number of refugees and displaced people around the globe.

In the immediate area of deviance, crime, and social control, democratic societies experience a lower level of corruption than non-democratic societies (Lederman, Loayza, and Scares 2005; Transparency International 2006). Toward its own people, a democratic government is less likely to commit violence and human rights abuses; and in the community of nations, it is more willing to resolve disputes or manage differences through peaceful negotiation. Because there exist more safety valves for social tension, there appears to be a lower likelihood that racial, ethnic, cultural, and religious clashes will balloon into barrages of terrorist attacks under democratic environments. In fact, despite public rhetoric, research shows that terrorism is least common in nations with the most political freedom (Powell 2004). There are, of course, causes for caution and concern. At a phenomenal level, countries in transition to democratic forms of government are witnessing increased individual freedom, growing private initiative in economic and political arenas, loosened state control, and diversified social regulations. This combinational dynamic is seen to be fueling unlimited personal motivation as well as ample social opportunity for deviancy and criminality. Even in established democracies, any initiative, either for a greater or smaller democratic exercise, can pose new challenges to establishments for social control. For example, a more democratic form of policing, as it gives offenders more of a legal leeway to avoid arrest or prosecution, often inadvertently motivates people to deviate from social norms and commit crimes.

On the other hand, in societies under a non-democratic form of government or with an authoritarian leadership, it is common to see patriarchal tradition, media censorship, civilian surveillance, restrictive laws, and even unusual punishments in place for the sheer purpose of social control. While authoritarian practices serve as deterrence to deviance and crimes in some countries, they spawn systematic human rights abuses and chronic civil liberties violations, a common form of crime by government against citizenry, in many others. Across Asia and the Pacific, Human Rights Watch (HRW) reports incidents ranging from disturbing to grave in association with authoritarianism, authoritarian government in particular, in various countries each year. In 2005, documented records by HRW include persecution of the Ahmadiyya community in Bangladesh, restrictions on AIDS activists in China, exploitation of child domestic workers in Indonesia, abuse of Internal Security Act detainees in Malaysia, disappearances of individuals arrested by security forces in Nepal, police beatings, rape, and torture of children in Papua New Guinea, and mistreatment of migrant domestic workers in Singapore. Moreover, authoritarianism often leads to civil disobedience, public riots, and social rebellion in such forms as terrorism and guerrilla warfare. The connection has been proved by one country after another in Latin America, South and Southeast Asia, and the Middle East, especially those caught between Western-style democracy in form and native, patriarchal, or Eastern authoritarianism in content (Lozada 2005).

An interesting observation, an exception perhaps, is that countries with a non-democratic form of government may have an indecisive leadership process or style, providing structural loopholes for criminality and deviancy by individual opportunists. In China, for instance, collective leadership and mass participation within the communist party's one-party framework not only hamper general political decision-making processes, but also hamstring social reactions to deviance and crime. Corporate and bureaucratic crimes take place frequently within a supposedly tightly controlled system. Many crimes of opportunity go undetected and untreated at the expense of victims and to the general harm of the state.

Finally, from a cross-border point of view, the contrast between democracy and authoritarianism among governments around the world provides motivation for migration of people, transfer of wealth, and exchange of information. It is widely known that some dictators send their children, relatives, and confidants to study and live in established democracies while ruling their country with an iron hand; some authoritarian business executives vacation in luxury resorts afforded by market economies while extracting pennies from their poor employees; some dogmatic intellectuals draw financial and intellectual support from the free media and from scholarships given in the West while defending control and authoritarian practices in their home society. Now on a grand scale, prostitutes leave traditionally patriarchal communities to practice in open, bustling metropolises; drug users enter free societies to continue a nonproductive habit; former social perverts engage in declared conversion to religiosity, manhood or womanhood, or citizenship in pursuit of the opportunity to follow their favored lifestyle; and even out-and-out criminals can move from one country to another to avoid prosecution or to face lesser punishment. Indeed, the coexistence of democracy and authoritarianism not only provides opportunities for normative deviation and criminal undertaking, but also creates pressures for law enforcement and social control on both sides of the political divide.

THE FUTURE

In spite of its growing popularity, democracy is not necessarily bound to become a universal model for government or other institutions in tomorrow's world. Similarly, authoritarianism will not disappear completely because it is out of fashion or trend. Even by a time when all governments in the community of nations adopt democracy in form, authoritarian leaders and leaderships will still find their way in both the making of substantive policies and the conducting of political affairs. Most important, humans are forever imaginative, innovative, and creative. Human civilizations are forever dynamic, evolving, and progressive. Besides democracy and authoritarianism, there will be many alternatives emerging for human organization, social institution, and political process. For example, voting over the internet not only raises the prospect of direct rather than representative democracy, but also points to the possibility of diversified versus centralized decision-making in the future.

In justice, a fundamental issue facing democracy is how it determines what is right by way of logic, according to established laws or principles, or in an absolutist sense. As it stands now, democracy essentially makes few assumptions about what should be or ought to be in terms of conscience, morality, historical tradition, or social convention. It remains open and ready to accept largely what is to emerge amid competition by various social elements and forces. It often follows whoever or whatever prevails out of competition even when the prevailing side or party is principally wrong. The matter of illegal immigration in the United States serves as an illustrative example. Many immigrants entered the country illegally. Once in the country, they seek employment, drive on public roads, use social services, and benefit from welfare programs, all against the terms of the law. However, when illegal immigrants stay long enough and their numbers grow large enough, they can go out to the streets or onto the political stage and demand amnesty, residency, protection, and citizenship. In front of a huge protesting crowd of illegal immigrants, mainstream society frequently yields, as do political parties and their leaders (Bernstein 2006).

For democracy to sustain and thrive, there obviously need to be some mechanisms in place to overcome excessive relativism concerning conscience, law, and morality. The need is especially evident where the balance between the majority and the minority changes constantly and neither major party seems to have settled set of beliefs, norms, and values. Even in established democracies, much work remains to be done before justice can be equitably delivered without weight unwarrantedly given to loud yet undeserving trumpeters. In the matter of law enforcement, there is also a great deal of work ahead to minimize discriminatory practices that so often exist. In other words, neither the majority nor the minority should bear more surveillance or punishment because they are more noticeable. For instance, use of obscenities on ethnic broadcasting networks should be monitored and penalized just as it is in the mainstream media under promulgated laws or regulations.

Authoritarianism, in contrast, needs to address the issue of what is wrong if it is to keep a place for itself in a more open and informed world. It becomes increasingly difficult for any diehard authoritarians, such as monarchists, despots, and warlords, who cannot see anything wrong in their rule, to continue their old ways to foster their own sense of security. For authoritarian leaders, facing what is wrong is to admit limits and exercise restraint while using the power inherent in their authority. Patriarchal authoritarians tend to claim that they work in the best interest of their subjects. If they do so, they need to know that they can err in their determination of a subject's best interest, that they can be wrong in striving for certain goals, and that they can be at fault in their disciplining of wayward subjects. For instance, just as standardized education does not suit every child of any household, economic modernization is not a universal answer to the problems of every community under a developmentally authoritarian government.

Similarly, leaders in favor of an authoritarian style in an essentially democratic form of government tend to bet on the political capital they assume they have won from an election. If indeed they do have legitimacy to pursue a particular agenda, they still must understand that they expose a nation to danger when they declare war without universal support, that they take a country to bankruptcy when they engage in drastic measures without open consultation, and that they poison public morale when they pursue overly partisan, sectarian, and otherwise divisive policies. Throughout Asia and the Pacific, there is no lack of negative precedents when authoritarianism gains currency in either democratic or non-democratic political contexts. The United States, for example, must keep itself fully aware of what can go wrong with its democratic form of government to avoid a repetition of history: being stuck in an unpopular war, being driven into a deep deficit, and being caught in various controversial policies or practices, such as eavesdropping against its own citizens without warrant and imprisonment of foreign suspects without trial.

Between democracy and authoritarianism, there will be far more mutual penetration and joint fusion of specific elements and forces besides the general interface of either democratic leaders pursuing an authoritarian style or authoritarian regimes seeking democratic legitimization. In the field of deviance, crime, and social control, while people are inclined to follow their authoritarian government to implement control and intolerance in every other sphere of life, they may take special efforts to foster, protect, and cherish some democratic practices against a generally authoritarian backdrop. Likewise, while institutions, businesses tend to model after their democratic state to collect input, resolve differences, and manage business affairs, they may use an often taken-for-granted democratic context to smuggle, justify, and cover various authoritarian practices. China is a non-democratic country. But it is only in China where power lies in a collective political bureau rather than a single-person presidency. Singapore is a democratic nation. But it is only in Singapore where caning juveniles for delinquent behavior, prohibiting chewing gums and drinking cokes in public places, and implementing other old-fashioned measures of social control are realities. Although some of its practices have drawn criticisms from human rights groups around the world, at times even prompted diplomatic interventions from foreign dignitaries, Singapore demonstrates that some Eastern forms of social control and patriarchal practices can go hand in hand with Western styles of democracy and development. In fact, with China, Vietnam, and other economies growing under developmental authoritarianism, Singapore's recipe of combinations may become a trend for social control in the future, especially across Asia and the Pacific.

Overall, democracy and authoritarianism are two contrasting forms of government and leadership in the world of power and politics. Democracy is popular but does not necessarily suit every nation through different stages of political evolution. Authoritarianism sounds out of fashion but still holds appeal to various states, organizations, and stakeholders, including some elected officials in democratic environments. As far as deviance, crime, and social control are concerned, democracy keeps government in check in such matters as corruption, abuse of power, violation of human rights, and use of repressive measures while promoting competition, conflict, and rivalry among individuals and interest groups. Authoritarianism, on the other hand, focuses a nation on one goal, commits a country to one agenda, and unifies a state under one ideology, often to a degree that deprives common citizens of their basic rights to freedom, property, and even silence. In the global dynamics of political reform, economic development, and social progress, however, it is fascinating to see how democracy and authoritarianism impact each other, resulting in new forms of government and new styles of leadership as well as new varieties of crime or deviance and new measures of social control around the world.

22

Citizen Initiative and the State Authority

Citizen initiative and community action may take different forms in crime and social control (Bursik and Grasmick 1993; Frate 1997). Citizens can take precautions against criminal victimization and the community can remain alert to it. When conflicts arise and crimes occur, citizens can take the initiative in dispute resolution, victim compensation, and offender rehabilitation, and the community can provide support (Xu 1994). State authorities, on the other hand, rely mainly on lawmaking, law enforcement, and the administration of justice for all walks of life in society. In relation to the citizenry, a weak state is likely to result in the resurgence of local tyrants and bandits. An unjust and corrupt state is likely to spawn mass vigilance, self-help, and local justice. Employing community groups as go-betweens, the state can install grassroots organizations for citizens to play a role in conflict resolution and crime prevention. It can also use group activities to limit individual initiative. It may even manipulate community actions and grassroots efforts in the service of social control or to the benefit of a favored social order.

THE PAST

Across Asia and the Pacific, there are undeveloped and developing societies where villagers guard their vital interests, resolve their daily disputes, and administer their age-old justice without any interference from the remote state. There are developed and developing countries where the state maintains a universal presence in every corner of society and citizens may have to expose every aspect of their private life, including domestic affairs and bedroom secrets, to legal scrutiny. There are socialist states that organize individual residents into neighborhood committees and mass campaigns to build a united defense against deviance and crime (Shaw 1996). There are capitalist corporations that advocate self-regulation as well as individualistic citizens who strive for private space and civil liberties.

The apparent diversity seems to provide an overview of what has happened over the course of history. Self-help represents the earliest and most widespread form of civil initiative by which individuals seek revenge, redress injustice, and build a network of control or support in the absence of authority and governmental protection. Reflective of the spirit of self-help is a tradition of vigilantism in the West. Vigilante, whose Latin root *vigil* denotes "awake" or "observant," is of Spanish origin, meaning "guard" or "watchman." Vigilantism, as practiced by vigilantes, is variously seen as "taking the law into your own hands," "secret policing" in the shadow of a formal law enforcement force, or "morally sanctimonious" behavior aimed at rectifying or remedying a "structural flaw" in society (Brown 1975). Examples of vigilantism hence abound, ranging from the Militia Clause of the United States Constitution, the Self-Defense Doctrine, the Right to Resist Arrest, Good Samaritan statutes, the Concealed Handgun Debate, and Road Rage to Digilantism in the high-tech era. As far as the state is concerned, however, vigilantes are often viewed as equally troublesome as many criminals, deviants, and other enemies of society despite the fact that vigilante groups see themselves as attempting to act as friends of society.

In North America, vigilantism arose during the 1700s when resident volunteers gathered in vigilance committees to blacklist, harass, flog, torture, mutilate, or kill those whom they perceived to be threats to their lifestyles, families, or communities. Vigilance committees became known as lynch mobs in some places where they carried out summary executions by hanging. In other places, they were called the regulators or given some exotic names because they worked to keep general social order or targeted specific groups or acts for revenge or punishment. With the absence of a formal criminal justice system, vigilantism developed into a way of life for much of the 1800s. In many American towns with seaports, vigilante groups openly looked for suspects in stealing, gambling, addictive use of alcohol, and other undesirable behaviors among newly arrived immigrants. Punishment was often meted out at will. Vigilante activities were particularly prevalent in frontier states or borderland areas, such as the Deep South and the Old West.

Montana, for example, witnessed some of the bloodiest vigilante movements in which hundreds of horse thieves were rounded up and killed in massive mob action (Karmen 1968).

Vigilantism declined overall in the early 1900s as the state rose to dominance. It, however, did not disappear totally from the scene of self-help. In new forms, neo-vigilantism has fueled such vigilante activities as antiabortionist movements, bounty hunting for fugitives, neighborhood crime watch, and border security patrols. While Pseudo-vigilantism continues to provide moral and legal justifications for cases of controversial self-defense where citizens kill suspected offenders to ward off anticipated attacks, cyber-vigilantism is just making its debut in the chase for auction defrauders, plagiarists, spammers, sexual predators, terrorists, and other lawbreakers on the internet.

On the other side of the Pacific, self-help at times evolved into localized controls by mountain bandits, territorial tyrants, or regional warlords. In China, bandits routinely took control of roads, mountains, and remote villages when imperial officials failed to perform duties in their sphere of power. There were rounds of organized rebellion against imperial establishments in the spirit of self-help, fueling the cyclical change of one ruling dynasty after another. One of the civilian self-help movements best known to the West was the Boxer Rebellion of 1900 in which people rose to expel all "foreign devils" as they watched Western powers encroaching further and further upon their land while the imperial Qing government fell more and more into total hopelessness (Preston 2001). The ultimate replacement of the feudal dynasty by the National People's Government, however, did not do much to stem the need for self-help. In fact, when famine struck the countryside, many law-abiding citizens turned to banditry as a means of survival. Compounding the problem of economic depression, the National People's Government sent the majority of its troops to put down rebellions in the major areas of revolt across the country, leaving a large number of places vulnerable to bandits and gangster attacks. For nearly half a century during the nationalist reign, bandit gangs remained chronically active in both rural and urban settings. While most of them held up local merchants and villagers for money, a few laid claim to territories as expansive as a few counties with members and associates numbered in thousands (Yuan 1995). As stated pointedly by Bishop D. T. Huntington of the American Church Mission, "the officials are doing nothing to help the people, reducing them to a state where banditry is the only means left to them to obtain a livelihood" (Associated Press 1930).

The founding of the People's Republic ushered in a new era of state control. Warlords, bandits, gangsters, and local tyrants were oppressed as reactionary elements. Drug addicts, prostitutes, gamblers, vagrants, and homeless beggars were reformed into productive citizens. Deviant behaviors were clearly defined, intensely shamed, and pointedly dealt with. For example, homosexuality was considered as taboo, belief in superstition was exposed as total ignorance, and inclination to practice religion was attacked as complete infirmity of purpose. Within the criminal justice system, thought reform was instituted as a standard procedure to transform inmates into socialist new men and women. Labor was uniformly forced upon convicts so that they could make useful contributions to the revolutionary cause. Throughout society, citizen initiatives were allowed only in areas where they were deemed necessary, manageable, and productive by the authority toward overall social unity. Grass-roots movements were nipped in the bud if they ever posed a threat to Communist rule. The Great Cultural Revolution provided a vivid illustration: Civil militia became ever popular and powerful because they were integrated into the official control apparatus whereas red guards soon lost favor and influence as they stayed loose from the state bureaucracy (Editorial Board 1990; Xu 1995).

In the West, although there was no openly staged revolution in domestic politics, the state was able to increase its strength, presence, and influence significantly in the climate of a Cold War with the communist world. The military machinery was forever growing and intimidating. The espionage network was forever expanding and penetrating. And technology for battleground confrontations as well as for non-battlefield controls was forever innovating and sharpening. On domestic fronts, public surveillance, curtailment of civil rights, media censorship, restriction on street protests, and other control measures were imposed from time to time in the name of resistance against communism, suppression of dangerous subversion, renewal of noble patriotism, or the war on terrorism. In the United States, McCarthyism gained currency in political affairs and threw the entire populace into the so-called Second Red Scare for almost a decade from the late 1940s to the middle 1950s. Blacklisting, purging, and imprisonment continued even through the 1960s for many identified social liberals, including artists, musicians, writers, scientists, and free-lance intellectuals, out of a simple suspicion of an alleged sympathy toward communism and the Soviet Union (Fried 1997).

In the more proper domain of crime control in the United States, the dominance of the state government was epitomized in the thriving prison industrial productions and later the popularity of the rehabilitation model throughout the correctional system. In the early part of the twentieth century, use of inmate labor was so widespread, systematic, and organized that the whole prison system developed into a prudent financial operation, turning out a variety of industrial goods for sale on the open market. It took the serious resistance of organized labor, the Great Depression, and restrictive clauses of law to push prison products out of interstate commerce (Flynn 1950). After a rather turbulent "period of transition," American corrections shifted its emphasis to the needs of individual prisoners. Treatment ideas and regimens were explored and tested; academic and vocational programs were designed and implemented; social workers, clinicians, and other trained professionals were brought in to administer social casework advisement, psychological counseling, and psychiatric therapies; special institutions were opened for youthful or amateur offenders in separation from adult or hardcore criminals; and prison facilities were overall expanded. The rehabilitation model reigned through the 1960s and the 1970s (Allen and Simonsen 1981). While it eventually lost its glory when critical evaluations seemed to reveal that nothing worked, the rehabilitation effort in a sense reflected the overreaching ambition of a full-fledged state in mobilizing all its social resources to transform control subjects in accordance with the desired social order (Lipton, Martinson, and Wilks 1975).

THE PRESENT

At present, most Asian and Pacific societies embrace a mixture of citizen initiative, community action, and state intervention in crime and social control (Bursik and Grasmick 1993; Dorfman 1997; Geiss 2001). In China, while the state-coordinated network of neighborhood committees is being loosened amid increasing social mobility, there appears a resurgence of local tyrants, mountain bandits, and clan-based justice in vast rural areas under the seemingly omnipresent communist authority. In the United States, middle-level community actions, such as the neighborhood watch, seldom gain popularity and momentum due to a lack of interest from citizens and a lack of incentives by the state. There are, however, two forces active in the relatively inactive community. American citizens stay vigilant and are long-habituated to self-help while various levels of American government remain alert and are well equipped to enforce the law in every corner of society. Gun control measures stall repeatedly in federal, state, and local legislatures because gun ownership is endogenously related to the deep-rooted tradition and sentiment of self-help (Kopel and Little 1999). The passage of a sweeping crime bill by Congress, on the other hand, provides strong evidence of the increased participation of the capitalist state in the field of crime and social control (Kramer and Michalowski 1995).

Against the backdrop of a phenomenal mixture of state policies with citizen initiatives, a few general observations seem valid and universal about crime and social control. First, the state, no matter whether it is strong or weak, whether it takes a civil law model or a common law framework, sits at the center of gravity for public order or lack of social control. The state makes law, legislating what people can do and what people cannot do. The state implements law, leaving one segment of the population to its likes or dislikes while placing another under surveillance, scrutiny, or custody. The state interprets law, delivering judgments as to whether a specific act constitutes a legal violation or whether a particular person deserves a penal treatment. In other words, the state takes a *de facto* lead in the definition of deviance, crime, and social problems as well as in the administration of punishment, justice, and control when it exercises its legitimate power of governance on a sovereign land.

Second, in the presence of an omnipresent state and its universally effective social control, citizen initiatives automatically become secondary, supplemental, or marginal. People make suggestions when they find loopholes in the system of law. Citizens voice concerns, worries, or resistance when they are left exposed, placed in danger, or pushed into deprivations of fundamental rights or basic interests by authority. People advocate for various social causes when they see critically important matters and issues drop out of the state policy loop. Citizens come together to clean the street, patrol the border, resolve disputes, fight crime, or reconcile victims with offenders when they are shortchanged in the delivery of justice, peace, and security by governmental bureaucracy. In a word, citizen initiatives take place often in times when public safety needs are not properly attended by the state or only at a place where there is a void left by the authority and its universal social control.

Third, depending upon the nature of the state, citizen initiatives can grow into either co-opted alliances or organized resistance, either citizen surveillance or civil disobedience, and either constructive supplement or disruptive challenge. Kinship groups, tribes, unions, occupational associations, religious organizations, and even interest clubs—each serves to discipline members, coordinate membership activities, and maintain rule or order within their respective spheres of influence. Communal surveillance, mediation, and citizen justice are natural, secular, and traditional forces to defuse friction, smooth relationships, and keep peace among ordinary citizens. The state may recognize, encourage, and support some civil organizations while discrediting, discouraging, and suppressing other grass-roots activities. As a result, some citizen initiatives take to the national stage of control and order while other such initiatives fall into disrepute and out of sight. Across Asia and the Pacific, people witness from time to time tribal or indigenous resistance against industrial projects or developmental plans by the state, state repression of religious movements headed by sectionalists or secret cults, and social approval or disapproval of action taken by various interest groups. On the side of cooperation, there are not only socialist states incorporating civil mediation and citizen justice in their overall social control machinery, but also capitalist governments co-opting aboriginals, labor advocates, civil rights activists, religious leaders, and people of professional or other fame in their general attempt to keep order and peace.

Fourth, citizen initiatives, when they are tempered, harnessed, and integrated, can make a strong state stronger in policymaking, policy implementation, and maintenance of social order. By the same logic, citizen initiatives can make a weak state weaker in running everyday affairs, managing regular ups and downs, or just maintaining its authority if these initiatives are left to grow or spread. Understanding the nature of citizen initiatives, state authorities often engage in channeling, containing, and stemming them to ensure that these initiatives operate beneficially among ordinary people, along their normal lines of action, and within their regular social networks. When they fail in active manipulation, some national leaders may lose their power totally to mass revolutions or they may continue in office but live in constant fear of civil disobedience, social rebellion, or organized guerrilla warfare. In China, the state becomes more powerful when it organizes youth leagues, women's federations, democratic parties, unions, neighborhood committees, and various other civil interests into the overall communist control network whereas in the Philippines, people's revolutions seem only to make the government less coordinated, less resolute, and less stable in its endeavor to move toward a much-needed national agenda of fighting corruption, crushing separatism, and pursuing development.

Finally, citizen initiatives and state authorities are essentially different forces with different agendas as well as different outcomes. The state is faced with a whole society. It aims at maintaining social order and perpetuating its power. For the sake of stability, the state tends to invoke, both implicitly and explicitly, suppressive measures to keep various population segments and their activities in check or balance. Citizens, on the other hand, are confined to specific locales. They aspire to grow, expand, and self-actualize. In the interest of self-development, citizens are inclined to engage in both individual and collective expressive acts to gain attention or draw support from the social establishment. There is then a potential danger to the state in utilizing citizen initiatives in the matter of social control. In specific areas, the state loses its due oversight when some parts of a national border are left to citizen patrol, some pockets of a local community are given to neighborhood watch, or some details of a commercial or cultural transaction are yielded to professional judgment. Generally, the state could find itself out of balance when it allows for the overgrowth of a particular grass-roots movement. During China's Great Cultural Revolution, for example, Mao used red guards to fight bureaucratism but soon found himself in urgent need of institutional or bureaucratic means to maintain order and control (Shaw 2000). Similarly, there is always a real risk for citizens to align their initiatives with the state, especially in the area of safety, security, and public order. While in the United States civil rights movements, illegal immigrant protests, and other sweeping social advocacies have grown and become absorbed into mainstream politics, in many other parts of the world citizen initiatives are often forced underground or banished as paganisms, taboos, or the work of social outcasts.

THE FUTURE

What lies ahead with regard to the manner in which citizens act as well as the way in which the state acts in the matter of deviance, crime, and social control? Is there a possibility for citizen initiatives to fuse with state law and regulation in the interest of overall social order, peace, and prosperity?

On the part of citizenry, there seem to be two major trends under way. One trend is for citizens to become more and more informed, interconnected, and yet individualized. On social issues such as crime and control, they tend to form or develop their own ideas and approaches with information received from different sources, including radio, television, magazines, newspapers, books, travel, interpersonal contact, the internet, and other mass media or channels. Indeed, in the information age, people not only can maintain independent minds with multiple input, but also can inject their individual initiatives into the general social process through active participation. For example, they respond to opinion polls, sample surveys, or population censuses, translating their individual likes into general preferences, of which political, economic, cultural, and other social establishments must take notice. They speak out in the media, demonstrate in the street, or protest in public arenas, turning their personal feelings into social sentiments to which politicians, business executives, knowledge producers, and other authority figures must attend. Most important, people head to official polling stations, voting in candidates or policies they favor or voting out officials or measures they do not like. In the United States, it is a clear belief that individual attitudes form public opinion, public opinion exerts pressure on social establishments, and social establishments make necessary adjustments in policy and practice. Even in China, civilians begin to chat in cyberspace, and neighborly gossips in a community begin to figure in formal policymaking forums or stages.

There is no doubt that American reforms in immigrant policy as well as the Chinese government's campaigns against corruption have drawn from individually conceived and expressed opinions, wants, or initiatives by respective citizens in the two rather different countries. These trends will continue.

The other trend is for citizens to actively organize and take their initiatives as a group to the public stage through every available effective means, in spite of increasingly available channels for individual expression or action. There are generally three forms of organizing efforts. First is to form interest groups, raise funds, and focus on political lobbying for policy change. In the United States, gun owners fight fiercely against gun control legislations just as corporate interests spend heavily on legal measures aimed at tightening or loosening governmental regulation of business, both through general as well as specific lobbying at Capital Hill or in individual state houses. The second form of organizing effort is to solidify occupational or professional associations or traditional labor unions, expand influence, and cultivate membership loyalty. For instance, a state medical board operates primarily to protect members rather than discipline those members implicated in malpractice. It also exists to maintain a general social impression that it is the only legitimate authority to render expert judgment on matters of medicine and medical treatment. The third form is to dramatize both ends and means, confront the state, and develop into known resistance organizations. In undemocratic or otherwise closed societies where institutional avenues to voice individual opinion or to realize civilian interests are often unavailable or become blocked, underground movements, outlawed bandits, localized gangs, and distanced guerilla bands rise to public attention, challenging the state from within or outside the system. While the situation serves to alert the authority as to what it should or must do in the face of an organizing or initiative-taking citizenry, it sends a clear message to the populace that in this era of state and state dominance they need to merge interests, pool resources, and increase public knowledge of their cause by organizing. It is through organization, either legitimate or illegitimate, that individual citizens can make their most powerful statements or take the most compelling action in relation to the state.

State authority has three dimensions. One is the dimension of centralization versus decentralization. Centralization overall means that the state keeps power in its hand, leaving little freedom or autonomy to civilians, civilian interests, and civilian organizations in running their own affairs. However, when this centralization is present only within the sphere of government, it may actually create opportunities for civil sectors to grow in various areas as it weakens local governments that directly oversee citizens and citizen activities. Also, when power shifts from local levels to the center, a strengthening central government may be able to reach out to the populace, spreading its message, promoting its agenda, and implementing its program mainly from communal support or citizen initiatives. For example, a popular mayor may call on people in the city to scrutinize police officers or to organize neighborhood groups to watch closely the municipal police department and its various community divisions to ensure that law enforcement does not abuse power or neglect duty to the detriment of the city and its governing authority or at the expense of residents and their fundamental rights or vital interests. Similarly, decentralization does not necessarily lead to an increased involvement in policymaking or social control by citizens and nongovernmental interests. In fact, when decentralized power ends up only in the hand of local governments, grass-roots groups and their routine activities are likely to face close scrutiny, direct interference, or intense containment in their immediate environment. What can people expect to experience in their lives when a decentralized municipal police department opens branch offices or patrol stations in downtown districts, mid-city neighborhoods, suburban communities, and satellite towns? More pointedly, in the case of a currently decentralized war against terrorism across the United States, what will most American citizens be likely to see in the near future as almost every local law enforcement agency is taking advantage of the war to increase its force, broaden its presence, and deepen its influence?

Another is the dimension of politicization versus de-politicization. As a political machine, the state has a natural tendency to politicize almost every policy or program it implements. In crime and social control, the state is likely to link citizen initiatives to patriotism, national interests, regional security, or world peace. Although a politicized agenda sounds lofty, abstract, and remote, average citizens often resonate well with it in a national context, especially during times of crisis or war. For example, the September 11, 2001 terrorist attacks in the United States may even have prompted ordinary criminals to make some adjustments to an emerging political environment of renewed patriotism and increased alertness as suggested by crime statistics in the immediate aftermath of the attacks. Indeed, many addicts, prostitutes, vagrants, drug dealers, thieves, or street troublemakers may feel as much ashamed of being unpatriotic as any ordinary law-abiding citizens when patriotism becomes a national sentiment under an aggressive state's political campaign. However, from a long-term point of view, a government will fare much better in winning public support for its policy goals and objectives if it can de-politicize its political will, communicate its agenda in language understandable to the populace, tie its goals to activities common in secular life, and implement its policies by means familiar to ordinary citizens. Instead of using political slogans, a government can present its goals—a national struggle against illicit drugs, a statewide campaign for clean government, or a five-year crackdown on urban gangs—in concrete terms such as reduced numbers of incidents, increased measures of monitoring or reporting, and expected improvements in service, access, public safety, or quality of life. Most important, specific programs, whether drug treatment, drug education, bidding on governmental contracts, limits on political contributions, neighborhood curfew, provision of after-school care, or delivery of youth services, can be designed and developed to give people at grass-roots levels direct opportunities to participate and to gain tangible benefits.

Still another is the dimension of control versus service orientation. Control is what the state begins with as well as what the state ends with. In other words, it represents both a goal and a means for the state and its authority. As a goal, control means that the state feels safe and secure in its authority over a populace or within a territory. As a means, control may necessitate such extreme measures as subjugation, oppression, and violence to keep people quiet for a kind of social order desired by the ruling authority of a country. On the matter of crime and criminal justice in particular, the state has set up law enforcement, the court system, the correctional complex, and numerous programs or regimens within and across all three branches in its design of order and control. Now a typical state automatically takes all these control apparatuses under its wing, leaving some of them idle, some of them in production of unnecessary control, and some of them in pursuit of excessive repression against the citizenry. Given the situation, should the state take a new approach to put its all-out control operation into some different use so that it can bridge traditional divides, reach out to the general public, and integrate once-disfranchised sectors into the social whole? For example, the police can assist lost tourists, stranded motorists, or stressed business owners in their search for direction, protection, opportunity, and resources. The court can lend support to people when it resolves disputes, redresses injustice, and renders retribution or restitution concerning their individual, business, and professional interests. And the correctional system can bring peace, harmony, and productivity back to the community when it works with families, schools, service agencies, treatment facilities, employers, and other social establishments to create a reforming, learning, and integrating environment for people under its care or custody. In fact, when the state takes a service orientation, especially in its crime control operations, it may gain more in terms of fostering trust, building solidarity, maintaining social order, and winning public support than it would from a control-centered approach.

In all, while citizens need to organize themselves to be heard and heeded for their ideas and initiatives in front of an increasingly omnipresent state, the state needs to de-politicize its agendas, decentralize its operations, and take a service orientation to keep its power, legitimate its authority, maintain social order, and stay in control in the face of an increasingly educated, informed, and assertive populace.

23

Formalism and Informalism

Formalism as a social control philosophy emphasizes the importance of the state in making, interpreting, and enforcing laws universally across the general population. In particular, formalism stresses that the state deal fairly with lawbreakers. Informalism, on the other hand, acknowledges the influence of non-state institutions, such as family, kinship, and voluntary groupings, in preventing crimes, resolving disputes, and maintaining local peace (Abel 1982; Xu 1994; Rountree and Warner 1999; Geiss 2001). While formalism and informalism may ideally coexist as complementary approaches to crime and social control, each oftentimes needs to be strengthened, restrained, and fine-tuned in relation to the other.

Across Asia and the Pacific, there are traditional tribes versus modern societies, small kingdoms versus large republics, war-afflicted territories versus peace-oriented sovereignties, mass-based revolutionary states versus law-centered political entities, democratic bureaucracies versus authoritarian regimes, and capitalist nations versus socialist countries. Formalism often fails to play its role when the state is either too weak to cope with kinships, chiefdoms, warlords, and mass campaigns or too strong in the hands of the king, the charismatic leader, the strongman, or the dictator. Informalism usually exists where there is either an absence of written legal codes or a lack of universal enforcement of law. Both formalism and informalism, however, tend to fare well when rules are established within a governmental entity and are interpreted at the will of those in power.

THE PAST

Formalism has been widely used in a variety of substantive areas. In art, formalism focuses on artistic or literary techniques, fashioning a unique style of criticism that goes above and beyond the social and historical context of any specific work. In science, formalism emphasizes the use of axioms, notations, and rules in the symbolic presentation of information, fueling an enchanted pursuit of logical simplicity, beauty, and universality that are believed to lie deeply in the truth of nature. In religion, formalism stresses the observance of rituals and ceremonial procedures, setting practitioners apart or aloof from the actual meanings or purposes that particular ceremonies or rituals are initially charged to convey or reinforce. Philosophy seems to have captured the essence of the contrast with its original distinction between form and content. In philosophical terms, formalism generally refers to the idea of privilege of form over content. A person who believes or practices formalism tend to show an indiscriminate regard for rules and their established uses.

In the matter of law and social control, formalism appears to have made two important distinctions in separating form from content. First as a theoretical orientation, legal formalism maintains that law is a set of rules and principles independent of substantive political, economic, and social processes or institutions. Second as a structural guideline, legal formalism seeks to keep checks and balances in the exercise of power by different branches of government. Specifically, it argues that the judiciary should never be invested with the power to say what the law should be; its duty is to explain what the law says. While it commands a widely acknowledged success of application in the rule of law across almost all Western democracies, legal formalism exhibits obvious shortcomings. Beginning with its assumption, formalism does not acknowledge the reality that there are contradictions, gaps, and loopholes in every system of law and that legal decisions in the mundane world are often deduced aside from the logical process of formal reasoning. Focusing on its operation, formalism creates a false impression that all legal rules are made by the state and its agencies on behalf of the common citizenry and therefore become automatically imperative to all the people within the sovereign state. Looking into its consequence, formalism leads to brutal indifference to substantive justice where political, economic, ethical, and social factors are found to weigh heavily in generating and sustaining legal inequalities across the populace (Fuller 1977; Brooks 2005).

Informalism, on the other hand, does not appear wherever there is a presence of formalism. Although it finds its way in a broad range of domains from architecture, music, painting, sound, writing, and customer service to software engineering, informalism as a whole hardly points to an intellectual orientation or a stylistic pursuit that only emphasizes content over form, the opposite of formalism. In fact, a common thread through informalism across different domains is "alternative." Informalism refers to an alternative approach to what is formal, bureaucratic, recognized, or dominant or what is inefficient, time-consuming, wasteful, or tedious. As to crime and social control, legal informalism entails use of informal justice, such as mediation, arbitration, and other dispute-processing mechanisms, outside or prior to formal legal procedures. With informalism, people resolve their disputes, the community keeps its peace, and the state frees itself to focus on the maintenance of general social order, thus creating a seemingly win-win situation for all. In the eyes of critics, however, legal informalism seldom serves as a genuine alternative to the formal adversarial legal process. Instead, it increases the organizational complexity when it adds alternative forums to traditional judicial institutions. From a political point of view, legal informalism extends the power of the state at the expense of individual freedom and civil liberty (Garth 1982; Harrington 1982).

In Asia and the Pacific, as elsewhere around the world, formalism takes the lead when society shifts from mechanical solidarity to organic solidarity or, generally, from traditional ways of life to industrialization, urbanization, and modernization. Western ideas and practices spread. A formal justice system is set up. The state rises to dominance as the center of power to make, interpret, and enforce the law. While uniformity makes formalism appealing and attractive, gridlock occurs from time to time, especially when the economy grows to scale and social life turns multidimensional. In the United States, commercial clients found it increasingly frustrating to deal with the courts on claims and disputes, fueling a growing hostility toward formalism at the turn of the century. Although formalist proponents made various efforts, such as application of scientific management and adoption of a "business-like" approach, to implement and improve an efficient kind of formality of law, the "crisis of the courts" seemed to continue unabated amid a ballooning volume of civilian transactions throughout the population. Informalism thus arrived upon the scene. First appeared the Children's Court, serving as a non-criminalizing alternative for minors who are assumed to be most amenable to reform and correction. Then followed the emergence of the so-called "socialized courts" in the areas of business contracts, small claims, domestic disputes, and civilian relations, bridging formal justice procedures with further outlying social measures such as education, prevention, diagnosis, and treatment (Harrington 1982).

In the 1970s, informalism grew to be on a par with formalism in a wide variety of fields, from family, welfare, administrative matters, commercial dealings, and professional exchanges to equal opportunity grievances. According to Richard Abel, informal justice as it eschews "official law in favor of substantive and procedural norms that are vague, unwritten, commonsensical, flexible, ad hoc, and particularistic," is in an actually advantageous position to deliver justice on a mass of issues that remain "relatively undifferentiated from the larger society" (1982: 2). Also, because it minimizes "the use of professionals," informal justice is even able to break into some of the traditional turfs of formalism, encompassing various formal legal institutions that are "non-bureaucratic in structure" (1982: 2). On dispute processing in particular, Silbey and Sarat (1989) saw joint participation from the rank and file of both formalism and informalism, bringing in the establishment Bar and legal elites, as well as the "access to justice" movement, opponents of the "improved quality of law," and other social advocacy groups. In a similar spirit, Harrington and Merry (1988) characterized community mediation as a combinational attempt by both formalists and informalists to increase their respective presence, efficiency, and influence. On the part of formalism, there is a pragmatic concern to improve the delivery of legal services so that costs can be reduced, court congestion can be relieved, and access to the formality of law can be promoted. On the side of informalism, there is a vested interest by individual citizens to take greater control over their own lives. It is generally believed that through community mediation people can enhance their personal skills in dealing with conflict and therefore can live a freer, better, and happier life. In between is a "hope that society could be restructured through new forms of popular justice." In other words, is it possible for community mediation to become "completely independent of the judicial system, with its authority based in the local neighborhood rather than in the state" (Harrington and Merry 1988: 715)?

The contradictory coexistence of formalism with informalism was once subtly identified by Peter Fitzpatrick as popular justice becoming "both opposed and integral to" the formal system (1992: 199). While in some capitalist contexts a greater integration of informalism with formalism may be achieved as in the case of Australia where informalism and its success in the Family Court, community justice, and the commercial sphere have given it some appeal in the criminal justice system, a total overhaul of the formal system with informal justice can happen only through extraordinary measures, such as revolution, war, and change of government (Astor and Chinkin

1992). There is seemingly one example in contemporary history. That is China where law, the entire justice system, and the whole legal profession were suspended for years during the Great Cultural Revolution to allow ordinary people in high revolutionary spirits to carry out popular justice for themselves and against bureaucratism, tradition, and various other reactionary elements or forces.

THE PRESENT

The state of affairs for formalism, informalism, and their interactions in Asia and the Pacific is a rather complicated mixture, featuring regional differences, development gaps, cultural contrasts, system-to-system variations, and within-system contradictions.

Throughout the region, there are areas and countries that serve as strongholds of formalism, showcases of informalism, or battlegrounds for formalism to either win or yield to informalism. While North America to the East of the Pacific Ocean operates under a somewhat omnipresent dominance of formalism, the Continent of Asia as a whole still struggles back and forth between the formality of law and the convenience of informal justice. As a few aboriginal societies or indigenous tribes in Oceania and across the Pacific live idyllically in the spirit of informalism, a great many secular states or modernizing nations from Latin America to Southeast Asia to the Middle East are abruptly breaking away from their informalist tradition for a formalist system. Older ways of life continue, perpetuating tension between formalism and informalism. New social orders emerge, creating opportunities for formalists to confront, contain, or control their informalist counterparts or vice versa. Overall, regional differences are so striking and phenomenal that it is far from clear whether there exists any uniformity in the presence of formalism versus informalism across Asia and the Pacific.

Development is another dimension to appreciate in the wide-ranging differentials of formalism, informalism, and their combinational influence. In developed countries, the state has long been a primary, if not always exclusionary, force in crime and social control. While non-state institutions often take blame for rising crime rates, they are never entrusted with power and necessary social resources to play an active role in crime prevention and intervention. In the United States, for example, it has become a well-institutionalized practice that domestic problems, such as child disciplining and spousal disputes, fall under the designated jurisdiction of the state rather than the customary court of the family when they take a violent or abusive form as defined by the state authority. In developing societies, although formalism has yet to prevail as an overarching social defense against crime and deviance, informalism seldom plays a sweepingly dominant role in general social control. Modernist critics attack age-old institutions and conventions as harmful and obstructive to the rule of law. Conservatives lament a decaying civil tradition, a declining family, and a crumbling community network in dealing with widespread social dislocation, deviance, and crime. Informalism is weakened with blame, suspicion, and distrust from both sides of the social mainstream.

Culture offers still another window through which to peruse the contrasts of formalism in comparison to informalism throughout Asia and the Pacific. Western culture permeates bureaucracy, organization, and other formal structural setups. In a governmental bureaucracy, there are first formal rules, positions, and responsibilities. Informal etiquette, roles, and obligations only fill in the space left out by an overreaching net of formality. In a corporate or professional organization, there is first a leading chain of command, then a formal channel of communication, and thirdly a systematic process of reward and penalty. Informal networks, the grapevine, and recognition or dislike by peers only grow in the outer space of off-work contacts, such as breaks, vacations, and incidental encounters at large. Eastern culture, on the other hand, permeates family, community, and the natural network of acquaintances, friends, schoolmates, workmates, teammates, or townsmen. Among closely related participants in a communal network, misunderstandings, disputes, and ill-feelings are handled informally through back-and-forth contacts, exchanges of gestures, or mediation of a trusted fellow. Appeal to law and an external authority can only be considered as a threat to the inner coherence that holds members where they are in their natural settings. Most important, the formality of law overall remains rather limited amid the abundance of informality in civilian affairs. Indeed, it is still essentially outside the culture to legislate family, community, and the way ordinary people go about their lives in the spirit of Eastern civilizations.

Finally, the social system determines how formalism operates with or without informalism as a viable alternative or a useful assistance. With regard to the two prevailing social systems that exist in Asia and the Pacific, capitalism seems to build primarily upon the formality of law while socialism from time to time tends to exhibit an idealistic enchantment with popular justice. Specifically, in capitalist countries, the scale of the economy, the emphasis on fundamental interests such as individual rights and property ownership, and the adversarial nature of law combine to make a formal legal system a public arena where power, influence, justice, and order can be contested, confirmed, and continued. Informal procedures step in only where the formal process leaves room for them. Alternative resolutions take effect only when the dominant system sanctions them. For example, a consent decree must become a court-sanctioned order before it holds any binding power over the parties who voluntarily choose informal settlement over formal adjudication. In socialist contexts, by comparison, as long as the idea of people as the masters of their country remains alive, it is simply against the system itself to set up a totally formal, intimidating, or alienating process out of the general social dynamics featuring equal access and full participation by the masses.

Within each social system, there are contradictions that could topple the system's hallmark of formality or informality for the opposite. Idealistically, socialism makes people masters of their society, enabling them to exercise power and justice among and for themselves. In reality, however, autocratic socialism often takes the center stage when power becomes concentrated in the hands of state managers, ultimately, in the hands of one or a few revolutionary families. As the state looms to keep an overarching net of control over the populace, informalism automatically recedes from the scene, giving way to formalism. For example, many nominally informal mechanisms in socialist countries, such as the people's militia, the people's reconciliation, neighborhood committees, or united village defense, are no different than formal state machineries in subjecting people to established social agendas. As a matter of fact, informalism often acts in a more penetrative, intimidating, and effective manner than formalism when it comes to serving the state and national interests. It customarily yields to formalism when it comes to dealing with people and their everyday life concerns. In capitalist countries, on the other hand, although power invested by voters becomes institutionalized in the formality of law, people can still take their reactions or opinions to the media, the streets, and other public arenas. Under democratic capitalism, people first can exercise their rights of political justice every few years at polling stations. They then can push for their version of order and justice through political lobbying. Most important, they always have the option to mobilize in the informality of street protests, mass demonstrations, and social movements. Even the most disenfranchised in the formal system can still inch their way toward mainstream society or the major political stage through informal acts. The situation manifests well in the United States through various civilian groups and their acts of informalism, from the early civil rights movements to the recent gay and lesbian rights advocacies and to the current immigrant rights demonstrations.

THE FUTURE

The sense of idealism inherent in formalism makes it an ideal to pursue by all who love the uniformity, formality, and sanctity of law, its making, enforcement, and interpretation. Likewise, the pragmatism associated with informalism makes it valued and convenient for those who cherish the accessibility and flexibility of local or popular justice. As the rule of law becomes fashionable and the state rises to dominance around the globe, the future seems to bode well for both formalism and informalism.

There is, of course, multilevel work ahead just to establish a proper position for formalism across Asia and the Pacific. First, the rule of law can be achieved only when a society is unified under a central state and is freed from tradition, mass activism, or dictatorship. In countries where a nominal or weak central government attempts to govern various warring sections or territories, there cannot be any encompassing constitutional base or framework for formalism. In places where modernization struggles with traditional forces, there cannot be any sound or solid cultural ground or atmosphere for complete formality of law. Polities where power is yet to be detached from mass movements or people's revolutions for institutionalization into bureaucratic structure obviously lack working governmental mechanisms or apparatus for uniform enforcement of law. States where dictators rule by will or with personal temperament often do not have any standard procedure or systematic process to ensure legal equity, impartiality, and fairness to all across different walks of life. Ironically, informalism does not necessarily flourish where formalism is yet to develop or where formalism remains fragile. In fact, because there is no reference, no comparison, and no ultimate source of legitimization, informalism practiced in isolated localities, fragmented polities, or unintegrated territories can only add irregularity, discord, confusion, or disillusion to the people who attempt to rise above their often chaotic social reality.

Second, it takes a rational division of labor among formal social control agencies to implement law across society. In developing countries, people see the law directly in the effects of law enforcement. Whether there are laws and whether they work fairly depend upon how they are implemented by the formal governmental authorities people have to deal with in their immediate environment. In developed societies, ordinary citizens often have the opportunity to watch the political stage where laws are made, revised, and enacted prolifically. However, because they are faced with so many different laws, people eventually have to use their own experience in the real world to judge whether a particular law is good or bad, fair or unfair, effective or ineffective. In other words, what counts or matters essentially rests ultimately in the

field of enforcement. To enforce the law uniformly, social control apparatuses must obviously be formalized with considerable size, differentiation,
and complexity. As for a division of labor, there ought to be regular forces as
well as special services, system-wide security as well as local policing, patrol
as well as investigation, and intelligence as well as enforcement. There must
be different agencies, divisions, departments, or sections for safety and security at various levels, in various sectors, and across various population segments. In the eyes of the general public, use of technology, adoption of professional protocols, and standardization of operational procedures can foster
a positive image of formality, order, and rightfulness about what social control agencies do in their sphere of duties and responsibilities.

Third, professional proficiency by formal agents of social control is key to
proving the amenability, effectiveness, and utility of formalism in everyday
life. At the outset, wearing uniforms, bearing firearms, and exhibiting professional manners evoke public awe and respect for law enforcement officers, court personnel, and correctional staff. Serious screening, rigorous
training, and strict disciplining make people think highly of social control
professionals. Most important, how agents of various justice sections conduct their job, relate to the populace, and connect to the state or general social order will eventually determine whether each contributes to the maintenance of the formality of law, order, and justice in their society. Specifically,
do social control professionals perform their job competently? Do they serve
people conscientiously and as role models? Do they convey a clear image of
the state as a protector and a source for justice through their work, conduct,
and professional integrity? In China, for example, the adoption of criminal
codes has led to a full-scale installation of the criminal justice system
throughout the vast governmental bureaucracy (Xu 1995). It now hinges
upon the professionalization of criminal justice personnel to demonstrate that
formalism takes root in Chinese society and works for the majority of Chinese people.

Informalism can and will grow strong and significant only when formalism becomes established and solidified in the first place. There are logical,
dialectical, historical, and practical reasons. Logically, informalism is informal. To be informal, there must be something that is formal as its background or reference. In a place where there is no government maintaining
social order for the interests of the general public, then any rule enforced or
lawlessness perpetuated by local bandits, gangsters, tyrants, or even noble-
men can be only considered either as typical anarchism or derivative formalism. Informalism, if there is any under the circumstance, would be whatever
deal, agreement, or self-protection observance is reached among ordinary
civilians for themselves.

From a dialectical point of view, informalism comes as an antithesis to formalism. While social turmoil motivates law and order, state dominance often leads to civil activism and mass movements. In an era when the state becomes a universal model for the claim of national sovereignty as well as the representation of civil authority, people also wonder what the government cannot do, will fail to do, or will overdo in the maintenance of order and justice. Informalism can therefore serve not only as a clearinghouse for whatever is left out of formalism by the government, but also as a springboard for whatever people feel necessary to do to the government with regard to its exercise of formal social control. In a sense, informalism signals the pulse of the people on general social orientations such as renovation, reform, and replacement as formalism implemented by the government can so often fall into abuse, corruption, bureaucratic ineptitude, and organizational waste. As a simple example, groups of people in the United States have organized to patrol their Southern national border against the entry of illegal immigrants mainly because they are so frustrated with the way formalism operates that they feel they need to counter it with their own action or informalism.

In historical development, formalism emerged as a reaction to informalism that had for so long existed as a universal phenomenon across human civilizations on the face of the earth. Now as formalism gains currency and commands dominance, it is only natural to ponder the fate of informalism. Will it pose a challenging comeback or will it optimize its supporting role? Specifically, does formalism serve well with an overarching presence in crime, deviance, and social control? What historical roles or opportunities are there for informalism when formalism takes dominance? What falls under informalism when formalism fairs poorly in fulfilling its charges? What is left for informalism when formalism handles everything handsomely? Finally, what is next when formalism serves out its term as a leading model for justice and social order? Is it informalism or something else? Although variations exist from country to country across Asia and the Pacific, informalism overall will assist, advance, amend, attack, or abolish formalism, whenever necessary and appropriate, in the general interest of people and their safety, security, and quality of life.

Practically, formalism needs informalism as an alternative, a supplement, an image builder, a bridge, a backup, and a reminder of the former's continuing presence and dominance in crime and social control. Generally, formalism draws the big picture. It leaves informalism to offer details. Formalism provides the large framework. It awaits informalism to fill in the blanks. And formalism strategizes relations with its constituents or clients. It calls upon informalism to smooth out and substantiate dealings with people amid their everyday reality. Specifically, as an alternative, informalism will have to resolve disputes and deliver justice in a time-sensitive and cost-effective manner. As a supplement, informalism will have to relieve the justice system and facilitate the formal process without any compromise on principle and integrity. As an image builder, informalism will have to soften the image of government, the justice system, or formalism as a whole in the eyes of the general public. As a bridge, informalism will have to aid formalism to reach out to different walks of life or bring ordinary citizens close to the seemingly intimidating machinery of formality. As a backup, informalism will have to step in when formalism fails, does harm, or causes alienation and animosity. And as a reminder, informalism will have to send warnings to the formal system so that the latter can stay away from operational rigidity, moral perfectionism, or relational apathy. Obviously, much is dependent upon informalism in its relationship to formalism.

All in all, as developing societies join developed societies by establishing the rule of law, installing a formal form of government on the basis of law, and undergoing other social transformations toward modernity, formalism will eventually take a dominant position in crime and social control across Asia and the Pacific. Informalism will also have to remain active, effective, and influential as an important supplement or alternative to universal state control and as a way of meting out justice on specific issues in people-to-people contact as well as in business-to-business transactions.

24

Procedural Fairness and Control Effectiveness

Procedural fairness begins with an assumption of innocence for criminal suspects before their conviction. It ensures that they be respected for their basic human rights, that evidence against them be properly collected, stored, examined, and presented to the court, and that they be afforded adequate legal and physical protection within the criminal justice system (Barlow 2000; Shaw 2003). Control effectiveness, on the other hand, requires that criminal offenders be apprehended and punished, that crime be deterred and contained, and that the general interests of society be protected and promoted. There are obviously various theoretical contradictions and pragmatic conflicts between the two value orientations in crime and social control. Theoretically, just deserts dictated by control effectiveness may necessitate deprivations of certain human rights. Pragmatically, in order to apprehend a criminal suspect in a timely fashion, law enforcement agents may sometimes take some extralegal actions, which may result in the inadmissibility of evidence in court and further the dismissal or acquittal of a real criminal from punishment.

Among societies in Asia and the Pacific, differences in the organization of law, in regulation of public order and social control, and in human rights standards are enormous. There are contrasting legal frameworks, common law versus civil law systems. There are opposing court traditions, inquisitorial versus procedural orientations (Terrill 2003). In human rights, whereas the United States and various democratic countries uphold the principles of privacy, civil liberty, freedom of speech, freedom of association, and freedom of movement, China and many developing societies argue that the most important human rights for their billions of common citizens are survival rights, that is, whether they are socially afforded food, drink, clothing, and shelter to live their lives in basic human dignity. China and the United States, along with their respective allies, seem to practice diametrically opposing philosophies of criminal justice. As pointed out by some America-China comparative scholars, the United States would rather set free one hundred murderers than kill one innocent person, whereas China would rather kill one hundred innocent people than set free one murderer. Population density, economic development, social custom, and public mentality are also major issues behind these two contrasting criminal justice approaches. In countries where large populations live on limited resources, people simply cannot understand why they have to spend public funds to defend and feed a criminal convict for years before his or her execution.

THE PAST

The idea of due process can be traced to Magna Carta Libertatum (Great Charter of Freedoms), an English document signed in 1215 at the end of a struggle between the English King and his barons. Magna Carta required the King to renounce certain rights and respect certain legal procedures to the extent that the will of the King would not capriciously go beyond and above the premises of law. Specifically, King John of England promised that "[n]o free man shall be taken or imprisoned or disseized or exiled or in any way destroyed, nor will we go upon him nor send upon him, except by the lawful judgment of his peers or by the law of the land" (Holt 1992).

As one of the most important legal documents in the history of democracy, Magna Carta has influenced almost every country with a common law system. The United States is an outstanding example besides England. The founders of the United States constitutional framework directly used the language of Magna Carta, including "the law of the land" phrase. Most important, they incorporated the spirit of Magna Carta, the "due process of law" provision, in the main body of the United States Constitution as well as in its amendments. The Constitutions of various individual states, such as Maryland and New York, also contain this provision (Jennings 1965; Holt 1992). As is widely known, the Fifth Amendment to the United States Constitution dictates that "no person shall be...deprived of life, liberty, or property, without due process of law..." by actions of the federal government. The

Fourteenth Amendment expressly extends the same protection to State actions even though State constitutions also have their own guarantees of due process for individuals living within the state jurisdiction.

In content, due process has two components: procedural and substantive. Procedurally, due process requires that an individual citizen be adequately notified of any charge against him or her, that he or she be necessarily afforded the opportunity to be heard at any court proceeding involving him or her, and that he or she not be subjected to cruel and unusual punishment as the accused in a criminal case. In other words, procedural due process imposes restrictions on legal procedures so that laws may operate in ways reflective of "fundamental fairness." Substantively, due process places limits on what laws may attempt to do or prohibit. With regard to individual citizens, substantive due process protects rights to life, to property, to vote, to travel, to freedom from imprisonment, and to privacy, the last of which may specifically include rights relating to bodily autonomy, private sexual activity, contraception, and abortion. As far as the government is concerned, substantive due process prohibits it from infringing citizens' fundamental right unless the infringement is narrowly tailored to serve a compelling interest. A consistent controversy surrounding substantive due process is that it is too ambiguous, rendering the Court excessive power to strike down state and federal statutes, especially those that govern criminal activities. As the jurist in *Connally v. General Construction Co.* rightfully pointed out, "[A] statute which either forbids or requires the doing of an act in terms so vague that men of common intelligence must necessarily guess at its meaning and differ as to its application, violates the first essential of due process of law."

Despite critics' concern that the due process doctrine, especially substantive due process clauses, might lead to an activist court, it is indeed through court proceedings and interpretations that a due-process model of the criminal justice system emerged in the 1960s. Under the leadership of Chief Justice Earl Warren, the United States Supreme Court incoporated nearly all of the Bill of Rights' provisions relating to crimnal violations into the due process clause of the Fourteenth Amendment, obligating the states to guarantee criminal defendants a wide range of constitutional safeguards, from the right to counsel, the right to be free from compulsory self-incrimination, the right to obtain witnesses, the right to confront hostile witnesses, the right to trial by jury, and a speedy trial, to proscription of double jeopardy. Two court decisions, *Mapp v. Ohio* and *Miranda v. Arizona*, were particularly instrumental in forcing states to institute procedural changes in their criminal processes. While the former established the basic parameters of illegal search and seizure in state cases, the latter set a series of procedural prerequisites for law enforcement agents to follow when they shift their inquiry into an unsolved crime from the investigative to the accusatory stage. For example, the police must warn the suspect of his or her right to remain silent and honor his or her request to consult with an attorney. In a nutshell, the due-process model considers the possibility of error in the stages leading to trial. It stresses the need to protect the accused and the rights of the accused to fairness and justice even if the implementation of various rights and protective procedures may prevent the criminal justice system from operating with optimal effectiveness and maximum efficiency (Packer 1968).

In the 1970s when crime and violence became less visible, the United States ironically moved into a direction seemingly opposite to what the due-process model would entail. With Chief Justice Warren Burger at the helm, the United States Supreme Court began issue rulings on cases that ultimately served to weaken *Miranda* and qualify other due process procedures. A crime control model took shape, putting a premium on the values of speed, managerial efficiency, repression of criminal conduct, and finality. For instance, *Michigan v. Tucker* established that evidence obtained from an interrogation in which the defendant has not received the full *Miranda* warning should nevertheless be admissible in the courtroom. *Kirby v. Illinois*, on the other hand, undercut the *Wade* guarantee of an attorney's presence whenever a suspect is ordered to participate in a police line-up to the point where the Sixth Amendment right to counsel no longer is a constitutional necessity for all but only for those defendants who have been indicted or otherwise formally charged with a serious crime. The crime control model, as a whole, recognizes that the curtailment of criminal activities is the most important function of the criminal justice process. It requires that suspects who have truly committed crime be convinced of the rationality of entering a guilty plea. Most essentially, it insists that an obviously guilty defendant should never go free because of some post-crime errors made by police or court personnel in their handling of the case. Beginning in the 1980s and continuing until the present, the crime control model has gained popularity as the federal government declares one war after another on crime, from war on organized criminality, war on drugs, and war on guns to war on terrorism (Marion 1994; Vila 1994; Pious 2006).

Across Asia and the Pacific, most countries recognize some form of due process for foreign visitors under customary international laws. Although the specifics vary and tend to be vague from country to country, there has been consensus that a nation must guarantee foreign nationals a basic minimum level of justice and fairness in civil and criminal proceedings. The doctrine of national treatment seems to provide justification for subjecting aliens to criminal justice processes by use of the same rationale for granting them the equal legal protections to which native citizens are entitled. For example, any country can legitimately argue that it is bound to grant no more rights to aliens than it does to its own citizens. Moreover, if foreigners enjoy the same due-process treatment as native citizens, they should by no means be less subject to any control deemed necessary by the national government. In other words, control and due-process go hand in hand when countries greet international migrants or when people traverse through the global community. The two perspectives have been kept in balance and will remain so unless the rapid growth of international human rights laws and the frequent use of bilateral or multilateral treaties usher in a new era of treatment for migrants across national borders on the world stage.

THE PRESENT

Procedural fairness contrasts with control effectiveness. But the former does not necessarily go against the latter. In fact, control enforced with procedural safeguards conceivably commands more legitimacy, acceptance, and influence while due-process procedures can only fare better under widely convincing and long-lasting control, peace, and order.

In the real world of crime, deviance, and social control across Asia and the Pacific, however, there exist mounting problems and challenges for either justice procedures to be fair or for social control to be effective. There are understandably more difficulties and obstacles for control effectiveness to be achieved under the due-process principle or for procedural fairness to be maintained with optimal control and orderliness. Procedural fairness alone requires a bureaucratized state, a well-trained legal profession, and a cultured civil society, as well as general social openness, economic accommodations, and political tolerance. First, a bureaucratized state depends upon an army of civil servants who themselves enter, move up, or exit the organizational hierarchy by way of standards and evaluations, who carry out their work duties in accordance with rules and regulations, and who remain aloof from political competitions yet are loyal, serious, and skilled in what they do on their specific job for fulfilling overall governmental functions in society. In Asia and the Pacific, bureaucratization of state apparatuses, routinization of governmental operations, and standardization of official services vary significantly from country to country. While a few modern, democratic states operate with a complex, rational-legal bureaucracy, a considerable number of governments are still in the hands of dictators, at the mercy of traditional forces or ideological currents, or in the service of economic convenience or political contingencies. Rules may be written but are often pushed aside whenever leaders want to protect some interests while repressing other interests. Procedures may be kept in place but are from time to time twisted or bypassed wherever the powerful, the rich, and the knowledgeable get their way to promote some agendas while disregarding other causes. No one would insist on procedural rightfulness when that person knows he or she can either have something in an extraordinary way at a particular time or lose it all through a normal process under every general circumstance.

Second, a well-trained legal profession consists of lawmakers, law enforcement officials, attorneys, prosecutors, judges, correctional officers, and other justice administrators or staff who go through a standard education, undertake systematic training, believe in the rule of law, specialize in specific legal duties, command a wealth of experience with the justice process, and follow a strict code of conduct on and off the job. In many Asian and Pacific societies, there is simply nothing in existence that is close to a legal profession. Commonly someone becomes a police officer purely because he or she used to be a military service person. It is taken for granted that someone can serve as a judge if that person once held an official position in the government. It is no surprise that someone finds a job in the legal field when the person looks fit, speaks well, or has a critical connection to the establishment. Even in a few developed countries where the rule of law has been in place for a considerable period of time, there are still institutional or operational backdoors, loopholes, malfunctions, or mishaps for the unqualified to sneak in, for the incompetent to stay on, or for the ill-intentioned to remain. In the United States, for example, recruitment campaigns driven by security contingencies occasionally recruit into law enforcement some individuals who otherwise would never qualify as police officers; political processes fueled by partisan divisions often place controversial figures in the justice system in such important positions as judge, attorney general, and chief prosecutor, positions that demand a professional adherence to legal impartiality, procedural fairness, and judgmental integrity. Given that these variations in personnel will affect the quality of justice and the delivery of social control, the attainment of due process or fair treatment in civil and criminal proceedings is obviously more of an ideal to pursue, less of a reality to enjoy, for the majority of people throughout Asia and the Pacific.

Third, a cultured civil society builds upon an educated, disciplined, and tempered citizenry who understand, respect, and pursue overall balances between activism and public order, individualism and the social contract, private rights and institutional constraints, as well as procedurally sound means and substantively important goals. In Asia and the Pacific, official languages, legal protocols, and social etiquettes are to a large degree still a rare luxury for a few privileged elitists in the upper class. For the majority of the populace, it does not matter what to say, how to perform, and whether to keep a sense of decency and dignity when they struggle in illiteracy, poverty, repression, and deprivation. An impoverished man does not have much time to ponder what means is most appropriate to obtain food, shelter, and a job in his day-to-day survival. A battered woman does not have much choice to make about what contractual relation is most sacrosanct to honor in her instinctual run for safety. Even an imprisoned intellectual would likely put aside his or her ideal of universal justice should the person find an opportunity for immediate personal freedom contingent upon agreeing to governmental policies at least temporarily. Now that a number of democratic countries are assured of a growing or increasingly mature middle class as the backbone of their respective civil society, will this literate citizenry be able to reconcile an idealistic penchant for procedural fairness with the realistic need for substantive attainment? The answer is still obviously negative for large parts of the Asian and Pacific region.

Finally, an emphasis on procedure and procedural integrity requires general social openness, necessary economic accommodations, and sufficient political tolerance. A closed society that always has something to hide from its ordinary citizens or tends to pit one of its population groups against another through surveillance and clandestine policing is not likely to put its civil or criminal proceedings on stage for public viewing nor would it place its government on equal footing with the accused over how the latter can be fairly treated by the former. A backward economy that struggles to feed people is not likely to afford a legal system that takes time and dispenses resources to gather evidence, attend procedural protocols, and ensure fair treatment for everyone involved in a civil or criminal case. An authoritarian regime that cares less about how people feel than what the regime desires is not likely to tolerate any procedural technicality that could curtail its exercise of power in any tangible way. Across Asia and the Pacific, there is no lack of polarities. Most pointedly, a great many countries have not yet developed the kind of social openness, economic conditions, and political infrastructure needed to support a justice system that is totally committed to due process, fair treatment, and comprehensive integrity. Even among the most advanced and supposedly freest countries in the region, from Australia, Canada, and Japan to the United States, it is still a common observation that national security, budgetary constraints, the war against terrorism, and other contingencies take priority, thus shortchanging fundamental principles of justice that a state holds in its constitutional obligations to the people.

Effectiveness of control per se depends not only on a united country, an organized justice system, and a synchronized public domain, but also requires general social cohesiveness, economic responsiveness, and political cooperativeness. A united country is assumed to concentrate much of its attention and energy on national defense, securing its borders and keeping out foreign terrorists, organized crime groups, and illegal immigrants. A united nation is expected to spend time and effort on domestic agendas, motivating ordinary citizens in their lawful pursuits while targeting extraordinary deviancy, illegality, and criminality. A united state is supposed to commit its resources and strength to peace, justice, and social order, containing social disturbances, punishing lawbreakers, and deterring potential offenders. In Asia and the Pacific, however, there are still countries whose governance is little more than nominal, whose resources are spent in quelling civil wars or in combating varying degrees of turbulence. A few nations united in territorial sovereignty are yet to be united on political, economic, and social fronts. Even some well-integrated countries must struggle from time to time just to stay unified, united, and focused on a national plan or a society-wide campaign for economic development, political reform, public safety, or crime control. For example, China is often held back by factional power plays in its crackdowns on corruption, political nepotism, and economic crimes; the United States is repeatedly hampered by partisan politics in its wars on drugs, guns, organized criminality, poverty, and terrorism.

An organized justice system is key to running control operations with effectiveness and efficiency. First, there is a rational division of labor among lawmaking, law enforcement, adjudication, and administration of justice. Each organizational branch specializes in its own sphere of work while cooperating with all other branches in the system. Second, there is a logically and naturally coherent process of recruiting, training, monitoring, and disciplining. Individual members perform their job duties in accordance with institutional rules and conventions. Third, there is a reasonable distribution of resources, rewards, and opportunities among sectors, departments, membership groups, ranks, and levels of productivity. Every unit or member fulfills its functions or carries out duties with adequate support. Fourth, there is a consistent and comprehensive system of expectations and standards of performance and productivity, a code of conduct for organizational integrity, effectiveness and efficiency, collegiality and cooperativeness, and other measurable indicators across units and throughout memberships. In a great many countries throughout Asia and the Pacific, however, an organized criminal justice system is far from a reality. In some countries it is not unusual that heinous crimes remain unsolved, truly guilty suspects walk free out of the court, convicted culprits are freed from the penitentiary, and professional criminals go undeterred under an apparently organized justice system. In other countries it is usual that people have no place to turn when they are victimized, judges serve as rubber stamps for decisions made by upper

political authorities, prisoners stay idle with no controls in rundown facilities, and territorial bandits or local tyrants exercise their version of justice
with no regard for humanity in the absence of any actually effective official
justice system.

A synchronized public domain is essential to ironing out differences and
securing consensus over control targets, strategies, and goals. As society develops, the mass media are likely to solidify, serving as a critical vehicle in
conveying news, information, civil debates, and exchanges with the outside.
Public opinion will diversify, becoming both assertive in content and color-
ful in form. In the meantime, when society grows mature, public opinion is
likely to be tempered, seasoned, balanced between ideological extremes, and
fixed in dynamic equilibrium. Similarly, as a country attains a greater degree
of integration, the mass media are more likely to operate on fundamental
goals of the state or serve vital interests of the nation. The public domain
will to a large degree be synchronized across different walks of life while
thriving in its apparently diverse dynamism. For instance, the United States
has had a public domain that features both highly active mass media and
enormously varied civic opinions. However, when it comes to national interests, individual freedom, democracy, peace, justice, and social order, the
United States from time to time can rise above discord and remain united,
purposeful, and effective as a nation. The majority of countries throughout
Asia and the Pacific are, in contrast, not always as clearly capable of national
unity in facing a crisis. There are nations where people hate and hurt each
other because they hold different beliefs and values. There are times when
groups sabotage each other's efforts because they embrace different ideologies, cultural frameworks, and world outlooks, and hence commit to different agendas. Often a city, a province, or a whole nation falls into total divid-
edness, ineffectiveness, or incapacitation on public safety, national security,
or general social order because politicians argue, intellectuals criticize, and
interest groups fight; the mass media are not able to find a common core of
consensus over what people need, how society benefits, where the future of
the nation lies, or how justice, peace, order, and prosperity may flourish for
the good of all in the land.

Finally, general social cohesiveness, economic responsiveness, and political cooperativeness provide a necessary atmosphere, an environment in
which social control can take place effectively and efficiently. Social cohesiveness builds on identification with a common heritage, solidarity around
fundamental principles or interests, and unity on challenging goals or pursuits among different population segments. Across Asia and the Pacific, a
lack of social cohesiveness is often to blame for civilian disputes and group
tensions from country to country. Only a few nations can legitimately take

pride in a considerable level of social cohesiveness for adequate crime control, citizen protection, and maintenance of social order within their boundaries. Economic responsiveness refers to the allocation of assets and effort on safety and security, the mobilization of materials and energy for emergency and crisis, and the contribution of resources and time to peace and justice by various social units or the society as a whole. In Asia and the Pacific, economic responsiveness hardly measures up to the pressing need for personal protection and social order when one state after another still struggles to meet more basic needs of food and survival for its citizens. Even some of the richest countries in the region sometimes find themselves scrambling to fix problems in social control on multiple fronts without adequate economic support. Finally, political cooperativeness involves the courage, the willingness, and the actual capability of diverse political elements and forces to put aside differences, expand common ground, and concentrate on essential goals and substantive tasks that bring about or facilitate unity, stability, and prosperity for all in a country. Throughout Asia and the Pacific, there is no lack of cases in which political division opens the door for foreign invasion, invites international interference, or ferments self-disorganization, subjecting ordinary citizens to genocide, national humiliation, personal insecurity, and various other day-to-day miseries. Only a small number of dictatorships in the region can say unequivocally they are in control of their population and country without any obvious political discord, dissidence, and resistance.

THE FUTURE

Given the fact that neither procedural fairness alone nor control effectiveness per se is close at hand, it will naturally be long into the future for control effectiveness to be achieved under the due-process principle or for procedural fairness to be maintained with optimal control and orderliness.

At the outset, a combinational attainment of control effectiveness and procedural fairness requires the presence or coexistence of all the conditions individually necessary for each of them. In other words, only when a bureaucratized state is in place within a united country, a well-trained legal profession in existence with an organized justice system, and a synchronized public domain in presence with a cultured civil society, can effective control be reached through equity, fairness, and justice. Only when political forces are cooperative while exercising tolerance, the economy stay responsive while providing various accommodations, and the entire society remain cohesive while exhibiting openness, can procedural fairness be kept and cherished under the general condition of control, order, and peace. A systematically organized criminal justice system in the absence of trained, disciplined professionals is likely to serve as a vehicle for authoritarian control; a combative, demanding, and divisive civil society without necessary synchronization from the mass media and other forces in the public domain may only debate or long for fair treatment and universal justice amid its generally disorderly and problematic day-to-day experience.

Developmentally, the process usually begins with control. Only when there is control or order, is there then the desire and the time to attend to procedure and its fairness or rightfulness. In a time of chaos or social upheaval when everyone is concerned with life and survival, there is obviously neither condition nor substance undergirding procedure and procedural matters. Moreover, only when there is control, are there then issues of what control is, whom it serves or targets, how it fares in public opinion, and whether it is open, fair, and appropriate in the way it is carried out. Control can often become excessive, prompting policy change, institutional reform, and social activism to keep it in check. Throughout Asia and the Pacific, a large number of countries are now in critical need of control and order as they strive for economic development, political democratization, and overall social modernization. Since it is natural, perhaps necessary, to exceed the proper limits in righting a wrong or in restoring and maintaining order during a tumultuous social transformation, there should be an adequate level of general awareness, preparedness, and tolerance for extraordinary, even occasionally extreme, measures taken by the authority to achieve control and control effectiveness. Intellectuals, liberal critics, and wishful idealists must understand that attempting a due-process model can be only counterproductive and even dangerous when a jurisdiction struggles to overcome its general disorganization. A premature scheme may not just actually delay a society's drive toward a legal system on the basis of procedural fairness, but also place the society under a permanent disability of divisiveness and disorderliness.

When society attains a minimum level of control, stability, and unity, it is then important to place control and control effectiveness in perspective with procedure and procedural fairness. Obviously, evidence can more likely be free from inappropriateness, controversy, or inadmissibility when law enforcement officials gather it in accordance with law, respect the civil rights of every party involved, and follow professional codes of conduct. Adjudication can more likely be free from question, manipulation, or partiality when judges conduct it with openness to legal input, with balance between defense and prosecution, and with regard for due process. Corrections can be more likely free from coercion, exploitation, or corruption when prison officers and other custodial personnel do their jobs following the principle of procedural fairness, respecting human dignity, and under the guidance of rules and regulations. In a word, control can be more convincing, effective, and self-perpetuating when it is achieved and maintained openly, fairly, rationally, and in the honest adherence to due process. Throughout Asia and the Pacific, as many developing nations are hardly able to keep control and many ordinary people rarely receive any fair treatment from their government, a simple attempt at procedural fairness under a newly established social order may serve surprisingly both as a powerful assurance for citizens and as a promised new beginning for control and law enforcement, paving the way toward long-term social stability and prosperity.

When a country establishes a complex system of law in the service of civil liberty, procedural equity, and judicial impartiality, it is crucial to keep procedure and due process practices in line with control and control objectives. Across Asia and the Pacific, although a few developed nations are able to entertain all the substantive sophistication as well as all the procedural technicality in civil and criminal proceedings, a streamlining of the justice system and its operations in light of control and control effectiveness may in fact alleviate individual pain, reduce social anxieties, save taxpayers' money, and bring about not only a much-needed vibrancy in control but also a renewed interest in due process and legal fairness. Without doubt, protection of a suspect's due process rights is more likely to fall into limbo when a police department is disorganized and unable to serve its jurisdiction effectively. With no question, respect for a defendant's constitutional privileges is more likely to diminish when a criminal court is overloaded and unable to meet the needs of its clientele in a timely manner. Attendance to a convict's basic living conditions will certainly become a problem when a correctional system is operating beyond its holding capacity. Overall, only when the guilty are brought to justice can the innocent be respected and protected for their rights to safety, security, justice, and peace in life.

In sum, control effectiveness and procedural fairness can either go against each other or work with each other. What happens in actuality depends on political climates, economic conditions, and overall social environments. Across Asia and the Pacific, it is especially important to take into account differences in cross-cultural communication. While people are generally able to perceive the rationality inherent in their own legal systems, value standards, and social contexts, they tend to misunderstand and express surprise, contempt, and even anger at practices in social control and the achievement of justice by citizens in other societies. For instance, American viewers and journalists, as seen in network television programs, are instinctually shocked by the use of flogging and hanging as punishment in Singapore, Malaysia, and other Asian and Pacific societies. It is inconceivable to them that a person caught in possession of a few ounces of a controlled substance at the airport is hanged or subjected to harsh punishment. Some American activists are so disturbed or infuriated by what they consider as unusual punishments in other countries that they organize public demonstrations to protest or lobby their elected officials to intervene. Similarly, people in many Asian countries have difficulty understanding why serial killers and heinous murderers are acquitted, why judges dismiss some serious cases while sentencing other rather minor offenders to long-term imprisonment, and why convicted killers on death row are seemingly given unlimited appeals for over twenty years in the United States. They assume that serious offenders should be put to death or kept behind bars as soon as possible, without question. To an average Chinese, it is simply ridiculous to dismiss a case on the basis of procedural inappropriateness. As some Chinese students argued at a legal seminar in the author's presence: Evidence is evidence; it may be collected or stored incorrectly; but evidence gathered with purely technical faults can nonetheless be entered as valid court records as long as it contains relevant, unaltered facts.

Conclusion

This study has examined the most critical types of cross-border crime in Asia and the Pacific. These include crime resulting from social disorganization, crimes of opportunity, corporate and entrepreneurial crime, governmental and bureaucratic crime, substance smuggling and the drug trade, human trafficking and illegal immigration, organized crime, and crimes of terror.

Beyond the specific findings presented on each type of crime with regard to its historical background, its socioeconomic cause, and its type, pattern, and characteristics, this study overall reveals ten important ideas about cross-border crime and deviance. First, there are development-generative crimes that occur inevitably in countries of similar levels of development regardless of a country's social system, geographic location, and historical heritage. Developing societies share social problems unique to lower levels of development whereas developed nations have to deal with deviations or violations common to higher levels of development. Second, there are system-generic crimes that are inherent in the way a country's political economy is organized regardless of the country's level of development, geographic location, and cultural tradition. Socialist countries experience some crimes that may not exist in capitalist nations. Third, there are culture-borne crimes and deviances that happen only within a culture no matter where, when, and over what group the culture holds its influence. Thus ethnic Chinese living in both capitalist and socialist nations, in both developed and developing economies, in both Western and Eastern societies follow almost the same course of action concerning their children's education; thus Muslims around the world share much tradition in the practice of their faith. Fourth, people move from one country to another to seek opportunity or commit crime be-cause of the difference in law, control, and punishment. While a few indi-viduals in developing or undemocratic societies travel to the West to enter-tain themselves with drugs and other deviant habits, a large number of com-mon tourists from the West now flock to other parts of the world for recrea-tion, exploration, sex, profit, or other perceived bargains. Fifth, people fall into trouble because of a change in employment, affiliation, or citizenship. Migrants are not only vulnerable to criminal victimization, but also likely to offend in the place of their passage or sojourn.

Sixth, countries export crime and criminals, deviance and deviants when they are at lower levels of economic development, closed to the outside, dis-organized socially, or displaced by natural disasters. An authoritarian regime sends away political dissidents routinely while a fragile government or a weak economy tends to drive people into international refugee camps in times of crisis. Seventh, countries import crime and criminals, deviance and deviants when they are at higher levels of economic development, open to the rest of the world, organized by long-established principles of law includ-ing due-process and recognition of human rights, or blessed with a generous welfare system. The United States is not only a melting pot for law-abiding immigrants of various cultural or national origins but also a gathering place for high-profile criminals and organized crime groups from all over the world. Eighth, increasing contact among people and between countries raises the likelihood for conflict and criminal victimization. Thus an American ser-viceman may commit forcible rape in Japan or South Korea when the United States puts him at an overseas military base within one of these countries. Ninth, widening gaps across cultural groups and national entities in the world fuel misunderstanding and hostility. International terrorism is thus deeply rooted not only in religious and other cultural divides, but also in the increasingly unequal distribution of power, wealth, and knowledge among countries across the globe. Tenth, globalization highlights comparisons and contrasts that exist among people of different cultures and between countries in different levels of development. Human trafficking, the drug trade, and organized crime all operate upon the known or recognized reality of differ-ences throughout the world population.

This study has touched upon the most fundamental issues in social con-trol. These include change of control ideologies, transfer of control tech-nologies, professionalization of control forces, modernization of control sys-tems, cross-border collaboration and cooperation, international organization and coordination, and civil penetration and global synchronization.

Beyond the concrete discussion developed about each fundamental issue and the context in which it arises, the both sides it involves, and the synthesis it may lead to, this study in general points to ten necessary conditions for cross-border social control. First, social control is to become ideology-neutral. For agents of social control from two or more countries to work on a case, they must put aside their ideological differences. Second, social control is to become technology-centered. Cross-border crime uses more and more technology as means. Nations that experience such crime must use technology in apprehending criminals and bringing them to justice. Third, agents of social control must embrace professionalism. Education, training, technical proficiency, and professional integrity will be essential elements of language when agents of social control cooperate on specific matters or interact with each other in general communication across national borders. Fourth, social control is to feature scientific management. Division of labor ensures specialization, operational effectiveness, and organizational scale for a domestic department of public safety and security. So will scientific management for any sizable international force of control. Fifth, social control must become open, borderless, and international. Just as the United States now sends anti-drug, counter-terrorist agents overseas for the sake of homeland security on American soil, many internationalized metropolises and some highly developed nations with a global reach in their economic and political affairs will have to dispatch specialized personnel to foreign destinations in normal criminal investigations and routine justice proceedings.

Sixth, learning from tradition is golden in the era of modernity. When disgracing or shaming takes center stage over profiting, attention, and publicity, exposure in the media can serve as deterrence to crime just as labeling did in the past. Seventh, using common sense is precious in the world of technology. An owner who counts on a security alarm system installed in his or her car will probably have to bear more severe damage if he or she parks the car in the public street and carelessly leaves a stack of currency in the driver's seat. Eighth, finding community and the accompanying sense of belonging in friendly association with kindred spirits is heart soothing in the shadow of organization and state. Migrants are more likely to turn to friends, relatives, and ethnic groups for advice and assistance in a place where the state and other formal organizations treat them as aliens or outsiders. Ninth, borrowing from the East is priceless when the West commands economic, military, and political domination around the world. The East offers common citizens as well as agents of social control valuable ideas and practices in safety, security, and general survival when it advises people to balance body with mind, nature with nurture, gain with loss, strength with weakness, and environmental sustainability with social progress. Tenth, an optimal state of order and control in the community of nations calls for a fusion of different, even opposing, elements and forces that are available in the totality of human civilizations. Indeed, as nations look hopefully to a future of prosperity and progress, they need to delve into their heritage from the past for insight and inspiration.

All in all, crime and social control in Asia and the Pacific are issues of a vast region and of the whole world. The study of crime and social control in Asia and the Pacific, correspondingly, has the significance of a vast region as well as of the whole world. Within the region, people and ethnic groups are brought closer and closer to one another, both physically and spiritually, by economic development, political liberalization, media penetration, cultural diffusion, and advanced means of communication and transportation. Countries and societies are integrated more and more into a common market, an interconnected block, or an interdependent union through trade, tourism, diplomacy, political agreement, military cooperation, and cultural exchange. Crime takes place within as well as across national borders, following the movement of people and the flow of materials. Reaction to crime, including prevention and intervention, therefore, has to be made and reinforced through both national and international social control forces.

For the whole world, Asia and the Pacific will be the center stage of the twenty-first century. The region provides a vast testing ground where Eastern civilizations meet with Western development, socialism with capitalism, authoritarianism with democracy, tradition with modernity, community with organization, patriarchal dominance with bureaucratic authority, and collectivism with individualism, for possible confrontation, fusion, or both. As these and many other apparently opposing forces come to face each other, they may not only establish their respective state of affairs, such as a complete bureaucratic state or a representative capitalist system, but also create new social situations, such as a market economy with a socialist flavor or a democratic government with a somewhat authoritarian leadership. Crime occurs in response to social change. While conventional crime tends to increase in number and severity, unconventional crime is likely to appear in a wide variety of forms and features. To mount a comprehensive, systematic, and effective offense against crime and deviance, social control in Asia and the Pacific will have to combine and fuse formalism with informalism, state authority with community resources, traditional restraints with modern control technology, Western form with Eastern content, and moral education with market incentives.

Without doubt, crime and social control in Asia and the Pacific provide both challenge and opportunity for academic research. Studying crime and social control in the context of country-to-country, system-to-system, ideology-to-ideology, and civilization-to-civilization interaction in Asia and the Pacific will not only generate critical insights about crime and social control in the contemporary era, but also enhance essential understanding of human adaptation, survival, and evolution across the globe.

References

Abadinsky, Howard. 1989. *Drug Abuse: An Introduction*. Chicago: Nelson Hall.

Abel, Richard L. 1982. *The Politics of Informal Justice*. New York: Academic Press.

Agee, Phillip. 1975. *Inside the Company: CIA Diary*. New York: Stonehill.

Agence France-Presse. 2000. "Organ Scam Doctors Charged." *The Western Australian* April 6.

Allen, Harry E. and Clifford E. Simonsen. 1981. *Corrections in America*. New York: Macmillan.

Amnesty International. 2005. *The State of the World's Human Rights*. London: Amnesty International.

Anderson, Elijah. 1990. *Streetwise: Race, Class, and Change in an Urban Community*. Chicago: University of Chicago Press.

Anderson, Malcolm. 1989. *Policing the World: Interpol and the Politics of International Police Cooperation*. New York: Oxford University Press.

Anderson, Nels. 1923. *The Hobo: The Sociology of the Homeless Man*. Chicago: University of Chicago Press.

Andersson, Martin and Christer Gunnarsson. 2003. *Development and Structural Change in Asia-Pacific: Globalizing Miracles or End of a Model?* London and New York: RoutledgeCurzon.

Arrarte, Anne M. 1992. "Noriega's Turn." *U.S. News and World Report* 111: 22.

Associated Press. 1930. "British Missionary is Slain in China." *New York Times* April 14: 10.

Associated Press. 2001. "Russia Says It Foiled Illegal Sale of Weapons-Grade Uranium." *New York Times* December 7: A6.

Associated Press. 2005. "Predators May Take Children." *Daily News* January 5: 17.

Astor, Hilary and Christine Chinkin. 1992. *Dispute Resolution in Australia.* Sydney: Butterworth-Heinemann.

Bal, Ihsan and Sedat Laciner. 2001. "The Challenge of Revolutionary Terrorism to Turkish Democracy 1960-80." *Terrorism and Political Violence* 13.4: 90-115.

Barker, Thomas and Julian Roebuck. 1973. *An Empirical Typology of Police Corruption: A Study in Organizational Deviance.* Springfield, IL: Charles C. Thomas.

Barlow, Hugh D. 2000. *Criminal Justice in America.* Upper Saddle River, NJ: Prentice Hall.

Bayley, David H. 1991. *Forces of Order: Policing Modern Japan.* Berkeley, CA: University of California Press.

Beccaria, Cesare. 1963. *An Essay on Crimes and Punishments.* Indianapolis, IN: Bobbs-Merrill.

Becker, Howard S. 1963. *Outsiders: Studies in the Sociology of Deviance.* New York: Free Press.

Beeson, Mark. 2002. *Reconfiguring East Asia: Regional Institutions and Organizations after the Crisis.* London: RoutledgeCurzon.

Beiras, Inaki R. 2005. "State Form, Labour Market, and Penal System: The New Punitive Rationality in Context." *Punishment and Society* 7.2: 167-182.

Beirne, Piers and Joan Hill. 1991. *Comparative Criminology: Annotated Bibliography.* Westport, CT: Greenwood Press.

Benekos, Peter J. and Alida V. Merlo. 2005. *Crime Control, Politics and Policy.* Florence, KY: LexisNexis.

Bentham, Jeremy. 1967. *A Fragment on Government and An Introduction to the Principles of Morals and Legislation.* Oxford, UK: Basil Blackwell.

Berg, Stanton O. 1970. "Sherlock Holmes: Father of Scientific Crime Detection." *Journal of Criminal Law, Criminology, and Police Science* 61.3: 446-452.

Berggren, Niclas. 1999. "Economic Freedom and Equality: Friends or Foes?" *Public Choice* 100.3/4: 203-223.

Bernstein, Nina. 2006. "Immigrant Rallies Stun even Organizers." *Daily News* March 27: 11.

Biggart, Nicole W. and Guillen Mauro. 1999. "Developing Difference: Social Organization and the Rise of the Auto Industries of South Korea, Taiwan, Spain, and Argentina." *American Sociological Review* 64: 722-747.

Birch, Anthony. 2001. *Concepts and Theories of Modern Democracy.* New York: Routledge.

Black, Donald. 1984. *Toward a General Theory of Social Control.* Orlando, FL: Academic Press.

Blum, William. 1995. *Killing Hope: U.S. Military and CIA Interventions since World War II.* Monroe, ME: Common Courage Press.

Bordua, David J. 1959. "Juvenile Delinquency and Anomie: An Attempt at Replication." *Social Problems* 6: 230-238.

Borkin, Joseph. 1962. *The Corrupt Judge: An Inquiry into Bribery and Other High Crimes and Misdemeanors in the Federal Courts.* New York: Clarkson N. Potter.

Braithwaite, John. 1984. *Corporate Crime in the Pharmaceutical Industry.* Boston: Routledge & Kegan Paul.

Braithwaite, John. 1989. *Crime, Shame, and Reintegration.* Cambridge, UK: Cambridge University Press.

Broder, John M. 1998. "Release just a Small Step, U.S. Aides Say." *New York Times* April 20: A6.

Brooks, Roy L. 2005. *Structures of Judicial Decision Making from Legal Formalism to Critical Theory.* Durham, NC: Carolina Academic Press.

Brown, Richard M. 1975. *Strain of Violence: Historical Studies of American Violence and Vigilantism.* New York: Oxford University Press.

Bureau of Justice Statistics. 1999. *Correctional Populations in the United States.* Washington, DC: United States Department of Justice.

Burgess, Robert L. and Ronald L. Akers. 1966. "A Differential Association Reinforcement Theory of Criminal Behavior." *Social Problems* 14: 128-147.

Bursik, Robert J., Jr. and Harold G. Grasmick. 1993. *Neighborhoods and Crime: The Dimensions of Effective Community Control.* New York: Lexington Books.

Busky, Donald F. 2002. *Communism in History and Theory: Asia, Africa, and Americas.* Westport, CT: Praeger Publishers.

Byrne, James M. and Robert J. Sampson. 1985. *The Social Ecology of Crime.* New York: Springer Verlag.

Cao, Feng. 1997. *The Fifth Peak: Crime Problems in Contemporary China.* Beijing: China Today Press.

Case, Karl E. and Ray C. Fair. 2004. *Principles of Macroeconomics*. Saddle Cliff River, NJ: Prentice Hall.

Chamlin, Mitchell B. and John K. Cochran. 1997. "Social Altruism and Crime." *Criminology* 35: 203-227.

Chen, Ji and Jing Deng. 1999. "Why Check on People from Other Places?" *Wuhan Evening News* August 24: 1.

Chepesiuk, Ron. 2003. *The Bullet or the Bribe: Taking Down Colombia's Cali Drug Cartel*. Westport, CT: Praeger Publishers.

Chilton, Roland J. 1964. "Continuity if Delinquency Area Research: A Comparison of Studies for Baltimore, Detroit, and Indianapolis." *American Sociological Review* 29.1: 71-83.

Chin, Ko-lin. 1999. *Smuggled Chinese: Clandestine Immigration to the United States*. Philadelphia: Temple University Press.

Choi, Ajin. 2004. "Democratic Synergy and Victory in War, 1816-1992." *International Studies Quarterly* 48.3: 663-682.

Clarke, Ronald. 1995. "Situational Crime Prevention." Pp. 91-150 in *Building a Safer Society: Strategic Approaches to Crime Prevention*, edited by Michael Tonry and David Farrington. Chicago: University of Chicago Press.

Clarke, Ronald and Ross Homel. 1997. "A Revised Classification of Situational Crime Prevention Techniques." Pp. 17-27 in *Crime Prevention at a Crossroad*, edited by Steven P. Lab. Cincinnati, OH: Anderson.

Clear, Todd R., George F. Cole, and Michael D. Reisig. 2005. *American Corrections*. Belmont, CA: Wadsworth Publishing.

Clinard, Marshall B. and Daniel J. Abbott. 1976. "Community Organization and Property Crime: A Comparative Study of Social Control in the Slums of an African City." Pp. 186-206 in *Delinquency, Crime, and Society*, edited by James F. Short, Jr. Chicago: University of Chicago Press.

Clinard, Marshall B. and Peter C. Yeager. 1980. *Corporate Crime*. New York: Free Press.

Clines, Francis X. 2001. "Man Arrested in Threats Mailed to Abortion Clinics." *New York Times* December 6: A20.

Cloward, Richard and Lloyd Ohlin. 1960. *Delinquency and Opportunity: A Theory of Delinquent Gangs*. New York: Free Press.

Cohen, Albert. 1955. *Delinquent Boys: The Culture of the Gang*. New York: Free Press.

Cohen, Stanley and Andrew Scull. 1983. *Social Control and the State*. New York: St. Martin's Press.

Cole, George F. 1989. *The American System of Criminal Justice*. Pacific Grove, CA: Brooks/Cole.

Cornish, Derek B. and Ronald Clarke. 1986. *The Reasoning Criminal: Rational Choice Perspectives on Offending*. New York: Springer Verlag.

Craig, Timothy. 2003. *The Shanghai Cooperation Organization: Origins and Implications*. Washington, DC: Storming Media.

Cressey, Donald A. 1969. *Theft of the Nation: The Structure and Operations of Organized Crime in America*. New York: Harper & Row.

Cressey, Paul G. 1932. *The Taxi-Dance Hall: A Sociological Study of Commercialized Recreation and City Life*. Chicago: University of Chicago Press.

Dahrendorf, Ralf. 1959. *Class and Class Conflict in Industrial Society*. Stanford, CA: Stanford University Press.

Daley, Suzanne. 2001. "Ex-Aide Guilty as France Ends Big Graft Case." *New York Times* May 31: A1.

Daly, Kathleen and Meda Chesney-Lind. 1988. "Feminism and Criminology." *Justice Quarterly* 5: 497-538.

Daniels, Roger. 1972. *Concentration Camps USA: Japanese-Americans and World War II*. New York: Holt, Rinehart, and Winston.

Davis, Nanette J. and Bo Anderson. 1983. *Social Control: The Production of Deviance in the Modern State*. New York: Irvington.

De Tocqueville, Alexis. 2003. *Democracy in America*. London: Penguin Books.

Demick, Barbara and Henry Chu. 2002. "China Letting N. Korean Defectors Leave." *Los Angeles Times* March 15: A11.

Desker, Barry and Arabinda Acharya. 2004. "Targeting Islamist Terrorism in Asia and the Pacific: An Unending War." *Asia-Pacific Review* 11.2: 60-80.

Deutsche Presse-Agentur. 2003. "Lid off Deadly Kidney Racket." *The West Australian* January 22.

Dewan, Shaila. 2005. "Victims Have Say as Birmingham Bomber Is Sentenced." *New York Times* July 19: A14.

Dorfman, Rachelle. 1997. "Taking a Walk: No Longer Safe for Elders in Urban America and Asia." *Journal of Aging and Identity* 2: 139-142.

Drucker, David M. 2004. "Fed Funds Needed for Immigrants Inmates." *Daily News* December 31: 7

Du Guerny, Jacques and Lee-Nah Hsu. 2002. *Towards Borderless Strategies against HIV/AIDS*. Bangkok: UNDP South East Asia HIV and Development Program.

Dunn, Stephen P. and Ethel Dunn. 1997. *Encyclopedia of Modern Separatist Movements*. Santa Barbara, CA: ABC-Clio Inc.

Durkheim, Emile. 1952. *Suicide: A Study in Sociology*. New York: Free Press.

Durkheim, Emile. 1964. *The Division of Labor in Society*. New York: Free Press.

Durutalo, Simione. 1992. Anthropology and Authoritarianism in the Pacific Islands. Pp. 205-232 in *Confronting the Margaret Mead Legacy: Scholarship, Empire and the South Pacific*, edited by Lenora Foerstel and Angela Gilliam. Philadelphia: Temple University Press.

Dutton, Michael R. 1992. *Policing and Punishment in China*. New York: Cambridge University Press.

Edelhertz, Herbert. 1970. *The Nature, Impact, and Prosecution of White-Collar Crime*. Washington, DC: National Institute of Law Enforcement and Criminal Justice.

Editorial Board. 1990. *China's National Conditions*. Beijing: Garden of Learning Press.

Editorial Staff. 1991. "Seven Lawmakers Charged in Bribe Sting." *Washington Post* February 7: A7.

Editorial Staff. 1993. "Paper Says Experiment Exposed 19 Retarded Youths to Radiation." *New York Times* December 27: A17.

Editorial Staff. 1996. "Rostenkowski's Downfall Ends in Prison Term." *Houston Chronicle* April 10: 7A.

Editorial Staff. 1999. "Litton Units to Pay $18.5 Million in Fraud Case." *Houston Chronicle* July 1: 3C.

Editorial Staff. 1999. "Organ Mafia Probe Ordered." *The West Australian* September 18.

Editorial Staff. 2001. "'Bankrupt' Berlin Could Change Tune over Rattle." *The Times* June 2: 17.

Editorial Staff. 2005. "Former Vans VP Admits Kickbacks." *Daily News* February 1: B4.

Editorial Staff. 2005. "Rebuilding a Hawaiian Kingdom." *Los Angeles Times* July 21.

Egan, Timothy. 2005. "Six Arrested Years after Ecoterrorist Acts." *New York Times* December 9: A18.

Elman, Benjamin A., John B. Duncan, and Herman Ooms. 2002. *Rethinking Confucianism: Past and Present in China, Japan, Korea, and Vietnam*. Los Angeles: UCLA Asian Pacific Monograph.

Engstrom, David W., Sarah A. Minas, Monica Espinoza, and Loring Jones. 2004. "Halting the Trafficking of Women and Children in Thailand for the Sex Trade: Progress and Challenges." *Journal of Social Work Research and Evaluation* 5.2: 193-206.

Ermann, M. David and Richard J. Lundman. 2002. *Corporate and Governmental Deviance: Problems of Organizational Behavior in Contemporary Society*. New York: Oxford University Press.

Evans, Peter and James E. Rauch. 1999. "Bureaucracy and Growth: A Cross-National Analysis of the Effects of Weberian State Structures on Economic Growth." *American Sociological Review* 64: 748-65.

Faison, Seth. 1998. "End of Line for Mob's Shuttle over the Hong Kong Border." *New York Times* August 3: A1.

Faris, Robert L. and H. Warren Dunham. 1939. *Mental Disorders in Urban Areas*. Chicago: University of Chicago Press.

Farley, Maggie. 2004. "Congo Sex Scandal Prompts Efforts for Reform in U.N." *Los Angles Times* December 18: A1, A18-19.

Fernandez, Carlos C. 2004. "Justice, Globalization, and Human Rights." *Peace Review* 16.2: 199-205.

Finckenauer, James O. 2004. "The Russian 'Mafia'." *Society* 41.5: 61-64.

Finckenauer, James O. and Yuri A. Voronin. 2001. *The Threat of Russian Organized Crime*. Washington, DC: National Institute of Justice.

Findlay, Mark. 1999. *The Globalisation of Crime: Understanding Transitional Relationships in Context*. Cambridge, UK: Cambridge University Press.

Fitzpatrick, Peter. 1992. "The Impossibility of Popular Justice." *Social & Legal Studies* 1: 199-215.

Flynn, Frank. 1950. "The Federal Government and the Prison Labor Problem in the States." *The Social Science Review* 24: 19-40, 213-236.

Forero, Juan. 2005. "Twenty Colombian Troops on Anti-Drug Mission Die in Copter Crash." *New York Times* January 14: A5.

Frate, Anna A. 1997. "Preventing Crime: Citizens' Experience across the World." *Issues & Reports-United Nations Interregional Crime and Justice Research Institute* 9: 1-16.

Fried, Albert. 1997. *McCarthyism, the Great American Red Scare: A Documentary History*. New York: Oxford University Press.

Fried, Joseph P. 1993. "Ship's Captain to Cooperate in Case of Immigrants' Death." *New York Times* December 21: B3.

Friedlander, Robert A. 1979. *Terrorism: Documents of International and Local Control*. Dobbs Ferry, NY: Oceana Pubns.

Friedman, Lisa. 2005. "Jail Costs for Illegals Sought." *Daily News* February 7: 3.

Frisby, Tanya. 1998. "The Rise of Organized Crime in Russia: Its Roots and Social Significance." *Europe-Asia Studies* 50.1: 27-49.

Fuller, Lon L. 1977. *Anatomy of the Law*. Westport, CT: Greenwood Press.

Gaouette, Nicole and Mary Curtius. 2005. "$31.8-Billion Homeland Security Bill Passes." *Los Angeles Times* July 15: A18.

Garland, David. 2001. *The Culture of Control: Crime and Social Order in Contemporary Society*. Oxford, UK: Oxford University Press.

Garth, Bryant G. 1982. "The Movement toward Procedural Informalism in North America and Western Europe: A Critical Survey." Pp. 183-211 in *The Politics of Informal Justice*, edited by Richard L. Abel. New York: Academic Press.

Geis, Gilbert. 1974. "Upperworld Crime." Pp. 114-137 in *Current Perspectives on Criminal Behavior: Original Essays on Criminology*, edited by Abraham S. Blumberg. New York: Alfred A. Knopf.

Geis, Gilbert, Robert F. Meier, and Lawrence M. Salinger. 1995. *The White-Collar Crime: Offenses in Business, Politics, and the Professions*. New York: Free Press.

Geiss, Paul G. 2001. "Mahallah and Kinship Relations: A Study on Residential Communal Commitment Structures in Central Asia of the 19th Century." *Central Asian Survey* 20.1: 97-106.

Gertz, Bill. 2005. "Syria, Iran Aiding Iraq Insurgents." *The Washington Times* March 18.

Gervassi, Frank. 1979. *The Life and Times of Menahem Begin: Rebel to Statesman*. New York: Plutnam.

Gethin, Rupert. 1998. *Foundations of Buddhism*. Oxford, UK: Oxford University Press.

Gibbs, Jack P. 1968. "Crime Punishment and Deterrence." *Social Science Quarterly* 48: 515-530.

Gibbs, Jack P. 1981. *Norms, Deviance, and Social Control*. New York: Elsevier.

Gilbert, Michael J. and Steve Russell. 2002. "Globalization of Criminal Justice in the Corporate Context." *Crime, Law and Social Change* 38.3: 211-238.

Glaser, Daniel. 1956. "Criminality Theory and Behavioral Images." *American Journal of Sociology* 61: 433-444.

Goddard, Michael. 2001. "From Rolling Thunder to Reggae: Imagining Squatter Settlements in Papua New Guinea." *The Contemporary Pacific* 13.1: 1-32.

Gold, George. 1958. *Theoretical Criminology*. New York: Oxford University Press.

Goodey, Jo. 2004. "Sex Trafficking in Women from Central and Eastern European Countries: Promoting a 'Victim-Centered' or 'Woman-Centered' Approach to Criminal Justice Intervention." *Feminist Review* 76: 26-45.

Goodman, David S. G. 1988. *Communism and Reform in East Asia*. Totowa, NJ: Frank Cass.

Gordy, Molly. 2000. "A Call to Fight Forced Labor." *Parade Magazine* February 20: 4-5.

Green, Gary S. 1990. *Occupational Crime*. Chicago: Nelson-Hall.

Greenwood, Peter W. 1982. *Selective Incapacitation*. Santa Monica, CA: Rand.

Halperin, Morton H., Jerry J. Berman, Robert L. Borosage, and Christine M. Marwick. 1977. *The Lawless State: The Crimes of the U.S. Intelligence Agencies*. New York: Penguin Books.

Hanlon, Joseph. 2004. "Is the International Community Helping to Recreate the Preconditions for War in Sierra Leone?" *The Roundtable* 94.381: 459-472.

Hanzich, Joey. 2003. "Dying for Independence: World Separatist Movements and Terrorism." *Harvard International Review* 25.2: 32-40.

Harrington, Christine B. "Delegalization Reform Movements: A Historical Analysis." Pp. 177-198 in *The Politics of Informal Justice*, edited by Richard L. Abel. New York: Academic Press.

Harrington, Christine B. and Sally E. Merry. 1988. "Ideological Production: The Making of Community Mediation." *Law and Society Review* 22.4: 709-735.

Hayner, Norman. 1936. *Hotel Life*. Chicago: University of Chicago Press.

Haynes, Dina F. 2004. "Used, Abused, Arrested, and Deported: Extending Immigration Benefits to Protect the Victims of Trafficking and to Secure the Prosecution of Traffickers." *Human Rights Quarterly* 26.2: 221-272.

Hirschi, Travis. 1969. *Causes of Delinquency*. Los Angeles: University of California Press.

Hodgson, Douglas. 1995. "Combating the Organized Sexual Exploitation of Asian Children: Recent Developments and Prospects." *International Journal of Law and the Family* 9.1: 23-53.

Holloway, Lynette. 1998. "Teacher Threatened over Book Weighs Switching School." *New York Times* November 27: 1A.

Holt, James C. 1992. *Magna Carta*. Cambridge, UK: Cambridge University Press.

Hopper, Elizabeth K. 2004. "Underidentification of Human Trafficking Victims in the United States." *Journal of Social Work Research and Evaluation* 5.2: 125-136.

Horwitz, Allan V. 1990. *The Logic of Social Control*. New York: Plenum.

Huntington, Samuel P. 1993. "The Clash of Civilization?" *Foreign Affairs* 72.3: 22-49.

Inciardi, James A. 1975. *Careers in Crime*. Chicago: Rand McNally.

Inciardi, James A. 1992. *The War on Drugs II: The Continuing Epic of Heroin, Cocaine, Crack, Crime, AIDS, and Public Policy*. Mountain View, CA: Mayfield.

Inciardi, James A. and Karen McElrath. 1995. *The American Drug Scene: An Anthology.* Los Angeles: Roxbury Publishing.

Inglehart, Ronald and Wayne E. Baker. 2000. "Modernization, Cultural Change, and the Persistence of Traditional Values." *American Sociological Review* 65: 19-51.

Inman, Keith and Norah Rudin. 2000. *Principles and Practice of Criminalistics: The Profession of Forensic Science.* Boca Raton, FL: CRC Press.

Israel, Jonathan I. 2002. *Radical Enlightenment: Philosophy and the Making of Modernity 1650-1750.* Oxford, UK: Oxford University Press.

Jacobs, Heidi H., Michael L. LeVasseur, Kate Kinsella, and Kevin Feldman. 2004. *Asia and the Pacific: Geography, History, and Culture.* Upper Saddle River, NJ: Pearson Prentice Hall.

Janowitz, Morris. 1975. "Sociological Theory and Social Control." *American Journal of Sociology* 81.1: 82-108.

Jayasuriya, Laksiri and David Sang. 1991. "Asian Immigration to Australia: Past and Current Trends." *Population Review* 35.1/2: 35-56.

Jennings, Ivor. 1965. *Magna Carta and Its Influence in the World Today.* London: British Information Services.

Jiang, Guorong. and Liang Wen. 2000. "A Criminal Suspect Extradited to Taiwan." *People's Daily* March 14: 5.

Jones, Daniel P. 1993. "Without Consent: The Government's Secret Experiments on Humans—Wartime Tests Leave Scars, Ethical Concerns." *Hartford Courant* October 17: A1.

Josey, Alex. 1973. *Asia Pacific Socialism.* Canberra: Asia Pacific Press.

Juska, Arunas, Peter Johnstone, and Richard Pozzuto. 2004. "The Changing Character of Criminality and Policing in Post-Socialist Lithuania: From Fighting Organized Crime to Policing Marginal Populations?" *Crime, Law, and Social Change* 41.2: 161-177.

Kaplan, David E. and Alec Dubro. 1986. *Yakuza: The Explosive Accounts of Japan's Criminal Underworld.* Reading, MA: Addison-Wesley Publishing Company.

Karmen, Andrew A. 1968. "Vigilantism." Pp. 1645-1649 in *International Encyclopedia of the Social Sciences,* edited by David L. Sills. New York: Macmillan.

Kohli, Atul, Chung-in Moon, and George Sorensen. 2003. *States, Markets, and Just Growth: Development in the Twenty-First Century.* New York: United Nations University Press.

Kopel, David B. and Christopher C. Little. 1999. "The Pros and Cons of Domestic Disarmament." *The Responsive Community* 9.3: 64-67.

Kramer, Ronald and Raymond Michalowski. 1995. "The Iron Fist and the Velvet Tongue: Crime Control Policies in the Clinton Administration." *Social Justice* 22.2: 87-100.

Kraul, Chris, Rich Connell, and Robert Lopez. 2005. "Nations Address Gang Violence." *Los Angeles Times* June 18: A9.

Ku, Agnes S. 2004. "Immigration Policies, Discourses, and the Politics of Local Belonging in Hong Kong, 1950-1980." *Modern China* 30.3: 326-360.

Kury, Helmut. 2002. "International Comparison of Crime and Victimization: The ICVS." *International Journal of Comparative Criminology* 2.1: 1-9.

Kyle, David and Rey Koslowski. 2001. *Global Human Smuggling*. Baltimore, MD: Johns Hopkins University Press.

Lander, Bernard. 1954. *Towards an Understanding of Juvenile Delinquency*. New York: Columbia University Press.

Lawrance, Alan. 2003. *China since 1919: Revolution and Reform*. New York: Routledge.

Lea, John and Jock Young. 1984. *What Is to Be Done about Law and Order?* Harmondsworth, UK: Penguin.

Lederman, Daniel, Norman V. Loayza, and Rodrigo R. Scares. 2005. "Accountability and Corruption: Political Institutions Matter." *Economics and Politics* 17.1: 1-35.

Lee, Jennifer. 2006. "The Basics: Human Trafficking, for a Hefty Fee." *New York Times* May 28: 2.

Lee, Kuan-Yew. 1966. *Socialism and Reconstruction in Asia*. Singapore: Ministry of Culture Publications.

Lemert, Edwin. 1951. *Social Pathology*. New York: McGraw-Hill.

Leuchtag, Alice. 1995. "Merchants of Flesh: International Prostitution and the War on Women's Rights." *The Humanist* 55.2: 11-16.

Lewis, Norman. 1964. *The Honored Society: A Searching Look at the Mafia*. New York: Putnam.

Lijphart, Arend. 1999. *Patterns of Democracy: Government Forms and Performance in Thirty-Six Countries*. New Haven, CT: Yale University Press.

Lipton, Douglas, Robert Martinson, and Judith Wilks. 1975. *The Effectiveness of Correctional Treatment: A Survey of Treatment Evaluation Studies*. New York: Praeger Publishers.

Liu, Jianhong, Lening Zhang, and Steven Messner. 2001. *Crime and Social Control in a Changing China*. Westport, CT: Greenwood Publishing Group.

Lotspeich, Richard. 1995. "Crime in the Transition Economies." *Europe-Asia Studies* 47.4: 555-589.

Lozada, Carlos. 2005. "Does Poverty Cause Terrorism?" *National Bureau of Economic Research Digest*, May 5.

Maas, Arthur. 1987. "U.S. Prosecution of State and Local Officials for Political Corruption: Is the Bureaucracy out of Control in a High-Stakes Operation Involving the Constitutional System?" *Publius: The Journal of Federalism* 17: 199.

MacMunn, George F. 1974. *Slavery through the Ages*. Lanham, MD: Rowman & Littlefield.

Madigan, Nick. 2003. "Cries of Activism and Terrorism in S.U.V. Torching." *New York Times* August 31: A1.

Magnier, Mark. 2005. "China Puts Focus on Security in Muslim Region." *Los Angeles Times* September 30: A3.

Mapes, Timothy. 2002. "Leaders Warn of Backlash from Abu Bakar's Arrest." *Wall Street Journal* October 21.

Marcus, Frances F. 1991. "U.S. Judge Convicted in New Orleans Bribe Case." *New York Times* September 7: 12.

Marion, Nancy E. 1994. *A History of Federal Crime Control Initiatives, 1960-1993*. Westport, CT: Praeger Publishers.

Marx, Gary T. 1997. "Social Control across Borders." Pp. 23-39 in *Crime and Law Enforcement in the Global Village*, edited by William F. McDonald. Cincinnati, OH: Anderson Publishing.

Marx, Gary T. 1997. "The Declining Significance of Traditional Borders and the Appearance of New Borders in an Age of High Technology." Pp. 484-494 in *Intelligent Environment*, edited by Peter Droege. New York: Elsevier Science.

Marx, Karl and Friedrich Engels. 1979. *The Communist Manifesto*. New York: International Publishers.

Matza, David. 1964. *Delinquency and Drift*. New York: Wiley.

McCargo, Duncan. 2004. *Rethinking Vietnam*. New York: RoutledgeCurzon.

McCarthy, Coleman. 1987. "The Consequences of Covert Tactics." *Washington Post* December 13.

McCormick, Barrett L. and Jonathan Unger. 1995. *China after Socialism: In the Footsteps of Eastern Europe or East Asia?* Armonk, NY: M. E. Sharpe.

McFeely, Richard A. 2001. "Enterprise Theory of Investigation." *FBI Law Enforcement Bulletin* 70.5: 19-25.

Meador, Daniel J. 2000. *American Courts*. Eagan, MN: West Publishing Company.

Merlin, Mark D. 1984. *On the Trail of the Ancient Opium Poppy*. Rutherford, NJ: Fairleigh Dickinson University Press.

Merriner, James. 1999. *Mr. Chairman: Power in Dan Rostenkowski's America*. Carbondale, IL: Southern Illinois University Press.

Merton, Robert K. 1957. *Social Theory and Social Structure*. New York: Free Press.

Mill, John Stuart. 1974. *On Liberty*. London: Penguin Books.

Miller, Walter. 1958. "Lower Class Culture as a Generating Milieu of Gang Delinquency." *Journal of Social Issues* 14: 5-19.

Mitford, Jessica. 1973. *Kind and Usual Punishment: The Prison Business*. New York: Alfred A. Knopf.

Molinski, Dan. 2005. "Colombians Seize 15 Tons of Cocaine Bound for U.S." *Daily News* May 15: 22.

Mon, Wei-Teh. 2002. "Causal Factors of Corporate Crime in Taiwan: Qualitative and Quantitative Findings." *International Journal of Offender Therapy and Comparative Criminology* 46.2: 183-205.

Moore, Jonathan. 1997. "Furor over Crime Could Topple Taiwan's Rulers." *Business Week* May 19.

Morley, James W. 1993. *Driven by Growth: Political Change in the Asia-Pacific Region*. Armonk, NY: M. E. Sharpe.

Morris, Norval and David J. Rothman. 1995. *The Oxford History of the Prison: The Practice of Punishment in Western Society*. New York: Oxford University Press.

Mowrer, Ernest. 1927. *Family Disorganization*. Chicago: University of Chicago Press.

Muller, Jerry Z. 2002. *The Mind and the Market: Capitalism in Modern European Thought*. New York: Random House.

Nadig, Aninia. 2002. "Human Smuggling, National Security, and Refugee Protection." *Journal of Refugee Studies* 15.1:1-25.

Nagel, Stuart. 2003. *Policymaking and Peace: A Multinational Anthology*. Lanham, MD: Lexington Books.

Newbold, K. Bruce. 2006. *Six Billion Plus: World Population in the Twenty-First Century*. Lanham, MD: Rowman & Littlefield.

Newman, Graeme. 1999. *Global Report on Crime and Criminal Justice*. New York: Oxford University Press.

Ni, Ching-Ching. 2000. "Chinese Dream of Escape to West Turning to Nightmare." *Los Angeles Times* February 20: A14-15.

Ni, Hua-Ching. 1998. *Tao: The Subtle Universal Law and the Integral Way of Life*. Los Angeles: Seven Star Communications.

Nossiter, Adam. 1994. "Judge Awards Damages in Japanese Youth Death." *New York Times* September 16: A12.

Office of Applied Studies. 1998. *National Household Survey on Drug Abuse Main Findings 1998*. Rockville, MD: Substance Abuse and Mental Health Services Administration.

Office of Applied Studies. 2004. *National Household Survey on Drug Use and Health*. Substance Rockville, MD: Abuse and Mental Health Services Administration.

Office of the Coordinator for Counterterrorism. 2005. *Country Reports on Terrorism*. Washington, DC: United States Department of State.

Office of National Drug Control Policy. 1998. *The National Drug Control Strategy 1998*. Washington, DC: The White House.

Oldenburg, Veena T. 2002. *Dowry Murder: The Imperial Origins of a Cultural Crime*. Oxford and New York: Oxford University Press.

Olive, Christopher. 2005. "The Treadmill of Production under NAFTA: Multilateral Trade, Environmental Regulation, and National Sovereignty." *Organization and Environment* 18.1: 55-71.

Packer, Herbert. 1968. *The Limits of the Criminal Sanction*. Stanford, CA: Stanford University Press.

Paoli, Letizia. 2003. *Mafia Brotherhoods: Organized Crime, Italian Style*. New York: Oxford University Press.

Park, Robert E. 1936. "Human Ecology." *American Journal of Sociology* 42: 1-15.

Park, Robert E., Ernest W. Burgess, and Roderick D. McKenzie. 1967. *The City*. Chicago: University of Chicago Press.

Parsons, Talcott. 1951. *The Social System*. New York: Free Press.

Paton, William. 2005. *Christianity in the Eastern Conflicts: A Study of Christianity, Nationalism, and Communism in Asia*. Whitefish, MT: Kessinger Publishing.

Pawar, Manohar S. and Rakesh M. Goyal. 1994. "Computer Crime in Bombay: Efforts to Alert This Problem." *International Journal of Offender Therapy and Comparative Criminology* 38.3: 241-246.

Peak, Kenneth J. 2006. *Justice Administration: Police, Courts, and Corrections Management*. Upper Saddle River: NJ: Prentice Hall.

Pious, Richard M. 2006. *The War on Terrorism and the Rule of Law*. Los Angeles: Roxbury Publishing.

Portes, Alejandro and Ruben G. Rumbaut. 1996. *Immigrant America: A Portrait*. Berkeley and Los Angeles: University of California Press.

Powell, Alvin. 2004. "Freedom Squelches Terrorist Violence." *Harvard University Gazette*, November 4.

President's Commission on Organized Crime. 2001. *The Cash Connection: Organized Crime, Financial Institutions, and Money Laundering*. Washington, DC: United States Government Printing Office.

Preston, Diana. 2001. *Boxer Rebellion: The Dramatic Story of China's War on Foreigners That Shook the World in the Summer of 1900.* New York: Berkley Publishing Group.

Rabasa, Angel M. and Peter Chalk. 2001. *Colombian Labyrinth: The Synergy of Drugs and Insurgency and Its Implications for Regional Stability.* Santa Monica, CA: Rand.

Ragavan, Chitra. 1999. "The Frantic Hunt for an Alien Killer." *U.S. News and World Report* 127.1: 23.

Ray, Oakley and Charles Ksir. 1996. *Drugs, Society, and Human Behavior.* St. Louis, MO: Mosby.

Reckless, Walter C. 1961. "A New Theory of Delinquency and Crime." *Federal Probation* 25: 42-46.

Reiss, Albert J. 1951. "Delinquency as the Failure of Personal and Social Controls." *American Sociological Review* 16: 206.

Renard, Ronald D. 1996. *The Burmese Connection: Illegal Drugs and the Making of the Golden Triangle.* Boulder, CO: L. Rienner Publishers.

Renfrew, P. 1980. "Introduction to Symposium on White Collar Crime." *Memphis State University Law Review* 10: 416.

Reza, H. Gil. 2004. "Orange County Man Guilty in Sex Tourism Case." *Los Angeles Times* November 20: B6.

Richter, Paul. 2005. "Poll Finds Less Support for Terrorism." *Los Angeles Times* July 15: A8.

Rigg, Jonathan. 2003. *Southeast Asia: The Human Landscape of Modernization and Development.* London and New York: Routledge.

Robinet, Isabelle. 1992. *Taoism: Growth of a Religion.* Stanford, CA: Stanford University Press.

Roebuck, Julian and Stanley C. Weeber. 1978. *Political Crime in the U.S.: Analyzing Crime by and against Government.* New York: Praeger Publishers.

Rosoff, Stephen M., Henry N. Pontell, and Robert H. Tillman. 2004. *Profit without Honor: White-Collar Crime and the Looting of America.* Upper Saddle River, NJ: Prentice Hall.

Ross, Edward A. 1901. *Social Control: A Survey of the Foundations of Order.* New York: Macmillan.

Ross, Edward A. 1965. *Sin and Society: An Analysis of Latter-Day Inequality.* New York: Houghton-Mifflin.

Roucek, Joseph S. 1978. *Social Control for the 1980s: A Handbook for Order in a Democratic Society.* Westport, CT: Greenwood Press.

Rountree, Pamela W. and Barbara D. Warner. 1999. "Social Ties and Crime: Is the Relationship Gendered?" *Criminology* 37.4: 789-814.

Schiray, Michel. 2001. "The MOST Project: Economic and Social Transformations Connected with the International Drug Problem." *International Social Science Journal* 53.3: 346-349.

Schlegel, Kip and David Weisburd. 1993. *White-Collar Crime: The Paral-
lax View*. Boston: Northeastern University Press.

Schneider, Keith. 1994. "Cold War Radiation Test on Humans to Undergo
a Congressional Review." *New York Times* April 11: D9.

Schultes, Richard E. and Albert Hofmann. 1979. *Plants of the Gods*. New
York: McGraw-Hill.

Schwartz, Martin and Walter DeKeseredy. 1993. *Contemporary Criminology*. Belmont, CA: Wadsworth.

Sebald, Hans. 1968. *Adolescence: A Sociological Analysis*. New York:
Appleton-Century-Crofts.

Segal, Jeffrey A., Harold J. Spaeth, and Sara C. Benesh. 2005. *The Supreme
Court in the American Legal System*. New York: Cambridge University Press.

Sellin, Thorsten. 1938. *Culture Conflict and Crime*. New York: Social Science Research Council.

Seow, Francis. 1990. "The Tyranny of the Majority." *Index on Censorship*
19.3: 3-8.

Shamir, Ronen. 2005. "Without Borders? Notes on Globalization as a Military Regime." *Sociological Theory* 23.2: 197-217.

Shaw, Clifford R. 1930. *The Jack Roller: A Delinquent Boy's Own Story*.
Chicago: University of Chicago Press.

Shaw, Clifford R. and James F. McDonald. 1938. *Brothers in Crime*. Chicago: University of Chicago Press.

Shaw, Clifford R. and Henry D. McKay. 1969. *Juvenile Delinquency and
Urban Areas: A Study of Rates of Delinquency in Relation to
Differential Characteristics of Local Communities in American Cities*.
Chicago: University of Chicago Press.

Shaw, Clifford R. and Maurice Moore. 1931. *The Natural History of a Delinquent Career*. Chicago: University of Chicago Press.

Shaw, Victor N. 1996. *Social Control in China: A Study of Chinese Work
Units*. Westport, CT: Greenwood Publishing Group.

Shaw, Victor N. 1998. "Productive Labor and Thought Reform: A Historical
and Comparative Analysis." *The Prison Journal* 78.2: 186-211.

Shaw, Victor N. 2000. "Mainland China's Political Development: Is the
CCP's Version of Democracy Relevant?" Pp. 177-200 in *The Trans-
formation of Chinese Socialism*, edited by Lin Chun. Dartmouth, UK:
Ashgate.

Shaw, Victor N. 2002. *Substance Use and Abuse*: *Sociological Perspectives*. Westport, CT: Greenwood Publishing Group.

Shaw, Victor N. 2003. "Within and Without National Borders: Crimes and Deviance in Asia and the Pacific." *International Journal of Comparative Criminology* 3.2: 119-148.

Shaw, Victor N. 2004. *Career-Making in Postmodern Academia*: *Process*, *Structure, and Consequence*. Lanham, MD: Rowman & Littlefield Publishing Group.

Shelley, Louise. 2003. "The Trade in People in and from the Former Soviet Union." *Crime, Law, and Social Change* 40.2/3: 231-250.

Shenon, Philip. 1994. "Singapore Affirms Teenager's Caning but Reduces Strokes to 4." *New York Times* May 5: A11.

Shenon, Philip. 1994. "Singapore Executes a Dutch Engineer Arrested on Drug Charges." *New York Times* September 24: 5.

Sheptycki, James and Ali Wardak, and James Hardie-Bick. 2005. *Transnational and Comparative Criminology*. London: Glasshouse Press.

Shlapentokh, Vladimir. 1997. "Bonjour, Stagnation: Russia's Next Years." *Europe-Asia Studies* 49.5: 865-881.

Siegle, Joseph T., Michael M. Weinstein, and Morton H. Halperin. 2004. "Why Democracies Excel?" *Foreign Affairs* 83.5: 57-71.

Sievers, Eric. 2003. *The Post-Soviet Decline of Central Asia*: *Sustainable Development and Comprehensive Capital*. London and New York: RoutledgeCurzon.

Silbey, Susan S. and Austin Sarat. 1989. "Dispute Processing in Law and Legal Scholarship: From Institutional Critique to the Reconstruction of the Judicial Subject." *Denver University Law Review* 66.3: 437-498.

Simpson, Sally S. 2002. *Corporate Crime, Law, and Social Control*. Cambridge, UK: Cambridge University Press.

So, Alvin Y. 1990. *Social Change and Development*: *Modernization, Dependency and World-System Theories*. Thousand Oaks, CA: Sage Publications.

So, Alvin Y. and Stephen W. Chiu. 1995. *East Asia and the World Economy*. Thousand Oaks, CA: Sage Publications.

Sollenberger, Richard T. 1968. "Chinese-American Childrearing Practices and Juvenile Delinquency." *Journal of Social Psychology* 74.1: 13-23.

Soothill, Keith. 1996. "The Growth of the Serial Killer Industry: A Study of the Asia-Pacific Rim Region." *Criminal Behavior and Mental Health* Supplement: 73-83.

Sullivan, Robert. 1998. "The Face of Eco-Terrorism." *New York Times* December 20: 46.

Sung, Hung-En. 2004. "State Failure, Economic Failure, and Predatory Organized Crime: A Comparative Analysis." *Journal of Research in Crime and Delinquency* 41.2: 111-129.

Sutherland, Edwin H. 1937. *The Professional Thief.* Chicago: University of Chicago Press.

Sutherland, Edwin H. 1947. *Principles of Criminology.* Philadelphia: Lippincott.

Sutherland, Edwin H. 1983. *White-Collar Crime: The Uncut Version.* New Haven, CT: Yale University Press.

Swedberg, Richard. 2005. "Capitalism and Ethics: How Conflicts-of-Interest Legislation Can be Used to Handle Moral Dilemmas in the Economy?" *International Social Science Journal* 57.185: 481-492.

Sykes, Gresham and David Matza. 1957. "Techniques of Neutralization: A Theory of Delinquency." *American Sociological Review* 22: 664-670.

Tannenbaum, Frank. 1938. *Crime and the Community.* Boston: Ginn & Co.

Taylor, Ralph and Jeanette Covington. 1988. "Neighborhood Changes in Ecology and Violence." *Criminology* 26: 553-589.

Taylor, Ralph and Jeanette Covington. 1993. "Community Structural Change and Fear of Crime." *Social Problems* 40: 374-392.

Terrill, Richard J. 2003. *World Criminal Justice Systems: A Survey.* Cincinnati, OH: Anderson Publishing.

Theoharis, Athan G. 2004. *The FBI and American Democracy: A Brief Critical History.* Lawrence, KS: University Press of Kansas.

Thomas, Gordon. 1989. *Journey into Madness: The True Story of Secret CIA Mind Control and Medical Abuse.* New York: Bantam Books.

Thomas, W. I. 1923. *The Unadjusted Girl.* Boston: Little, Brown & Co.

Thomas, W. I. and Florian Znaniecki. 1920. *The Polish Peasant in Europe and America.* Boston: Gorham Press.

Thorwald, Jurgen. 1967. *Crime and Science.* New York: Harcourt, Brace & World.

Thrasher, Frederick M. 1927. *The Gang.* Chicago: University of Chicago Press.

Times Wire Reports. 2005. "Australian Smuggler Hanged Despite Appeals." *Los Angeles Times* December 2.

Toby, Jackson. 1957. "Social Disorganization and Stake in Conformity: Complementary Factors in the Predatory Behavior of Hoodlums." *Journal of Criminal Law, Criminology, and Police Science* 48: 12-17.

Tokyo Correspondent. 1989. "In the Land of the Rising Gun." *The Economist* August 26: 23-24.

Transparency International. 2004. *Global Corruption Report 2004.* London: Pluto Press.

Transparency International. 2006. *Global Corruption Report 2006*. London: Pluto Press.

Tyler, Patrick E. 2004. "Nineteen Die as Tide Traps Chinese Shellfish Diggers in England." *New York Times* February 7: A3.

United Nations Economic and Social Commission for Asia and the Pacific. 2003. *Combating Human Trafficking in Asia: A Resource Guide to International and Regional Legal Instruments, Political Commitments and Recommended Practices*. New York: United Nations Publication.

United Nations Office for Drug Control and Crime Prevention. 2000. *World Drug Report 2000*. Oxford, UK: Oxford University Press.

United Nations Office on Drugs and Crime. 2005. *Legislative Guides for the Implementation of the United Nations Convention against Transnational Organized Crime and the Protocols Thereto*. New York: United Nations Publication.

United States Department of State. 2005. *Trafficking in Persons Report*. Washington, DC: United States Government Printing Office.

United States Senate Committee on Governmental Affairs. 1990. *Organized Crime: Twenty-Five Years after Valachi*. Washington, DC: United States Government Printing Office.

United States Sentencing Commission. 2002. *Sourcebook of Federal Sentencing Statistics*. Washington, DC: United States Government Printing Office.

Vankin, Jonathan and John Whalen. 1997. *The Sixty Greatest Conspiracies of All Time*. Secaucus, NJ: Citadel Press.

Vartabedian, Ralph. 2005. "U.S. Soldiers, Law Officers Snared in Border Drug Sting." *Los Angeles Times* May 13: A1, A18.

Vila, Bryan. 1994. "A General Paradigm for Understanding Criminal Behavior: Extending Evolutionary Ecological Theory." *Criminology* 32.3: 311-359.

Vining, Joseph. 2003. "Corporate Crime and the Religious Sensitivity." *Punishment & Society* 5.3: 313-325.

Vitello, Paul. 2006. "Local Officials Seek Help from U.S. on Immigration." *New York Times* March 7: B5.

Walker, Samuel. 1980. *Popular Justice: A History of American Criminal Justice*. New York: Oxford University Press.

Walker, Samuel. 1992. *The Police in America*. New York: McGraw-Hill.

Wallerstedt, John. 1984. *Returning to Prison*. Washington, DC: United States Department of Justice.

Wallerstein, Immanuel. 1979. *The Capitalist World-Economy*. Cambridge, UK: Cambridge University Press.

Ward, David. A. and Charles R. Tittle. 1993. "Deterrence or Labeling: The Effects of Informal Sanctions." *Deviant Behavior: An Interdisciplinary Journal* 14: 43-64.

Ware, Robert B. and Enver Kisriev. 2001. "Ethnic Parity and Democratic Pluralism in Dagestan: A Consociational Approach." *Europe-Asia Studies* 53.1: 105-131.

Warner, Mildred and Jennifer Gerbasi. 2004. "Rescaling and Reforming the State under NAFTA: Implications for Subnational Authority." *International Journal of Urban and Regional Research* 28.4: 858-873.

Wayne, Leslie. 2005. "Report Faults Air Force on Proposed Boeing Deal." *New York Times* June 8: C4.

Weber, Max. 1968. *Economy and Society*. Totowa, NJ: Bedminster Press.

Weber, Max. 2001. *The Protestant Ethic and the Spirit of Capitalism*. New York: Routledge.

Weinberg, S. Kirson. 1976. "Shaw-McKay Theories of Delinquency in Cross-cultural Context." Pp 167-185 in *Delinquency, Crime, and Society*, edited by James F. Short, Jr. Chicago: University of Chicago Press.

Weitzer, Ronald and Steven A. Tuch. 2006. *Race and Policing in America: Conflict and Reform*. New York: Cambridge University Press.

Welsh, Wayne N. and Philip W. Harris. 2005. *Criminal Justice Policy and Planning*. Florence, KY: LexisNexis.

White, James D. 1996. "The Map of the City: Putting an Asia Face on Crime." *Technological Forecasting and Social Change* 52.2/3: 199-219.

Whyte, William F. 1943. *Street Corner Society: The Social Structure of an Italian Slum*. Chicago: University of Chicago Press.

Williams, Phil. 1999. "Emerging Issues: Transnational Crime and Its Control." In *Global Report on Crime and Justice*, edited by Graeme Newman. New York: Oxford University Press.

Wilson, William J. 1987. *The Truly Disadvantaged*. Chicago: University of Chicago Press.

Wirth, Louis. 1928. *The Ghetto*. Chicago; University of Chicago Press.

Wirth, Louis. 1931. "Culture Conflict and Misconduct." *Social Forces* 9.4: 484-492.

Wolfgang, Marvin E. and Franco Ferracuti. 1967. *The Subculture of Violence: Toward an Integrated Theory in Criminology*. London: Tavistock.

World Almanac. 2006. *The World Almanac and the Book of Facts 2006*. New York: Work Almanac Education Group.

World Bank. 2006. *World Development Indicators 2006*. Washington, DC: World Bank Publications.

Xu, Xinyi. 1994. "People's Conciliation: A Mode of Conflict Management of Civil Disputes in China. *International Journal of Conflict Management* 5.4: 326-342.

Xu, Xinyi. 1995. "The Impact of Western Forms of Social Control on China: A Preliminary Evaluation." *Crime, Law and Social Change* 23: 67-87.

Xu, Xinyi. 1996. "The Role of the State in Economic Development: Japan, South Korea, and Taiwan." *International Quarterly for Asian Studies* 27.1/2: 51-68.

Yao, Xinzhong. 2000. *An Introduction to Confucianism*. Cambridge, UK: Cambridge University Press.

Yin, Shun. 1998. *The Way to Buddhahood: Instructions from a Modern Chinese Master*. Somerville, MA: Wisdom Publications.

Yuan, Guanghai. 1995. *Chinese Bandits, 1911-1950*. Chongqing: Chongqing Press.

Zaitseva, Lyudmila and Kevin Hand. 2003. "Nuclear Smuggling Chains: Suppliers, Intermediaries, and End-Users." *American Behavioral Scientist* 46.6: 822-844.

Zhang, Sheldon and Ko-lin Chin. 2002. "Enter the Dragon: Inside Chinese Human Smuggling Organizations." *Criminology* 40.4: 737-768.

Zhao, Bingzhi. 1997. *Drug Crimes and Punishments in the World*. Beijing: Chinese People's Police University Press.

Zhou, Xueguang. 2000. "Economic Transformation and Income Inequality in Urban China: Evidence from Panel Data." *American Journal of Sociology* 105.4: 1135-1174.

Zorbaugh, Harvey W. 1929. *The Gold Coast and the Slum*. Chicago: University of Chicago Press.

Zvekic, Ugljesa. 1995. "The International Crime Victim Survey in the Developing World." *Overcrowded Times* October 6.5: 5-7.

Index

About the Author

Victor N. Shaw, Ph.D., is an associate professor of sociology at California State University-Northridge. Dr. Shaw is interested in the study of crime, deviance, social control, organizational behavior, higher education, academic careers, and public policy, and has published widely in those areas. Dr. Shaw's 2002 book, *Substance Use and Abuse: Sociological Perspectives*, appeared in "Outstanding Academic Titles, 2003," *CHOICE: Current Reviews for Academic Libraries*, the Association of College and Research Libraries. His most recent book, *Career-Making in Postmodern Academia: Process, Structure, and Consequence* is at the top of some academic advisors' list of books to read for postgraduate students and professionals.